Psychological Assessment of Dyslexia

Martin Turner

Head of Psychology, Dyslexia Institute

Consultant in Dyslexia. Professor ......g ......ing, University of York

Whurr Publishers Ltd

© 1997 Whurr Publishers
First published 1997
Whurr Publishers Ltd
19B Compton Terrace, London N1 2UN, England

Reprinted 1997 and 2000

British Library Cataloguing in Publication Data
A catalogue record for this book is available from the
British Library.

ISBN 1-897635-53-2

Printed and bound in the UK by Athenaeum Press Ltd,
Gateshead, Tyne & Wear

Psychological Assessment
of Dyslexia

This book is dedicated in memory of my father:

H.F. Lawrence Turner

Born 30 December 1908   ~   Died 17 December 1977

We shall not cease from exploration
And the end of all our exploring
Will be to arrive where we started
And know the place for the first time.

(T.S. Eliot, *Little Gidding*)

Contents

Acknowledgements

Although 'a man will turn over half a library to make one book',[1] a production such as this is the work of an invisible team as much as of a sole author. Where possible the work of others is made visible at appropriate points in the text, but let me acknowledge here also the significant contributions of Liz Brooks, Director, and Dr John Rack, Regional Psychologist – Northern Region, both of the Dyslexia Institute; and Professor Maggie Snowling of the Department of Psychology, York University; and Demian Turner: all read portions at various stages and made improving comments; Dr Rack in addition provided the intercorrelation matrix in Chapter 8; Michael Biddulph, Gary Howl and Michael Lock, consulting psychologists, all shared knowledge, expertise and vital information; Dr Colin Elliott, Senior Clinical Scientist with American Guidance Service, contributed the Wechsler factor analyses drawn upon in Chapter 3; Dr Ian Deary of the Department of Psychology, Edinburgh University, provided an analysis of 30 school entry-age children reported in Chapter 10; DLM Riverside gave permission for reproduction of portion of the Woodcock-Johnson record form in Chapter 6; my teacher colleagues at the Dyslexia Institute, too numerous to list, have surrounded me for five years with examples of teaching excellence, together with occasional glimpses of the ethic that sustains it; while those of the Institute's trainees on our postgraduate diploma course whom I have taught have made me understand the professional and technical problems that teachers face, while responding with appreciation and a willingness to undertake almost any challenge. Finally, the children and their families who have come to the Institute for consultations, together with those of student age and other adults, some of whom will recognise themselves in these pages, are those to whom I owe the most: they have trained, schooled and groomed me to know what was needed.

Notes

[1] James Boswell: *The Life of Dr Johnson* for 6 April 1775.

Chapter 1
Introduction

The nature of the enterprise

The nature of dyslexia is much clearer than it used to be. There may one day be hard, physical criteria for its detection, given, for example, that it is now possible using specimens of sweat or hair to test how much zinc has been absorbed by the body. But until then we must continue to use *behavioural measures* that are, by their very nature, imprecise, even slippery. For this reason it is necessary, in assessing individuals for dyslexia, to use measurement resources to their utmost. The path to precision has meant that qualitative observation and comment long ago ceased to be adequate, by themselves, as a mode of assessment.

A psychological test is rather like an experiment. The person giving the test is exposed to the possibility of learning something new. Indeed the decision to administer a test implies that the outcome is not wholly predictable.

In this sense the psychological assessment of dyslexia seeks to escape from subjectivity and the bias of prejudices. This quest, of course, is that of science itself. In common with procedures in other fields where the phenomena are not entirely understood, the psychological assessment of dyslexia takes a cautious measurement approach.

Psychometrics – the science of the measurement of mental attributes such as attitudes and abilities – is not the subject of this book. Unusually within educational psychology, psychometrics offers some of the certainties of closure and finality; its procedures are robust, disciplined and well developed. However, a frequent criticism is that psychometric science is detached from the concerns, especially the theoretical concerns, of psychology. It has rejoiced in the status of troublesome republic on the borders of the motherland.

Psychometric technology is amply covered in many authoritative texts. The focus of this book will be the careful measurement and detection of dyslexia, using psychometric methods where these address the problems satisfactorily but drawing on other experimental procedures where they do not. The lure of the well-understood procedures of psychometric investigation will be resisted, except in so far as these help in the difficult task of puzzling out reality. The theoretical concerns of psychology in relation to the nature of dyslexia will remain uppermost.

Over many years the world of applied educational psychology has become somewhat detached from its host discipline of experimental psychology, even acknowledging that many of its people-based concerns are less amenable to scientific enquiry. But over the same period the success of cognitive psychology, within the family of the life sciences rather than that of 'social science', has nowhere been more apparent than in the field of learning: reading, dyslexia, memory, perception, language, information-processing. Those engaged in the fundamental research have worked in classrooms with children and teachers in their instructional environments, examining carefully the actual materials and methods in use. Reciprocation seems overdue: applied psychologists should learn once again the value of the methods and logic of experimental science.

Almost accidentally the discipline of psychology has become the main knowledge base and resource for understanding dyslexia. Cognitive psychology has been a victim of its own success. In common with other previously strange disciplines – neurobiology, cell physiology, quantitative genetics – it has been absorbed into the 'cognitive neurosciences', that Voyager II of inner space which promises to supplant even astrophysics in the public imagination.

This book aims to satisfy psychologists by bringing into an organised framework the main techniques, theories and operations in diagnosing dyslexia. It also hopes not to frustrate or disappoint those numerous other lay people, parents, teachers and members of other professions, whose unwavering attention to developments in this field is so impressive.

The present view of dyslexia is illuminated by its history

It is humbling to revisit the early descriptions of dyslexic children, written in the late nineteenth and early twentieth centuries, and see how well observed these were and how little, in some respects, we have improved upon them since. The emergence of interest in and public awareness of dyslexia is a notable success story, one which is often told (see for instance Richardson, 1992; Thomson, 1990).

Essentially the earliest view of the dyslexic child, however, is of someone with an *unexpected failing*. The individual, that is, came to notice because of an inconsistency between intellectual gifts manifested in various ways, especially oral discussion, and miserably inadequate written language skills. The discrepancy between the two very early became the hallmark of the phenomenon for which the term *dyslexia* would later be preferred (or avoided).

This discrepancy explains how, historically, the problem came to be conceptualised and how, to a significant extent, it is still recognised today. We will see, in a subsequent chapter, that the mathematical treatment of a discrepancy (between general abilities and specific literacy abilities) may be implemented in various different ways; and we will tackle the fundamental question of whether such a methodology (discrepancy evaluation) is actually justified.

But for now this historical perspective leads us to the simple and useful working definition of dyslexia given by Margaret Snowling, in which developmental dyslexia is

> ... the unexpected failure of a child to acquire written language skills. (Snowling, 1987, p. 1)

It is usual to cite the quarter-century-old definition of 'specific developmental dyslexia' given by the World Federation of Neurology:

> ... a disorder manifested by a difficulty in learning to read, despite conventional instruction, adequate intelligence and socio-cultural opportunity [which is] dependent upon fundamental cognitive disabilities which are frequently of constitutional origin. (Critchley, 1970, p.11).

This latter definition begs, at the outset, many of the questions with which this book will be concerned: the relationship between teaching and literacy learning, the cognitive developmental imbalance which may underlie literacy failure, the negativity of definition by exclusion. In contrast and with deceptive simplicity, the Snowling definition highlights *literacy* failure and proposes only the 'unexpectedness' of such a failure. Given the current expansion of knowledge of the genetic components in literacy failure, it could be objected that for many families with a history of specific learning difficulties there is nothing at all unexpected about literacy-learning problems in the latest generation.[1] However, the problems are held not to be unpredicted, only *improbable*, in the sense of showing an unexpected imbalance or inconsistency in cognitive development.

In November 1994, the Research Committee of the Orton Dyslexia Society (ODS) consolidated what appears to be a new consensus, as well as signalling agreement with it, by adopting a new definition of this 'most common and best defined' learning disability, as follows:

> Dyslexia is one of several distinct learning disabilities. It is a specific language-based disorder of constitutional origin characterized by difficulties in single word decoding, usually reflecting insufficient phonological processing abilities. These difficulties in single word decoding are often unexpected in relation to age and

other cognitive and academic abilities; they are not the result of generalized developmental disability or sensory impairment. Dyslexia is manifested by variable difficulty with different forms of language, often including, in addition to problems reading, a conspicuous problem with acquiring proficiency in writing and spelling. (ODS, 1994)

This represents a considerable shift in thinking, towards the viewpoint adopted in this book, and reflects progress in the base sciences that inform dyslexia studies. In this sense the negotiation of definitions is *post hoc*, following rather than leading the way. We will return to the question of definitions before long but, always preferring matters of substance, may want in the end to concur with the proconsul Gallio:

> [b]ut if it be a question of words and names . . . I will be no judge of such matters.[2]

Describing and explaining dyslexia

The assessment of dyslexia, then, reflects the way we think about it. Some sort of contrast is sought between the range of an individual's normal abilities and the faulty processes and disappointing attainment in skills of literacy: reading, spelling and other aspects of writing. Even while controversy still surrounds the use of the IQ or general intelligence statistic, the most frequently proposed alternative continues to highlight a discrepancy between reading and the important linguistic ability of listening comprehension. The essential contrast, so keenly noted by Pringle Morgan 100 years ago,[3] remains at the centre of the detective effort engaged in by psychologists.

However, the demonstration of such a discrepancy in a school-age child only sets the descriptive scene. It describes, after all, underachievement that might plausibly have been caused by prolonged non-attendance at school or by internal exile once there. We are inclined to agree with one expert that:

> . . . determining a severe discrepancy does not constitute the diagnosis . . . it only establishes that the primary symptom . . . exists. (Reynolds, 1990, p. 574)

As the 'primary symptom' is merely underachievement, we can perhaps go further and say, with Frith, that:

> While a discrepancy definition remains at best descriptive, it is possible to move towards a more explanatory definition by applying a developmental framework. (Frith, 1985, p. 306)

The psychologically meaningful work of diagnosis remains to be done: that of discovering whether one or more of the fundamental cognitive anomalies implicated in dyslexia is present in an individual. It is at this level that a psychological assessment – in effect a single-case study – explains as well as describes the disturbance of normal learning and reconciles the facts of the case with accepted clinical knowledge.

Parents and teachers alike stand to gain from the light thus shed on the problem. Both have rights: the teacher to be delivered from the confines of the sort of school-based assessment that can be conducted in the classroom, and the parent to be taken beyond the confines of common-sense redescription. Indeed it should be emphasised that psychological investigation aims to achieve the solution of a problem, not merely to make recommendations for forms of remedial action such as teaching. The aim of diagnosis is a worthwhile one *in its own right*, not merely as a stepping-stone to other purposes. A psychological assessment remains valid even if bereft of implications for action. The scientific problem is to determine what is revealed about a child's learning problem in the light of the best contemporary knowledge. This needs to be solved before considerations of action even arise.

The question, 'What, if anything, is wrong with this child's learning?', is a serious one, whose answer will have intense personal consequences for each family. This goes some way to explaining a phenomenon that seems to puzzle many observers: the immense relief and gratitude of parents whose child's learning difficulty has been successfully identified during a psychological consultation, regardless of whether the exercise has resulted in any labelling. The question of which label applies, though of frequent tactical importance in ensuing social negotiations, is often a secondary one for families.

The criteria for a successful psychological assessment are stringent. The facts of the developmental and educational history must be marshalled; new, relevant evidence must be generated by the investigation itself; the combined story of new and old findings must be correctly interpreted and the explanation must reconcile observational data with the best contemporary theoretical understanding. It must be said that theory is not some luxurious extra which may optionally be added for *aficionados*, as is sometimes implied; a theory is a kind of lamp without which a correct understanding is not to be had. It is in this sense of true understanding that an explanation should be sought for the release and alleviation so often expressed by children, parents and teachers following a psychological consultation.

Before leaving the subject of explanation, we may like to remind ourselves what explanation is *not*. In one of Molière's medical comedies, a candidate doctor is asked why opium puts people to sleep. His reply is that the medicament contains 'a certain dormitive principle'. Whilst not strictly inaccurate, it may be thought that this explanation does not take us much further forward. Equally, recourse to a sophisticated but unsupported system of hypothetical constructs may sound scientific but is open to the charge of explaining the doubtful by the uncertain, *obscura per obscurius*. In the case of dyslexia a complex explanation in terms of cerebral lateralisation, hemispheric imbalance, visual-motor memory, cross-laterality, and so on, is quite common but ventures far beyond what is known and agreed.

Why should earthquakes frequently occur in the same places, such as the Japanese islands and the San Andreas fault in the western United States? In this example, the study of plate tectonics illuminates known phenomena and furnishes an explanation – movement of the Pacific plate – that carries implications and predictions. An effective explanation in terms of dyslexia, though not necessarily complete, will tend to simplify the chaos of phenomena by distinguishing relevant from irrelevant information. It will also account for essential information by recourse to underlying mechanisms and developmental processes and it will serve to predict a child's likely response to intervention, its pattern of school adjustment in future years and its degree of eventual success in overcoming the learning difficulty.

Science and diagnosis

Diagnostic procedures must embody the best current theoretical knowledge. In 1976 Yule and Rutter could say:

> There has been a complete failure to show that the signs of dyslexia constitute any meaningful pattern. There is no evidence for the validity of a single special syndrome of dyslexia.

There is no longer quite the collateral there was for this degree of agnosticism. It is the position of this book that dyslexia *is* a syndrome, a learning disorder consisting of a meaningful constellation of symptoms, and that it is to be distinguished from other 'specific learning difficulties'. The latter term has served to keep open the scientific options pending a greater degree of knowledge. As such it may have served its day.

As much of the rest of this book will be concerned with the increasingly sophisticated methods used to diagnose dyslexia, we would do well to consider first the status of dyslexia as a scientific concept.[4] Issues in syndrome validation receive detailed coverage in Pennington (1991); here the position will be only summarised. Though operational definitions vary, dyslexia may be replicated across techniques and samples, with reliable classification procedures (if consistent criteria are employed) and good homogeneity (allowing for habits of including in 'dyslexia' subjects with possibly heterogeneous aetiologies). Dyslexia therefore meets Fletcher's (1985) criteria for internal validity to an impressive extent. Of course these are claims that are contestable: for example a recent epidemiological investigation (Shaywitz *et al.*, 1992) finds that a discrepancy definition (of reading with intelligence) identifies largely different children as a group passes through successive primary years; but conversely it is argued (for example by Miles, 1994) that such a definition may be too loose and ignore diagnostic features of dyslexia such as poor information management skills.

Dyslexia also meets most of the criteria for external validity. A meaningful causal chain has been identified across different levels of analysis (genetic, neurophysiological, cognitive, behavioural: for a recent outline see Rack, Hulme and Snowling, 1993). The hypothesis of a core deficit in phonological processing (Stanovich, 1988) is fruitful in guiding interpretation of behaviour in both normal and abnormal domains. A dyslexia diagnosis has implications for course of development and response to treatment at different ages; other syndromes have different implications. Useful distinctions can be made between primary and secondary symptoms. Concomitant, secondary and artifactual symptoms may all be discriminated.

Dyslexia is usually discussed in terms of heterogeneous aetiology; but

> If the different etiologies affect the same or similar brain mechanisms and produce the same underlying neurological deficit, then it seems reasonable to retain the concept of the behavioural syndrome and not divide it into subtypes. (Pennington, op. cit., p. 26)

A dilemma occurs in the undoubted cases where damage to, for instance, the visual cortex produces a kind of 'visuospatial dyslexia', but here behavioural convergence is not confirmed by a common neuropsychological deficit and wider consideration of the acquired dyslexias applies.

It is unlikely that recent scientific evidence from different disciplines will be able to satisfy all interested parties as to the syndrome of dyslexia. Its status may be regarded as provisional but its validity is a working assumption in all that follows:

> [A] valid . . . syndrome is a construct below the level of observable behaviours or symptoms, which provides a meaningful explanation of why certain symptoms co-occur in different patterns across development, as well as a meaningful explanation of why some treatments are efficacious and others are not. (Pennington, op. cit., p. 24)

Because of 'the degree of covariation across levels of analysis' (ibid., p.30) (symptomatic, neuropsychological, genetic), the burden of evidence is taken to favour dyslexia as a distinct syndrome.

Accordingly, psychometric and diagnostic techniques will be

constantly evaluated in the light of a theoretical understanding of dyslexia. Such techniques, it will be argued, are a great deal more purposeful than any blind psychometric routine. The nature, causes and characteristics of dyslexia will, therefore, be encountered incidentally in the course of discussion of its diagnosis, rather than the other way round. General dyslexia studies are now probably too voluminous to be encompassed within a single book, especially one primarily concerned with assessment.

Dyslexia and specific learning difficulties

As much as 15–25% of the population may have learning disorders which can be described as 'specific learning difficulties'. Dyslexia is but one of these. As mentioned, both convergent and discriminant criteria validly differentiate dyslexia from other specific learning difficulties.

Figure 1.1 illustrates the relative prevalence of the major categories of specific learning difficulty within the learning-disordered population.

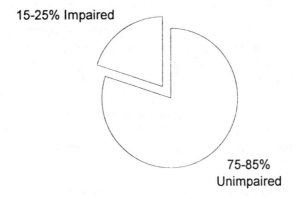

Figure 1.1: Relationship of impaired to total population. After Pennington (1991).

The term dyslexia will therefore be distinguished from the more general term, 'specific learning difficulties', of which it is a subset.

Figure 1.2 illustrates the variety of these specific difficulties.

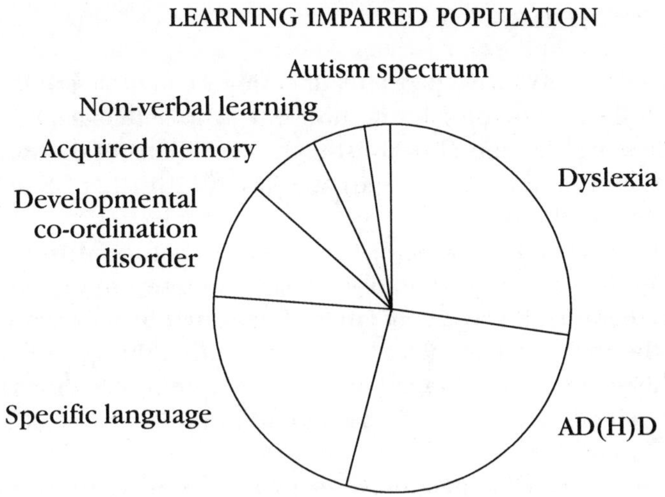

LEARNING IMPAIRED POPULATION

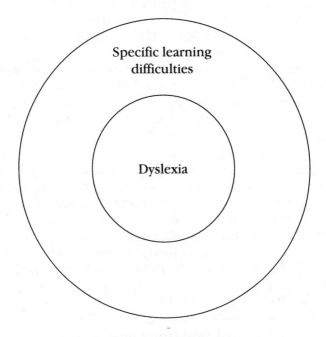

Figure 1.2: Learning impaired population: dyslexia and other specific learning difficulties. After Pennington (1991).

The relationship between the *set* of specific learning difficulties (SpLD) and the *subset* of dyslexia is shown in Figure 1.3.

Figure 1.3: Dyslexia is a *subset* of specific learning difficulties.

Beyond definitions

If questions of definition have proved something of a cul-de-sac in this field, this may be because of their inherent scholasticism (Turner, 1994a). Pumfrey and Reason (1991) list eight definitions of dyslexia or its aliases and discuss Hammill's (1990) analysis of 11 further US definitions of 'learning disability'.

When Richard Owen, creator of the Natural History Museum in South Kensington, London, invented the term 'dinosaur' in the middle part of the last century, it was a convenience designed to accommodate new facts in the form of some lizard bones recently dug up in Lewes. For a long while controversies raged over the definition of a 'dinosaur'. We should be surprised today, 150 years later, at any revival of such interest.[5]

Many problems can be disguised as problems of definition. In Guatemala indigenous Indians make up some 60% of the population but literacy rates, nationally about 50%, are much lower among them, in some areas 10–20% by one account.[6] There are of course different ways of defining 'Indian' and 'indigenous'. At the individual level problems of definition may be acute but these figures are unlikely to alter very much depending upon the definition chosen.[7]

Definitions are a matter of convenience and the most apparently unambiguous phenomena are subject to definitional uncertainty. Only in the last few years has the World Health Organization agreed on a definition of migraine (Wilkins, 1992).

To give substance to the discussion of dyslexia, while avoiding definitional pirouetting, it may be said that dyslexia is a specific learning difficulty in which a disorder of phonological processing, frequently inherited, compromises the development of internal phonological representations. This difficulty affects, first of all, various low-level aspects of speech processing (phonological manipulation: rhyming, blending, segmenting and articulatory sequencing) and latterly the acquisition of the written language sequences which depend upon these skills (reading – more specifically phonological decoding – and spelling). To the extent that there is a close match with verbal and auditory sequences, this learning difficulty affects all written symbolisation routines (number, musical notation). As verbal strategy and rehearsal progressively become, in middle childhood, the vehicle for more varieties of learning (Hitch, 1990), so the dyslexic finds the barriers to curricular learning rising.

In March 1996, after extensive consultation, the Dyslexia Institute published its own revised definition of dyslexia, as follows:

DEFINITION OF DYSLEXIA

Dyslexia is a specific learning difficulty that hinders the learning of literacy skills. This problem with managing verbal codes in memory is neurologically based and tends to run in families. Other symbolic systems, such as mathematics and musical notation, can also be affected.

Dyslexia can occur at any level of intellectual ability. It can accompany, but is not a result of, lack of motivation, emotional disturbance, sensory impairment or meagre opportunities.

The effects of dyslexia can be alleviated by skilled specialist teaching and committed learning. Moreover many dyslexic people have visual and spatial abilities which enable them to be successful in a wide range of careers.

The Dyslexia Institute
March 1996

Obviously, this has much in common with other contemporary approaches to definition. No longer do such definitions arouse controversy or mark off well-defended positions; instead they tend to occupy common ground and aspire to communicate to a lay audience.

The research picture has, as mentioned, begun to achieve consistency across disciplines and levels of analysis but many mysteries remain. Quite why information, subject to decay in the short-term verbal store, should transfer successfully to longer-term memory remains obscure, though clinically there can be little doubt that it does. Intact long-term procedural memory seems able to assist skills insecurely established in immediate memory, for instance through multisensory teaching. The cortical networks that first process information consolidate it by means of a boost called long-term potentiation and, with the involvement of the hippocampus and amygdala in the transfer, consolidate it thereafter on a distributed basis as declarative (semantic and episodic) memory, also usually unimpaired in dyslexics. This is harder to disrupt but, in any case ,the information must remain in working memory (visible in the pre-frontal cortex in PET scanning) to begin with.

Mechanisms of transfer are more vulnerable but, in dyslexics at least, operate normally. In the bodies of the limbic system, especially the hippocampus, the weights of the connections between nerve cells are altered, rather as in the process used to train artificial neural nets. Rehearsal and renewed stimulation preserve the learning long enough for transfer into long-term memory, perhaps during REM or dreaming sleep. The implications of this are understood by teachers who employ repetition, frequent revision and 'overlearning'.

Another puzzle concerns the role of attention. This has not proved as fruitful a terrain as memory (but see Whyte, 1994, for a recent review), though it remains tantalising. Psychological testing of working memory tends to be 'convergent', in that it challenges vigilance and concentration as well as sensitivity and the capacity of the phonological store. Such testing is notably affected by impulsiveness and anxiety. Thus far theory can best explain the role of attention by reference to the sharing of attentional resources between the central executive and the phonological loop (Baddeley and Hitch, 1974). As the challenge to working memory capacity increases, for instance where digit sequences must be repeated backwards, so attention is drawn away from the 'supervisory attentional system' (Shallice, 1988), whose resources are limited. Reduced efficiency of both memory and attention results. Much remains, however, to be explained in the relationship between dyslexia and the neuropsychologically distinct attention deficit (hyperactivity) disorder (ADHD).[8]

Most experienced teachers of children with specific language disorders (SLD) observe poor motor control ('clumsiness') in their pupils, though this is true to a lesser extent of dyslexics. I recall asking the non-special children what was different about pupils attending the Language Unit, a model of integration, attached to their primary school in East London. The children replied that the SLD pupils arrived in taxis and often fell over in the playground. It may simply be the case that articulatory dyspraxia tends to occur with general dyspraxia, leading to problems with both speech and balance. Otherwise a singularly strong version of the theory that language regulates all behaviour must be required to explain such striking and consistent problems with motor coordination.

A measurement approach to a cognitive deficit

As this discussion implies, dyslexia is part of the conversation between cognitive psychology and the neurosciences. Indeed 'cognitive neuropsychology' has become an accepted name for this domain. Whilst this conversation would appear to neglect social and interpersonal factors, particularly in aetiology, it must be said that social and cultural explanations of learning difficulties have made remarkably little progress in the last 15 years, at least in comparison with genetics and the neurosciences. In addition to dyslexia, this conclusion may be held to apply to various other areas also, such as schizophrenia and autism.

Rourke and Fuerst (1991), in a recent treatment of psychosocial functioning, contrast what they designate as:

- Hypothesis 1, that 'socioemotional disturbance causes learning disabilities', with
- Hypothesis 2, that 'learning disabilities cause socioemotional disturbance', before turning to

- Hypothesis 3, that 'specific patterns of central processing abilities and deficits cause specific manifestations (subtypes) of learning disabilities and specific forms of socioemotional disturbance'.

In relation to Hypothesis 1, the conventional fall-back position in British educational psychology,[9] Rourke and Fuerst instance 'excellent examples' of primary emotional disturbances causing the learning difficulties which they antedate. However, they characterise most of this evidence as 'clinical', as assuming that improved socioemotional functioning would bring about improved academic performance and as violating the 'exclusionary' definition of 'learning disability' (LD):

> ... these factors are not properly considered within the context of socioemotional correlates of LD. (Rourke and Fuerst, 1991, p. 6)

It may be felt that this exclusion is unsatisfactory by definition. Experience of exclusionary definitions of dyslexia has shown that there is no reason *a priori* why children of below average intelligence from poor homes, who may have missed school through illness, who have been inadequately taught, speak English as a second language and have emotional problems, may not also be dyslexic. The exclusionary definition belongs to an era when it was not clear what dyslexia was. As the nature of dyslexia becomes better understood, so the first, descriptive *discrepancy* half of the assessment methodology can be taken as read (except in the case of young or compensated dyslexics) and the second, explanatory half comes into its own: the *diagnosis* of low-level information-processing anomalies.

The rationale for measurement may be too well known to need rehearsal. The book of nature, said Galileo famously in *The Assayer*

> ... is written in the language of mathematics, and its letters are triangles, circles, and other geometric figures; without which it is humanly impossible to understand a single word of it.[10]

It is also commonly said that whatever exists, exists in a certain amount; and whatever exists in a certain amount, can be measured. But many things that can be measured are not. Why this preoccupation with numbers?[11]

The perception of number seems to be an important tool at a primitive stage of becoming aware of the external world. Wynn (1992) has demonstrated something like a grasp of number series in infants only a few months old. Given that thought is by no means dependent on language, moreover, this awareness of *number* may antecede and influence language itself:

> When we construe an aspect of the world as something that can be identified and counted or measured and that can play a role in events, language often allows us to express that aspect as a noun, whether or not it is a physical object. For example, when we say, I

have three reasons for leaving, we are counting reasons as if they
were objects (though of course we do not literally think a reason
can sit on a table or be kicked across a room) (Pinker, 1995, p. 106)

Identifying (naming) things often, but not necessarily, precedes awareness of their quantity. If we select aspects of the world for counting or
measurement, then, it may be as a response to what has interested us or
as a bet on what will turn out to be of importance for theory, the total
sense we make of the world.

Numbers, of course, *are* words and their written representations
must be learned as whole symbols. Dyslexics typically have difficulty
with the packed verbal routines in the earlier stages of mathematics.
Ruskin, considering how the fords of English rivers had given their
names to many beautiful villages, allowed himself to digress:

... the difference between ford and bridge curiously – if one may
let one's fancy loose for a moment – characterizing the difference
between the baptism of literature, and the edification of mathematics, in our two great universities . . .[12]

It may be that he meant by this that literature represented an immersion
in experience, mathematics a dignified and dry detachment.

Of course rational explanations go out of date, and along with them
the perspective of any given training. Experience, with its penumbra of
unschooled observation, is perhaps less prone to obsolescence but the
important principle is simply that words are inherently imprecise. Their
meanings change, as may be seen from a remarkable study of just eight
words (Lewis, 1960). Numbers are inherently precise – their meanings
do not change.

There is at present an enthusiasm for 'qualitative method' but this
usually seems to entail saying what *kind* of thing a given phenomenon
is. As such it belongs to a nominal level of measurement, when one thing
is discriminated from another and given a different name. Ordinal, interval and ratio levels of measurement may follow.

By choosing the modest and provisional path of empirical enquiry,
psychologists are obeying the dictum of Sir Isaac Newton: 'Do a little
with certainty.' The same imperative constrains those who would now
apply some of the lessons of the host discipline. All the more reason,
then, why apathy in relation to cognition and the psychology of learning
should no longer hold back educational psychology.

Naturally developing abilities for unnaturally acquired skills

All children are not the same; all school curricula, all associated methods
of teaching reading are not the same. Skills in literacy, held by the

community to be important, are implanted in children with differing patterns of learning abilities at different ages, inside and outside school. In this symphony of variation, what sense can be made of any individual's developmental progress?

Amidst the variation there are two constants: the nature of written English and the method of science. But these may be in conflict. Indeed they seem to offer radically different paradigms of development. Science is accustomed to observing objects in their natural state, attributing meaningful variation to laws and random variation to 'chance'. In many instances, including in developmental child psychology, such a 'natural science' stance is successful and beneficial. In newborn human infants motor programming of eye movements is already as sophisticated as that of adults and undergoes no further development. The perceptual system, however:

> . . . already capable of making functional categories of experience, may undergo great refinements after birth. (Trevarthen, Murray and Hubley, 1981, p. 227).

Such natural development may be theorised as innately programmed and under the control of a gene or genes, but subject to developmental opportunities afforded by an environment which, by the same token, will allow other genes to remain unexpressed but for human beings the environment is largely a cultural affair and development follows a sometimes thornily specific and unnatural path.

For instance, the propensity to speak a known language may be thought of as innately given. Though it appears that initial acquisition of speech is subject to far more 'teaching' and maternal fine-tuning than had been thought (Moerk, 1992), and that therefore the Chomskyan language acquisition device is far more dependent on human intervention than, say, walking, the innate nature of this gift, and its evolutionary advantage, are no longer in question. However, within the first weeks after birth babies become selectively sensitive to the functional phonological units of their community language. Thus Japanese babies attend preferentially to *moras*, French babies to syllables and English babies to prosodic 'feet' (Mehler, 1994).

Because it is innate – an 'instinct' (Pinker, 1995) – and apparently universal, language is a denizen of the psychological World 2 but, by virtue of the cultural uses which it serves, language contributes to a World 3 domain of objective cultural products (Popper, 1979).[13] Psychological science, a family member of the life sciences, is limited to the study of phenomena which are the products of biological, not cultural, evolution. It may study the behaviour of children at arcade games, but can relate this only distantly to cognitive and motivational mechanisms which have adaptive significance.

Cultural creations, such as language, tend to preserve the steps that led to their creation. Their survival is a testimony to the values that brought them forth. The Trinidadian novelist, VS Naipaul, commenting on the labourer working in the fields of rural India, pointed out that the Western values so disparaged in Eastern religious traditions, which teach that reality is not objective, that daily experience is an illusion, and so on, are asserted by the very transistor radio to which he is listening.

Cultural objects, further, may embody self-evident functions. This might be called the principle of the safety-pin. The existence of a steel industry is implicit in a safety-pin; its function is implicit in its design, requiring a minimum of instruction; and as an object it might be thought an epitome of unnaturalness.

There are important lessons here for a consideration of written English. Early in the history of writing, basic features of text – vowel markings and divisions between words – were introduced and esoteric abbreviations removed to ensure uniformity of interpretation among a widening readership for sacred texts (Venezky, 1993). More recently, arbitrary orthographic conventions 'evolved' (in the senses of Hayek and Popper) or were gradually agreed by Norman scribes and Flemish print-ers, culminating in the sixteenth century. 'Irregularly' spelled words, such as *love* and those with *-gh-*, turn out to obey consistent conventions designed apparently to avoid visual confusions (Ramsden, 1993).

Far from being a naturally 'developed' skill, therefore, literacy depends directly upon mastery of an arbitrary code of conventions. These seem to posit a developmental path of their own: morphology recapitulates orthography, orthography recapitulates phonology. The evolution of the structures of written English turns out to create a struc-ture for learning.[14] English, with a uniquely large[15] vocabulary compris-ing many loan-words (McCrum, Cran and MacNeil, 1992), offers hurdles, obstacles and rewards to the pupil writer different from those of other written languages.

In this sense, then, dyslexia may have a very great deal to do with the objective stages and difficulties of the English language in its written form. Yet theorists have, understandably, preferred to ignore the artifi-cial, instructional aspects of learning to read and write, and the safety-pin-like aspect of written English as a fact of life, in favour of quasi-developmental theories of acquisition. For instance, in a theoreti-cally adventurous chapter that has become justly influential, Frith (1985) seeks to move away from a structural model of skilled reading on the grounds that:

> [i]f one ignores the question of acquisition . . . one would have to
> believe that the brain is equipped from birth with a grapheme-to-
> phoneme converter. (Frith, 1985, p. 304)

Among 'developmental factors', 'maturational and educational' ones (ibid., p. 311) are subsequently distinguished, as too are 'maturational and environmental causes of change' (ibid., p. 317) but a biologically based sense is consistently given to notions of developmental stages of reading acquisition. Thus the developmental stages 'are hypothesized to follow each other in strict sequential order' (ibid., p. 309), and consist in 'underlying step-wise improvements in skill' (ibid., p.311), in which there may be an 'arrest at a particular phase in the developmental sequence' (ibid., p.327). Moreover, the dyslexic who is taught phonics (i.e. skills belonging to a stage not yet attained) acquires only a *'resemblance* of alphabetic skills . . .' (ibid., p.318; emphasis added).

However, the natural science project of establishing a normal developmental model for learning to read may be doomed. Learning to read is not natural. Learning to read English is not like learning to read Italian (Thorstad, 1991) or Spanish (Manrique and Signorini, 1994). Pupils' strategies may reflect primarily the particular teaching methodology to which they have been exposed (Johnston and Thompson, 1989). Individuals may learn to read in a plurality of ways, not all of them optimal, at virtually any age and stage. In a remarkable refutation of theories of 'reading readiness', the Steinbergs taught their young son, Kimio, to recognise nine words by his first birthday and 181 words by two-and-a-half years (Steinberg and Steinberg, 1975).

Yet it cannot be doubted that the given nature of written English is learned by means of developing abilities that may properly be called natural. Cognitive neuropsychologists have been clear that these abilities have not developed through natural selection to support literacy skills. Equally, the 'unnatural' and cross-modal linking up of disparate abilities required for the skills of reading and writing soon produces functioning units that behave as if they were modular, that is, composed of dissociable cognitive subsystems (Ellis and Young, 1988).

The paradox at which we have arrived, the surface antagonism between a natural science preference for the study of development and the arbitrary and objective nature of written English, has immense implications for assessment and teaching. One opportunity afforded in principle is a wholly curriculum-based rationale for assessment. This could perhaps follow the given sequence of learning tasks dictated by the 'nature' of written English, rather than a more psychological analysis of the 'nature' of spelling abilities. This is consistent with an analysis of learning which stresses the primacy of the instructional component, rather than the passage of idiosyncratic skills along some spontaneous course of development. Similarly, competing teaching methodologies can be subjected to rational comparison on the basis of the analyses of English they offer, of the 'learnability' of their teaching sequences.

Within the confines of a 'thought-experiment', there might be agreement that, school, instructional and other conditions being equal, progress in learning depends solely upon the intra-individual variables of intelligence, cognitive development and information-processing efficiency. Similarly, with such innate and developmental variables being equal, progress will depend solely upon the nuances of teaching technique and curriculum rationalisation. Indeed, most practitioners could agree that in the real world an inevitable admixture of the causal brew must operate in each individual case. Everyday examples of aptitude–instruction interactions abound. At the ideological extremes the proponents of a genetic IQ-based account of learning, and, alternatively, of a purely curriculum-based approach to assessment, remain influential. Among teachers, the experience of teaching retarded readers, 'garden' variety (easy), contrasts with the experience of teaching dyslexics (hard). No amount of research scepticism as to discrepancy definitions and cognitive profiles is likely to shake this common-sense lesson of experience, and it is a matter of observation that specialist dyslexia teaching, though seldom evaluated, is often effective with hard-to-teach individuals. Indeed, response to intervention is an important additional criterion in differential diagnosis.

An important unexplored premise of this book, however, remains that instructional and curriculum variables are very much more important in the causal mixture than individual cognitive foibles. After all, school and teaching arrangements offer the only way forward for the pupil with learning disabilities (pending the arrival of chemical cognitive enhancers) and may have contributed largely to the predicament in the first place. It seems likely that, except in the extreme case, sound early instruction in literacy may serve to 'suppress' the dyslexia, whilst late, scarce and 'holistic' instruction may serve to exacerbate it. School history is a salient feature in children who seek assessment for dyslexia. Indeed, beyond the margin of children who may need special educational services, there is a large proportion of the school population, usually put at 40%, whose persistent low achievement in literacy seems to have little to do with innate abilities and rather more to do with inadequacy of instruction.

This is properly subject-matter for a different, and complementary, book. In later chapters we will therefore attend very carefully to what implications for instruction an individual psychological assessment may have, with precise examples of teaching method, material and mode of delivery. Before then we must make the huge assumption of 'other things being equal' (in whose favour weighs only a certain tendency in schools towards conformity) and seek and interpret evidence of individual differences in learning ability and style of a kind which bears on the question of the nature of dyslexia.

Notes

1 Dr J Rack, personal communication, 1994.
2 Acts 18:15 Authorized Version.
3 '. . . [H]e seems to have no power of preserving and storing up the visual impression produced by words . . .' (Morgan, 1896; quoted in Thomson, 1990, p. 5.)
4 A recent publication, *Dyslexia: An EPS View* (London Borough of Havering, March 1995), chooses 'not to introduce this term into a discussion about a child'

because 'most people are unclear about what the word means', 'there is no single accepted definition', it has 'a medical ring to it', it 'helps to reinforce the view that those without the dyslexia label are simply unintelligent' and because 'teachers should not be misled into believing that there is some special expertise which is beyond their reach'. That there may be more to this denial is suggested by the further comment that 'if the term were used for all children who experience difficulties in learning to read and write, *regardless of measured intelligence*, then most of our concerns would disappear' (emphasis added). The measurement of intelligence evidently remains emotion-laden (see subsequent chapters). Yet nothing so mystifies ordinary members of the public as aversion to the *word* dyslexia by professionals. Any explanation in terms of attitude should address the Fabian approach to social planning, egalitarian flight from IQ and resentment of the claims of middle-class families. The latter, however, have historically made negligible demands on personal social and educational services, accustomed not to consuming but, through taxation, to paying for them. Nowadays the *dyslexia doesn't exist* doctrine serves to assert Party solidarity, rather like showing a badge. And when the *System* is mentioned, it is always the *Party* that is meant.

5 The *Oxford English Dictionary* credits Owen with inventing the term and with its first published reference in 1841. The story is told again in Janet Browne's review of Nicholaas Rupke's biography, *Richard Owen* (Yale University Press), in *The Times Literary Supplement*, 12 August 1994.

6 See 'An Indian who can read?' in *The Economist*, 7 May 1994, p. 70.

7 Professor Peter Pumfrey points out to me that the figures will vary considerably depending on the definition of 'literacy' chosen.

8 Recent theoretical work explores the 'interactive cognitive subsystems' of propositional meaning and more generic, implicational meaning. Together these specify the 'resources required to fulfil central executive functioning' and 'provide the core central engine driving thought'. Interestingly for dyslexia studies in particular, the propositional subsystem 'interacts with a phonological subsystem' (Barnard, 1995).

9 A recent article, 'To test or not to test, that is the question', by Carolyn Blyth and Joy Faulkner, in *Newsletter* No. 26 of the Division of Educational and Child Psychology (British Psychological Society, August 1994), cites 11 sources in support of the '. . . well-researched and established link between emotional disturbance and the inability to learn appropriately . . .'; the date of publication of these sources is, on average, April 1972. Might it not be doubted whether, mediated solely by 'concentration' and 'self-esteem', '. . . emotional problems [could] produce exactly the same pattern of reading failure in a child as so-called specific learning difficulties'? No: just as specific learning difficulties are 'so-called', so the well-established link is 'without doubt' (Blyth and Faulkner, op. cit., p. 31).

10 Cited in Flew (1994, p. 147).

11 Human behaviour has from ancient times been fertile ground for omniscience, and systems of thought which explain too much, rather than too little, have, like Marxism and psychoanalysis, betrayed their adherents to cults. Psychology, by choosing the harder path of the behaviourist programme, gradually triumphed until it could afford to discard some of the self-inflicted unrealism.

12 This excerpt from *Fors Clavigera* (1873) is included by Kenneth Clark in his anthology, *Ruskin Today* (Harmondsworth, Middlesex: Penguin Books, 1982, p. 101).

13 Popper differentiates the world of physical objects (World 1) from that of psychological events (World 2), and both from the world of autonomous cultural

products (World 3). The latter category embraces symphonies and scientific theories, language ('a bird's nest') and gardens; all, like 'an animal path through the jungle', are the unintended consequence of actions directed at other aims (Popper, 1979, p. 117).

14 The exposition of even a determinedly contrary view concludes: 'although reading and writing are typically "taught" in the formal setting of a classroom, and although the emergence of mature skill is no doubt influenced by teacher–child interaction, the basic *prerequisites* are grounded in human biology' (Marshall, 1987, p. 27, emphasis added). This formulation seems quite compatible with the point of view of this book.

15 Gwyneth Fox, Director, Birmingham University COBUILD Dictionary project, interviewed on ITN News on 13 July 1994, spoke of 200 million words already logged, with about 12 new words being added each week.

Chapter 2:
The Concert of Abilities

Why measure intelligence?

A serious case against intelligence measurement has been sustained and, by many practitioners, accepted for some time now. One purpose of this chapter is to defend intelligence measurement, but both tentatively, on pragmatic grounds and not always directly connected with dyslexia, and provisionally. It is necessary to keep under review this basic procedure of cognitive psychological assessment. Further it may need to be shown that IQ, the summary measure of global ability, though sometimes a distraction, nevertheless has a serious statistical utility.

Let us deal briefly with controversial aspects of intelligence testing which are not really our concern. In a conformist era, ever more preoccupied with political correctness, intelligence testing has become anathema: it furnishes valid and reliable information about human inequality! Group differences, including racial differences, are apparently highlighted (though the technical literature is complex) and simplified (though most popular generalisations cannot, in fact, be supported).[1] The results are certainly unhappy: pundits describe a future dominated by 'cognitive stratification' (Herrnstein and Murray, 1994) and surveys appear to reveal countries where more than half the population meets traditional European psychometric criteria for subnormality (Zindi, 1994).

The usual argument against such psychometric pessimism is cultural. To impute quantities of primarily verbal intelligence to Zimbabwean children who speak little English, using the (untranslated) English-language Wechsler Intelligence Scale for Children – Revised (WISC-R), seems little short of foolhardy. Modern theories of intelligence (about which more shortly) distinguish between fluid and crystallised ability (Horn, 1985, 1989, 1991; Horn and Cattell, 1966). Verbal skills of vocabulary and social comprehension provide good examples of problem solving and factual learning that are dependent on formal schooling and cultural experience (crystallised intelligence).[2] Bilingualism is a factor of massive importance in any such survey or assessment (Cline, 1993; Valdes and Figueroa, 1994). The role of verbal mediation and rehearsal (Turner, 1994c), not to mention familiarity with task materials and their demand characteristics, remains a big dilemma even when the cognitive tests administered across a large cultural distance are non-verbal and culture-reduced.

Yet popular and conformist attitudes, however ethically noble, are not always helpful when evaluating new and unexpected findings in science. Intelligence tests *should* perhaps be discussed as tests of achievement of one kind or another. But learning cannot be attributed solely to environmental conditions, however important opportunity and adequacy of instruction might be. Sophisticated twin and adoption studies show that individual differences in intelligence are, in the main, inherited (see, for example, Bouchard et al., 1990), whilst the environmental influences that count are more often those of nutrition than of education (Lucas et al., 1992; Lynn and Hampson, 1989; Lynn, Hampson and Mullineux, 1987; Todman, 1993). During its period of unfashionableness, psychometric testing has become ever more technically efficient; and experts from all pertinent disciplines have moved closer to consensus on intelligence, its definition, transmission and measurement.

Nor can the facile equation of hereditarian analyses of intelligence and IQ with attitudes of political conservatism be accepted any longer. In his remarkable and detailed survey of the origins and early progress of educational psychology, the historian Adrian Wooldridge sustains virtually the opposite thesis:

> The argument [that hereditarians are natural conservatives whilst environmentalists are habitual progressives] repeats the characteristic fallacies of the Whig interpretation of history, ignoring intricacies of circumstance and context, sacrificing understanding for moral outrage, and mistaking consequences for intentions. If we approach the inter-war period without this set of contemporary assumptions, a very different pattern emerges. The inter-war educational psychologists were meritocrats rather than conservatives and reformers rather than reactionaries. They found their most committed supporters on the left and their most stubborn opponents on the right. They maintained that intelligence testing would open up opportunities and guarantee social justice, and combined a belief in IQ testing with a commitment to a general programme of social reform: the raising of the school leaving age, the expansion of the welfare state, improved scientific education, and a progressive and child-centred approach to teaching. (Wooldridge, 1994, p. 165)

It is often overlooked that intelligence testing began, and continues, as a clinical resource for identifying and planning for learning difficulties. It was not for research, survey or selection purposes, let alone as social or political sorting devices, that tests were originally designed. We will therefore limit ourselves to applications of ability measurement in which the sole question is the best interests, within the province of special education, of the individual concerned. Though such testing is normative, that is, concerned with the average development of representative individuals, the performance on tests of the majority of people concerns us only as a background to that of exceptional individuals.

What is IQ?

IQ, a statement of a person's overall intellectual ability, is an arithmetic average of his or her scores on several tests of ability. Such an average begins to stabilise – for purely numerical reasons – after 4–6 such tests, and thereafter it is difficult, even by the addition of several highly discrepant new results, to shift it far either up or down. However, any pattern of scores will show the effects of *regression to the mean* and these are particularly apparent far from the mean, at the extremes of high and low ability.[3] IQ and other composite scores are adjusted to take into account regression effects. But this is the only qualification needed to the statement that IQ is the mean of the subtest scores that comprise it.

The IQ measurement is therefore a composite score (a score composed of other, direct measurements) which has, above all, the property of stability. One psychologist may examine a child and find him/her to have high verbal and low non-verbal abilities; another examiner may find the reverse: high non-verbal, low verbal abilities; but the IQ may well remain constant across the two assessments. The accuracy of the process can be uncanny. A child tested by one psychologist at one age on one instrument obtains, on another instrument with another examiner at a later age, an IQ score only a point or two different from the first.

This summary of an individual's general level of performance across a range of ability tests has become well known not least, perhaps, because two letters (two or three digits) appear to render superfluous the vast number of observations that comprise it. Further, the history of psychometrics and its continuing technical development would appear to be disposable. Though such simplicity may commend itself to the popular mind, it is only a relief from knowledge.

Nevertheless some such summary of *potential* (a word that has been making a comeback) has obvious general appeal, given the history, outlined in Chapter 1, of dyslexia as a *contrast* between literacy and other developments. Accordingly a *discrepancy* (statistically crude or otherwise) between IQ and one or more measures of attainment has

served as an operational definition of the condition. It is against this definition that eloquent voices have been raised.

The case against IQ in dyslexia assessment

Professionals uncomfortable with general notions of cognitive inequality
have welcomed the critique of IQ in dyslexia assessment, but this
critique is founded on a precise analysis of diagnostic methodology,
rather than on generalised objections to the measurement of individual
differences in ability.

Let us take a recent and representative statement of the case against
the discrepancy definition of dyslexia. Stanovich (1991a, 1991b) claims
that

> . . . most psychometricians, developmental psychologists and
> educational psychologists long ago gave up the belief that IQ test
> scores measured potential in any valid sense . . . (1991b p. 126)

though such scores

> . . . are gross measures of current cognitive functioning. (op. cit.,
> p. 127)

Yet intelligence is both a 'foundation concept' and 'superordinate
construct', without which 'the notion of reading disability . . . dissolves
into incoherence' (op. cit., p. 130). Different authorities recommend
different versions of IQ. Attainment discrepant with Performance IQ
(Wechsler's non-verbal scale) will 'necessarily lead to broad-based
deficits on the verbal side'; that is, the definition will produce children
with a range of linguistic difficulties of which poor reading is but one.
Yet a discrepancy with Verbal IQ will not, conversely, lead to generalised
non-verbal deficits, because fewer of these are associated with reading
failure. Visual-orthographic deficits might be more easily isolated.

Though opposed to one discrepancy methodology, Stanovich
presents another (as do most such critics). This is based on a discrepancy between reading and listening comprehension:

> We surely do not expect a child who does not understand spoken
> language to *read* well. (op. cit., p. 135, original emphasis)

Recently several studies have emanated from the Yale, Connecticut
longitudinal investigation into children with learning disabilities (for
example Fletcher et al., 1994; Shaywitz et al., 1992; Shaywitz et al., in
press). These try to address the issue of definitional variability in the
light of empirical observations of different groups. For instance in the
study by Fletcher et al. (1994) 199 children aged 7:5–9:5 were selected
according to criteria of:

- simple difference between ability and attainment scores;
- discrepancy between ability and attainment, using the score on one test (ability) to predict the score on another (attainment) through observed correlations between the two measures (regression);
- both criteria (when children identified by both methods are subtracted, simple difference leaves higher ability, regression leaves lower-ability individuals);
- low achievement (IQ 80 or above, attainment 90 or lower); and
- normal children without any reading impairment.

All children were given nine cognitive measures, five of them linguistic. Group profiles were obtained using multivariate profile analysis to yield dimensions of shape, elevation and flatness. This investigation confirmed that children with and without reading disabilities could be reliably discriminated and that two linguistic measures (phoneme deletion and word finding) characterised such reading disabled children. However, support was not forthcoming for the distinction between low-achieving and under-achieving poor readers.

In a more recent study by the same Yale team summarising findings from the Connecticut longitudinal sample (Shaywitz, Fletcher and Shaywitz, in press) , it is concluded that dyslexia is dimensional rather than categorical. This is because low-achieving and under-achieving poor readers show no qualitative differences (individual growth curves) and because a normal distribution model fits well data showing continuity between reading ability and reading disability. There need be no difficulty in living with this conclusion. To take the authors' own example of hypertension, the condition is as deserving of treatment if it is dimensional as if it is categorical. The data and argument leading to the conclusion are unconvincing however: out of a sample of 445 children, 46 (10.3%) are identified as poor readers by discrepancy *and* low achievement methodologies[4]. This is not at all what is usually meant by dyslexia and it comes as no surprise that Shaywitz et al. are soon claiming that 'reading disability is as prevalent in young girls as in young boys' (pp. 28–29). Dyslexia (not 'reading disability') is a more extreme matter than this and, in common with other extreme conditions, includes more boys but it is doubtful whether the small size of the Connecticut cohort could yield an unambiguously dyslexic sample of more than about a dozen children.

Severity may be of more consequence than a mere reduction in the ambiguity of definition. It may also be a necessary ingredient of aetiological distinctness. In their discussion of whether dyslexia is dimensional or categorical, Maughan and Yule (1994) cite evidence from genetic modelling techniques which evaluate differences between group and individual heritabilities (Plomin and Rende, 1991):

> [G]roup heritability [reflects] the extent to which average differ-
> ences between probands and individuals in unselected popula-
> tions are due to genetic effects . . . group heritabilities are only
> about half the magnitude of individual heritabilities . . . This
> pattern is consistent with a model of reading disability as aetiolog-
> ically distinct from the continuous dimension of reading ability.
> (op. cit., p. 654)

A methodologically innovative study by Stanovich and Siegel (1994)
came to a conclusion similar to that of the Yale studies. In this study ability and attainment data for some 1500 children aged 7–16 years were
reanalysed to permit reading-level group matches with younger controls
for both under- and low-achieving pupils. As a test of Stanovich's phonological-core variable-deficit model (Stanovich, 1988),[5] dependent variables both within (pseudoword reading, orthographic coding) and
outside (arithmetic, grammatic closure) the 'word recognition module'
were included. This permitted an examination of the hypothesis that:

> . . . other processing deficits emerge as one drifts in the multidi-
> mensional space from children with a discrepancy toward chil-
> dren without a discrepancy. (Stanovich and Siegel, op. cit., p. 28)

Other processing deficits did emerge, but the two groups (defined with
and without an IQ discrepancy) seldom differed with regard to the
nature of the reading disability itself. They did differ, however, in respect
of other cognitive abilities not directly implicated in literacy learning,
such as arithmetic skill and tasks of working memory (for rhyming and
non-rhyming letters, lists of numbers and words). Here the discrepancy
group performed better than the non-discrepancy group and reading-
age match controls, though their level of performance would not be
equal to that of chronological-age match controls. The implication,
though the authors do not say so, is that the main difference between
disabled readers defined by means of a discrepancy and 'garden variety'
disabled readers is one of intelligence. This is a criterion, of course, for
drawing up the groups in the first place: because IQ has played a part in
definition, this particular difference is entirely the result of the selection
process. In any group there will be variation of one kind or another,
including this kind.

Reply to these criticisms

The issue of the definition of dyslexia by aptitude-achievement discrepancy is, unfortunately, one on which the research and service-providing
communities seem to be steaming in opposite directions. Researchers – or

some researchers – the issue remains contentious – warn of the lack of empirical foundation for this methodology. Meanwhile country after country and, in the USA, state after state, vote such definitions into legislation.

On the professional view of intelligence and its measurement, matters are a good deal less 'signed-and-sealed' than Stanovich would have us believe. Fortunately there is plentiful recent evidence as to what 'experts' think which makes it unnecessary for us to rely on his assertion. His position on the lay view of 'potential' is advanced notwithstanding a 'scholarly consensus' regarded as 'overwhelming . . . that IQ is a significant predictor of academic success . . .' (Snyderman and Rothman, 1988, p. 51). Though no topic eludes definition so persistently as the nature of intelligence:

> . . . there is a consensus among psychologists as to the kinds of behaviour that are labelled intellectual. (Cleary et al., 1975, p. 19)

Robert Sternberg and colleagues published, in 1981, the results of a survey among research psychologists from the intelligence research community *and* among lay persons which found broad agreement in the ways 250 kinds of intelligent behaviour were rated.[6] Furthermore, Sternberg and Detterman (1986) found good agreement in a symposium of 25 intelligence researchers, in that:

> . . . the most frequently mentioned elements of intelligence are higher-level cognitive functions, such as abstract reasoning and problem-solving. (Snyderman and Rothman, 1988, p. 45)[7]

On intelligence *testing*, however, the views of experts and lay people, especially those influential in the media, tend to diverge. Towards the end of 1984, Snyderman and Rothman surveyed 1020 scholars, academics and practitioners in the United States: education researchers, developmental psychologists, sociologists of education, behaviour geneticists, industrial and organisational psychologists and cognitive scientists. These scholars, over half of them faculty members of universities and colleges, were sent a detailed questionnaire dealing with all aspects of intelligence, intelligence testing, heritability and group differences. Snyderman and Rothman sum up thus:

> [M]ost experts continue to believe that intelligence can be measured, and that genetic endowment plays an important role in individual differences in IQ. Whilst experts believe that IQ tests are somewhat biased, they do not believe that the bias is serious enough to discredit such tests, and they believe that measured IQ is an important determinant of success in American society. Indeed . . . the weight of evidence supporting such views, to judge from the scholarly literature, is probably greater today than it was in the 1950s. (Snyderman and Rothman, op. cit., p. ix).

Moreover:

> . . . such tests tap the most important, general way in which
> people differ psychologically . . . [I]n normal circumstances the
> reliability of Binet and Wechsler IQs is still around .93: such
> reliability is far higher than is found for any other important indi-
> vidual, non-biographical measurement across the entire range of
> twentieth-century psychology and indeed social science . . . The
> striking central phenomenon, however, is twentieth-century
> psychology's overwhelming and continuing vindication of Binet's
> main finding . . . Binet's common sense and empiricism arguably
> netted the key reality of human mental differences. Like heat, intel-
> ligence has proved satisfactorily quantifiable; and measurement
> should yield the same sorts of advance as occurred in science and
> medicine after the development of the thermometer...As much as
> household thermometers or kitchen scales, IQ tests are generally
> reliable and make distinctions that are not interpretable as
> discriminatory . . . IQ has undoubtedly been more fully checked
> out for possible bias than has any other variable in psychology.
> (Brand, 1996, pp. 1–2, 33, 41–2)

There may be reasons for including intelligence testing in the psychological assessment of dyslexia over and above those afforded by agreement
that it can be done. But before we consider these, what about the negative evidence of distinctive cognitive profiles in individuals identified by
means of aptitude-achievement discrepancies?

The Fletcher et al. study described above itself depends upon a
narrow definitional base of reading disability. Two reading tests were
used, word and non-word reading from the Woodcock–Johnson Psycho-
Educational Battery – Revised (WJ-R) (Woodcock and Johnson, 1989,
1990). Both word recognition and phonological decoding have a direct
relationship to the likely 'profile' that was being sought. Though full
WISC-R assessments were used to generate IQs for discrepancy purposes,
other profile data were sought from nine variables with 'well-attested
relationships with reading ability and disability' (Fletcher et al., 1994, p.
9). No real attempt, however, was made to address, in the light of theory,
likely information-processing differences other than in phonological
processing. Evidence of the latter, certainly, was a single clear-cut finding.

Raw scores were converted to standard scores based on the performance of only 33 children in the original sample enrolled as the normal
group but regression equations were generated from a larger epidemiological cohort of Connecticut school children. The regression cut-off,
however, described underachievement throughout the sample, given that
at an IQ level of 100 a reading quotient of 80 is predicted. By this standard possibly as few as 10 of the so-called unimpaired readers would fail
to be described as relatively poor readers by a discrepancy criterion of

some magnitude in a clinic setting using WISC-R and WJ-R measures in the usual way. The absence of normality in the control group does rather undermine the absence of distinctive pathology in the disabled groups.

The Stanovich and Siegel study referred to, through greater sample size and age variety, overcomes some of the shortcomings of the Fletcher et al. analysis. The principal conclusion, that there is no evidence of greater *severity* in the discrepancy group, need not necessarily be challenged. Again, there is some question about the 299 children selected as normal controls: there is an (unweighted) average of about −0.3 of a SD between IQ and WRAT-R reading among them – unexplained general underachievement. In spite of technical sophistication the study is of course unable, being cross-sectional, to address the most compelling class of evidence of severity: differential response to treatment and differential cognitive progress with and without treatment.

Stanovich and Siegel are keenly aware of the importance of the former: they refer to a study by Cole, Dale and Mills (1990) of children with developmental language disorder. Here there is evidence that enables them to conclude: 'In short, there was no differential response to treatment' (Stanovich and Siegel, op. cit., p. 47). Elsewhere, however, Stanovich admits that there are:

> no good data indicating that discrepancy-defined dyslexics respond differently to various educational treatments than do garden-variety readers of the same age or than younger non-dyslexic children reading at the same level (Stanovich, 1991b, p. 129).

Without necessarily rejecting the hypothesis that dyslexics may differ only in position on a quantitative continuum (rather than qualitatively as members of a unique category), it must be asserted here that there is no single teaching experience better agreed than that non-dyslexic retarded readers are easy to teach! Response to intervention remains an important criterion, among others, for diagnosis of dyslexia.

In fact a major distinction between retarded and disabled readers is a common finding. For instance in a recent evaluation of the effectiveness of Reading Recovery in several English local education authority settings, Sylva and Hurry (1995) found that Reading Recovery benefited children from socio-economically disadvantaged homes more, by virtue of its book experience approach. They speculate:

> For children from homes and communities where reading is more highly valued but who still find reading difficult, the explanations of their problems are more likely to include internal causes, for example, some genetic factor. It is plausible that those children will be more difficult to help, and that the widening of their reading experience for a fixed time is not sufficient to overcome their long-term problems. (Sylva and Hurry, op. cit., pp. 15–16)

One or two studies will not suffice to settle such continuing arguments. As I have suggested, the formidable weight of history, and its foundling, common sense, incline to the contrast view of dyslexia. Those with a fundamentally different conception of the phenomenon have an uphill struggle to persuade others that a different method is required for a different problem.[8]

It is instructive that Stanovich couches his criticisms in the language he does. He asks: 'Do we really want to look for a group of poor readers who are qualitatively differentiable in terms of etiology and neurophysiology?' He goes on to refer, though he doesn't share it, to: 'enthusiasm for the quest to isolate . . . a select group (Stanovich, 1991b, p. 131). With a non-verbal IQ-based discrepancy, he complains: 'A behaviourally and neurologically differentiable core deficit will be virtually impossible to find, given such a classification' (op. cit., p. 132). And a 'conceptually justified discrepancy-based classification . . . will be maddeningly tricky to carry out in a principled fashion' (op. cit., p. 136).

Implicit here is a *research agenda*. However, the researcher's agenda is not the clinician's.[9] Both are interested in careful definition of dyslexia. The clinician ultimately depends upon research elucidation of the problem, as the researcher depends upon the clinician for knowing *what matters*. Yet the experimental construction of virtually pure samples of one or another type of poor reader, or subtype of dyslexia, or definition of deficit, so that hypotheses may be subjected to ever more stringent tests, must seem to the clinician a will-o'-the-wisp.

The researcher serves abstract truth. The clinician hopes to resolve a child's problems in the light of research. The researcher aims to clear up uncertainties. The clinician hopes to tolerate them. The researcher lives with a small cluster of issues and focuses on these with absolute cunning. On the clinician's shores are washed up ever-varying examples of familiar problems. There are, for the researcher, improbable theories that no amount of data will finally clinch. For the clinician there are home truths no absence of data can undermine. For the researcher the boundaries of dyslexia must be drawn before the centre can be defined. For the clinician every dyslexic individual's position can be mapped in relation to the centre of a circle – the classical dyslexic – whose outer boundaries dissolve through shades of grey to indistinctness.

Uses of discrepancy

In fact the contrast principle is the cornerstone of the individual cognitive assessment. There are many possible discrepancies to be evaluated – discrepancy with IQ is but one kind – and all are descriptive rather than definitional.

This may be seen readily enough in cases where an individual is dyslexic but where no discrepancy is to be expected. The compensated or remediated dyslexic continues to show clear symptomatology (poor everyday memory, deterioration of skill under stress, phonological confusions) but may no longer show literacy levels at variance with other abilities. The younger child, not yet at school or in the early stages of schooling, cannot be expected to qualify on the grounds of inability to score on a reading test: children of this age in the main do not score on reading tests.

Careful use of statistics will define the degree of exceptionality in most cases of children of school age (Turner, 1994a) but this may sweep many more children into the dyslexia net than are actually dyslexic. Discrepancy statistics describe *underachievement only*. An individual may have missed school through long illness, suffered frequent moves of home and school during the years crucial to instruction in literacy (5–7), or through emotional problems has not engaged with the teaching he/she has received, or may simply have spent several years shipwrecked happily on a desert island free from schooling. Such a child will show up, on any battery which includes ability and achievement measures, as underachieving in literacy relative to ability.

This is why dyslexia diagnosis seeks, in addition, evidence of a processing deficit. Broadly speaking, there are two classes of such evidence: phonological processing and speed of information processing.[10] Evaluation of any such deficit proceeds along the same lines (normatively if possible) as evaluation of reading and other abilities. Without such evidence, the description remains one of underachievement. But by the same token the discrepancy criterion must in most cases be met: a case can hardly be made for a dyslexic-type learning difficulty in a pupil whose reading and spelling are not exceptional.

Normative testing provides for precise comparisons between an individual and his or her contemporaries; this is so for ability and attainment. The same methodology also enables a comparison to be made of the size of any gap there may be between the two. For this purpose a summation of development of general ability (IQ) is probably the most convenient measure but further types of discrepancy come to light during the assessment and these may be significant. They may be between verbal and non-verbal abilities, between non-verbal and spatial abilities, between performance on visuo-spatial tasks with and without a motor component. They may also be between different kinds of attainment: between reading and spelling, between decoding and comprehension, between literacy and number skills.

Several such 'minor discrepancy' methodologies have been well developed. Sometimes published tests contain contrast pairs of measures along with the statistical apparatus with which to interpret them. Word and non-word reading may turn out to be the most important of these (Rack, Snowling and Olson, 1992). If so, both the Woodcock–Johnson Psycho-Educational Battery – Revised (WJ-R) (Woodcock

& Johnson, 1989, 1990) and the Woodcock Reading Mastery Tests (Woodcock, 1987) offer the user co-normed tests of high quality, designed to yield detailed programme-planning information. The Wechsler Memory Scale – Revised (Wechsler, 1987) provides for an evaluation of any difference between verbal and visual memory in adults.[11] Similar possibilities exist for children in the Wide Range Assessment of Memory and Learning (WRAML) (Sheslow and Adams, 1990) and in the recent Test of Memory and Learning (TOMAL) (Reynolds and Bigler, 1994).

The discrepancy favoured by Stanovich and others, that of reading with listening comprehension, shows equal promise and limitation. One can see from tables of subtest intercorrelations for the British Ability Scales (BAS) and Differential Ability Scales (DAS) that, in the years in which reading skills are first acquired, they are mainly associated not with overtly linguistic measures (vocabulary, verbal reasoning) but with perceptual and pattern-recognition skills such as Basic Number Skills, Matrices, Block Design and Recall of Digits (see Tables 2.1–2.2). In the main, the activities involved in these tests are associated with verbal strategy, for instance applying names to shapes and storing verbal sequences in immediate memory (for a closer examination of these processes, see Chapters 3 and 4). Only at about age 9–10 does Word Definitions, a vocabulary measure, become strongly associated with reading.

Table 2.1: Three highest correlations at each age of the Word Reading scale with other British Ability Scales; decimal points omitted. For abbreviations, see Appendix 1. After Elliott (1983, Ch. 9).

Age	WDe	Sim	Mat	BDL	RDi	SIP	BNS	Mean
5:0–5:11	41				44		51	45.3
6:0–6:11		39			41		50	43.3
7:0–7:11			39	43	39		56	44.3
8:0–8:11	38		38		38	46	41	40.2
9:0–9:11	67	59					62	62.7
10:0–10:11	56	51			53		51	52.8
11:0–11:11	67	55					67	63.0
12:0–12:11	67	52	54				54	56.8
13:0–13:11	68	58					61	62.3
Mean	57.7	52.3	43.7	43.0	43.0	46.0	54.8	

Though measures of listening comprehension are promising and should be pursued (see, for instance, Bedford-Feuell et al., 1995), when used to provide a discrepancy with reading attainment they require *greater failure*. This is because the separation of reading technique and linguistic sophistication takes longer to establish developmentally and is more evident in children who are older or more advanced. Only at greater

Table 2.2: Three highest correlations of Word Reading with all other Differential Ability Scales and composites; decimal points omitted. For abbreviations, see Appendix 1. After Elliott (1990, Tables C9–C24, pp. 314–29).

Age	WDe	Sim	Mat	SQR	RDi	BNS	Spe	VC	NVC	GCA	Mean
5:0–5:11		42		46	39			42	42	44	42.5
6:0–6:11			46		48	75	88			59	63.2
7:0–7:11	45					67	90			58	65.0
8:0–8:11	45	49	39			56	85	52			54.3
9:0–9:11	59	51	51	48			85	61		61	59.4
10:0–10:11	49			50	47		80	55		54	55.8
11:0–11:11	60	44		47			81			59	58.2
12:0–12:11	58	41	41	56			78				54.8
13:0–13:11	64	57		54			84	67		68	65.7
14:0–14:11	56	47		46			75	57		56	56.2
15:0–15:11	60	49		48			79			61	59.4
16:0–16:11	73	64		60			77	75			69.8
17:0–17:11	70	51		44			78	67			62.0
Mean	58.1	49.5	44.3	49.9	44.7	66.0	81.7	59.5	42.0	57.8	

ages and higher levels of linguistic complexity, in other words, does this methodology come into its own as a measure of dyslexia.

It seems to have been overlooked, however, that such a comparison, using objective normative data, has been possible since 1983. The British Ability Scales (BAS) (Elliott, Murray and Pearson, 1979, 1983) will be discussed more fully in the next chapter but it may be observed here that a measure of reading/vocabulary discrepancy was designed into the system by giving an identical set of words to a short form each of Word Definitions (F) and Word Reading (E). Measures of vocabulary are by common consent among the most highly g-loaded tests of both verbal and general intelligence and describe one aspect, at least, of listening comprehension. The short all-age Form F of Word Definitions does excellent duty as a measure of verbal comprehension. The same set of 20 words serves as the stimulus set for one of several alternative word-sets in the test of word recognition, Word Reading. Thus the words whose meaning a child knows serve also to measure those the child can read. Given a reading age of about 7:2 (two words read correctly), the number of words that must be correctly *defined* at different ages to obtain a discrepancy large enough to be found in only 5% of the standardisation sample may be given for different ages as in Table 2.3.

Table 2.3: Numbers of words that must be correctly defined on BAS Word Definitions Form F at different ages to give, at a reading level of 7:2, a discrepancy frequency of 5%.

Years	Words	Years	Words
8.0	3	11.0	8
8.5	4–5	11.5	8–9
9.0	5	12.0	9
9.5	5–6	12.5	9
10.0	6	13.0	10
10.5	7	13.5	10

The psychologist, then, will want to evaluate all possible inconsistencies in the development of cognitive skills, by means of contrasts or discrepancies, using the measurement resources available to the fullest extent.

The case for an IQ component to the individual assessment

The modest case for IQ is soon made. First, there is the role of IQ in summarising the abilities of an individual across a range of task domains, especially those abilities *unaffected* by any learning impairment (the contrast principle: impaired skills contrast with unimpaired ones).

However, it may be that there is so much inter-subtest scatter that the global IQ is seriously misleading: it may represent a level of ability at which the subject never performs. In this case the segregation of abilities is best explained at a level below that of the summary. It is usual not to report Full Scale (global) WISC IQ but only Verbal, Performance or Index scores where these are widely disparate. However, overall IQ is always derived by the same procedure and is therefore fair to all children, however heterogeneous the contributing scores. Intermediate-level composite scores on the Differential Ability Scales (DAS) permit analysis of three factors or clusters, Verbal, Non-verbal Reasoning and Spatial and, within these, of discrepant individual scales. The DAS, like other modern tests, permits higher-level abilities, such as vocabulary and social comprehension, to be measured separately from lower level information skills, such as immediate verbal memory, sampled through diagnostic tests.

Such intra-individual or *ipsative* variation may reveal much of significance in the profile of an individual referred for a learning difficulty. But global IQ, an individual's total or mean score, is, by a universally accepted procedure, the summary of performance across all areas of ability measured.

Perhaps *because* schools of thought differ as to whether the discrepancy with reading (say) is best made by a verbal, non-verbal or some other stable summary of cognitive performance, it is best to retain the simplest general summary measure – IQ. In experimental terms, this provides an easily understood measure of control. There is little difficulty in explaining to the lay person, parent or teacher that in relation to *age and ability* their child is performing at an unexpectedly low level. Even for those individuals for whom the global IQ is misleading, because it conceals what the clinician has been at pains to reveal, for instance a large difference between verbal and non-verbal abilities, IQ-achievement discrepancy can provide a generous framework within which to draw finer distinctions, such as a discrepancy of achievement with verbal IQ or some more particular strand of linguistic ability. It seems reasonable to make the IQ the starting point of the analysis however.

Factor-analytic studies, of course, have long proposed that something is being measured by IQ, namely *g* or a higher-order general factor in intelligence. Colin Elliott, co-author of the original British Ability Scales (Elliott, Murray and Pearson, 1979, 1983) and author of many subsequent developments (Elliott, 1983, 1990, 1992), writes (1995, p.1) that

I have changed my view . . . 'Intelligence' and 'IQ' . . . have so many meanings that finally they have none . . . I consider that they should be defined as psychometric *g* . . . 'the general ability of an individual to perform complex mental processing that involves conceptualization and the transformation of information'.[12]

One corollary of this view is that IQs measured by different tests are not all measuring the same thing. A Stanford-Binet IQ has different characteristics[13] from a Wechsler IQ; WISC-III[UK] yields a different IQ from WISC-R; and so on. On this view, the validity of newer, better tests is not to be adjudicated by how well their IQs correlate with Wechsler or Binet IQs. But all such tests may be evaluated to the extent that their IQ or global summary scores approximate to psychometric g. This will be done for three major tests in Chapter 3.

An obstacle is that many intelligence tests contain a lot of 'noise', that is, data on cognitive functioning whose importance derives from their measurement of something other than intelligence. Only five of WISC-III's 12 scales, for instance, measure intelligence (psychometric g) to an acceptable extent (loadings on the unrotated first factor in principal components analysis of 0.70 or above: see Kaufman, 1994, pp. 42–3). Generally, technical progress in this area has favoured the redesign of IQ tests to reflect modern intelligence theory and to measure varieties of intelligence more directly and to a better extent. The next chapter will include discussion of one-, two- and three-factor tests and their evaluation. Whether one prefers to think of intelligence as unitary or plural, however, the irrelevance of much material in major tests warns against the too-close identification of general intellectual ability with 'IQ'. This is particularly an issue with dyslexic individuals, whose higher-order reasoning and abstract conceptual understanding often contrast wildly with their low-level information-processing efficiency.

Historically this has posed a considerable dilemma for consulting psychologists. How is one to interpret a child's Wechsler IQ when this composite includes scores on Digit Span and Coding, subtests that are poor measures of g but efficient if unintended indicators of learning difficulty? Are IQ tests biased against certain groups? Should IQs be computed with certain subtest scores omitted at the examiner's discretion? That this dilemma runs well beyond dyslexia is shown by the example of the child with poor fine motor skills whose scores on timed tests are depressed, slowness being a prime feature of developmental co-ordination disorder (DCD). Should one group of subtests be divided into the timed and the untimed, each yielding a composite? There is considerable collateral support for doing just this nowadays: WISC-III scoring software and other publications give detailed methods for producing just such measures of 'shared abilities'. But perhaps all such special pleading, especially in the pressures of the consultation situation in which IQ is far from being a dead issue, however ingenious, impartial and well justified, should always be accompanied by an estimate of IQ accomplished in the conventional way and left unadjusted. Rather than *suppressing* IQ for any of the reasons now popular, none of them free, either, from forms of special pleading, perhaps the independent-minded examiner should consider the *multiplication* of IQs and intermediate-level composites, such as WISC-III Index scores and DAS Clusters. Such composites are simply closer to the evidence, to the facts of the child's particular case.

But why survey an individual's *g* or general intellectual abilities anyway? The answer to this is twofold. The IQ, first port of call in analysing the pattern of performances on a test of general cognitive ability, is the midpoint of a person's profile (Kaufman, 1979, 1990, 1994) and therefore a point of reference for all other results, including those that diverge so widely as to call the midpoint in question. Then there is another important principle to which we shall return: *it is important not to miss the problem you are not looking for*. Specific tests for dyslexia should be interpreted in the context of an analysis of all of a person's cognitive abilities and difficulties, as the person may have a learning problem that has nothing to do with dyslexia, or other learning problems in addition to dyslexia. It is hardly the responsibility of the person referring him- or herself to identify the difficulty correctly in advance. It must be true, given correlations of reading with IQ between 0.6 and 0.7, that 'most reading problems are caused by low intelli-·gence'.[14] Moreover, tests of general ability enable us to map much of the spectrum of a person's verbal, non-verbal reasoning and visuo-spatial abilities, in any area of which may lurk the explanation of a more local learning difficulty.

IQ should be computed, banded with error and reported. If it is notably unrepresentative of the level at which the individual characteristically performs, it may, after providing a first point of reference for the regression matrix, be set aside in the interpretation process. Dyslexia, not IQ, is the focus of the assessment. IQ-attainment discrepancy is descriptive, rather than definitional, and insufficient by itself for diagnostic purposes.

A further point in support of a summary measure of intelligence is the often cathartic effect this information has on dyslexic individuals who have long been given to understand they are stupid. There is no *a priori* reason to associate dyslexia with any particular level of intelligence; and careful use of regression methods is necessary to achieve fairness with respect to all levels of ability (Turner, 1994a). Though the differentiation of specific from general learning difficulties has been the preliminary to the establishment of dyslexia as a meaningful diagnostic entity (Hornsby, 1995), it seems misconceived to attempt to recruit, posthumously, Leonardo da Vinci, Einstein, Rodin, Yeats and others to the dyslexic cause. This is sometimes done, notwithstanding the absence of educational and other evidence that might enable later ages to reach a judgement on whether or not such heroic figures may have been dyslexic. Moreover there is a risk that such positive role-models may render their condition still more daunting to the dyslexics they are supposed to encourage! Dyslexia is a deficit, rather than a 'different way of thinking' and an association with artistic ability has been suggested rather than demonstrated. But the view that normal intelligence makes dyslexia 'élitist' is perversely the opposite of the truth. Accusations of stupidity and laziness continue to be the most common after decades of 'awareness' work, and consistent experiences of dyslexic children in today's schools. The demonstration of significant unimpaired areas of cognitive ability remains important both as assurance and as part of the diagnostic process.

Finally, to return to our larger dilemmas, there is the view that it 'it is not necessarily the case . . . that individuals with lower IQ scores should inevitably be poorer readers' (Frederickson and Reason, 1995, p. 197). Indeed not. Ample evidence of reading gains obtained proportionately for lower-IQ pupils with Direct Instruction techniques is contained in Engelmann and Carnine (1982, Ch. 30) and as Frederickson and Reason argue, reading can itself lead to gains in verbal ability, just as reading disability can lead to intellectual deprivation. Furthermore it is not the case that so-called *garden variety* poor readers are necessarily lacking in intelligence. Poor readers who have *nothing wrong with them* abound in schools,[15] but the exceptions mentioned by Frederickson and Reason are exceptions to a rule they wish not to mention: the obvious but much-avoided proposition that intelligence may have something to do with learning! A rare acknowledgement of this state of affairs is to be found in Kline (1993):

> The cause of academic failure may be relatively straightforward – low intelligence. Thus a first step is the intelligence test. Until the intelligence of a subject is known, it is impossible to decide how she ought to be performing at school. Thus in cases of educational difficulty an intelligence test is a good first test. (p. 313)

The omission of cognitive ability by social scientists considering such problems as malparenting (abuse and neglect of children) leads Herrnstein and Murray to comment: 'The reluctance of scholars and policymakers alike to look at the role of intelligence . . . may properly be called scandalous' (1994, p. 213). They consider intelligence 'a reasonably well-understood construct, measured with accuracy and fairness by any number of standardized mental tests' (op. cit., p. 1).

Some indication of the scale of the neglect is given by these authors' isolation of the major independent contribution made by cognitive ability to poverty, unemployment, accident proneness, divorce, illegitimacy and crime, as well as to academic success. This contribution is analysed, using standard regression analyses, so that all other hypothesised contributions are taken into account.[16]

For many purposes, too, that are of immediate relevance in psychological assessment

> [o]ther more specific abilities . . . [when they do not] involve g . . .

are irrelevant to capturing more than a small fraction of the practically important differences between random members of the population (Brand, 1996, pp. 51–2)

Measured intelligence, then, may be an important variable in many realms of human behaviour, including learning. Beyond dyslexia, most cognitive abilities should be considered in relation to most kinds of learning. In assessing for dyslexia, the psychologist will be particularly interested in the development or non-development of groups of skills of known diagnostic significance. This is consistent with the turning of research endeavours towards the elucidation of manifold abilities and their interrelationships, for instance in literacy learning. These efforts do not necessarily weaken the position of psychometric g nor negate a half-century of related empirical research. But the explanatory power of g is not strong at the level of the average individual. Children perform within very broad limits and teaching is tuned only in rather general ways[17] to the styles of initiative and dependency associated with different ability band-widths.

IQ, then, is a first port of call: a summary measure of performance on all tests of ability; an anchor for a regression matrix which includes, in good modern tests, co-normed measures of attainment in basic skills; reassurance for individuals and families that failure in literacy does not have to imply mental retardation; and the broadest possible guide to setting expectations in teaching. From now on we shall refer principally to tests of specific abilities and distinctive processes. These hold out promise of what has become known as *profiling*.

Notes

1 Jensen (1981), a popular yet reliable book on psychometric matters, is a welcome corrective to the usual conflict-laden accounts furnished in the media.
2 Recent experience in black South African classrooms (Turner, 1994b) made abundantly clear to me the ubiquitous nature of language in mediating cognitive skills, especially the skills of reading or writing in English, as opposed to one of the 11 African languages which were the children's mother tongues. The latter, with their small vocabularies, oft-repeated grammatical links and infinitival forms, are part and parcel of the non-literate cultures to which they belong, speaking of other ways of life, other values.
3 For a good recent treatment of regression to the mean, in a discussion of statistical arguments in general reasoning, see Garnham and Oakhill (1994).
4 Some 75% of the children identified by an evidently loose discrepancy criterion are also identified as low achievers, yet the authors note (p. 35) that 'children who do meet discrepancy criteria but who are not low achieving . . . also require assistance'.
5 This holds that though the features of reading disability may vary widely with individuals, there is always a core deficit present of difficulty with the processing of speech sounds.
6 Sternberg et al. (1981) cited in Snyderman and Rothman (1988, p.45).
7 'Psychologists must know from ordinary experience what human intelligence is ,before they can devise tests for measuring it scientifically, and should they mea-

sure instead something that ordinary experience does not recognize as intelligence, they would be constructing a new subject matter which could no longer claim the intrinsic interest attached to that which they originally chose to study.' Polanyi (1958, p. 139).

8 '. . . we must always remember that the idea of 'unexplained' reading failure is the puzzle that enticed us into the idea of dyslexia in the first place' (Stanovich, 1991b, p. 134).

9 For instance the most common clinical finding that major imbalances in cognitive development, e.g. between spatial and verbal ability, exist in dyslexic *and non-dyslexic* children, would seem to justify for many continued use of such tests in describing and explaining learning difficulties.

10 It may, indeed, turn out that the two are the same: McDougall and Hulme (1994) already speak summarily of 'speed of phonological processing' (p. 41).

11 I am indebted to Dr Beverley Steffert (personal communication) for this methodology: she is able to illustrate the utility of this approach by reference to large quantities of data from adult dyslexics.

12 Elliott (1995) is here quoting his own earlier definition from the manual of the Differential Ability Scales (Elliott, 1990).

13 Aside from a standard deviation of 16.

14 Chris Brand, personal communication. In social science terms, these are remarkably high correlations.

15 In many cases no explanation is needed beyond that of curriculum deprivation.

16 Among psychologists, the distaste for intellectual measurement may have no basis more substantial than egalitarian animus. But, as is so often the case, a gap exists between rhetoric and reality. A survey of local education authority psychological services by Fife Psychological Service in 1990 found that intelligence tests were used 'often' or 'very often' by 70.9% of respondents. Nevertheless some ambivalence may be gauged in the purposes psychologists imputed to their test use, including that of 'structured interview techniques'. Results of this postal survey are contained in a paper, with an accompanying letter of explanation dated 10 October 1990, both signed by Mrs Ingeborg Stobie, Fife Regional Council Psychological Service, 1 Swan Road, Kirkcaldy, Fife KY1 1UZ.

17 To deny the importance of these, however, would necessitate also denying that there are *aptitude-instruction interactions*. The significance of these was authoritatively discussed in Snow and Yalow (1982); more recently Pumfrey and Reason (1991) have returned to the part such interactions may play in explaining dyslexia.

Chapter 3
Describing Individual Variation

Unusual but not unique?

All human individuals can be classed together (as human beings), as members of broad classes (such as males), more narrowly as members of select groups (mathematically gifted) or as unique individuals. Great emotion attaches to almost any partition of human beings into categories. At the other extreme the uniqueness of the individual, logically incommunicable, has a basis in religious vision.[1]

But the category is to social science what the billiard ball is to physics. Enabling a comparison of any individual with *all* others of the same age, evaluation on the major intellectual assessment systems, permits finer and finer discriminations, moving from the universal to the unique, of the individual as a member of smaller groups. An assessment, of course, will include consideration of the individual as unique, as well as being a member of large and small categories.

To identify membership of the small group *dyslexic* is to move in another direction as well, from the descriptive one, of underachievement in need of explanation, to the cognitive neuropsychological one, of diagnostic features in need of clarification. Criteria for identification, therefore, are twofold: an underachievement criterion, where this can be applied, and a deficit criterion of one or more positive signs consistent with the known information-processing characteristics of dyslexia.

Diagnosticity

Fortunately or unfortunately there is no single test for dyslexia. The assessment process involves building up, in *pointilliste* fashion, innumerable small bits of data until the picture, one way or another, becomes clear. This can be difficult as children frequently present inconsistent and contradictory profiles. Indeed the best contemporary psychological assessments may draw on 20–30 individual test results. By comparison with the best, reports which base their judgements on, say,

41

only 80% of this information can fail entirely to demonstrate the real nature of the problem. Thoroughness and comprehensiveness remain, for the present, the hallmarks of the most highly developed assessment.

Quality of psychological assessment, however, is not transparent to the user. There may be a measure of agreement, nowadays, as to what constitutes a *bad* psychological assessment: thinness of evidence, absence of argument, vague conclusions, lack of useful recommendations. On these features all can perhaps agree, but there is little recognition, even within the profession, of what constitutes a *good* psychological assessment. Comprehensiveness, at least, is recognised by families (the primary users) as a virtue. A difficulty to which we shall return, however, is that other concerned users of assessments – teachers, befrienders, administrators, advocates – have little of the technical grasp necessary to discriminate between a good and a *less good* assessment.[2] Given the educational level required to do so, it may be that standards should first be established within the applied psychology professions themselves.

A diagnostic test for dyslexia is a task at which dyslexic people perform badly and non-dyslexic ones perform well. No more sophisticated definition of a diagnostic test for dyslexia is available. Refined, this becomes a test on which, selectively, dyslexic people perform badly, who otherwise perform normally (that is, unexceptionally), and on which non-dyslexic people perform no less well or badly than on other tests. This remains, for the moment, a behavioural criterion: there is no histological test of tissue culture, no blood test, no hair test.[3] So long as dyslexia remains a performance-based educational and cognitive deficit, behavioural tests will be employed. The sharper the contrast between the performance of dyslexic and non-dyslexic people on any test, the fitter the test for this purpose.

Clinical use of ability tests

There are now *nine* major psychological assessment batteries suitable for use with school-age children. (Technology available for assessment of pre-school children and post-school adults is discussed in separate chapters.) These are:

1. Wechsler Intelligence Scale for Children – Third Edition (WISC-III) (Wechsler, D. *Wechsler Intelligence Scale For Children* – Third Edition. New York: Harcourt Brace Jovanovitch, The Psychological Corporation, 1992).
2. British Ability Scales (BAS) (Elliott, C.D., Murray, D.J. and Pearson, L.S. *British Ability Scales*. Windsor, Berks: NFER-Nelson, 1979, 1983); this will shortly be available in a second edition, BAS-II.
3. Differential Ability Scales (DAS) (Elliott, C.D. *Differential Ability*

Scales. New York: Harcourt Brace Jovanovitch, Psychological Corporation, 1990) is a US revision of the BAS .

4. Woodcock–Johnson Psycho-Educational Battery – Revised (WJ-R) (Woodcock, R.W. and Johnson, M.B. *Woodcock–Johnson Psycho-Educational Battery* – Revised. Allen, Texas: DLM, 1989, 1990).

5. Stanford-Binet Intelligence Scale: Fourth Edition (Binet-4 or SB:FE) (Thorndike, R.L., Hagen, E.P. and Sattler, J.M. *Stanford-Binet Intelligence Scale: Fourth Edition*. Chicago: Riverside, 1986).

6. Das–Naglieri Cognitive Assessment System (Das, J.P. and Naglieri, J.A. *Das–Naglieri Cognitive Assessment System*. Chicago: Riverside, in press).

7. Detroit Tests of Learning Aptitude – Third Edition (Detroit-3; Hammill, D.D. *Detroit Tests of Learning Aptitude* – Third Edition. Austin, Texas: Pro-Ed, 1991).

8. Kaufman Assessment Battery for Children (K-ABC) (Kaufman, A.S. and Kaufman, N.L. *Kaufman Assessment Battery For Children*. Circle Pines, Minnesota: American Guidance Service, 1983).

9. Kaufman Adolescent and Adult Intelligence Test (KAIT) (Kaufman, A.S. and Kaufman, N.L. *Kaufman Adolescent and Adult Intelligence Test*. Circle Pines, Minnesota: American Guidance Service, 1993).

These test batteries, which may sometimes be referred to by their abbreviations as these become familiar, exist for the most part in editions with fully *co-normed* tests of achievement (reading, spelling, number). That is, tests of achievement in these basic skills were given to individuals in the standardisation sample at the same time as the major tests of ability. This permits comparisons to be made between ability and achievement *from within the standardisation sample*. This can be done because of the observed tendency for such measures to correlate; the prediction of achievement, based on ability, depends on the strength of the correlation and requires a simple calculation. Regression effects – the tendency for scores further from the mean to fall closer to it – are crucially taken into account. Accordingly the batteries are published with an apparatus for calculating and interpreting the frequency of occurrence of any gap between expected and observed levels of performance (regression analysis). This will be central to the discussions that follow.

Woodcock–Johnson (WJ-R), for instance, consists of 35 tests of cognitive ability and achievement (core and supplementary), with full regression apparatus for interpreting discrepancies between related individual test scores, between test scores and clusters, and between achievement and ability composites. It is developed wholly on the basis of modern theories of intelligence (Horn-Cattell theory of *fluid* and *crystallised* ability: see below). The Kaufman Adolescent and Adult Intelligence Test (KAIT), too, follows the Horn–Cattell theory, with some influence of Luria–Golden theory on 'block 3' higher-order planning and analysis and a Piagetian emphasis on formal operational thinking. It yields Fluid and Crystallised IQs as well as a Composite IQ, but has not been standardised with any integral achievement tests.

The technical advantages and disadvantages of each system in this wave of new tests, and new editions of old tests, which has altered the user's vista in the 1990s, will not be reviewed in detail, nor will the varying possibilities that exist for addressing discrepancies between abilities and achievements. For the most part we will be concerned with the two systems which are most popular in Britain: Wechsler Intelligence Scale For Children – Third Edition (WISC-III[UK]), a British edition of WISC-III, and the British Ability Scales (BAS), revised in the USA as the Differential Ability Scales (DAS), and forthcoming in a further revision in September 1996 in Britain as BAS-II. Occasionally we shall be referring to Woodcock–Johnson or KAIT, when these address some difficulty or present some opportunity that cannot easily be paralleled.

The Wechsler legacy

David Wechsler (1896–1981) published his first test of adult intelligence, the Wechsler-Bellevue Intelligence Scale in 1939. In 1955 he published its revision, the Wechsler Adult Intelligence Scale (WAIS) and in 1981 a further revision, the Wechsler Adult Intelligence Scale – Revised (WAIS-R). A new edition (WAIS-III) is in prospect though not yet close to publication.

This early model introduced a structural distinction between Verbal and Performance intelligence, summarised in summary scores, IQs. Various non-verbal tests employing visual-motor skills and depending to a lesser extent on words for their instructions and the subjects' responses were gathered together in a Performance scale. This contrasted with the Verbal scale, which typically measured vocabulary, verbal reasoning and social comprehension. The Full Scale IQ was an average of the two, always allowing for regression effects.

This model provided the pattern for the first such test for children, the Wechsler Intelligence Scale for Children (1949) which, in 1974, became the Wechsler Intelligence Scale for Children – Revised (WISC-R) and, in 1990, the Wechsler Intelligence Scale for Children – Third Edition (WISC-III). For nearly 50 years these tests have provided the standard by which all others have been judged. Adapted, translated and used worldwide, they have accrued a unique body of research literature around them whose value, nowadays, tends to transcend that of the tests themselves. For instance, the measurement of the verbal and visuospatial groups of abilities would not always now be done using Wechsler's measures of Verbal and Performance IQs. Nevertheless the psychological literature that has evaluated this major developmental contrast is built largely upon these IQs.

It is important to understand that the intentions and methodology of David Wechsler were those of a clinician. He worked for the most part not before the era of factor analysis (this dates to the 1904 work of Pearson and Spearman, under both of whom Wechsler studied in London after the First World War), but before the era in which powerful computing allowed the large-scale development of such methods and their application to psychometric problems. He died only five years after hand-held programmable calculators first appeared in the high street.[4]

Wechsler long resisted the revision of his scales along statistical lines, clinging to WISC items he liked[5] on grounds that they drew forth revealing answers during clinical assessment (Kaufman, 1994, Preface). In this he was taking sides in a dispute that has gone on for most of the century between defenders of clinical and intuitive judgement and psychometricians who advance purely statistical arguments about test construction, based on item analyses and sampling theory. This argument has in fact clearly been won by the statisticians.

The Wechsler scales are virtually the prisoners of their illustrious and prestigious tradition because of (a) their continuity across pre-school, school-age and post-school populations; (b) their historical position as constant reference points in innumerable research studies; and (c) their world-wide institutionalisation in cultures remote from the Coney Island that provided the 'standardisation' for the first Wechsler-Bellevue Intelligence Scale. They cannot be revised as radically as they need to be. Nevertheless, in an attempt to adapt in an era of rising technical standards, the Wechsler scales have acquired an exo-skeleton, the factorial structure that provides basic psychometric credibility.

Although the WISC was conceived before the ascendancy of factor analysis within psychometrics, it has now received the attention of sophisticated statisticians whose task was to revise WISC-R without changing it. Like squaring the circle, this has in fact, in WISC-III, been accomplished. It is to the rationale for such revision that we now turn.

Structure of the WISC

Much of what has been applied to the development of WISC-III was learned from its predecessor, WISC-R. Publications on WISC-R's factorial structure – the tests' observed measurement tendencies when applied to differing groups of abilities – date from 1975 (Kaufman, 1975). WISC-R was then one year old and the work was an analysis of data from its standardisation, on which Kaufman had worked. The earlier WISC had simply claimed to measure general intellectual ability and express the result in two ways, as Verbal and Performance (non-verbal) IQs.

Before we take a critical look at this factorial structure, upon which dyslexia diagnosis has traditionally relied so heavily, we should first consider the performance of the tests *as measures of intelligence*. Factor analysis is a mathematical technique, greatly facilitated by modern computing power, which identifies what gives rise to patterns of inter-correlation, across large bodies of data. To give a well-known illustration, if you fed the measurements for each of innumerable but different sized shoe-boxes into a computer program, the analysis would conclude, without of course naming them, that there were three 'factors' (length, breadth and height).

Thus out of the 'noise' of innumerable child performances (for instance those of the 2200 American standardisation sample children on all 12 subtests of WISC-R, some 26 400 data-points) there emerges a tendency – g – to measure a higher-order factor of general intellectual ability. Children who are good at one test tend to be good at another.[6]

However, David Wechsler worked before the widespread application of factor analysis and the example he had in mind was that of the Binet-Simon Intelligence Scale (1916) and its revision, the Stanford-Binet or Terman-Merrill (1937). His belief was that any activity could serve to demonstrate intelligence, which he defined as 'the *aggregate or global* capacity of the individual to act purposefully, to think rationally and to deal effectively with his environment' (1939, p. 3; emphasis added).

This rather conventional account does not describe *high* intelligence very well, however. Free intellectual enquiry is often *purposeless*, under-taken for its own sake. And the exercise of intelligence may often bring the individual into *conflict* with his/her environment, interrupting the smoothness of transaction.[7] Wechsler's definition is a great deal more general (and correspondingly vague) than the formulations of Spear-man. Moreover in minimising considerations of item content, he explic-itly attributed an influence to Binet:

> One of the greatest contributions of Binet was his intuitive assumption that in the selection of tests, *it made little difference what sort of task you used*, provided that in some way it was a measure of the child's general intelligence. (op. cit., p. 6; emphasis added)[8]

Not surprisingly, a number of the subtests on the WISC (and, therefore, its revisions) are rather poor measures of psychometric g or the general factor in intelligence. Though the test was built upon the search for IQ (unitary global ability), it relied upon arithmetic settlement[9] to furnish a stable composite from item content of variable quality. Because of the difficulty, already mentioned, of revising the WISC, this remains the case. In factor analysis, all the observed correlations of each test with every other test may be subjected to an analysis of how each one loads on a *factor* or principal component, for instance *verbal ability*. Such load-ings, varying like correlation coefficients within the range 1.0 to −1.0, enable an evaluation to be made of the strength of each relationship. Strong positive relationships vary towards 1.0; neutrality or an absence of relationship is represented by 0.0 and strong negative relationships tend towards −0.1. Further *rotations* may be performed, which reveal second and subsequent factors or groupings within the data. Such factor analysis leaves to human discretion the decision as to what identified factors actually mean, but the method brings out stable patterns of relationship within large sets of data. A factor is a *controlled generalisation*.

Taking by convention a median loading across all age-groups of 0.70 or above on the unrotated first factor in principal components analysis, the *g*-loadings of the WISC-R subtests (with and without Mazes) are as given in Table 3.1. Equivalent values for WISC-III are compared in Table 3.2.

Table 3.1: Median loadings on an unrotated first factor (*g*-loadings) of WISC-R subtests. For abbreviations, see Appendix 1.

	with Mazes	without Mazes
Inf	0.77	0.78
Sim	0.74	0.75
Ari	0.62	0.62
Voc	0.85	0.86
Com	0.72	0.71
DSp	0.48	0.48
PCo	0.62	0.63
PAr	0.45	0.44
BDe	0.74	0.71
OAs	0.61	0.61
Cod	0.47	0.47
Maz	0.45	
Mean	0.63	0.64

The WISC-III revision has improved the *g*-loading of Arithmetic (from 0.62 to 0.70) and Picture Arrangement (from 0.44 to 0.54), and reduced that of Vocabulary (from 0.86 to 0.79) and Comprehension (from 0.714 to 0.676), while leaving others much the same. Still only five out of 12 tests measure psychometric intelligence to an extent judged 'good' on the conventional criterion.

Alan Kaufman, the guru of two generations of WISC research, complains that the excellent psychometric properties of the new test, Symbol Search, should have been allowed to usurp the much more ambiguous Coding in IQ calculations, relegating Coding to 'supplementary' status. Moreover Mazes should have been dropped altogether. Although it is already hard to get some of the Wechsler tests to measure what one wants them to measure, Mazes in particular appears not to measure anything at all. But as we have seen, the position worldwide of the WISC is such that caution and conservatism have been forced on the publisher.[10]

By contrast the six core and four diagnostic tests of the Differential Ability Scales (DAS), to be discussed later in this chapter, load as given in Table 3.3 on an unrotated first factor (*g*-loadings).

Table 3.2: Median loadings on an unrotated first factor (*g*-loadings) of WISC-III subtests. For abbreviations, see Appendix 1.

Equivalent values for WISC-III may be compared:

	with Mazes	without Mazes
Inf	0.76	0.77
Sim	0.76	0.77
Ari	0.72	0.70
Voc	0.79	0.79
Com	0.67	0.68
DSp	0.46	0.46
PCo	0.62	0.61
Cod	0.42	0.40
PAr	0.55	0.54
BDe	0.73	0.71
OAs	0.63	0.61
SSe	0.59	0.59
Maz	0.32	
Mean	0.62	0.64

Table 3.3: Median loadings on a first unrotated factor of the six core and four diagnostic subtests in the school-age DAS. From Elliott (1990, Table 9.11, p. 206).

Word Definitions	0.68
Similarities	0.69
Matrices	0.71
Seq. and Quant. Reas.	0.76
Recall of Designs	0.63
Pattern Construction	0.70
Mean (n = 6)	0.70
Speed of Info. Proc.	0.28
Recog. of Pictures	0.42
Recall of Digits	0.36
Recall of Objects	0.35
Mean (n = 10)	0.56

Here the intelligence-measuring properties of the core tests are such that they *average* a median loading of 0.70.[11] Tests of diagnostic significance, by contrast, show among the lowest *g*-loadings for tests in a major psychometric battery but, owing to their administrative separation from intelligence-measuring tests, this is by design.

All subtests in these three major batteries may be ranked according to the extent to which they load on the *g*-factor, as given in Table 3.4.

Such an analysis brings out the effectiveness of the verbal subtests on both editions of the WISC, together with the ineffectiveness of some, at least, of the visuo-spatial tests.

Table 3.4: Loadings on a first, unrotated principal component of all subtests in the three major batteries: WISC-R, WISC-R-III and DAS (WISC-III subtests in capital letters) in rank order. For abbreviations, see Appendix 1.

WISC-R	WISC-III	DAS	g-loading
Voc			.86
	VOC		.79
Inf			.78
	INF		.77
	SIM		.77
		SQR	.76
Sim			.75
Com			.71
BDe			.71
		Mat	.71
	BDE		.71
	ARI		.70
		PCo	.70
		Sim	.69
		WDe	.68
	COM		.68
		RDe	.63
PCo			.63
Ari			.62
	OAS		.61
	PCO		.61
OAs			.61
	SSE		.59
	PAR		.54
DSp			.48
Cod			.47
	DSP		.46
PAr			.44
		RPi	.42
	COD		.40
		RDi	.36
		ROI	.35
		SIP	.28

Despite their provenance as 'IQ tests', however, WISC-R and WISC-III claim to measure intelligence in at least two contrasting ways, Verbal and Performance. How well do they do so? Imposing a two-factor solution on the analysis allows this claim to be tested empirically (see Table 3.5).

Evidently a two-factor solution for WISC-R supports Wechsler's description of it as principally measuring two dimensions of ability, verbal and visuo-spatial, though only six subtests correlate with their own factor better than the two factors do with each other ($r = 0.59$).[13] The position of the Verbal subtests has improved somewhat, though the

Table 3.5: Loadings of WISC-R subtests (Mazes omitted) on two factors; Oblimin rotation,[12] factor pattern matrix; together with correlation for both factors. For abbreviations, see Appendix 1.

	Verbal	Visuospatial
Inf	0.68	0.17
Sim	0.58	0.25
Ari	0.77	−0.12
Voc	0.80	0.13
Com	0.56	0.23
DSp	0.61	−0.11
PCo	0.15	0.58
PAr	0.10	0.41
BDe	0.10	0.74
OAs	0.12	0.86
Cod	0.42	0.10
Mean (n = 6)	0.67	
Mean (n = 5)		0.54
$r\,F_1F_2$	0.59	

median loading of the Performance (visuo-spatial) subtests has declined, thanks largely to Coding, an anomalous test in search of a third factor.[14]

How does WISC-III fare in such a comparison? We know a four-factor solution is claimed for WISC-III but it may be examined along the same lines as its predecessor (see Table 3.6).

Because of the inclusion of a new test of perceptual speed and decision, Symbol Search, the second factor to appear here is that of Speed: both Coding and Symbol Search load on the new, second factor, the former redeemed at last from its factorial obscurity, but with the new test registering at the higher level.

Thanks to the pioneering work of Kaufman (1975), the three-factor solution for WISC-R brought the test into its own, with a vital role – suspected by clinicians since Bannatyne (1974) – for the anomalous 'diagnostic' subtests. We shall look at some actual case profiles before long, but first the loadings on three factors may be examined. In Table 3.7, Kaufman's own Varimax[15] loadings are used.

This is the classical background to dyslexia assessment. Now purity of the Verbal and Performance dimensions is factorially improved, with separation of the awkward – but revealing – diagnostic subtests, Digit Span and Arithmetic, which seem to measure mainly verbal memory, and Coding, which measures clerical speed and eye–hand coordination. This triad of tests of diagnostic significance has long been the engine within the ACID profile[16] of folklore. Three factor scores can 'efficiently describe' (Sattler, 1988, p. 127) the performance of the standardisation group on the WISC-R. Selected subtests may be added together, given weightings according to the well-established

Table 3.6: Loadings of WISC-III subtests (Mazes omitted) on two factors; Oblimin rotation, factor pattern matrix; together with correlation for both factors. For abbreviations, see Appendix 1.

	Verbal	Speed
Inf	0.86	-0.08
Sim	0.87	-0.09
Ari	0.58	0.18
Voc	0.89	-0.10
Com	0.71	-0.02
DSp	0.33	0.18
PCo	0.47	0.21
Cod	-0.05	0.60
PAr	0.33	0.29
BDe	0.41	0.41
OAs	0.34	0.37
SSe	0.03	0.74
Means (n = 6)	0.71	0.44
$r\,F_1\,F_2$	0.58	

Table 3.7: Loadings of WISC-R subtests (Mazes omitted) on three factors; Varimax rotation. After Kaufman (1990, Table 8.10, p. 252). For abbreviations, see Appendix 1.

	Verbal	Visuo-spatial	Distractibility
Inf	0.63	0.25	0.41
Sim	0.64	0.34	0.28
Ari	0.37	0.20	0.58
Voc	0.72	0.24	0.33
Com	0.64	0.30	0.24
DSp	0.18	0.12	0.56
PCo	0.35	0.57	0.11
PAr	0.33	0.41	0.12
BDe	0.27	0.66	0.28
OAs	0.21	0.65	0.12
Cod	0.15	0.20	0.42
Mean (n = 4)	0.66		
Mean (n = 4)		0.57	
Mean (n = 3)			0.52

method of Tellegen and Briggs (1967) and deviation quotients obtained for Verbal Comprehension, Perceptual Organisation and Freedom from Distractibility. The first two of these *factor scores* provide marginally better measures of verbal and visuospatial ability than the Verbal and Performance IQs, whilst the third, the distractibility factor, corresponds to the *ACID profile* or memory-and-attention dimension appreciated by clinicians (see below). Statistical significance of discrepancies may be evaluated, and frequency rates assessed, for any exceptionality using data from Clampit, Adair and Strenio (1983). Of course, all these values may be entered once only on a spreadsheet and used with ease to generate individual profiles thereafter.

A three-factor solution for WISC-III, however, brings back the familiar visuo-spatial or Performance factor, albeit with negative loadings (see Table 3.8).

Table 3.8: Loadings of WISC-III subtests (Mazes omitted) on three factors; Oblimin rotation, factor pattern matrix; together with intercorrelations for all factors. For abbreviations, see Appendix 1.

	Verbal	Speed	Visuo-spatial
Inf	0.79	–0.06	–0.07
Sim	0.79	–0.07	–0.07
Ari	0.51	0.12	–0.17
Voc	0.91	–0.01	0.07
Com	0.74	0.06	0.07
DSp	0.31	0.15	–0.08
PCo	0.18	–0.06	–0.56
Cod	0.00	0.77	0.07
PAr	0.21	0.16	–0.28
BDe	0.01	0.05	–0.79
OAs	–0.06	0.02	–0.77
SSe	0.03	0.63	–0.19
Mean (n = 6)	0.68		
Mean (n = 2)		0.70	
Mean (n = 4)			–0.60
$r\,F_1\,F_2$	0.46		
$r\,F_2\,F_3$	–0.49		
$r\,F_1\,F_3$	–0.70		

This three-factor solution already achieves the separation of visuo-spatial tests into two groups: tests of motor and perceptual speed (Factor 2) and tests of conventional visual-perceptual organisation (Factor 3). But WISC-III is presented as a test battery with *four* fully fledged factors: this apparatus has been included in the test manual in the form of Index Scores which, for dyslexia assessment, are much to be preferred. So we may inspect the last stage of factorial clarification of the structure of the WISC in this four-factor solution (see Table 3.9).

The development of the third edition of WISC seems to have refined the structure of the first, verbal dimension, but to have sustained only the two-subtest heart of the visuo-spatial second dimension (Block Design, Object Assembly), with a loss of clarity for the two 'picture' subtests. Beyond these first two factorial dimensions, the two editions of WISC are not fully comparable. The speed dimension remains the least correlated of the four, perhaps because speed of execution is on the whole engaged. Where speed of mental intake of information is

Table 3.9: Loadings of WISC-III subtests (Mazes omitted) on four factors; Oblimin rotation, factor pattern matrix; together with intercorrelations for all factors. For abbreviations, see Appendix 1.

	Verbal	Speed	Visuo-spatial	Distractibility
Inf	0.67	−0.06	−0.08	0.15
Sim	0.69	−0.06	−0.09	0.12
Ari	0.09	−0.01	−0.04	0.75
Voc	0.88	0.02	0.03	0.00
Com	0.70	0.08	0.03	0.02
DSp	0.05	0.07	−0.01	0.44
PCo	0.21	−0.03	−0.55	−0.03
Cod	0.01	0.79	0.07	0.01
PAr	0.25	0.19	−0.30	−0.06
BDe	−0.08	0.02	−0.72	0.21
OAs	−0.02	0.03	−0.75	0.00
SSe	−0.01	0.57	−0.19	0.12
Mean (n = 4)	0.73			
Mean (n = 2)		0.68		
Mean (n = 4)			−0.58	
Mean (n = 2)				0.60

Intercorrelations

	Verbal	Speed	Visuo-spatial	Distractibility
Factor 2	0.38			
Factor 3	−0.64	−0.43		
Factor 4	0.69	0.45	−0.59	

measured one might expect a more central relationship with intelligence (see, for example, Brand, 1996).

The evolution of Coding over the years is a lesson in how perceptual and clerical speed exists as a psychometric dimension independent from g.[17] However, it should be noted that the symbol-set used in Coding A for children aged 6–7, which has fewer linguistic elements, loads on its 'processing speed' factor better (0.98) than either Coding B or Symbol Search does at any age. Indeed it might be taken almost to define this factor.[18] Conversely the deterioration of Digit Span is something of a mystery given that the stimulus set has not changed, apart from the addition of some two-digit items, and the performance of the normative group is much like that of its predecessor 16 years earlier. Clearly Digit Span was happier on a more widely than on a more narrowly defined *distractibility* factor.

To summarise, the progress of each of the 12 WISC-III subtests, as it loads, first, on a single factor, then on two, then three, then four factors, each time on the factor most appropriate to it,[19] may be followed visually by means of the diagram in Figure 3.1.

WISC–III Subtests loading on 1,2,3 and 4 factors

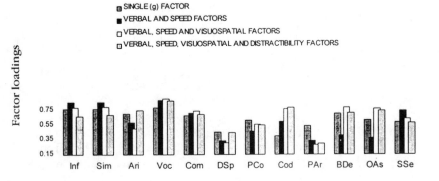

Figure 3.1: Progressive migration of each of the 12 WISC-III subtests to its closest factor in successive 1-, 2-, 3- and 4-factor solutions. For abbreviations, see Appendix 1.

This way of examining the factorial vicissitudes of WISC-III development shows, at least, that the structure has been altered to accommodate the most recalcitrant of the 12 subtests: Coding. Coding alone is unequivocally happier with a four-factor solution than one based on a single, general factor. Other subtests, such as the unsatisfactory pair of Picture tests, progressively lose their justification. Notably, Arithmetic and Digit Span, for many the clinical *raison-d'être* of WISC administration, improve their status rather little on a fourth, distractibility actor compared with a first, general one. If intelligence assessment is the aim, contemporary norms the rationale, and time scarce as ever, then one would do just as well to use Vocabulary, Information, Similarities and Block Design – the four subtests that load above 0.70 on g – to obtain an efficient short-form IQ.

Much of what is known about the psychometric assessment of different abilities is reviewed in John Carroll's monumental *Human Cognitive Abilities* (1993).[20] Yet curiously, the large WISC literature is scarcely mentioned. Carroll remarks in parentheses: 'I chose not to include Kaufman's matrices in my datasets for reanalysis because of the limited character of the WISC battery, by itself, for factor analysis purposes' (p. 258). Further, 'the scales are not designed for factor-analytic investigation; the factors derived in studies that employ only the subscales of this battery are not well defined'; and three-factor interpretations 'must be regarded with caution because the WISC-R battery is too restricted to permit iden- tification of all the factors it measures' (p. 702).

If this is so, it would seem to be the result of David Wechsler's 'common-sense' approach to the definition of intelligence.

In the words of Frank, whom Carroll quotes, the Wechsler test is 'unable to remain viable in a psychometric age which has passed it by in conceptualization' (Frank, 1983, p. 126).

Yet not only does a three-factor interpretation of Wechsler subtest patterns dominate learning disability and dyslexia assessment, but in the WISC-III revision the fourth factor, Processing Speed, is an important addition to the exoskeleton. Because of their clinical significance, the third and fourth so-called 'small' factors deserve a closer look.

The 'small factors': Processing Speed

Claims that there is a distinctive 'dyslexia profile' rest heavily upon the third (and fourth) factors of the WISC. Yet this test originated in an era when a single factor occupied the foreground of intellectual assessment. What is one to make of further factors, especially ones with claimed diag- nostic utility?

The fourth factor, Processing Speed, may best be dealt with first. This is a factor based on the combined results of Coding and Symbol Search, the new addition. In the five years since publication some clinical research has accrued but Symbol Search is a new test with an old prove- nance. Tests of speed of processing are well understood and, more importantly, the psychology of speeded cognitive performance is more secure than that of most abilities. Experimentally a distinction must be made between *mental* and *motor* speed; the former is implicated in dyslexia and is well measured by Symbol Search; the latter has incidental clinical relevance to writing difficulty (of which, however, spelling is usually the most important component), and is measured by Coding.[21]

A criticism of the limited visuo-spatial tests in the WISC has been that they are in the main visuo-motor tests; that is, speed of motor response plays much too large a part in the scoring. The historic emphasis – for instance in the Stanford-Binet and the Wechsler Preschool and Primary Scale of Intelligence (WPPSI) – on *verbal* skills leaves vocabulary, in most batteries, as the central and most highly g-loaded intellectual measure; but in recent years recognition has grown that less culturally specific (or 'crystallised') forms of general reasoning ability are to be valued. The modernity of tests often shows itself in their non-verbal measures, though all continue to survey vocabulary and verbal reasoning abilities in similar ways. In any case neither motor co-ordination nor vision are indispensable components of spatial ability: blind people maintain an awareness of the position of objects in space. Yet 'the number of possible bonus points [for speed] has grown from 51 on the WISC-R to 83 on the WISC-III' (Kaufman, 1994, p. 191).

One corollary of reward for speeded performance is the relative triviality of the tasks: as children mature in intellectual depth in the early secondary years, they tend to plateau in numbers of items correctly solved on Wechsler's Performance scales, so additional points must be awarded for speed. It is impossible to obtain more than a mean scaled score of 10 earning no bonus points for speed after about the ages of 10–12 on Picture Arrangement, Block Design and Object Assembly.

Wechsler's Performance scales, in Piaget's terms, are (with the important exception of Block Design) rooted in the sensorimotor stage rather than the formal operational stage, but to have tests that explicitly sample mental speed on an 'elementary cognitive task' (Carroll, 1993) is a major asset. Coding has long been recognised to have an important diagnostic function, though it is a poor measure of intelligence. Fifteen years of research and experience with the British Ability Scales (BAS) have shown that its Speed of Information Processing test is an important indicator of learning difficulty. So the WISC Processing Speed pair, Coding and Symbol Search, are a welcome additional reserve of diagnostic power.[22]

The nature of the difficulty children may show on tests of speed of information-processing needs some explanation. If the problem is neither *motor* speed nor, in normally intelligent pupils, *mental* speed, there remains the ambiguous visual–verbal character of the tasks to consider. As so often, we find help from the neuropsychological and (especially) PET-scan findings, which implicate language processing areas in these successive, serial, left-to-right, item-by-item tasks. It may be their digital or *language-like character* that poses difficulties for dyslexic children. In this case, measures of speed may offer a summation of the efficiency of the whole language-processing system.

The 'small factors': Freedom from Distractibility

Since at least 1975 it has been recognised that low scores on Arithmetic, Digit Span and Coding signal an information-processing difficulty. Nevertheless the WISC-R manual provided no help with this or other possible clusterings (alternative factorial groupings of subtest scores), even when these were as well established in the dyslexia and LD field as Bannatyne's clusters (1971, 1974). For the dedicated assessing psychologist there must be recourse beyond the WISC-R apparatus, perhaps to Sattler (1988, Table C-4), who draws on the influential analyses of Kaufman (1975). Kaufman's was to be the first of many attempts, aided by research, to extract 'meaningful psychological dimensions' (Sattler, op. cit., p. 130) beyond IQ from the Wechsler tests.

Factor score calculation on the WISC-R, though not always performed routinely by consulting psychologists, has been immensely helpful to

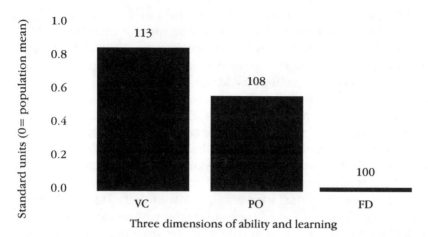

Figure 3.2: WISC-R Factor scores for JG (April 1991). VC = Verbal Comprehension, PO = Perceptual (Visuo-spatial) Organisation, FD = Freedom from Distractibility (Learning Difficulty).

the diagnostic cause. Indeed, as WISC-R data form an important item in the case histories of individuals presenting for reassessment today, it still is. Consider the WISC-R factor profiles of two dyslexic individuals, a brother and sister, now both young adults. The elder of the two, the brother, is of above average intelligence, though reading and spelling levels remain poor. His younger sister is of low ability and this forms a component of her difficulties just as intense as that of her dyslexia. She has been given the WISC-R on three occasions.

Figure 3.2 gives a historic WISC-R three-factor profile for JG, the brother.

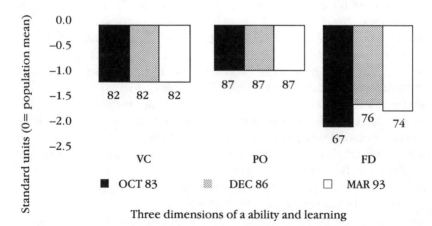

Figure 3.3: WISC-R Factor scores for KG on three separate occasions. VC = Verbal Comprehension, PO = Perceptual (Visuo-spatial) Organisation, FD = Freedom from Distractibility (Learning Difficulty).

Figure 3.3 gives three such profiles for KG, the sister.

In the case of all four WISC-R administrations, the third factor, Freedom from Distractibility, is statistically discrepant from one or both other factors (Verbal Comprehension and Perceptual Organisation) at the 1% level (P = <0.01). The children are from a family with an incidence of dyslexia, both have repeatedly met the criteria for dyslexia when assessed and have received specialist help over long periods. The diagnostic utility of the Freedom from Distractibility factor survives equally its comparison with above-average general abilities, in the case of the brother, and with low abilities, in the case of the sister, a considerable achievement given that dyslexia in individuals of low ability is harder to isolate. In the case of the sister, moreover, the independent contribution of the intelligence test to an explanation of her intense difficulties with schooling is clear.

Calculation of factor scores is not at all the same thing as identifying an 'ACID profile', a concept whose popularity seems somewhat undeserved.[23] Scores on A (Arithmetic), C (Coding), I (Information) and D (Digit Span) are, indeed, often depressed in dyslexic children but their interpretation should not be a matter of subjective pattern recognition. (We will discuss a more rational approach to profile analysis shortly.) The Information component of A-C-I-D is the most loosely implicated in specific learning difficulties (the phonological sequences of days of the week, months of the year and four seasons are all required in the first nine items). With Arithmetic, Information is more often among the lowest scaled scores for girls than for boys (Nichols et al., 1988). With WISC-III, 30% of Information items are new or highly modified, and the test is no longer administered first in the sequence.

Just as Information has changed its factorial character, no longer, as in WISC-R, loading substantially on an FD (Freedom from Distractibility: see below) or ACID factor, so on the revised WISC-III, Coding has drifted away from this 'clinical' factor. Using a criterion loading of 0.40 or above, the three subtests (A-C-D) define FD on WISC-III only at ages 13.5 and 16.5. At the lower loading of 0.30, still only four out of 11 age-groups define a triadic FD. On WISC-R, seven of the 11 age-groups showed a Freedom from Distractibility factor at a loading of 0.40 or above (Kaufman, 1994, p. 57). The split in the Verbal scale that has been apparent since the 1939 Wechsler-Bellevue, between the tests that engage verbal comprehension and those that engage attention and memory, has settled down, in WISC-III, to a Freedom from Distractibility factor comprising simply Arithmetic and Digit Span.

Debate continues as to the nature of this 'third factor'. From the beginning psychologists have had difficulty agreeing what to call it, and this seems symptomatic.[24] Kaufman himself labelled the FD factor, Freedom from Distractibility because

> in the early to mid-70s I was a practising and devout coward.
> Jacob Cohen and Irla Lee Zimmerman called the factor by the

mouthful label of Freedom from Distractibility, and I lacked the courage to split with tradition. In truth, that label should have been trashed years ago. I cringe whenever I read 'Kaufman's Freedom from Distractibility factor.' It's not mine and I don't want it. (Kaufman, 1994, p. 212)

The name is particularly inappropriate because, as Kaufman further argues:

It is easy to see how children may score very poorly . . . because of distractible behaviour, but it is more difficult to visualize children scoring very well . . . merely or primarily because of close attention to the task. 3 . . . The Psychological Corporation should have taken a risk and called Factor 3 by a proper cognitive name. (op. cit., p. 212)

At this point it may be well to remind ourselves of Carroll's comment that: 'the factors derived . . . are not well defined [and] the battery [is] too restricted to permit identification of all the factors' (1993, p. 702).

It should be emphasised that these neuropsychological uses for WISC subtests are accidental and unplanned: test item areas were intended only as further domains in which cognitive performance could be sampled for IQ. That there is now quite an apparatus for converting WISC tests to uses other than ones for which they were intended does not mean that conscious design has no role to play in test construction.

A full apparatus has been provided (even if *post hoc*) to evaluate significance and frequency of low scores on all four factors (Wechsler et al., 1992, Tables B1–2, pp. 265–6). So what is the relevance of the Freedom from Distractibility factor for dyslexia? Sadly, the most exhaustive investigation of subtest fluctuation patterns on the WISC-R concluded that: 'no regrouping scheme was found exhibiting a uniqueness for learning disabilities that might be useful in differential diagnosis' (Kavale and Forness, 1984, p. 136).[25]

In particular, profile patterns, including the ACID, were found *not* to discriminate reliably between dyslexic and non-dyslexic children. A list, given by Kaufman (1994, pp. 212–13), of groups of children showing selective impairment on the Freedom from Distractibility factor includes those with leukaemia who have received cranial irradiation therapy, others with unilateral cerebral lesions, with ADHD, with epilepsy, with autism, with specific language disorder, with emotional problems, with conduct disorders, with schizophrenia and with Duchenne muscular dystrophy.[26]

However, the Freedom from Distractibility factor does signal a learning difficulty *of some kind*, because exceptional groups of many kinds, but not unimpaired children, show difficulty with the tasks comprising it. The specific processes with which children struggle remain unclear and, given the pot-pourri of subskills in Arithmetic and Digit Span, there may be no definitive answer. For different individuals a numerical, a verbal memory, an anxiety or an executive function problem may cause difficulty. Indeed one minimal role for the third and fourth[27] factors is that of validation. A child's performance on these factors helps interpretation on the main VC (Verbal Comprehension) and PO (Perceptual Organisation) factors, suggesting reliability or not, as the case may be.[28] But a pupil without significant difficulty on the Freedom from Distractibility factor is unlikely to have a learning difficulty of cognitive origin.

For dyslexia purposes, most psychologists seem to regard Arithmetic and Digit Span as tests of working memory. They should nevertheless be aware of the complexity of the discussions over Freedom from Distractibility and the tendency for this important diagnostic indicator to signal trouble for many, quite different reasons with different children.

Perhaps *general working memory* (WMG) and *special working memory* (WMS)[29] bring the discussion of cognitive architecture close to the dyslexic's area of difficulty. Problems with the 'visuo-spatial sketchpad' (the other dedicated WMS system) are not important in dyslexia: when a 'visual memory' deficit is apparent, it is usually the linguistic (naming or retrieval) component which is at fault.[30] The purer the measure of visual memory – BAS Visual Recognition, for instance, uses in later items purely abstract shapes and configurations – the better the dyslexic is at doing it. The mean standard score on the spatial cluster of the DAS for 136 reading disabled pupils is 100.5 (Elliott, 1990, p. 260). This cluster is made up of two tests, Pattern Construction (block design) and Recall of Designs, a test of visual memory with a verbal mediation component.[31]

In summary, the two 'diagnostic' index scores, Freedom from Distractibility and Processing Speed, are at least indicators of *low-level information-processing difficulties*. The WMS system of 'phonological memory' (Gathercole and Baddeley, 1993) may be the heart of the matter for Freedom from Distractibility, given the almost unlimited central role of verbal learning and mediation.[32] In this case there are more direct and developmentally relevant tests of phonological processing – non-words, rhymes, spoonerisms. Specific diagnostic tests will be discussed in a later chapter.

But as we take leave of the famous WISC 'small factors' and the ACID profile,[33] it seems wise to remind ourselves of what we are doing. We give intelligence tests to determine intelligence. This provides a kind of *general cognitive survey*. If the intelligence test describes a contrast between two or more different kinds of ability, so much the better. On the WISC, some tests have an accidental diagnostic significance. This is a bonus. But to ask that this vintage[34] test (or any other) should in addition support all specialised diagnostic requirements and provide the basis for differential diagnosis, with such large administrative decisions as may hang on the results, is unreasonable.

WISC-III and WISC-IIIUK

Many professional users of psychological tests in the UK, unaware of the prohibitive smallness of the British market for test development, are less than friendly towards the products of North America. When such a test cannot be avoided, they convince themselves that it has been *standardised* in the UK. Some educational psychologists have been using WISC-R for years, apparently in the belief that they were using a British standardisation. Experts, too, are careless. Kline (1993, p. 403) comments, about the WAIS-R that 'British norms have been provided for the test'. They have not. Both WISC-R and WAIS-R received a cosmetic treatment called Anglicisation, by means of which items employing US usage (visual or linguistic) were deleted and replaced by culturally British items which were then trialled for order and approximate level of difficulty. British versions of the manuals were supplied to purchasers.

The only full-scale standardisation of a Wechsler test ever to be carried out in these islands is the WISC-R(S) (Scottish Council for Research in Education, 1987). Norms obtained then for the WISC-R showed the familiar world-wide rise in IQ and composite, especially Performance, scores (Flynn, 1984, 1987a, 1987b; Lynn and Hampson, 1986) but no significant difference otherwise between American and Scottish children.

With the revision of the WISC, a different strategy was adopted by the publisher. In the USA a battery of eight achievement tests, the Wechsler Individual Achievement Test (WIAT; 1992), was standardised alongside WISC-III and appeared at about the same time. This 'co-norming' allows for well-defined predictions to be made from within the standardisation sample and, therefore, for exceptionalities to be fully quantified using regression methods. In the UK a decision was taken to procure a 'validation sample' of 824 children (37 boys and 37 girls in each of the 11 age-groups), stratified, as well as by age and sex, by four ethnic groups, seven levels of socio-economic status, 12 regions and three areas. Three (only) of the eight WIAT tests were given at the same time as WISC-III: the literacy trio of Basic Reading, Spelling and Reading Comprehension. All these materials were appropriately Anglicised.

The UK data permitted the construction of transformation tables and the publication, in the UK version of the manual, of locally valid, albeit little different, norms.[35] However, a notable opportunity was lost to standardise all eight of the WIAT tests in Britain, given that differences in attainment of cultural origin are to be looked for more than differences in ability. The others[36] have subsequently been administered to a comparable sample to obtain UK norms and reissued with an appropriate garlanding of acronyms (WOND, WOLD: see Rust, 1996).

Almost no contemporary data on differing international standards in literacy attainment in English are published.[37] In principle a comparison of US and UK children on recently constructed, well standardised tests, administered close together in time, is of considerable interest. The three WIAT tests thus far published in Britain (called here WORD: see Rust, Golombok and Trickey, 1993) are unchanged from WIAT originals in terms of item number (order and wording are altered) so some comparison is possible, but inspection of the norm-tables for the two standardisations reveals no interpretable pattern because all effects have already been removed by statistical smoothing. Tables comparable to 4.1 and 4.2 in the WISC-IIIUK Manual, which apply US norms to UK raw data, have not been published. However, in spelling at least, a slight UK advantage, due no doubt to earlier school entry, is apparent through the primary years, but fades at about age 10–11.[38]

Scoring software

A comprehensive scoring programme, WISC-III Writer, is available for WISC-III and WIAT and is to be recommended. Computer scoring obviates clerical work and UK norms can be entered as scaled scores.[39] In addition, the calculation of higher-level cluster scores – which a half century of research makes possible and which renders continued use of the Wechsler tests advantageous – is effected almost to the point of superfluity. More than 50 'shared ability' cluster scores (alternative factorings) are optionally provided.[40] Expected and observed attainment scores, if WORD or WIAT tests are given at the same time, are regressed and exceptionalities reported. All main significance and prevalence computations are performed and a simple graph is shown, on screen and in a print-out.

Procedure for interpreting WISC-III composites

With or without computer assistance, however, the assessing psychologist needs a rationale for plotting his or her way through the technical complexities of WISC-IIIUK. None is provided in the manual. In what follows the enormous contribution of Alan Kaufman must be acknowledged. His *Intelligent Testing With The WISC-R*, first published in 1979, proposed a rational and research-based method for profile attack, intra-individual or 'ipsative' testing.[41] Kaufman argued from the Wechsler research base that individual cognitive profiles on the WISC were susceptible to systematic interpretation. This view has since met with widespread acceptance and respect, especially hard-won given the coldness of the anti-psychometric climate during those years. The 1994 edition, *Intelligent Testing With The WISC-III*, completely rewritten, contains guidance on scoring and interpretation so detailed that I refer the reader straight to this source.[42] Here I shall present a synthesis and statement of principle to make clear what is involved.

A first principle, familiar in research methodology, is that no procedure is resorted to after the event. The plan of attack, to be principled, must be formulated in advance and adhered to, rather than varied *post hoc* in the light of the findings.

Generally one wishes measurements to be as factor-pure as possible. The most highly *g*-loaded of the measurements is the Full Scale IQ itself, so a full administration is required. There is a mini-literature on shortening WISC testing (and tests) but reliability is soon sacrificed and the factoring or clustering of scores requires a full administration.

However, the Index scores, Verbal Comprehension, Perceptual Organisation, Freedom from Distractibility and Processing Speed, are very much to be preferred, on grounds of factor purity, to the traditional framework of IQ composites. (The Full Scale IQ need be retained only as an anchor for the regression matrix and as the single most highly *g*-loaded statement about the child's intelligence.)

Statistical significance is assumed throughout. Anything not statistically significant should not feature in any psychometric analysis. It is known that 40% of the normal population, for instance, show statistically significant Verbal–Performance discrepancies (Kaufman, 1976b). This means only that there is some phenomenon to be interpreted, beyond meaningless noise. For instance, a significant discrepancy between Verbal and Performance IQs means that a true difference exists which may be interpreted. All interpretations should proceed, only on the basis of statistical significance, to actual prevalence levels, reporting on the frequency or rarity of the phenomenon observed.

Some rules of parsimony may be invoked as to when, by default, a level of interpretation simpler than that of Index Scores is permissible. The Full Scale IQ should be interpreted while noting any significant variation among the scaled scores; the average range (difference between the highest and lowest of IQ-contributing scaled scores) in the general population is a substantial 7 points (+/–2) (Kaufman, 1976a). Verbal and Performance IQs should be interpreted only if there is no interference from, for the Verbal scale, a Verbal Comprehension and Freedom from Distractibility discrepancy (13+ points) and, for the Performance scale, a Perceptual Organisation and Processing Speed discrepancy (15+ points). In addition any other scatter (range greater than 7 points for the Verbal tests and 9 points for the Performance) may invalidate interpretation. To report and interpret Verbal and Performance IQs they must be fairly homogeneous.

Values for interpreting Verbal–Performance and Verbal Comprehension–Perceptual Organisation discrepancies are given in Kaufman (1994, Table 3.2). Differences of 19+ points are unusually large.

The 'small factors' (Freedom from Distractibility and Processing Speed) may be interpreted if their component pairs, similarly, are fairly homogeneous. A difference of 4 or more points in either case argues against interpretation.

At the bottom level, individual subtests may justify some comment (subtest specificity permitting) if they deviate markedly from the mean scaled score – a strength or a weakness. The least *g*-loaded tests deviate most freely: Coding must deviate by at least 5 points to be interpretable.[43]

Procedure for interpreting measures of scholastic underachievement

Co-norming permits an optimal investigation of underachievement, the first criterion of dyslexia diagnosis. The basic procedure, described here for WISC-IIIUK, is the same in principle for all test batteries that offer this facility.

As most test manuals explain, there are two methods of comparing ability with attainment. The first, that of *simple difference*, subtracts the lower – usually attainment – score from the higher – ability – one, if they are in the same units. The distance between the two can be expressed in Ds, standard deviation units, and a value looked up in a table of the normal distribution.

For instance, a pupil obtains an IQ of 110 and a reading standard score of 80. There are 30 points of standard score between the two, or 2 SDs. About one pupil in 44 (2.3%) would be expected to obtain two scores this discrepant.

Close to the centre of the distribution this method works well enough and, in the case of two test results from different systems, this may, by default, be the only method of evaluating such a difference, but it is rough and ready, may ignore margins of error and associated values required for statistical significance, says nothing about the relationship between the two scores and is sometimes unfair to pupils of lesser ability.

Much to be preferred is a *regression analysis*. This employs two useful sets of assumptions: first, the strength of relationship between the two variables being compared; and second, the tendency for a second observation to fall closer to the mean than the first (regression to the mean). Actual regression effects observed in the standardisation sample are used to predict expected scores from observed scores.

Innovative tests have, for some time, made clear the assumptions built into such evaluations. For instance, the Woodcock Reading Mastery Tests (WRMT-R) (Woodcock, 1987) offer a table of aptitude–achievement correlations, some of them estimates, for users to pick among and enter into their calculation (Manual pp. 54–7, Table 3.2; the WRMT-R does not incorporate ability measures)[44]. Both WISC-III and DAS provide the apparatus for evaluating discrepancies by simple difference (with margins of error taken into account) and by full regression.

To give another example: an 11-year-old pupil obtains on the DAS a GCA (IQ) of 85 and a Word Reading standard score of 71. A GCA of 85 predicts a reading score of 91 (because of regression to the mean). The difference between observed (71) and expected (91) scores of 20 points is found in only 5% of the population; a difference of 11.7 points is significant at the 0.01 level.

Clearly the simple difference method, faced with this second example, can only quantify the difference between the two scores, 14 points or 0.93 SD, and report that about one individual in six (17%) would show such a gap. The full regression method is not only more precise and more realistic but it is fairer to pupils of lower ability. This may be seen in the following way. A discrepancy definition is used to isolate individuals in a large population who read less well than expected in relation to their ability. Both methods – regression and simple difference – are used. Pupils who are identified by *both* methods are subtracted. Who is left? Only high-ability pupils predicted by simple difference, and low-ability pupils predicted by regression, remain. Exactly this exercise was performed in the Fletcher et al. (1994) study referred to in Chapter 2 whose authors provide a graph (Figure 1, p. 11) showing the different subpopulations identified by various methods, including these two.

Clearly tests such as the Woodcock–Johnson or DAS that have at least three measures of basic skill attainment built in (in the case of the DAS, measures of word recognition, arithmetic and spelling) can provide full regression evaluation possibilities for all individual circumstances. With WISC-IIIUK only literacy measures are available for comparison and, though co-normed in the UK as in the USA, the literacy tests, WORD, must be purchased separately.

Further cluster analyses

We have now looked at rational procedures both for evaluating an individual's cognitive profile using WISC-IIIUK, and for evaluating any discrepancy there may be between expected levels of achievement, based on Full Scale IQ (or such other composites as may be warranted), and observed levels. Thus far we have followed the course of traditional IQ-based methods of approaching dyslexia diagnosis. Yet far from being the end of the story, this is little more than the beginning.

WISC-III, then, like WISC-R, needs the research-based provision of factorial structure (index scores), with strict procedures for interpretation, in order to tame its wayward power and get it to measure what it is required to measure. With patience a reasonable job may be done. Nevertheless, as Lynn says:

> The problem is that the Wechsler consists of an arbitrary collection of subtests which has no theoretical rationale . . . Faith in [IQ effects] is only as strong as faith in the representativeness of the subtests as a good example of cognitive abilities. (1994, p. 260)

In addition to the notorious Mazes, further examples can be given. Object Assembly is deficient in specific variance. Picture Arrangement sits uneasily between verbal and non-verbal factors and loads poorly on *g*. Coding, which is the weakest measure of *g*, has ambiguous diagnostic significance and shows a larger sex difference than any other subtest (see below).[45]

So what other means are there for coercing the WISC into measuring clinically significant abilities and difficulties? Since the early efforts of Bannatyne (1971, 1974), research lore on the WISC has led to many alternative clusters or groupings of scores. Among the best known are those by Bannatyne (verbal conceptualisation, spatial ability, acquired knowledge, sequencing ability); Horn and Cattell (crystallised ability, fluid ability, broad visualisation, short-term acquisition and retrieval, broad speediness); and Guilford's classifications (operations: cognition, memory, evaluation, convergent production; and contents: figural, symbolic [auditory, visual], semantic and behavioural).

There are many others however. A convenient listing may be found in Kaufman (1994, Tables 6.1–6.6, pp. 274–82), where the Tellegen and Briggs (1967) method is used to derive standard scores from small clusters of 2–4 subtests. This means adding the scaled scores concerned, applying a weighting and adding a constant. The subtests' known reliabilities enable a standard error of measurement and a confidence interval to be constructed for each of these derived measures. Users of spreadsheets will find it convenient to incorporate this information once only for repeated analyses of clinical profiles. Alternatively WISC-III Writer scoring software routinely provides virtually all the same cluster analyses to the point, it must be said, of some redundancy. However, I have found this higher-order analysis of WISC subtest profiles almost always to be more informative than the first-order listing of subtest strengths and weaknesses. The clusters can be rank ordered on a spreadsheet and redundancy eliminated, as several clusters close together will define the same set of attributes. In some cases a strategic weakness (such as motor skill) which has gone unnoticed through many psychological assessments, can become apparent in the reordering by clusters.

Sex differences

The complex role of sex differences in cognition is now widely acknowledged (Ansara et al., 1981; Daly and Wilson, 1983; Moir and Jessel, 1989; Halpern, 1992; Silverman and Eals, 1992; Born and Lynn, 1994; Lynn, 1994). The sex ratio in dyslexia is so imbalanced[46] that all possible contributions to it should be investigated. It does now seem that, in part, there is a genuine imbalance and that definitional studies (such as the Yale) that produce equal numbers of male and female dyslexic people may be suspect (Miles, 1994). Hormonal, intrauterine factors may be involved. Males are more prevalent at the extremes of many distributions – female variance in IQ is typically about one point of standard deviation less than male. Female advantage in certain aspects of language skill may be important but genetic transmission nevertheless is likely to be autosomal, that is, not directly sex-linked.

However, another consideration, little mentioned, is that of test bias. For many years male–female equality in IQ has been widely accepted and dismissed as an non-issue.[47] This may now be changing. Lynn and colleagues (Born and Lynn, 1994; Lynn, 1994) are able to show consistent male advantage in Verbal[48] and Full Scale WISC IQ, though not in Performance. The small IQ difference, which is put at about 4 points, has little bearing on individual assessments. That it has hitherto been overlooked is attributed to masking by girls' earlier maturation (Lynn, 1994).

In test construction various decisions are taken which have a bearing on whether or not male–female differences can be regarded as artefacts (Kline, 1993, pp. 141–2). Sex differences are expected in many areas, for instance on tests of personality, interests, personal preferences and so on. Such differences may be deliberately excluded by judicious selection of items. If differences are allowed to appear, separate norms may be provided for the sexes. This procedure is well accepted for personality tests.

The abundant recent literature on cognitive sex differences (or *preferences*) has thus far made little impact outside the laboratory. Perhaps this is as well, as established findings seem open still to periodic doubt. An influential early study is that by Maccoby and Jacklin (1974); a recent review is provided in Halpern (1992). To risk summarising the position, visuospatial superiority (with mathematical ability to which it appears to be linked) is shown by boys at least from adolescence onwards. Language advantage, especially in synonyms and, to a lesser extent, verbal memory, is shown by girls at all ages, together with certain perceptual sensitivities (smell, sound, colour, dark vision).[49] There is an extensive neuropsychological literature which relates cognitive sex differences to contrasting degrees of brain localisation and specialisation.

What seems not to have attracted comment is the particular role of the WISC Digit Span and Coding tests in diagnosing dyslexia. Figure 3.4 shows subtest scores for three standardisation samples for WISC-R: the original 1974 US norms, widely used in Britain and elsewhere; the 1987 Scottish standardisation; and the 1982 Dutch standardisation.

On all three occasions and with all populations, there is a female advantage on Coding of about half a standard deviation. This is a large difference even in an individual assessment, equivalent to 1.5 points of WISC scaled score, 5 points of T-score, or 7.5 points of standard score. For Digit Span there is also a female advantage, though a lesser one.[50]

Given that WISC has been the foremost instrument used in dyslexia diagnosis, the implications for identification of girls are impossible to ignore. Individuals in assessment have their test scores compared with the combined scores of boys and girls in the standardisation sample.

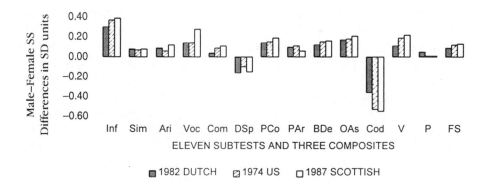

Figure 3.4: Mean scaled scores on WISC-R for the sexes in three standardisations. Data from Born and Lynn (1994).

Thus boys are more likely, and girls less likely, to have their scores deemed as exceptionally low. To attract a dyslexia diagnosis, a girl must perform at a lower level than a boy on these two tests.

Where normative sensitivities appear, a desirable prophylactic may be the provision – in the interests of fairness – of separate norms for the sexes. Some examples are strategic tests for deciding on special education services, or reading tests at seven – an age at which girls are often more advanced as several surveys have shown, or tests of writing speed and productivity more generally.

Major test publishers and developers have yet to consider the provision of this essential facility. Existing tests which do take into account cognitive sex differences are rare indeed. Personality tests for children (such as the Eysenck Personality Questionnaire: Eysenck and Eysenck, 1975) do normally provide separate norms for the sexes. Otherwise the Edinburgh Reading Test at Stage 1 is a noteworthy exception (Godfrey Thomson Unit, 1972–7).

Because, as already mentioned, higher-order clustering may help to make sense of the atheoretical WISC subtests, the Jastak Cluster Analysis may be mentioned here (Jastak and Jastak, 1979). This procedure for clustering WISC or WAIS subtests together with WRAT Reading, Spelling and Arithmetic commends itself, especially with adults, for whom the testing repertoire is limited. Normative differences for the sexes are built into the interpretation at all ages by means of separate tables, though the empirical basis, beyond the authors' own clinical experience, is not always clear.[51]

Other major batteries: the Woodcock–Johnson (Revised)

Essential psychometric and diagnostic procedures have thus far been illustrated by reference to the WISC tests. This is for straightforward reasons of historical precedence and familiarity. However, the procedures that have evolved out of 50 years of experience with Wechsler's tests have been incorporated at the design stage in newer, technically more efficient tests. Two will be described in some detail: the Woodcock–Johnson Psycho-Educational Battery – Revised (WJ-R) (Woodcock and Johnson, 1989, 1990) and the Differential Ability Scales (DAS; Elliott, 1990).

The Woodcock–Johnson has grown, partly in response to criticism since the publication of its first edition (Woodcock and Johnson, 1977), into a kind of ultimate monument to the psychometric possibilities of educational diagnosis. The 1977 Woodcock–Johnson was the first fully developed test which included co-normed tests of ability and achievement with the means of evaluating discrepancies between the two. In that edition, there were 27 tests in all: 12 of ability, 10 of scholastic achievement and five of interest or motivation. The tests could be clustered in various (though non-independent) ways and a Relative Performance Index (RPI) score was available, which described the percentage of mastery likely for an examinee when the reference group achieves 90% mastery. However, factorial support was not forthcoming for the cluster scores, though these were as usual more reliable. The segregation of ability, aptitude and achievement was imperfect, with ability tests (in particular) being weighted towards academic achievement. In addition, the Cognitive Abilities Full Scale score was some 9 points *lower* for learning disabled children than their WISC-R IQs (McGrew, 1986). If construct validity was lacking, the test battery was excellently standardised. Professionals have tended to use the system selectively, with special interest being shown in the many, ingenious tests of academic achievement. In 1985 Woodcock published alternative – and preferable – clusterings, Oral Language and Broad Reasoning (Woodcock, 1985).

The revision of 1989–90 is notably radical. In addition to the elimination of numerous minor problems, the factor structure explicitly attempts to base itself on modern psychological theory. The number of tests has risen to 35 (21 cognitive ability and 14 scholastic achievement, with additional measures of punctuation, capitalisation, spelling, usage and handwriting derived from three of them). The tests of 'interest' have gone. The scope of the norms (from ages 2 to 79) means that materials suitable for assessment of early years and, a major consideration nowa-

days, adults, are no longer a problem. Given the tendency of the elaborate Woodcock–Johnson scoring apparatus to put off many users, the
provision of a computerised scoring system is especially welcome.[52]

Even more than before, the measures of academic learning and school
achievement are admirable. Results from tests of word and non-word
reading may be compared, a more important diagnostic feature, perhaps,
than the developers may have realised.[53] Reading comprehension now
transcends the limited sentence completion items which had been criticised. There are now synonym and antonym problems and passages for
silent reading which require, at higher levels, spoken single-word
responses that often hinge on an understanding of syntax. There are three
tests of number: conceptual, word and calculation problems are separated.[54] Brave attempts to sample higher curricula are ventured for
science, social studies and humanities. Best of all, the area of writing,
conventionally thought of as the most resistant to psychometric incursion,
is approached in two ways. In Writing Samples, the prompts take several
forms: short, highly predictable sentences which must be completed;[55]
picture items; and passages in which a deleted but implied middle section
must be furnished. In a second, timed test, Writing Fluency, several
prompt words must be combined in meaningful sentences.

Such relevant and ingenious achievement tests will continue to tempt
the eclectic user. However, it is the cognitive ability tests that deserve
special comment. These 21 ability tests exemplify seven Horn-Cattell
factors: Gf (fluid reasoning), Gc (comprehension-knowledge), Gv (visual
processing), Ga (auditory processing), Gs (processing speed), Glr (long-
term retrieval) and Gsm (short-term memory). Seven clusters are therefore derived, with the addition of another, Oral Language, and three
composites of Broad Cognitive Ability – 11 altogether. The highest level
clusters, the composites of Broad Cognitive Ability, approximate most
closely to IQs and are made up as follows. The Standard Scale is based
on seven tests, each representing one Horn-Cattell factor; the Early
Developmental Scale is based on five tests (the fluid reasoning and
processing speed tests are inapplicable); and the Extended Scale is available if the seven supplemental, as well as the seven standard, tests of
ability are administered and is of course to be preferred on grounds of
reliability.

As 'both the theory and the model are evolving' (Woodcock and
Mather, 1989, 1990, p. 20), and without purporting to evaluate factorial
studies which must remain its ultimate test, it is suggested provisionally
that this ambitious seven-factor apparatus may resolve, for the user, into
six clusters and two IQs with greater utility. This is because of the uneven
quality of the cognitive tasks and their relationship to tests with known
g-loading and other characteristics (g-loadings for the Woodcock–
Johnson tests are not published in the manual). This alternative clustering is as follows:

1.	Verbal (Picture Vocabulary, Oral Vocabulary, Verbal Analogies);
2.	Visuo-spatial (Picture Recognition, Spatial Relations);
3.	Non-verbal reasoning (Analysis–Synthesis, Concept Formation);
4.	Speed (Visual Matching, Cross-Out);
5.	Verbal Short-term Memory (Memory for Sentences, Memory for Words, Numbers Reversed);
6.	Verbal Strategy (Memory for Names, Visual-Auditory Learning).

These dimensions have a tried significance for the diagnosis of dyslexia (see the next section on the Differential Ability Scales). In particular the separation of higher-order *g*-loaded tests from lower-order tests of 'information skills' is an established distinction of clinical importance, though it is seldom advanced by reference to Jensen's Level 1 and Level 2 theory which is its natural theoretical base (Jensen, 1968, 1970). Moreover among the latter group, a third group of information skills may be as important as the recognised ones of verbal memory and speed of processing: that of 'verbal strategy'. The Woodcock–Johnson cognitive tests include two original tasks which involve verbal learning in relation to novel visual stimuli (cartoon aliens, linguistic rebuses).[56] As this entails attaching names to pictures, it may be supposed that the tests will be dyslexia-sensitive (Ellis, 1981). Memory for Names, in particular, requires the memorisation of *non-words* in relation to the cartoon-like pictures of aliens. Suspicion attaches, too, to a larger class of tests in which a verbal strategy seems indispensable in solving visual problems and on which dyslexic children do unaccountably poorly.

These six proposed clusters, then, correspond better to known dimensions of learning and ability, where *Gf-Gc* theory has only partially resolved the mappings (or lack of them) between the fluid/crystallised distinction and the verbal/performance, verbal/visual and fluid/quantitative ones. One parsimonious mapping of abilities is along a continuum between verbal and visuo-spatial extremes, with non-verbal reasoning (closely associated with *Gf*) in the middle.

The first three clusters can be combined into an IQ or general ability composite; the second three give a combined measure of information skills. Any disparity between the two, as between General and Short Form IQs on the British Ability Scales (BAS) or between Verbal Comprehension/Perceptual Organisation and Freedom from Distractibility factors on the WISC, may be an indication of learning difficulty. Woodcock–Johnson otherwise lacks an explicit diagnostic rationale (though not a factorial apparatus) for its cognitive ability tests.

To see the effect of this cluster analysis by comparison with cluster analyses for the same child using WISC-III, consider Figures 3.5–3.7. The child, a girl, was tested on WISC-III at age 8:6 years and again on WJ-R at 9:2 years. Free from dyslexic underachievement, her reading and spelling were excellent and she obtained a Verbal IQ (WISC-III) of 137;

nevertheless she took a long time to learn her multiplication tables. Figure 3.5 shows her index scores on WISC-III.

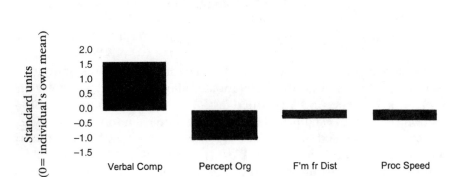

Figure 3.5: Cognitive profile for TM based on four WISC-III Index Scores.

Figure 3.6 shows selected clusters derived from the work of Bannatyne, Horn and Kaufman.

Figure 3.7 shows the six clusters and two summary IQs proposed for the WJR-COG.

In all three graphs, the subject's scores are *ipsative,* that is, adjusted to her own mean, so that strengths and weaknesses appear in relation to her own characteristic level of performance. In all three representations of TM's cognitive functioning, it can be seen that her high verbal abilities stand in contrast with weaknesses in visuo-spatial and information skills – speed, verbal strategy and the Freedom from Distractibility factor – though not verbal memory. There is reasonable agreement between the clusterings, with the exception that 'non-verbal reasoning' on WISC-III clearly lacks the fluid ability character it has elsewhere, and 'verbal strategy' on WJ-R consorts better with WISC fluid and visuo-spatial subtests than it does with WJ-R non-verbal reasoning.

The British/Differential Ability Scales (BAS/DAS)

In its day the British Ability Scales (BAS) (Elliott, Murray and Pearson, 1979, 1983) represented a refreshing change and innovation in the measurement of cognitive abilities. Although IQs were imposed upon the test developers by inertial force in the late 1970s, the principal author has now come to the view that *g* is the only acceptable definition of psychometric 'intelligence' (Elliott, 1995). A literature quickly grew

WISC–III UK: Selected cluster analyses
Profile for TM (8:6)

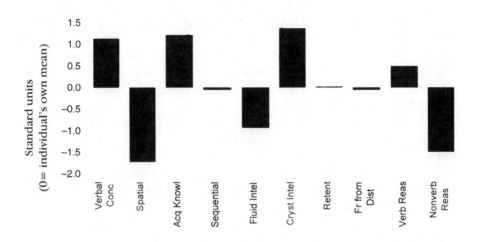

Derived composite measures

Figure 3.6: Cognitive profile for TM using cluster scores based on three alternative methods of deriving composites of shared abilities: clusters 1–4: Bannatyne; clusters 5–7: Horn; clusters 8–10, Kaufman.

WJ–R Cognitive abilities: Alternative clusterings
Profile for TM (9:2)

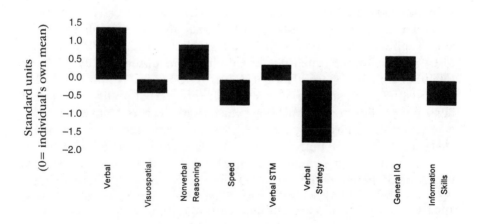

Composite measures

Figure 3.7: Cognitive profile for TM using alternative clusterings of WJ-R standard scores.

up around the compromise 'Short Form IQ', which proved to have fatal limitations. In terms of the present discussion, there was confusion between its two g-loaded contributing scales (Matrices, Similarities) and the other two measures, which were primarily of information skills (Recall of Digits, Speed of Information Processing). The composite rapidly proved to be highly dyslexia-sensitive (Thomson, 1982). Nevertheless, it was the fixed point of reference for the regression matrix which, at that time, was an important innovation, permitting discrepancy analysis. Tests of word recognition and number were integral, allowing quantification of underachievement; a test of spelling has been added (Elliott, 1992).

Two current developments may be mentioned. First, the BAS scoring software has been issued in a new edition, allowing a regression matrix to be calculated around a new, fifth IQ, the 'g-enhanced' short form IQ;[57] and, second, NFER-Nelson the test developer and publisher is bringing out in the autumn term of 1996 a UK-normed revision, BAS-II, which builds upon the innovations and strengths of the DAS.

Meanwhile the BAS has been superseded by its reincarnation in the USA, the Differential Ability Scales (DAS). The Psychological Corporation, with Colin Elliott, recreated the BAS – unfettered by tradition – to a technical and production standard that no other psychometric battery approaches. As this is the assessment system that some regard as the state of the art, it will be worth taking a little time to describe it.

At school ages (6–18) the DAS comprises six 'core' (ability-measuring) tests, four 'diagnostic' tests of information skills and three tests of school achievement – word recognition, number and spelling. This is economical: assessing three dimensions of intelligence (the DAS is a three-factor test) takes about 40 minutes; diagnostic and attainment testing takes perhaps a further 20 minutes. Even a slow-working child can be assessed in an hour and a quarter. For pre- or early-school children (2½–6), there is a different selection of tests: six 'core' tests (five of them different) and five 'diagnostic' tests (two of them different). At all ages (2–18) the core tests give a summary measure of General Conceptual Ability (GCA or IQ), with abilities differentiating into Verbal Ability and Non-verbal Ability composites or clusters at 3½ and again into Verbal Ability, Nonverbal Reasoning Ability and Spatial Ability clusters at 6:0 years. Nonverbal ability was found in confirmatory factor analyses to represent an intermediate factor associated with both verbal and spatial factors at age 6 and above.

In fact the factor structure of the DAS is based on only the six core tests, one of them (Sequential and Quantitative Reasoning, SQR) an innovation not developed from the BAS. There are thus three pairs of tests, each supporting a designated factor. All six school-age tests load highly on a g factor, as we have seen (Table 3.3). Three of these six core tests meet the 0.70 criterion for 'good measures of g', with Recall of Designs being the weakest from this point of view, whilst all six are either 'fair'

(0.50–0.69) or 'good'. The newcomer, the apparently 'scholastic' scale, Sequential and Quantitative Reasoning, has the highest g-loading of all. We have seen that WISC subtests tend to resolve in contradictory fashion into multiple factor structures. This is not the case with DAS core tests: in a three-factor resolution they come into their own (see Table 3.10).

Table 3.10: Three-factor loadings for DAS core test battery; after Elliott (1990, Table 9.12, p. 207).

	Verbal	Non-verbal reasoning	Spatial
Word Definitions	0.79		
Similarities	0.81		
Matrices		0.74	
Seq. and Quant . Reas.		0.80	
Recall of Designs			0.69
Pattern Construction			0.82
Mean (n = 6)	0.78		

Now five of the six tests appear as clear measures, in addition to g, of their specific factors or 'group' abilities as they used to be known. Even the memory-contingent Recall of Designs hovers close to excellence in this analysis based on 2400 cases. It is an important achievement of the DAS that it measures more distinct kinds of intelligence more purely (without time wasted on 'noisy' scales) than other comparable tests.

Most structural theories of human cognitive ability, at least those with a psychometric base, posit an ability hierarchy of some kind, with a general factor (g) at the apex of the pyramid. The verbal factor, at the next level, is the group or component factor about which there is the best agreement. Indeed, measures of vocabulary are commonly the class of tests most highly g-loaded within the ensemble. The contrasting group of *visual* (BAS), or *Performance* (Wechsler) or *k:m* (spatial-mechanical, Vernon) or *fluid* (Cattell–Horn) abilities has always been more ambiguous. Not least, this is because different kinds of spatial ability have different relationships with the kinds of verbal reasoning required to exercise them; what I have here called verbal strategy.

In the DAS the Nonverbal Reasoning cluster comprises a multiple-choice untimed matrix completion test (Matrices) of the traditional kind, and a mainly abstract test of quantitative reasoning whose early items involve sequences of figural stimuli (Sequential and Quantitative Reasoning). Mathematical ability, of course, has a familiar if enigmatic closeness to spatial ability, though early *arithmetical* and calculation skills have a largely verbal, even phonological character. Though factor-analytic model-fitting with the DAS standardisation data confirmed that this intermediate, Non-verbal Reasoning cluster partook of both spatial and verbal qualities, a distinctive place is allowed for tests 'that measure inductive reasoning and therefore allow for verbal mediation in the solution of [spatial] problems' (Elliott, 1990, p. 21).

But how do these intermediate verbal–spatial abilities fit within other theories, for instance *Gf-Gc* – or fluid and crystallised – theory? Some work already confirms that the distinction between DAS Spatial and Nonverbal Reasoning clusters maps well onto that between Horn's *Gv* (broad visualisation) and (fluid) abilities respectively (Keith, 1990). Another study drawing on concurrent administrations of DAS, WJ-R and Detroit-3 finds that this is particularly the case with a three-factor solution (McGhee, 1993). Furthermore the DAS Spatial pair of tests (but not the Nonverbal Reasoning pair) joins the Perceptual Organisation subtests on the Wechsler scales in a *Gv* factor (Stone, 1992). This is useful confirmation that the Perceptual Organisation subtests lack the non-verbal reasoning element in fluid ability. Moreover:

> The DAS's two subtests are quite different from the subtests that compose the WISC-III, and they measure nonverbal reasoning without using time limits or requiring visual-motor co-ordination. In that sense, they provide a good measure of the kind of uncont-aminated tests of Gf that Horn prefers. (Kaufman, 1994, p. 171)

The DAS intermediate factor, then, has higher-order properties of fluid reasoning that combine elements of mental (visuo-spatial) manipulation of shapes with verbal mediation and problem solving. There matters might rest, were it not for the fact that dyslexic children show a mysterious inability to apply just such a verbal strategy to visual problems. Indeed as we will see in a later chapter their collective score on the Nonverbal Cluster is significantly lower than their score on the Verbal and Spatial clusters. In the face of this phenomenon, some speculation is necessary. Possible explanations include:

- some sort of rigidity of thinking, leading to inferior Gf (fluid ability) in dyslexic individuals;
- another general factor such as lack of absorbed attentiveness (non-verbal reasoning skills remain demonstrably beyond the reach of impulsive, ADHD children);
- specific cognitive factors such as a working memory component involved in the control of operational sequences (steps in reasoning) and a phonological element in the use of naming (retrieval) and other verbal strategies (Turner, 1994c).

Factor analytic studies reported in the DAS Handbook (Elliott, 1990, pp. 225–9) confirm a relationship between the Nonverbal Reasoning cluster and the WISC-R Fourth Factor. Two studies are reported of concurrent DAS and WISC-R administrations, one with 63 8–10-year-olds, another with 52 14–15-year-olds. Matrices bears little relationship to any of the WISC-R composites, perhaps for the reasons suggested above. But the Nonverbal Reasoning cluster correlates with the Fourth Factor almost as highly (0.70 and 0.69) as with Verbal (0.77, 0.68) and Full Scale (0.75, 0.79) IQs. In particular, the Fourth Factor correlates highest with Sequential and Quantitative Reasoning (0.58, 0.69), Recall of Digits (0.58, 0.60) and Basic Number Skills (0.69, 0.63) at these two ages. As well as confirming some unintended 'diagnostic' behaviour on the part of the cluster, this rather highlights the numerical character of the Freedom from Distractibility factor on WISC-R and WISC-III, not an aspect much emphasised by psychologists. Factorists will have to decide for us whether quantitative ability, so impressively central in analyses such as those referred to here, is in fact somewhere out on a diagnostic limb in factor space, as in *Gf–Gc* theory, or is a neglected but principal element in all rational activity. Do numbers fall midway on a spectrum between words and images?

The DAS's diagnostic repertoire

We turn from considerations of intelligence and the core DAS tests to look next at the selection of diagnostic tests that form an integral part of the DAS repertoire. These are presented as tests of a different ('diagnostic') class, form no factorial clusters (including that of memory: Elliott, 1990, p. 21) and have low correlations with *g*. Though a rational method for evaluating exceptional performances on all tests is central to the DAS, no basis, other than a common-sense descriptive one, is offered for the inclusion of these particular tests.

In the pre-school battery there are two diagnostic tests aimed at skills thought to be important in the early acquisition of basic skills. Recognition of Pictures is a test of short-term visual memory, using pictures of objects (domestic implements, parts of the body, animals) instead of the abstract figures that were a feature of later items in the BAS's Visual Recognition, its predecessor test. The theory is that the verbal strategy of naming will not interfere because usually several similar objects with the same name are pictured. However, it seems that a naming strategy is stimulated by any pictured object and is hard to inhibit thereafter. Matching Letter-like Forms, the other test, entails identification of a target shape from among distractors, a test of perceptual matching. In fact, very few dyslexic children actually seem to have difficulty with this.

Three other tests are available at all age levels. Evidence of memory functioning is provided by Recall of Objects – Immediate (formerly Immediate Visual Recall) in which words and pictures are linked. A card with familiar objects is displayed for one minute while the objects are named. The card is then removed and the individual is asked to recall as many as he or she can. There are two further presentations followed by recall. Recall of Objects – Delayed occurs after 10–15 minutes, when a fourth, unexpected recall is attempted. The task, although a visual array, is principally a verbal list. As a difficulty with naming is characteristic of many dyslexic people, and problems of retrieval are separated from problems of storage, the test is of clinical interest. In addition, the subject's performances on the Immediate and Delayed versions of this test may be significantly different. If there is an exceptional decay in items recalled, we may interpret a failure to consolidate in memory information recently acquired. In the case of an exceptional recovery of items, the problem may be one of retrieval rather than storage. This pair of tests seems to have particular value with younger children, when it is sometimes the best warning indicator that something is wrong.

The third test common to all ages is Recall of Digits. In this test, digits must be repeated, forwards only, after presentation at the rate of two per second. This low-level language task requires no transformation of the stimuli, but language memory capacity is vital for comprehension of speech and print. This version of digit span correlates with Digit Span from the WISC-R (Elliott, 1990, pp. 227–9); the correlations were 0.72 (8–10 year-olds) and 0.74 (14–15 year-olds).

Speed of Information Processing, the last of the DAS diagnostic tests, comes into play at 6 years. The highest in a row of numbers must be marked with a pencil; the action is repeated for a series of rows; time per page (in seconds) is the raw score. In the case of the younger child, the circle containing the most squares in each row must be marked. This is a clerical checking task, requiring only threshold levels of arithmetical ability (place value). Like Visual Matching and Cross Out (WJ-R) and Symbol Search (WISC-III), this 'elementary cognitive task' requires mental rather than psychomotor speed, though any pencil-and-paper task will compromise certain children. The relation with writing and spelling seems to be weaker than that of Coding (WISC-III). But the test is particularly descriptive when, as is often the case, dyslexic children seem to process all information slowly.

The DAS attainment tests

There are three of these: the tests of written calculation skills, spelling and reading (given in that order) are of a conventional kind. Arithmetical problems give way to word problems in number only in the later stages; spelling consists of dictated words, with single sentence contexts; and reading is once again a matter of word recognition. The main improvement over the BAS prototypes is the extension of the normative range to take in all individuals aged up to and including 17:11 years. However, the gradient of difficulty of later Word Reading items is steep and the test is severe with older, poorer readers.

Tracking exceptionality: a consistent method

The DAS offers a clear rationale for examining individual profiles that is both simple[58] and direct. With the separation of g-measuring from diagnostic tests, contrasts are available between three classes of test (intelligence, diagnostic and attainment) and between three levels of test score (summary, cluster and individual). Moreover a clear, if succinct, procedure for analysing individual profiles is suggested in the *Introductory and Technical Handbook*, though not the Manual.

In summary, this is as follows. First, at the top level, the GCA or IQ is contrasted with cluster scores, exposing any unusual imbalance in cognitive development such as, good spatial or poor non-verbal reasoning abilities. Second, contrasts are evaluated within clusters. Given that Matrices and Sequential and Quantitative Reasoning correlate highly and so form a cluster, any contrast in scores between the two may be noteworthy: a pupil's difficulties with written number symbols relative to his or her non-verbal reasoning skills may be unusual, found only once in 5% of individuals, say. Third, his or her performance on one or more diagnostic tests may be interpretable; perhaps a low Recall of Digits result contrasts with the mean T-score on the core tests, for instance. Fourth, one or more attainment test result may be highly unexpected in relation to overall GCA (IQ). For all exceptionalities, criteria are provided clearly on the record form for whether a discrepancy is statistically significant; and Tables B6–8 in the Handbook give percentages of the standardisation sample with discrepancies as large as that observed or larger.[59]

Conclusion

This concludes our examination of some of the major cognitive assessment systems, their uses and interpretation, with regard to the patterns of unusual cognitive development that are believed to be important in the diagnosis of dyslexia. On the principle that it is important *not to miss what you are not looking for*, the general cognitive survey is performed without prejudice as to whether a dyslexia diagnosis is likely or not. All major sets of cognitive skills known to be relevant to progress in school subjects are sampled and individual profiles are respected: a child may have significant specific learning difficulties regardless of how these are categorised and *dyslexia* will in many cases seem a wrong description of the difficulties.

In the clinical sample discussed at length in Chapter 8, the average number of DAS subtests, out of a maximum of 10, that are discrepant[60] from the mean T-score on the six core or ability-measuring tests is, for 346 cases, 2.4. That is, each individual referred for a psychological assessment for whatever reason is likely to have between two and three subtest scores that are significantly high or low in relation to his or her characteristic level of performance. Although the DAS documentation does not allow us to say how this compares with overall prevalence rates, it may be an indication that imbalance in cognitive development is an important first level of observation in a cognitive assessment, and further justification for the use of a good modern ability measurement system. With or without an associated under-performance in number or literacy skills, inconsistent intellectual development in non-verbal[61] or verbal learning constitutes a *specific learning difficulty* in its own right, one apparently far from rare.

The diagnostic enterprise, however, must go beyond the descriptive features delineated by a general cognitive survey. Because many of the finer-grained diagnostic features of dyslexia are linguistic, they are properly considered in the context of attainment testing. It is to diagnostic testing that we turn next.

Notes

1 '. . . our ideas of human personality, of that *personal* quality which makes every human being unique, to be expressed only in terms of itself: this idea of *person* comes to us from Christian theology . . . The human person cannot be expressed in concepts. It eludes all rational definitions, indeed all description, for all the properties whereby it could be categorized can be met with in other individuals. Personality can only be grasped in this life by a direct intuition; it can only be expressed in a work of art' Lossky (1957, p. 53; original emphasis).

2 This does not prevent ardent espousal of one or other particular touchstone favoured by the teacher, befriender, administrator or advocate: the ACID profile, for instance, or 'digits backwards'.

3 Analysis of a specimen of hair provides an excellent test of zinc levels in the body and this in turn is linked with behavioural and learning problems (Grant *et al.*, 1988); but as yet such a procedure falls short of the specificity needed for a test for dyslexia.

4 I recall being shown, at about this time, how to perform factor analysis on a pocket calculator by Dr Alec Walbridge, then unretired and still training educational psychologists at North East London Polytechnic's Department of Psychology.

5 For those familiar with them: the boxing match, the burglar and 'Why should women and children be saved first in a shipwreck?'.

6 Stephen Jay Gould in his best-seller, *The Mismeasure Of Man* (1981), trenchantly argues the sceptical case on this methodology. However, though his book won the National Book Critics Circle Award and 'so successfully cemented the received wisdom about IQ in the media . . .' (Herrnstein and Murray, 1994, p. 296), it has failed in the longer term to halt the uphill struggle to establish often painful facts in a contentious scientific area. His case, which he scarcely develops, is that IQ is a 'reification' of a first principal component in the construct of intelligence.

7 I owe these reflections to Demian Turner.

8 Cited in Elliott (1990).

9 The tendency of any average to stabilise after four or so items, so that new additions to the calculation, unless extreme, find it progressively harder to make an alteration.

10 Kaufman (1994). Comments on Symbol Search, Coding and Mazes may be found on pp. 58–62.

11 It is surely unwise, therefore, to speak, as Lynn (1996, p. 272) does, amongst other minor errors, of the DAS being 'less g-loaded' than WISC-R and WAIS-R.

12 An Oblimin rotation allows the factors to become correlated, as we know them to be in reality.

13 On WISC-R, only the Block Design subtest correlates with Full Scale IQ at a level better than Performance IQ correlates with Verbal IQ. See the WISC-R Manual (Wechsler, 1974, p. 47).

14 The distorting effect on dyslexic IQ of subtests with unintended 'diagnostic' significance has long exercised clinicians. The solution is a regrouping of scores along three-factor lines, to be discussed.

15 Varimax is an orthogonal rotation: it forces factors to be uncorrelated.

16 Arithmetic, Coding, Information and Digit Span.

17 See, for example, the recent summary in Draycott and Kline (1994).

18 Its lesser popularity with psychologists for assessing dyslexia perhaps owes little to factor purity and more to the interesting mixture of challenges presented by Coding B. See Chapter 4 for more discussion on this.

19 For example, in four successive factorial solutions, Picture Arrangement is assigned, first to the general factor, next to the verbal factor, finally to the visuo-spatial factor, where it remains.

20 As Carroll pools and reanalyses psychometric data from many of the best quality studies of intelligence and component abilities, his is truly a meta-analysis.

21 In studies of group ethnic differences in average performance, a similar distinction – between reaction time (cognitive processing) and movement time (small motor skills) – is important: white reaction, but black movement, times are faster. Movement time is much less well correlated with g than is reaction time. As an entrée to an extensive literature see, for example, Barrett, Eysenck and Lucking (1986).

22 Psychologists wishing to resolve ambiguous clinical problems centring on speed of information processing may turn to the Woodcock–Johnson Psycho-Educational Battery – Revised (WJ-R) (Woodcock and Johnson, 1989, 1990). Well constructed and normed tests of cognitive ability include Visual Matching (two 1–3 digit numbers the same must be detected in a row of six), Test 3 in the Standard Battery; and Cross Out (five figures the same as a target figure must be identified in a row of 19), Test 10 in Supplemental Battery Tests 8-14. Both tests are of course timed and the numbers of items correct within three minutes constitute the raw scores.

23 Specialist teachers seem especially prone to assimilating inaccurate concepts of dyslexia profiling: errors abound, for instance, in Edwards (1994), an otherwise interesting book.

24 *Freedom from Boredom* would seem appropriate, given that it is mainly composed of low-level, convergent processes. More seriously, I cannot see why the Third Factor was not from the outset called simply, accurately and comprehensibly the Learning Difficulty (LD) factor; Learning Difficulty rather than Learning Disability since not all learning difficulties are disabling.

25 The same difficulty, of course, has been encountered in utilising the subtest structure of the Wechsler Adult Intelligence Scale (WAIS) to obtain information about cognitive deficits. Kay (1989), too, puts forward the view that this is not a purpose for which IQ tests were designed nor one which they can perform satisfactorily. The issue is discussed in Kline (1993, p. 294).

26 Low scores on the Freedom from Distractibility factor are also characteristic of 'normal children, especially girls, living in the Western part of the United States' (Kaufman, 1994, p. 213).

27 As an alternative name for the fourth WISC-III factor, Kaufman suggests 'Freedom from Bad Attitude'.

28 Kaufman (1994, pp. 210–11).

29 Baddeley's terms: see Baddeley (1986).

30 I wonder to what extent the expression 'visual sequential memory' is a contradiction in terms.

31 The use of BAS/DAS Recall of Designs as a diagnostic test cannot be supported. Pattern Construction and Recall of Designs do not register significantly discrepant mean scores for any of the four 'clusters' of reading-disabled pupils in this disjoint cluster analysis from the DAS standardisation sample. For the whole subsample of 136, mean T-scores on the two tests are 50.4 (PC) and 50.8 (RD). That Recall of Designs has a memory component cannot, from a factorial point of view, be doubted however. In confirmatory factor analyses, a three-factor solution produced Verbal, Non-verbal and Memory factors, with Recall of Designs loading 0.70 on the memory factor, together with Recognition of Pictures (0.47), Recall of Digits (0.37) and Recall of Objects (0.38), though much more highly g-loaded than these other tests. Transferring Recall of Designs to a separate spatial factor produced a better fit for a three-factor solution; an independent memory factor could not be justified (Elliott, 1990, pp. 205–6 and Table 9.11).

32 Currently discussion centres on whether phonology mediates the learning of letter shapes in the early stages of learning to read. Theorists wishing to make sense of the ubiquitous role of language in learning face an uphill struggle because inner language is unlimited and language, like love and intelligence, tends to explain too much. But given Luria's proposal that language is the 'regulator of behaviour', attempts to do so should persist.

33 Kaufman now commends a SCAD Profile for WISC-III: Symbol Search, Coding, Arithmetic and Digit Span. He provides (Kaufman, 1994, pp. 219–4) statistical support for this combination of all the troublesome tests in the form of deviation quotients for sums of these four scaled scores (Table 5.3) and cumulative percentages for normal and exceptional children of the difference between sums of these scaled scores and the sum of scores on the four Perceptual Organisation subtests (Table 5.2). My own experience is that speed of processing is a more inconsistent diagnostic feature in dyslexia than verbal memory and so this index, S-C-A-D, will probably not have quite the appeal of the A-C-I-D profile.

34 Like many psychometricians, Kline suggests, in relation to the Stanford-Binet and WISC tests, that 'both these tests should be retired. It is simply more efficient to measure the primary factors separately and derive from them overall IQ measures of both crystallized and fluid intelligence' (1993, p. 408).

35 British children obtained slightly higher composite scores at the 6- and 16-year-old levels, which the Manual attributes to different patterns of statutory schooling at entry and exit ages (Wechsler et al., 1992, pp. 57–58).

36 Mathematics Reasoning, Numerical Operations, Listening Comprehension, Oral Expression and Written Expression.

37 A valuable exception is the work of Rhona Johnston and Brian Thompson, who have compared Scottish with New Zealand children and found an overall advantage for phonically taught Scottish pupils over book-experience-taught New Zealand pupils of ten months (1989, 1995).

38 Rust, J. Personal communication, 1994.

39 It is to be hoped that the program will be issued in the UK with British data tables.

40 Among these WISC-III Writer selects according to rational criteria: at least one scaled score in the cluster must be significantly different (higher or lower) than

the mean on the scale (Verbal or Performance) from which it is drawn; the other scaled scores in the cluster must all differ from the scale mean in the same direction. Thus the clusters reported by the software are fewer than the total number that can be calculated following, for instance, formulae given in Kaufman (1994, Tables 6.1–6.6, pp. 273–282). Reliabilities of the Shared-Ability Composites are given in the Manual, sections 2.11–2.12.

41 The term is used in not quite the same sense as traditionally with personality questionnaires in clinical psychology. In the latter, if a forced-choice response is imposed, the subject's own needs contend with each other and the test is said to become 'ipsative', meaning the relevance of norms may be questioned. Kaufman's method relies squarely upon the provision of accurate norms.

42 Kaufman, 1994, Chapter 3: 'Seven steps for interpreting the WISC-III profile: from IQs to Factor Indexes to scaled scores'.

43 That statistical criteria must be applied to each individual subtest and grouping of subtests shows why the pattern-recognition approach to the ACID profile is unacceptably imprecise: given the power of the instrument, often overlooked, WISC-IIIUK interpretation should not proceed in casual and parochial fashion as if it were a game anyone can play.

44 Of course the subsequent Woodcock–Johnson Psycho-Educational Battery – Revised (WJ-R) (Woodcock and Johnson, 1989, 1990) contains full sets – 35 in all – of ability and achievement measures. For each of the WRMT-R and WJ-R there is a useful set of scoring software which, in the case of WJ-R, performs all the many possible discrepancy comparisons and can be printed via an ASCII file onto paper.

45 In particular the Wechsler batteries may be criticised for an absence of tests of reasoning, working through steps in a logical sequence. Only when one encounters newer tests, such as the Kaufman Adolescent and Adult Intelligence Test (KAIT) (Kaufman and Kaufman, 1993), with its four excellent fluid reasoning tests, does one see fully what this lack means.

46 Many estimates agree on a male:female ratio of 4–5:1. My own casework sample, analysed in a subsequent chapter, is no exception: 4.6 males to 1 female.

47 Sattler (1988), in his otherwise excellent and compendious work on assessment technique, dismisses, for each test he reviews, male advantage in IQ as 'less than 3 points'. Nothing at all is said about cognitive sex differences.

48 This, of course, runs contrary to the accepted view of a female advantage in most aspects of language skill.

49 Unless, of course, the Born and Lynn view of a slight general male, including language, advantage prevails.

50 Data are from Born and Lynn, 1994. Aggregate female are subtracted from aggregate male scores and the differences expressed in units of standard deviation (Ds). Items in both tests are essentially all of one type: the decision to retain the tests as a whole means that sex differences, expected on theoretical grounds (female advantage in short-term auditory–verbal memory and in what Horn calls clerical speed), are real. There have been opposed views on the female verbal memory advantage but the WISC data seem consistent.

51 References in the manual are largely to the authors' own publications.

52 'Compuscore for the WJ-R' is available from the publisher, Riverside (Houghton-Mifflin, Chicago). The neat graphics which show, aligned on a single bar, standard scores and percentiles must, however, be printed from a separate ASCII file after exiting the main program.

53 The Woodcock–Johnson Battery provides, however, for intra-achievement discrepancy analysis only between one higher-order cluster in this category and the

other three; the clusters have higher reliability. Thus a discrepancy between an expected standard score for Broad Written Language of 78 and an actual one of 69 represents a difference in SD units of 0.93 or about one child in six. Evaluating a discrepancy between Word Attack (non-word reading: Test 31) and Letter-Word Identification (word reading: Test 22) or Reading Comprehension (passage reading: Test 22) is a matter of evaluating statistical significance based on the standard error of the difference(SE_{diff}). A table for evaluating three-way inter-subtest significance levels is presented in Chapter 5, Table 5.1. Beyond this, there is no way of establishing, by reference to the normative group, what the frequency of occurrence of such discrepancies might be.

54 In combination these three, although 'achievements', give a measure of quantitative ability – or Gq.

55 Robin Hedderly has over many years in Kirklees gathered normative data on writing productivity for large samples of children aged between 9 and 18, together with comparable data for the 'average adult', using incomplete sentences as 'seeds' or prompts ('I want to know . . .', 'My greatest fear . . .'). This has now been published (Hedderly, 1995).

56 In the manual for the KAIT (Kaufman and Kaufman, 1993), the authors acknowledge the primacy of Woodcock–Johnson in the development of their own Rebus Learning test.

57 There is, therefore, the General IQ with eight contributing scales at most ages; a Verbal IQ of four scales (including Speed of Information Processing, which transferred in 1983 from the Visual list, and Recall of Digits, a one-per-second forwards-only measure of digit span); a Visual IQ of four fairly unproblematic scales; the Short Form IQ, as mentioned, a combination of two good g measures and two 'diagnostic' scales; and the new g-enhanced four-scale IQ, consisting of Matrices, Similarities, Block Design Level and Word Definitions. A new diagnostic feature, unexploited by the software, therefore appears: a contrast between the Short Form and the g–enhanced IQ. The IQ of the first dyslexic child whose BAS results I examined using the software revision rose 12 points. Another pupil, RE, had obtained a BAS IQ in April 1992, aged 12, of 119; in August 1995, aged 15, he obtained a DAS GCA of 111. Reanalysed by the scoring software which had appeared in the meantime, the earlier IQ, now g-enhanced, was revised to 113, an impressive testimony to the validity of the DAS.

58 Unusually, however, no software is yet available for the scoring and analysis of the DAS, so possibilities of error remain amid the joys of clerical exercise.

59 In the case of the three attainment tests, differences are one-tailed, that is, scores are expected to fall *below* the level predicted. Unusually *high* or *low* core and diagnostic tests are evaluated according to a two-tailed criterion.

60 Statistically significantly so, at the 5% or $P = 0.05$ level.

61 Rourke (1989).

Chapter 4
Detecting Cognitive Anomaly

The field

It is strongly suspected that dyslexia is a cognitive deficit (Frith, 1992, 1995). That is, the dyslexic suffers from an inefficiency – normally inherited, sometimes acquired – in a relatively peripheral set of automatic information-handling processes. These seem to converge on linguistic processes and their analogues: auditory memory, word perception, linear sequencing, rate of articulation, auditory comprehension and timing. Not all current theories and descriptions of these are mutually compatible.[1] Complete understanding of how this ensemble of subservient skills operates is awaited. But in the meantime impressive opportunities invite the assessing psychologist.

The criteria

Some of the processing faults or anomalies are already familiar to us. For any one in particular there may or may not be a choice of instruments. The purpose remains the same: to detect and demonstrate a specific processing weakness beyond natural variation. This calls, as always, for a cautious measurement approach to establish the phenomenon in question in ways that allow public verification.

At the outset let us be clear that the same criteria apply to diagnostic testing, some of which explores sensitive frontiers of knowledge, as to conventional educational and other psychological testing. Tests should be published,[2] constructed to the highest modern technical standards and should measure variables identified in advance as significant by theory. They should also permit full statistical interpretation, so that the effect of interest should be discriminable above the noise of natural variation and its rarity or otherwise quantified in the ways we have been considering.

Nevertheless, psychometric publishing is somewhat conservative and the use of *informal diagnostic procedures* is likely to be a necessity for some time to come for the sensitive observer. In this case results should not be overinterpreted. Limits of the normative base, for instance, should be made explicit and the findings treated as merely suggestive.

Throughout the rest of this chapter, some lines of inquiry into major diagnostic areas are outlined, with reference to specific tests or procedures. Inevitably the possibilities are a great deal wider than can be satisfactorily indicated in such a survey, but the scope of the individual assessment can be widened by this means to include virtually all considerations of theoretical importance, the *general cognitive survey* often being, as we have seen, something of a necessary distraction. The technology of intelligence testing represents a completed art; little remains to be achieved, at least without further advances in the study of intelligence, beyond economy savings, as administration time is shortened, but almost the whole interest of the assessment of dyslexia resides in the linguistic and other discoveries to be made in which otherwise sound and unexceptional individuals demonstrate inexplicable limitations in their ability to process certain kinds of information.[3]

Verbal repetition and memory

Most obvious among many such limitations is that of immediate verbal memory. With good reason this has long been seen as the hallmark of dyslexia. The psychometric hallmark, correspondingly, has been a low score on Digit Span (WISC) or Recall of Digits (BAS, DAS). Results on these two tests, however, though reliable, are also somewhat enigmatic. Let us first look at what they purport to measure, however.

Stimuli for immediate verbal repetition may be familiar (numbers) or unfamiliar (contrived non-words). The requirement to repeat actual words is susceptible to the influence of prior vocabulary and hence cultural difference. Long-term lexical knowledge has been shown to influence performance on such short-term tasks (Hulme, Maughan and Brown, 1991). A purer measure of capacity, therefore, has been obtained by using neutral stimuli such as numbers. In English all digits between one and 9 (zero is omitted because of multiple names: nought, nothing, 0) have a single syllable except seven. Capacity is therefore measured well by the *number* of digits presented.[4] Different digit span norms have been obtained in Wales; digit names may have several syllables in Welsh.

At younger ages a non-word repetition task may be more reliable and yield individual differences that are more stable than digit repetition (Gathercole et al., 1994; Gathercole, 1995b). Moreover the vocabulary influence is lower, and the memory component higher, when unword-like non-words are used (Gathercole, 1995a). Just what the memory component is remains disputed. One view is that internal phonological (speech-sound) representations are built up from infancy and operate in normal individuals as a well-constructed processing system (Mehler,

1994; Mehler and Dupoux, 1994). Individuals with impaired or non-intact speech-sound processing have complex difficulties in remembering utterances as well as learning the mappings between sound and print. Another view is that a dedicated auditory-verbal memory system, the phonological loop, acts as a buffer with degrees of sensitivity and capacity. On the latter view, as mentioned in Chapter 1, overload will affect the way attentional resources are shared between the phonological *memory* and the supervisory attentional system.

These considerations are germane to the varying nature of the digit repetition task. On Recall of Digits (BAS, DAS) the numbers are repeated at half-second intervals, with risk of overcrowding or congestion. On Digit Span (WISC) numbers are repeated at one-second intervals, with less risk of overcrowding but more risk of decay. Moreover, repeating digits *in reverse order* (WISC Digit Span) is, in the main, another task altogether:

> Cognitive psychologists . . . and neuropsychologists . . . have known for decades that Wechsler's Digits Forward and Digits Backward measure a different set of skills. Repeating digits in the same order as they are spoken is an automatic task that requires an immediate response with some mediation (chunking the numbers) and does not tax the individual's working memory. Reversing digits, in contrast, requires number manipulation and spatial visualization to recode the information in working memory . . . Digits Forward is generally a poor measure of *g*; Digits Backward serves as a much better measure of general intelligence. (Kaufman, 1994, pp. 232–3)

Note that this account implies a model of 'working memory' in which two things are done at once, sometimes referred to as multitasking. It is additive demands of this kind that locate WISC Arithmetic, as well as Digit Span, on the third factor, though Arithmetic, unintended diagnostic consequences aside, is frequently a good measure of *g*.

Psychologists used to familiar psychometric instruments may overestimate attentional, 'working memory' aspects and underestimate linguistic aspects of this diagnostic activity. Non-word repetition is 'highly associated with both current and later reading development' (Gathercole, 1995b, p. 162) to a greater extent than digit span. Yet it is unusual to find practising psychologists also taking the next logical step and confronting the frequent numerical component in such tasks as Digit Span, Arithmetic, Speed of Information Processing and Coding. If this is done, as discussed in Chapter 3, the question arises of an overlap between dyslexia and attentional or executive function (frontal lobe) disorders. It may be that the inner language component in logical reasoning or *Gf* tasks is sufficient to explain why they seem to be especially difficult for dyslexic people. Nevertheless the verbal strategy requirement of planning tasks remains a major unsolved element in the cognitive research.

Non-word repetition and digit span are useful diagnostic tasks which are readily available in psychometrically acceptable form.[5] A test that mixes letters *and* numbers is Test 9 of Wide Range Assessment of Memory and Learning (WRAML) (Sheslow and Adams, 1990): Number/Letter Memory. A span of seven numbers and letters increases over the 11-year age range to about 16. Internal reliability (alpha coefficient) is good (0.83–0.90); standard error is only 1.0–1.2 points of scaled score (1.3 points of raw score across the age range). Letters may be less neutral than numbers and the only polysyllabic letter, W, is used freely. But the test consistently loads highest among the nine tests in this battery on a verbal factor (0.85 typically).

Among many other tests of verbal learning the California Test of Verbal Learning – Children's Version (CVLT-C) (Delis et al., 1994) may be mentioned. This battery evaluates consolidation of list learning across task types and over varying intervals. However, the test has been criticised for transferring uncritically to children an adult verbal learning paradigm (Fennell, 1994).

The tests in the British Ability Scales that are most commonly used as supplements by practitioners who do not use the main battery are Immediate and Delayed Visual Recall. In a permutation of Kim's Game, the pupil is shown 20 pictures on a card for two minutes and then must recall as many as possible in a further two minutes. A second recall is requested, without forewarning, 15–20 minutes later. In the revised version in the Differential Ability Scales three initial exposures (1 minute, 20 seconds, 20 seconds) are given and shorter recall times are allowed (1 minute, 40 seconds, 40 seconds). The Delayed Visual Recall trial is similar. It is common practice to treat this exercise as a 'visual memory' test, and results are often reported as supporting evidence for memory problems additional to those of verbal memory. Dyslexics' reading techniques include, we know, much guessing from limited, especially visual, cues and this strategy, though maladaptive, makes sense as a developmental compensation for limited sound-symbol decoding skills. Dyslexics may well use visual memory to a greater extent on this test but the character of the test is surely a *verbal list* more than a *visual array*. (The pupil hears the objects named before attempting to memorise them.) This makes it an interesting diagnostic instrument, especially for the kinds of errors made by children with learning difficulties. Renaming is common (*wine* for *bottle*, *rat* for *mouse*). Errors that reveal a semantic strategy in memory are common in dyslexic children (*wind* for *flag*), who often show no phonological ordering principle, such as initial letter (*bird, book, bottle*), in recall.

Another dimension is entered with the Delayed Visual Recall, after 15–20 minutes. Although quite a stringent statistical criterion is applied to the significance of a discrepancy between T-scores obtained on the two occasions,[6] a difference in either direction often sheds light on the classroom functioning of a child. On the one hand, a child who consolidates information poorly is able to recollect many fewer items after the lapse of time; this often corroborates the picture of him or her presented by the class teacher. On the other hand, dyslexic children often seem to recover more items on the later occasion than would be expected. This is broadly consistent with a verbal deficit interpretation of the problems in dyslexia. Under the stress of the demand for immediate recall (immediate verbal memory), the dyslexic often exhibits word-finding difficulties. These are also apparent on tests with little diagnostic profile, such as Similarities. This strategy of attaching names to things seems, especially in the preschool and earlier primary years, to be a useful diagnostic indicator of dyslexia. When a later recall is requested, however, there has been no preparatory effort or build-up of test-taking set. Consequently the dyslexic freely recalls many names, demonstrating that the problem the first time was one of *retrieval*, not of *storage*.

As *rapid automatised naming* (RAN) is well established as a difficulty in dyslexia (Denckla and Rudel, 1976),[7] it is to be hoped that the third generation of this test battery, BAS-II, will include as a sequel a timed trial on which the pupil names the pictures of objects with the card in open view. A trial in which the pupil arranges cut-out versions of the objects on a grid will serve to control to some extent the element of visuo-spatial strategy.

Other measures of phonological processing

Although tradition strongly favours memory as the chief descriptor in dyslexia diagnosis, it may not be necessary to employ this construct at all in relation to phonology. All that is necessary is to posit a processing system that degrades linguistic stimuli and to give some test of current phonological processing that will demonstrate the accuracy or otherwise of the system. Obviously immediate verbal memory will be affected if the stimuli are modified before they reach it.

Non-word repetition is a major asset in assessing the phonological processing of children as young as four years. However, the ability to repeat five-syllable non-words plateaus at about 9–10 years and other phonological manipulation tasks are needed for the older or more able child or adult. Among the most commonly used tasks in research into phonological sensitivity are phoneme deletion, rhyming (including rhyme generation), blending, oddity (which word ends with a different sound?) and others which involve the initial phoneme. Stanovich, Cunningham and Cramer (1984) gave a comprehensive selection of such tasks to preschool children and identified a single phonological factor. An adaptation of 10 of these tasks is given in an appendix to Aaron and Joshi (1992). The latter authors give a mean and standard deviation obtained on the first four tests (final phoneme same, substitute initial phoneme, initial phoneme not same, supply initial phoneme) for children aged 7–8 after a year of statutory schooling in the USA. They thus provide a serviceable test of phonological skill for this age-group.[8] As a resource for assessing reading difficulties, Lynette Bradley provides a test using rhyme oddity (Bradley, 1980). Frith, Landerl and Frith (1995) recently demonstrated in a dyslexic sample the poverty of phonological generation ('Tell me as many things as possible beginning with *s*'). Mean and standard deviation for this age-group (12-year-old boys) again allow direct comparison. One of the best short measures of phoneme deletion ('Say *play*; say it again, but don't say *p*'), the Test of Auditory Analysis Skills, is to be found in Rosner (1993). Phoneme deletion usefully combines several aspects of phonological processing: segmentation (*p-l-a-y*), blending (*lay*) and rhyme (*lay, play*). Segmental phonology seems closest to the processes of literacy (Muter, Snowling and Taylor, 1994) but measures that include single phoneme deletion may correlate too highly with reading skill, functioning as concomitants of reading ability rather than predictors or precursors.

Though these phonological assessment procedures are useful with older school pupils who are failing in some aspect of literacy, they are still aimed at younger children. This is because phonemic awareness and phonological skill have come to the fore in the research literature in recent years as precursors of literacy learning. Typically measures are taken preschool and evaluated in the light of literacy attainment a year or two later, but in assessing dyslexic pupils of all ages it is important to be able to detect age-inappropriate lack of phonological skill on age-appropriate tasks.

One such is the spoonerism task devised by Dolores Perin (Perin, 1983). Her subjects were 14-year-old pupils at London schools: good spellers and readers, poor spellers and readers, and good readers but poor spellers. The task involved some practice at devising spoonerisms (*Polores Derin*), followed by 18 names of singers and pop groups, culled from the *New Musical Express* of the day, to be spoonerised (*Mob Barley*). This exercise is ready-made, in cultural and age-appropriate interest, to be used with today's adolescents. Especially critical to administration is the five-second time limit within which spoonerised names must be produced. Pupils' total scores may be compared with those of Perin's three sample groups.

It may often be observed how much time and conscious effort, calculation even, it takes a dyslexic to arrive at correct responses to spoonerism items. In many ways the spoonerism task combines the most challenging but literacy-free demands of phonological processing. Because onsets and rimes must be transposed across syllables, this task assorts well with Goswami's claim that phonological skill above the individual phoneme level is possible for the child before school, but awareness and manipulation of individual phonemes tend not to develop

except in relation to alphabetic literacy teaching (Goswami, 1992).[9]
Forms of systematic phonological manipulation, such as *ag*-slang, where
-ag- is interpolated before the rime in each syllable (*black = blagack*),
or *havergav*, where *-uvug-* is interpolated (*bluvergack*),[10] periodically
sweep through primary schools, apparently without causing most children any difficulty in accomplishment. The spoonerism ought not, after
some initial learning trials, to cause serious difficulty to the average
child.

One especially ingenious implementation of this task, suitable for all
ages, is from the Phonological Assessment Battery (PhAB) (Brook and
Dalton, 1995). The child is asked to perform, within time limits, progressively harder substitutions of the initial sounds in words: first a new
initial consonant or consonant cluster is substituted (*crime* with *ch*
becomes *chime*); next the substitute consonant or consonant cluster is
extracted from another word (*fight* borrows *br* from *branch* to become
bright); lastly two complete words are spoonerised (*plane crash*
becomes *crane plash*). This procedure permits a gradient of difficulty.
The Phonological Assessment Battery as a whole exists in an experimental, unnormed version only,[11] but initial statistics are encouraging: the
spoonerism task relates closely to reading ability and reading difficulty.

Another useful but unnormed exercise in metalinguistic analysis
appropriate for older individuals is Townend's Syllable Perception Task
(Townend, 1994). Here the pupil is presented with words and non-
words, orally and in written form, and must say how many syllables
there are, or must isolate the stressed syllable, in each. In the surge of
popularity for a phonological account of dyslexia, it is often overlooked
how poor dyslexic people are at other aspects of linguistic processing,
notably of morphemes (Elbro, 1989). The Syllable Perception Task
demonstrates how even older, brighter dyslexic people show extraordinary difficulties with the counting of syllables, a trivial enough task for
many younger children.

Tests of speed of processing

We have already considered that an individual's linguistic system is
involved in many other forms of cognitive behaviour. Speed, therefore,
can be a sort of index of the efficiency of the whole. Obviously linguistic
tasks, such as rhyme and other phonological generation, illustrate
clearly how slowness may be a sign of difficulty, as when pupils are asked
to produce words beginning with a given sound, or ending with a
certain rime, within a set period, perhaps 10 seconds (Frith, Landerl and
Frith, 1995).

Other tasks may be more mixed, less obviously linguistic. WISC
Coding and WAIS Digit Symbol, for instance, involve recognition and
naming of numbers, opportune naming of some, but not all, symbols,

transcoding skill in making repetitive substitutions, and some visual memory, as symbol pairs become familiar. Because of considerable fine, rapid movement of the pencil, this test appears to load on a motor control factor as well as *G*s (clerical speed). But the linguistic character of the task remains strong. The explicitly named BAS/DAS Speed of Information Processing involves numerical sort; it therefore has a greater cognitive or mental speed component. Other tests clearly have more to do with visual search, Symbol Search on WISC-III and the two speed tests in Woodcock-Johnson[12] being good examples.

In principle any low-level cognitive operation, which above a given age is usually found as a well- automated skill, would serve the purpose of a test of speed. An example is the One Minute Addition–One Minute Subtraction Test (Westwood et al., 1974).[13] Here pupils are asked to perform with pencil and paper at speed very simple, largely one-digit calculations from sets of 30 and are stopped after one minute. Means and standard deviations are available for the primary age range and, given the nature of the task, are unlikely to have changed much since the early 1970s. Inspection of the norms confirms that *all* children do fewer subtraction than addition sums in the time available. Reasons for this are clearer than they used to be and pertain to the greater working memory demands of subtraction (Boulton-Lewis, 1993). But in relation to their peers dyslexic people are *very much* less able to perform even simple subtraction operations.[14] The test serves both as a measure of automaticity or fluency and, given this internal contrast, as a dyslexia indicator. The effect may be partly attributable to phonological memory, number bonds being for dyslexic people in this respect rather like the notoriously unlearnable times tables.

Diagnostic tests of written language

From a research point of view, tests of anomalous cognitive processing and tests of distortion in reading skill are part and parcel of the same investigation. However, in the field psychologists are able to use 'restricted' tests of 'underlying cognitive ability' whereas others, for instance specialist teachers, are not. The latter, however, may use varieties of diagnostic reading test. In practice, therefore, there appears to be a large categorical divide. In deference to this convention, testing of attainments (in reading, spelling, number skills) is dealt with more fully in a subsequent chapter, with as much information as possible on specific tests that may be used without 'restriction'.

However, it should be borne in mind that in reality this is often an artificial distinction. Tests of achievement sometimes turn out to be better measures of *g* than tests supposedly of ability. An example is the Kaufman Assessment Battery for Children (K-ABC) (Kaufman and Kaufman, 1983). Various analyses, of which the earliest was that by

Jensen (1984), have shown that the K-ABC is less saturated by *g* and more dependent on memory than conventional measures of IQ. Moreover certain of its tests of 'achievement' appear to be more *g*-loaded than its tests of 'mental processing' (Keith, 1985). Similarly, the Armed Forces Qualification Test (AFQT) consists in selected subtests of 'arithmetic reasoning, word knowledge and paragraph comprehension' (Herrnstein and Murray, 1994, p. 570). It was given as part of the National Longitudinal Survey of Youth in the USA, which yields such rich analyses of covariance of IQ in Herrnstein and Murray's *The Bell Curve*.

A better analysis, in other words, may once again be in terms of *Gf* or fluid intelligence and *Gc* or crystallised ability (Kline, 1991). Moreover it may be presumed that *all* dyslexia studies will one day be subsumed by the study of intelligence, as the phylogeny and ontogeny of the various intellectual abilities become better understood. From this point of view, the educational context is somewhat secondary, though properly attracting research interest for the large differences in achievement that may be attributed to curriculum design and teaching technique (Engelmann and Carnine, 1982).

Here we may take up the speed of processing issue in relation to speed of reading and speed of writing. At least one ambitious general theory of dyslexia turns upon dyslexic people's alleged inability to automate all learned skills, including the 'primitive' skills, such as balance (Nicolson and Fawcett, 1990; Fawcett and Nicolson, 1994). That this is so within the narrower range of acquired literacy skills should be easily agreed. Accordingly, how can we examine more closely the fluency or otherwise of these skills?

At least one test published in the UK claims to offer a standardised measure of speed of reading. The revised Neale Analysis of Reading Ability (Neale, 1989) offers three measures, derived from the same performance of the child in reading passages aloud: *accuracy* (number of decoding or pronunciation mistakes); *comprehension* (number of questions answered correctly about the mainly literal detail in the passages read); and *rate* (speed of reading on passages below that on which the child's errors exceed a limit).

This has its interests. In a single case study, Bodien (1996) shows marked improvements in reading accuracy and comprehension to be associated with a *decrement* in rate. Her pupil, in other words, had first to learn to slow down in order to decode and comprehend effectively. But this pupil showed, over the period of intensive instruction, no change in cognitive profile in WISC-III Index scores in terms of his marked preference for verbal over non-verbal tasks. However, he *did* show an improvement in processing speed – in effect, an improved score on Symbol Search.[15] This, it might be argued, arose from improvements, associated with specialist teaching, in his discipline of left-to-right scanning (sometimes called *tracking*) and analytic strategy.

There will no doubt continue to be pupils with learning difficulties whose rate is high or low in relation to their accuracy, each eventuality deserving interpretation. But, in the main, rate or fluency of reading is an artefact of accuracy. This is because of the longer times taken by poor readers over unfamiliar words. This will affect their times on all passages, not just the one on which they reach an error ceiling. Measures of *rate*, therefore, become to some extent a proxy measure of decoding in less able readers.

Aaron and Joshi, who have drawn attention to this problem, have also proposed a solution in the form of word lists (Aaron and Joshi, 1992; Aaron, 1994). Standard stimulus sets, that is, are given to pupils under controlled conditions. There are two sets of words, easier and harder, appropriate for less and more able readers, respectively. Each set consists of function and content words matched for letter length and frequency. Dyslexic readers make more errors on function words (*also, once, ever*), as well as reading them more slowly than content words (*book, bird, gold*). This enables an interesting internal contrast to be made, of potential diagnostic significance. Eye-movement studies have shown that all readers fixate slightly longer on content than on function words; this is because content words disproportionately carry the information in a sentence, whereas function words enact the sentence structure itself. As measures of reading speed are distorted by time taken over unfamiliar words, these four lists of 20 words each offer a good alternative. The individual's reading of the words in each set is timed and the total is divided by 40 to give a measure of seconds per word. A skilled adult reader reads silently at a speed of about 0.25 seconds per word or less (Adams, 1994).

Another possibility is the One Minute Reading Test (Transvaal Education Department, 1987). The child is asked to read across in rows, as quickly as possible, high-frequency one-syllable words for one minute. Norms are provided for English-speaking children of primary age and seem to increase from 2 seconds per word at age six to 0.5 seconds per word at age 10.

Speed of writing is quite another matter, though of considerable practical importance given that dyslexic pupils must sit exams and may have special arrangements, including extra time, requested by psychologists (Hedderly, 1992). Measures of writing have long been thought psychometrically unapproachable, given the difficulty in agreeing on such subjective dimensions as quality and style. However, since 1979 the Assessment of Performance Unit has made commendable progress in this field, in the course of wide-ranging assessment of language skills of school pupils (Department of Education and Science, 1988). Moreover the Wechsler Individual Achievement Tests (WIAT, 1992) include a fully developed psychometric instrument, Written Expression, normed from 8 to 17 years. The writer's ideas, sentence construction, vocabulary, grammar and narrative progression – but not spelling – are each assessed on a scale of 0–4 and the sum of such assessments compared with the performance of a normative group. The reliability of this measure is surprisingly high.[16]

As administration time for Written Expression is 15 minutes, the writer's words may be counted and divided by 15 to give a measure of productivity (words per minute). What is the value of such an estimation of writing speed? In a recent review, Alston (1994) found quite good agreement on 'norms' for both primary and secondary pupils but reliability of the various measures is unknown. Moreover productivity measures obtained from a limited writing exercise bore little relationship to actual examination performance among older secondary pupils.

Compromise is possible only if psychometric reliability is achieved. Two tests of writing, Writing Samples and Writing Fluency, from the Woodcock-Johnson battery have been mentioned. The requirement to complete in writing a set of printed incomplete sentences is comparable. In Kirklees, a set of 40 sentences has been given annually, and results collected, since 1972. For this set of incomplete sentences, 'test–retest reliability is high (0.93). In an untimed situation most people write between 190 and 220 words . . .' (Hedderly, 1995). The norms displayed in Table 4.1, for ages 9–18, including the 'average adult' (i.e. one not in higher education), are inferred from the slightly varying proportions of those falling under various portions of the normal curve.

Table 4.1: Means and standard deviations of writing speeds at 10 age-levels, including for those in and those not in full-time education at 17 and 18. Source: after Hedderly (1995).

Age:	Mn	SD
9	8	2.21
10	10	2.64
11	12	3.06
12	14	3.48
13	14.5	3.40
14	15	3.32
15	17	3.48
16	20	4.33
17Ed	23	4.92
17NotEd	19	4.75
18Ed	25	5.07
18NotEd	20	5.85

Linguistic aspects of reading and spelling

Conventional standardised tests of literacy have their critics.

> The inadequacy of such tests is now increasingly acknowledged. They are not rigorous enough to be fully accurate, and they are too coarsely calibrated to be fully informative. Merely to allocate a

precise 'reading age' to a child means very little *functionally*. To pitch a test at the level of sentence-comprehension is to neglect the needs of precisely those most needing help – children with more basic difficulties, such as problems of word recognition. And to take the traditional off-the-peg approach and offer a 'broad picture' diagnosis is to encourage rough-and-ready remediation rather than a tailor-made course of treatment. (Doctor and Stuart, 1995, p. 1, original emphasis)

In an understandable effort to promote a finer-grained assessment of reading, these strictures propound a number of errors. Global tests of reading should be doing rather more than assigning reading ages, a pseudo-metric to whose use researchers themselves continue to lend credence (Turner, 1996). Beyond this, to be acceptable, such tests must in fact be rigorous, accurate, well-calibrated and fully informative about the individual's relation to his or her peer group. Without such a *preliminary evaluation*, Doctor and Stuart's finer-grained assessment may be lavished on *the wrong child*.

Moreover, standardised literacy tests nowadays include among their number exceptionally powerful diagnostic instruments, including tests of word and non-word recognition. The latter, often designated tests of word attack, deserve first mention.

Non-word reading tests

Unfortunately for dyslexic people, tests of non-word reading represent the most stressful, because the most diagnostically acute, episode in any assessment. Fortunately, they do not take long. The requirement to *decode phonologically* an orthographically realistic but actually contrived letter-string highlights all the dyslexic's difficulties in the most conspicuous way. If ever there was a marker for dyslexia, this is it.[17] The methodology deserves to be an integral and routine part of every dyslexia assessment. There is an excellent recent review (Rack, Snowling and Olson, 1992), a provisional stimulus set (Turner, 1994d) and a diagnostic procedure based on single-case studies specialist teachers can follow (Turner, 1995b).[18]

The most familiar set of non-words is that of Snowling, first encountered in appendices to journal articles and reprinted selectively in Klein (1993). A psychometrically fully developed version, allowing the vital regression between word and non-word reading, most significant of all discrepancy methodologies, is forthcoming (Snowling, in press). In the USA there already exist, however, two fully developed and normed tests of *word attack*, both by Richard Woodcock: Test 31 in the Woodcock-Johnson battery, already mentioned; and two parallel tests (in forms G and H) in the Woodcock Reading Mastery Tests – Revised (WRMT-R) (Woodcock, 1987).[19]

The Woodcock-Johnson is, as we have seen, a most elaborate and ambitious psychoeducational assessment repertoire, with 35 tests of cognitive ability and achievement (core and supplementary). Test 31, Word Attack, is a fully developed non-word reading test that may be used, for comparison, alongside Test 22, Letter-Word Identification. Conormed, this pair of tests offers the firmest base for comparison short of actual regression. Given that the WJ-R is a resource principally for psychologists and that to use it thus selectively is like removing a penny whistle from an orchestra, the dimensions of these two tests are attractive. Letter-Word Identification has only 57 items, the first four of which require identification of rebuses[20] and the next nine naming of capital and lower-case letters. There are thus 44 word recognition items. Word Attack consists wholly in non-words, none shorter than three letters, and is content with 45 items.

For non-psychologists, concerned to seek evidence from the literacy domain alone, however, the WRMT-R is a uniquely powerful instrument. It will be discussed more fully later but it covers, through two parallel sets of six tests, attainment in decoding, word reading and comprehension, the latter at word and passage level. There are, in addition, three 'readiness' tests appropriate for beginners. Of interest here are the two parallel forms (G and H) of tests of Word Identification, each with 106 items, and Word Attack, each with 45 items, including some two-letter *vc* ones. As with the WJ-R, basal and ceiling rules apply, so reliability associated with additional length is not bought at the expense of efficiency of administration. Performances in reading words and non-words can be compared, though again without an actual regression apparatus. Dyslexics' comprehension is typically better than their word recognition, as their recognition of words is better than their decoding of non-words. This one battery, therefore, enables profile information relevant to a dyslexia diagnosis to be gathered without recourse to restricted 'cognitive' tests.[21] Moreover error analysis is facilitated through a systematic record form, so the fine-tuned teaching that Doctor and Stuart were referring to is carefully supported.

Further linguistic assessment

The issue of precisely targeted teaching, however, is not quite as Doctor and Stuart would have it. Although remedial instruction must be the least theorised area in education, there is widespread (if unconscious) acceptance of the rationale of *teaching to the defect*. That is, one should identify as precisely as possible what the pupil cannot do, and then devise teaching focused on this area. In adult neuropsychological work, this is called *rehabilitation* and the same rationale of devising therapy programmes keyed to details from the assessment applies.[22]

However, this is seldom what most experienced teachers of dyslexic children actually do. There is often a reluctance to accept that middle-range literacy skills are *secure*, as children may have learned later structures unsupported by logically earlier ones. As a result the skills are shaky and intermittent. So a teaching programme will start at an earlier point in the sequence and secure earlier structures as a firm basis for more complicated later learning.[23] This is the principle of *cumulativeness*. An approach that aims at fluency, automaticity or *mastery learning* in dyslexic children may be differentiated from the approach that by convention is applied to adults with acquired problems.

Nevertheless Doctor and Stuart are quite right to seek to disclose the *linguistic components* of a literacy-learning problem. Though not always necessary for accurate teaching, and liable to extend the time taken for the assessment session, the fine-grained analysis of a reading/spelling difficulty comes much closer to the theoretical understanding[24] we have of such problems. There are certainly *varieties* of dyslexia if there are not distinct *subtypes* and it will always be valuable to distinguish, among the host of skills which must contribute to literacy, those that are consistently weak or strong.[25]

Perhaps the most elaborate *psycholinguistic* assessment resource is PALPA-*Psycholinguistic Assessments Of Language Processing In Aphasia* (Kay, Lesser and Coltheart, 1992). Based on dual route theory and essentially a cognitive neuropsychological assessment tool for adults, the collection includes a whole volume of stimulus lists for use with reading and spelling. Such norms as there are derive from adult patients and their spouses; as emphasised at the beginning of this chapter, informal diagnostic procedures may be successfully used in an exploratory and descriptive way, but absence of norms proves a recurrent stumbling-block with this resource.

PALPA's five booklets offer a cornucopia of possibilities. They cover:

1.   the theoretical background
2.   sentence comprehension
3.   picture and word semantics
4.   auditory processing
5.   reading and spelling. Obviously the contributions to assessment of reading and spelling are of greatest interest, but as abilities in relation to written language are contingent upon wider language skills, it will be worth looking briefly at all areas sampled.

Auditory processing consists of seventeen tests:

•   four discrimination tasks involving minimal word and non-word pairs (van/fan) with both word and picture selection;
•   two lexical decision tasks (real versus made-up words, with real words of high and low frequency and imageability);
•   six tests involving verbal repetition of words, non-words and

sentences, controlling for syllable length, imageability, frequency, grammatical class and morphological endings;

- a digit span task involving both repetition (forwards only) and a decision on whether two strings match or not;
- two rhyme judgement tasks, one with pictures;
- and two segmentation tasks for initial and final sounds ('Find the letter that stands for the first (last) sound in the word.')

Although occasionally entailing aspects of literacy, this assortment of phonological tasks ranges admirably over memory, phonological manipulation, auditory discrimination and word and sentence grammar.

Sentence comprehension comprises six sets of diagnostic procedures:

- auditory sentence comprehension, a TROG-like exercise in picture selection,[26] in which 'The girl is taller than the dog' describes only one picture (others show a girl shorter than a dog and a man taller than a dog);
- written sentence comprehension, in which the sentences are printed;
- 'auditory comprehension of verbs and adjectives from the sentence set' for those who had difficulty with the previous task, in which correct definitions ('indicating . . . pointing something out') must be accepted and incorrect ones ('keen . . . not bothering') rejected;
- auditory comprehension of pictured locative relations ('bucket inside box . . . square inside circle');
- written comprehension of pictured locative relations;
- and pointing span for noun-verb sequences, in which successive items ('pin . . . boil . . . shed . . . mouse') must be pointed to.

Like most investigations involving meaning, this collection risks behaving much like an IQ test in practice, but may be useful in individuals with some specific semantic impairment.

Picture and word semantics offers eight tests:

- spoken and written picture-word matching (two tests), in which distractor items may be visually or semantically related (or not), in order to isolate any perceptual deficit;
- auditory and written synonym judgements (two tests), controlled for imageability;
- word semantic association, in which the word closest in meaning must be chosen from four alternatives;
- spoken word-written word matching ("Please tick the word I have just said"), which reverses the usual print to speech route of word recognition tests;

- and two tests of picture naming, in which responses are spoken, written, read or repeated, in which words are controlled for regularity and frequency.

Again a literacy component enters into some of these tasks, while dyslexic subjects would not often evince difficulty with the semantic aspect.

Finally, *reading and spelling* includes 29 tests:

- five involving letters, which must be matched or discriminated, named or sounded;
- one of spoken/written letter matching, where the target spoken letter must be selected from four written letters;
- four tests of visual lexical decision, pencil and paper tasks in which subjects must recognize real words among non-words, in which the dimensions varied include orthographic legality, imageability, frequency, morphology and regularity of spelling;
- nine involving reading aloud words, non-words and sentences which vary by letter and syllable length, imageability, grammatical class, morphological endings (regular, derived) and orthographical regularity;
- two tests involve printed homophones ('Do sore and saw have the same sound?', 'Define and read aloud chute, gait');
- and eight tests of spelling in which letter and syllable length, imageability, grammatical class, morphological endings and orthographical regularity are again varied, while a further task requires 'disambiguated homophones' to be spelled ("suite . . . furniture to sit on").

Clearly, some of these procedures are more relevant to developmental dyslexia than others. The collection as a whole, drawn from the MRC Psycholinguistic database, is yet scarcely normed: indicative norms show, as often as not, that most normal adults can do most of the tasks. Provision is therefore for adults with marked acquired disabilities who cannot do so. But numerous possibilities exist where a developmentally dyslexic individual shows complicating factors, especially linguistic factors, such as difficulty with spoken or written morphology. Homophone confusion seems to be in part a consequence of an insecure grasp of the nature (especially the spelling) of written words. The useful test of regular versus exception words may, however, show not which of the two 'routes' is impaired, so mush as the degree of severity (or recovery through tuition) that may be present in a dyslexic pupil.[27]

  There are sixty informal diagnostic procedures in total. In all cases, presenting forms enable the test to be administered, while marking forms enable an analysis of errors by type, so that the subject may, for instance, show a selective impairment with a particular class of phoneme or grammatical structure. There are also suggestions as to 'where to go next' along the trellis-work of hypotheses and references to main sources in the clinical and academic literature. Throughout, the paradigm is that of the controlled experiment which, as clarified at the outset, is the only rational basis for the assessment enquiry.

Worthy of mention also is the rather undervalued Boder Test of Reading-Spelling Patterns (Boder and Jarrico, 1982). This incorperates in its methodology the contrast between regular and exception words, as part of the effort to define words which the individual can read but cannot spell. This test classifies individuals into four diagnostic catergories; the dubious subtype of visual or *diseidetic* dyslexic people would today in most cases be described as *surface* dyslexic people, able to read regular but not exception words and prone to errors of regulation. The absence of norms in this test, and the archaic use of complex ratio quotients, are less of a drawback since the interest is in a ipsative evaluation of contrasts within the individual's own profile.

This completes our tour of the major areas of diagnostic sensitivity in the assessment of dyslexia, together with a selection of the better quality instruments that guide the search for cognitive anomaly.

However provisional or psychometrically undeveloped some of these probes may seem, they all play a directly explanatory role; that is, they account for the information-processing difficulties which are at the heart of the condition. As we turn next to the array of conventional tests of attainment, we may feel that, logically, this is slipping back a step, since these all serve once again to describe the dimentions of the presenting problem - lack of expected attainment. But as with the range of abilities, so an accurate job of description is worth doing well and serves, in a theory-free way, to resolve what ambiguities and disagreements there may be about the individual who is the starting point of the assessment process.

Notes

1 Paula Tallal, for instance, reports that children with early specific language delay often show later reading disability. Such children take longer to perform auditory processing tasks such as language segmentation; temporal processing rate correlates highly with *receptive* language ability. Such differential temporal processing rates may be heritable: see Tallal (1994). In Britain greater emphasis has been placed on *output phonology*.

2 That is, not esoteric, obscure, inaccessible or home-made. As with any book, the full reference should be given to allow tracking and inspection of the item through library services. However, exceptions are sometimes forced on the intrepid user who should be allowed the benefit of the doubt if necessary. Commercial interests forbid emulation of research papers in archived, refereed journals, which often print in full, as appendices, the stimulus items used in an investigation. But this standard is one to aspire to. There is, however, an uphill struggle to be waged to achieve in libraries, subject to considerations of security, the same terms of respect and consideration for tests as for books.

3   The assessing psychologist will often have observed that, after an administration of WISC-III lasting an hour-and-a-half, the most useful information relevant to the learning difficulty is obtained in the last five minutes of the assessment by a task involving non-word repetition or spoonerisms.

4   Otherwise differences arise from the *phonotactic* requirements of pronouncing their names; that is, from the differing vocalic and mouth movements involved.

5   Gathercole et al.'s CNRep (1994) has 'reasonable test–retest reliability' (Gathercole, 1995b, p. 162). Psychological Corporation's plans to publish this invaluable instrument are advanced.

6   Fourteen points.

7   This has even led to the inclusion of a naming, word-finding task in the Phonological Assessment Battery (PhAB).

8   Given the mean score (m) and standard deviation (s) of a given population, a child's observed score (x) can be expressed as a standard or z-score (whose mean is 0 and standard deviation 1) by applying the formula: $(x-m)/s$. This in turn can be expressed as a standard score with mean 100 and SD 15 by multiplying by 15 and adding 100. Any standard score can, in turn, be expressed as the *percentile*, which experience suggests is most comprehensible to the lay mind.

9   But the related claim, that phonic teaching cannot be used with children who as yet lack awareness of phonemes, is surely misconceived: phonic teaching directly creates such awareness. See Chew (1994).

10 The more contemporary *havergav*, which triples the number of syllables, is less comprehensible to bystanders and adults.

11 This has not stopped it from being given a widespread airing as the dyslexia-diagnostic methodology designed to render superfluous the testing of intelligence! One large English county currently forbids its educational psychology service to purchase tests of general ability, but pins its diagnostic credibility on the Phonological Assessment Battery. This combines healthy respect for the sophistication of IQ tests with cavalier disregard for the individual child's right to be assessed with properly developed instruments.

12 See note 12, Chapter 3 for details.

13 I am indebted to my colleague, Michael Biddulph, for his rediscovery of this test.

14 Dyslexics go to great lengths to avoid subtraction. One boy in the North East, faced with 54 –7, performed the operation as follows: 40 + (10 – 7) + 4, as he explained to his baffled teacher.

15 This dyslexic pupil's PS Index score rose from 75 to 91 across an interval of 22 months; his FD Index, on the other hand, remained much the same, as did a 26-point difference in his other scores (VC > PO).

16 0.81 is the average across the age-range for split-half; 0.77 for test–retest (WIAT, 1992, Manual, Tables 5.1 (p. 139) and 5.11 (p. 144).

17 '*Non-words* are by definition *unreadable*.' J. Hynds, personal communication, 29 September 1993 (original emphasis).

18 Votaries of *Meaning*, in service to their solemn and somewhat exclusive cause, often object on principle to tests of non-word decoding. In deference to all such scruples I suggest the following item set: *tod, dunt, gleg, tenty, gliff, raxing, gowls, wyte, gants, kittle, tirls, deave, pitmirk, slockens, rickle, trokings*. A test based on these 16 words, all of which were glossed as footnotes in the first edition of R.L. Stevenson's *Kidnapped* (1886), might properly be known as the Louis (pronounced *Lewis*) Test in honour of this enterprising and free-spirited author.

19 Purchase of the latter, unrestricted, test does not of course entail an investment in a large-scale assessment resource. Non-word reading tests exist, although not

known to me, in two further batteries, both published in 1985: Richardson and DiBenedetto's *Decoding Skills Test* and the *K-TEA* of Alan and Nadeen Kaufman.

20 A rebus, an important concept in the WJ-R and WRMT-R, is a graphical symbol to which a name or function is attached through preliminary teaching. In the early Letter–Word Identification items, the symbol is straightforwardly representative of an object, for instance a cat or a book.

21 Profile information obtained on the WRMT-R is discussed in relation to a single case study in Turner (1995b).

22 Professor Andrew Ellis summarises contributions to a recent symposium on such cognitive remedial work with adults in Ellis (1995). A notable book-length contribution is Riddoch and Humphreys (1994).

23 Perhaps the most elaborately developed teaching sequence is that found in the Dyslexia Institute Language Programme (Walker et al., 1993). A letter-order optimal for teaching has evolved thorough trial and error and been exemplified with every known instance of a particular pattern or rule, complete with detailed word lists and well-tried methodologies for teaching. The issue of such *sequences* is discussed further in Turner (1996).

24 Theory: making sense.

25 An inspiring account of one such detailed study, of a 10-year-old French girl, Olivia, with whom careful hypothesis-testing over many months using single-case experimental designs revealed, not a conventional phonological dyslexia, but a peripheral, visual attentional difficulty, is contained in Valdois et al. (1995).

26 The comparison is with the *Test For The Reception Of Grammar* (Bishop, 1982).

27 At one time I classified the 90 words of the British Ability Scales (Elliott, Murray and Pearson, 1979, 1983) Word Reading scale Form A into 61 regular and 29 irregular words, arranging them along the 202 point interval or *ability* scale. Given the probabilistic nature of this Rasch scale and the availability of published difficulty values for each word, the difference between the values obtained by a child reading his or her highest regular and highest exception word could be evaluated using the apparatus described in the test manual (Elliott, 1983, Chapter 2). One child, for instance, read the two kinds of words rather differently, such that the odds against such a difference would be about 30 to one (probability = 0.032).

Chapter 5
Charting Individual Attainment

Orientation

Conventional testing of attainment of basic skills is a task familiar to many teachers. Although this may be better done through tests that are 'restricted', that is, available for purchase and use only by those with a recognised postgraduate professional qualification in psychology, many serviceable tests are put to good use daily to measure progress in one or another attainment. We will therefore content ourselves with an overview of attainment testing and a tour of some, but of course not all, the technical issues that recur. Others, notably those pertaining to the communication of statistical data, are dealt with in a subsequent chapter.

The placement of a child in a literacy teaching programme, so-called *placement testing* or curriculum-based or curriculum-referenced testing, is properly the province of the specialist teacher. As with the fine-grained psycholinguistic assessment discussed previously, this belongs in a separate, later place in the assessment sequence. Before accepting the child (or adult) for teaching, the specialist teacher will want to know the dimensions of his or her dyslexia problem, the severity or otherwise of memory and other problems and the extent of retardation in reading and spelling. Aware of the ambiguous literature regarding subskills, the psychologist is often sceptical about this apparently uncritical acceptance of diagnostic features in which older elements of the dyslexia tradition live on.[1] But it seems to me that skilled teachers use terms in ways that correspond to their experience, and that teaching requires attention to many other features of learning difficulties than those that are clearly markers for dyslexia.

As placement in a specific programme will depend upon the dimensions of that programme,[2] this kind of auditing of skills is perhaps beyond the scope of the general purpose psychological assessment. Moreover, as discussed in the previous chapter, only the most secure and automatic skills will be taken as capable of supporting a high-powered literacy programme. Placement will depend, too, on the level below which there is an *absence of gaps*.

So it is necessary to consider the range of literacy tests from a *normative* point of view, comparing any individual's acquisition of skills in relation to that of *all* other comparable individuals, to see what short-falls or inconsistencies there may be. As spelling and writing are best taught concurrently with reading, according to best multisensory princi-ples, they will be considered together, in approximately the order in which they are learned, in what follows.

Letters and sounds

Most sophisticated modern reading and spelling tests include some early items (or subtests) that elicit knowledge of letters, written, named or sounded. For instance *WORD* (Rust, Golombok and Trickey, 1993) Basic Reading initially asks the child to 'point to the word with the same beginning sound' and 'ending sounds' as stimulus pictures. Spelling begins with four letters that must be written from the dictated letter names, followed by two 'letters that spell some sounds', after presenta-tion of the letter-sounds with exemplar words. In The Wide Range Achievement Test (WRAT-3) (Wilkinson, 1993), Reading allows 15 points for capital letter *naming*. Spelling similarly gives 15 points for *just two* letters of the individual's name, presumably first name, together with 13 letters which the child is asked to 'write or print'.

As we saw in the last chapter, the Woodcock–Johnson battery includes (Test 22) Letter–Word Identification, the first four of whose 57 items require identification of rebuses and the next nine naming of capi-tal and lower-case letters. However, the same author's fuller Woodcock Reading Mastery Tests – Revised (WRMT-R) (Woodcock, 1987) includes, in Form G, some excellent tests of early learning. Visual-Auditory Learn-ing is a series of rebuses that are attached to words, including function words (*and, the, is*), whose complexity increases, through seven test stories, until 10 word elements are visually represented by rebuses. Letter Identification presents 51 capital, lower case and *script* letters in a variety of typefaces. The Supplementary Letter Checklist is simpler, presenting *all* the letters of the alphabet in sans-serif upper and lower case, with alternative *q*s, followed by seven of the commonest digraphs, which must be sounded.

Though unnormed, the four Supplementary Diagnostic Tests that appear at the end of the Neale Test (Neale, 1989) have been found useful by many. Discrimination of Initial and Final Sounds requires the child to select, below a stimulus picture, the printed letter which corresponds to the initial and final sounds of a spoken word. Names and Sounds of the Alphabet proceeds without pictures but with sans-serif upper- and lower-case letters. Graded Spelling offers 60 words, but no letters. Auditory Discrimination and Blending asks, for each set of 16 words that differ in beginning, medial or ending sounds, whether they 'sound the same or different' (minimal pairs). Although this diagnostic battery is carefully prepared, little guidance is offered as to what to do with the results.

Word recognition and spelling

As rapid, context-free word recognition is the engine that drives more complex reading processes, as well as the principal locus of difficulty in dyslexia, a sophisticated word-reading test is an essential component in the assessment of reading attainment.

Two may be mentioned which occupy a foremost place in Britain: the Word Reading scale of the British Ability Scales (Elliott et al., 1979, 1983) and its extension in the Differential Ability Scales (Elliott, 1990). Both have 90 items but with a steeper gradient of difficulty the latter is normed on the full age-range of the test, 6:0 to 17:11 years.[3] Similarly BAS Spelling (added in 1992)[4] consists of 69 items though short forms, not the full set, would in most cases be given. DAS Spelling comprises 70 items,[5] though there are many substitutions at the harder end of the scale. A basal and ceiling administration method allows much greater precision of assessment than the BAS's choice of two alternative ranges of items. A third generation of this test, BAS-2, is currently in production and will retain and build upon the technical advances of the DAS.

Along with previously mentioned tests of Word Attack and Letter Identification, the Woodcock family offers two word-reading tests that are well-established internationally, though less well known in Britain. Test 22 in the Woodcock-Johnson Psycho-Educational Battery – Revised (WJ-R) (Woodcock and Johnson, 1989, 1990) is Letter–Word Identification which, as mentioned in Chapter 4, comprises 44 word recognition items. Also mentioned, the Woodcock Reading Mastery Tests – Revised (WRMT-R) (Woodcock, 1987) offers two parallel forms (G and H) of tests of Word Identification, each with 106 items. The length of the latter, the most considerable test of its kind, means that reliability is gained whilst, because of basal and ceiling rules, efficiency is not lost. Essentially a valuable instrument because of its versatility, the WRMT-R needs to be noted here as, amongst other things, an excellent single-word test for all ages, adults as well as children.

Widely used because of its association with WISC-III is *WORD* (Rust, Golombok and Trickey, 1993). Basic Reading and Spelling are two tests of the conventional kind, the former with 55 items, the latter with 50. Normed from 6;0 to 16;11, the data tables incorporate information from a UK validation sample of 824 pupils. *WORD* norms are often the best way of demonstrating poor progress in younger children relative to British expectations; US norms tend to err on the side of optimism below 8 years.[6]

Again, basal and ceiling rules allow appropriate concessions to economy.

Stretching brevity to its technical limit, the third generation of the Wide Range Achievement Test (WRAT-3) (Wilkinson, 1993) assesses individuals aged from 5:0 to 74:11 with a mere 42 words for reading and 40 for spelling. However, alternative *tan* and *blue* forms allow progress retesting; by combining the two (*red* form) maximum reliability is achieved.[7] Because Rasch scaling is again used, an *absolute* scale is provided, along with the usual forms of standard score, and this probably represents the most accurate scale along which to measure progress. But the WRAT has always been designed and used as a *screening* device and should not be strained to purposes beyond its capacity.

Graded word tests, like old soldiers, never die. Indeed some (Burt) appear in new editions or achieve posthumous importance in research. Others (Schonell) slip out of copyright and appear in popular editions of diagnostic tests (Aston Index: Thomson and Newton, 1982). But such veterans appear to work only for 'reading ages' 6–8 and serious measurement purposes are beyond them. Not that there is anything wrong with the words: words rise and fall in the stock exchange of usage (Shearer and Apps, 1975) but most would do duty in a well-constructed modern test. It is just that the scale of normative reference, if it ever existed, has degenerated beyond recovery. Spelling ages obtained on the Schonell and Vernon tests come adrift by a year at age 11 and 2.5 years at nearly 16 (Turner, 1991). Teacher-usable alternative tests of word recognition and spelling are discussed in a later chapter.

Passage reading

Beyond word recognition, the child must match written to spoken language in terms of sentence structure and must make some sense of what is read as soon as sense may be made. The Salford sentence-reading tests (Bookbinder, 1976), though they lack a questioning, comprehension-checking component, remain popular, presumably because of speed of administration. 'Reading ages', alas, are the sole outcome.

Worth mentioning here are the silent, pencil-and-paper tests of sentence completion. Group tests of reading have technical profiles only a little less excellent than individual ones and individual administration of a group test achieves higher reliability. Because they may be given with a minimum of supervision before or after the main assessment interview, they are often a useful supplementary check on *vocabulary and comprehension* aspects of the child's reading. Prominent among tests in this class is the Suffolk (Hagley, 1987), which is timed to 20 minutes. A test timed to 9 minutes for its sentence-completion items (earlier items require printed words to be selected to match simple pictures) is the neglected reading component of a test better known for its spelling: SPAR (Young, 1976).

It is no longer true that such group tests, in the main multiple-choice *cloze*,[8] necessarily lack item variety and concentrate on a limited, unnatural set of reading activities, little met with outside the testing situation. They are *global* tests of reading, in that they require the child to *decode* each sentence, *comprehend* propositional content and, because the test is timed, perform a number of such tasks with *fluency*. But modern variants utilise passage structure and the cloze exercise often turns on local syntactic constraints. This immediately highlights more complex reading skills, including *anaphor*, the referring back in a passage to what was stated earlier, and specifically *grammatical* meanings. The Macmillan Group Reading Test 9–14 (Macmillan Test Unit, 1990) includes both sentence-completion and context-comprehension tests, with two parallel forms of each. These are interesting to the child and can easily be completed in solitude.

The main contributions, however, are the passage-reading tests. Three will be considered. The best known and most widely used has for many years been the Neale Analysis of Reading Ability, first in its 1958 edition, then in a modernisation by NFER (Neale, 1989). The economy of the older version was missed by practitioners as a significant loss to the onslaught of complexity in the modern world. In some regions an orchestrated return to use of the older test has been supported by some thin but persistent controversy regarding the newer norms: these are held to be *harder* for younger children in the 1989 version. However, in 1985, before the new edition, the 'old' Neale was given a local standardisation in the London Borough of Croydon as a basis for annual testing of reading attainment in the Year 2 age-group.

Table 5.1 shows the reading advantage young children have today after 30 years of rising living standards including ever-earlier admission to formal education.

It is both a strength and a weakness of the Revised Neale that it attempts to measure all aspects of reading through a single performance by the child. Essentially a primary test (one can obtain a percentile rank of 97 in Accuracy on Form 1 at 11;11), the pupil is presented with a well-illustrated book with up to six connected passages to read, all notable for an avoidance of unhappy endings. There are two parallel forms, to permit retesting.[9] The test offers three dimensions of reading assessment: *accuracy* (mistakes are penalised in reading aloud), *comprehension* (the child must answer questions about the passage just read, in which words not read within 5–6 seconds or read incorrectly have been supplied) and *rate* (essentially number of words read per minute on all passages read except the last, on which the child's errors exceed a given ceiling).

Difficulties in *comprehension* are nowadays taken very seriously. Estimates of numbers of children who do not fully understand what they read, based largely on the memory for accumulation of literal detail required in

Table 5.1: Comparison of scores on the 1958 Neale Analysis of Reading Ability between Year 2 children in the London Borough of Croydon in 1985 and comparable children in the original standardisation. Source: London Borough of Croydon.

Neale Analysis of Reading Ability: 1985 Croydon standardisation		
Points of raw score required to obtain an age-appropriate score (100; or RA = CA)		
	Accuracy	Comprehension
Neale 1958		
6 years 6 months	4	2
7 years 0 months	12–13	5–6
7 years 6 months	21	9
Croydon 1985		
6 years 6 months	22	8
7 years 0 months	25	10
7 years 6 months	29	11–12
Reading age gain (months) in 1985 over 1958 norms:		
6 years 6 months	13	10
7 years 0 months	9	10
7 years 6 months	7	10

the Neale test, vary in the range 10–15% (Oakhill and Yuill, 1991; Stothard, 1994). The term *non-specific reading difficulty* has been introduced by Aaron and Joshi (1992) to cover such eventualities and to differentiate them from *dyslexia*. The gains to be made in measured comprehension ability by the teaching, in particular, of *inference* skills and comprehension monitoring, are impressive (Oakhill and Yuill, 1991).[10]

Rate or fluency is to a large extent, as we have seen, a function of decoding ability, in that time taken to puzzle out less familiar words lowers the average reading speed. We have suggested that standard stimulus sets – word lists – offer a more reliable and independent measure, if it is indeed desired to measure reading speed as a separate dimension.[11]

Accuracy is the heart of the matter for most dyslexia assessments. The Neale test performs well here but by the same token high intercorrelations with tests of single-word reading, witnesses to validity, suggest that this, too, may just as well be disaggregated and measured directly by tests of word and non-word reading. However, against this view there is persistent evidence that connected meaningful prose reading is preferable, and not just from an ideological, Whole Language standpoint. Progress in reading may actually be measured far more effectively by the Neale test (Hatcher, Hulme and Ellis, 1994; Turner, 1995a).

As a general-purpose, *global* test of naturalistic reading ability, then, the Revised Neale continues to deserve its primacy of place in the hearts and testing schedules of British practitioners. But for the assessment specialist, who may want to concentrate to a significant extent on reading processes in relation to possible *dyslexia*, the question remains whether the 15–30 minutes spent on the Neale is actually justified, given that each aspect of interest may be better measured separately.

What are the possible consequences of addressing separately these three aspects of reading? We have seen that word and non-word reading, and especially any contrast between them, provides one crux of the dyslexia assessment. The Neale could never hope to displace this focus on word-level processes. We have also seen that fluency can, with distinct advantage, be evaluated using a rather different methodology. What of comprehension?

One saving that should probably *not* be expected is in time. There seems to be a law that cognitive complexity inevitably entails extended processing time. Rapid tests of reading comprehension have thus far eluded the ingenuity of psychometricians. But time is only one of the dimensions of awkwardness contained in what is, after all, a most slippery, 'higher' dimension of ability. For a long time comprehension processes, like creativity in writing, were thought not to be measurable. Scoring criteria for comprehension items on passage-reading tests are notorious: ' . . . *make sure that the sense is identical with that of the answers supplied in the Answer Key on p. 62 of this Manual . . .*', say the instructions (Neale Manual, p. 14, original emphasis). But on the designated pages we find that *any similar response* is authorised five times, *etc.* occurs six times, *explanation required* once and once even *any sensible answer*. In these cases what may 'identical sense' mean? Acceptable responses for one item are 'Frightened/Curious/Anxious/Scared/Worried/Upset'. It may be thought that these are three different things, but then the question that has been asked is: 'How do you think Kim felt?' Comprehension assessment, then, is a very open-ended business.

Some radical alternatives will be considered in a moment, but first let us look at two other passage tests, both from the Macmillan stable, now taken over by NFER-Nelson. The pair are siblings: the New Macmillan Reading Analysis (NMRA)[12] appeared in 1985 and its junior, the Macmillan Individual Reading Analysis (MIRA), in 1990. The earlier New Macmillan Reading Analysis (Vincent and de la Mare, 1985) became popular before the Revised Neale had appeared and serves many of the requirements of a prose reading test. Passages increase in length and complexity and comprehension questions must be answered correctly. (There is no *rate* or fluency measure.) By some misfortune in the construction process, results allow only wide-band reading ages to be reported which, because of their width, convey rather little. The calculation of mid-points is the commonest solution. An embedded Rasch scale, little used, allows scoring to be based on the reading of certain words in each passage.

But it is the junior sibling, the Macmillan Individual Reading Analysis (Vincent and de la Mare, 1990) which is of especial interest. One would not recommend the administration of either the Revised Neale or the NMRA to younger or less able readers, because the result can so easily be a massacre. Steps in the administration occur only with 'levels' (discrete passages) and the floundering reader must soldier on until the requisite number of errors, on the Neale typically 16, allows the level to be discontinued and the test scored. In its hardest passage the MIRA, in common with its elder sibling, offers three parallel forms with five passages of ascending difficulty in each, but the point from which the difficulty ascends is truly impressive: the earliest passages each have 13 words, none longer than five letters. Large, intriguing illustrations dominate the pages but thankfully the comprehension questions do not seek to elicit interpretation of pictures. They twice, however, ask 'How do you think the girl [or *she*] felt' and 'Any appropriate/relevant response' is authorised no fewer than six times, leaving the test administrator afloat on a swell of initiative. Unfortunately only reading ages are reported but, in an independent development, standard scores have been supplied for Form Z (Sawyer and Potter, 1994).

This is a niche test, a genuine contribution to the assessment of younger or less able readers. It enables them to approach connected passages, and make interpretations of meaning, early on in the process of learning to read.

Dedicated comprehension assessment

It has long been noticed that a distinctive *profile* may be obtained on the Neale and comparable tests with dyslexic people. These individuals typically do poorly on any measure of decoding, such as *accuracy*, and comparably poorly (the two measures are not independent) on *rate*, but obtain *comprehension* scores that are mysteriously higher. Quite how dyslexic people surmise correct interpretations of passages of which they have but a patchy knowledge is not known, unless it is a question of piecing out missing information by compensatory use of unimpaired verbal intelligence. At any rate, comprehension ability is usually at a higher level.

This lends weight to the cause of separate investigation of decoding and comprehension processes in reading. If they were not contingent, that is, if the measures were as independent as possible, the gap might be even wider. In Chapter 4, it will be remembered, dyslexic people's comprehension was described as typically better than their word recognition, just as their recognition of words is better than their decoding of non-words.

Another of the *WORD* trio of literacy tests, co-normed in Britain in the WISC-III validation exercise, is Reading Comprehension. It offers 38 short passages, which may be read either silently or aloud and about which short, fairly convergent questions must be answered. Only the first eight items are pictured and employ single sentences. Thereafter several short sentences serve to build up meaning in the passages. Basal and ceiling rules aid economy. Scoring criteria, though a welcome advance in precision, are not always intuitive and do not provide for all dilemmas. But given that for the first time an alternative to the Neale comprehension measure is being adopted, Reading Comprehension's greater variety of item content is very much to be welcomed, as a result of which the pupil has to predict, infer, understand cause and effect or combine new with old knowledge to reach a synthesis. Whilst accuracy and vocabulary remain important, these are the higher functions that serve the purposes of the mature reader.

It will have been noticed that the Woodcock Reading Mastery Tests – Revised (WRMT-R) make an appearance under every heading. This is because they offer unparalleled versatility in the assessment of reading. Earlier versions of the Woodcock reading tests were criticised because comprehension was ill served, it was felt, by a series of cloze items of the kind that, in Britain, is familiar from many global tests of group reading. In response to criticism, the revised edition of the WRMT includes a variety of tests of comprehension at the *word level*, together with a test of *passage comprehension*. The word comprehension tests include Antonyms (each word must be read and another, opposite in meaning, supplied); Synonyms (single words must be read and 'another word that means the same thing' as each supplied); and Analogies (one word-pair must be read and an analogous word found to complete a second pair, as in *snow–white, coal—*). All these item formats are familiar from innumerable verbal reasoning tests. In this case reasoning processes are developed from single-word reading to give a composite measure of 'word comprehension'.

Better still, Passage Comprehension remedies many of the defects mentioned in reading comprehension tests so far. This test retains the cloze format and so circumvents the subjectivity of scoring decisions, with its associated unreliability, whilst escaping early from the picture and single-sentence formula. In a total of 68 items, there are 11 in the first half of the test that include more than one sentence and 13 that do not have a picture. None of the items in the second half of the test is pictured and all are multi-sentence (with one exception, a single sentence 33 words long). Complex passages are offered, non-fictional but of general interest, with scoring procedures convergent enough for acceptable and unacceptable responses to be specified in short lists that cover every eventuality.

The utility of this *combination* of reading tests can hardly be overstated. I have described elsewhere the superior profiling information that, even more clearly than on the Neale, allows the *three levels* of decoding, word recognition and comprehension ability to separate in a way highly diagnostic of dyslexia (Turner, 1995b). Moreover this instrument is not being kept assiduously out of the hands of teachers; parallel forms offer retesting facilities and all-age norms at last fill the serious gap where adult assessments are concerned.[13]

Analogous tests within the slightly more recent Woodcock–Johnson Psycho-Educational Test Battery – Revised (WJ-R) are, however, restricted to psychologist users. All three tests of interest exist in streamlined versions, one with an altered name: Letter–Word Identification (so-called because earlier items in this all-age test require first rebuses, then single letters to be named) appears as Test 22, Word Attack as Test 31 and Passage Comprehension as Test 23. For psychologists this trio represents the most sophisticated repertoire of reading assessments available. Though no regression apparatus internal to the reading module is supplied, statistically significant discrepancies among the three may be evaluated as shown in Table 5.2.

Table 5.2: Differences in points of standard score required at seven age-levels for statistical significance at $P = 0.15$, $P = 0.10$ and $P = 0.05$ levels. SEMs are derived from split-half reliabilities given in Woodcock and Mather (1989b, 1990b); formula for SEdiff is given in Friedenburg (1995). LWId = Letter–Word Identification; WAt = Word Attack; PCo = Passage Comprehension.

	LWId v WAt			LWId v PCo			WAt v PCo		
Age	15%	10%	5%	15%	10%	5%	15%	10%	5%
6	6.2	7.1	8.4	6.4	7.3	8.7	6.8	7.7	9.2
9	8.3	9.4	11.2	9.1	10.4	12.4	9.7	11.1	13.2
13	10.7	12.2	14.5	12.6	14.4	17.2	12.7	14.5	17.3
18	9.4	10.7	12.7	10.1	11.5	13.8	9.5	10.9	13.0
30–39	10.2	11.7	13.9	9.9	11.4	13.5	10.7	12.3	14.6
50–59	8.3	9.5	11.3	7.8	8.9	10.6	9.2	10.5	12.5
70–79	6.9	7.9	9.4	5.5	6.3	7.6	7.5	8.6	10.2
Median	8.9	10.1	12.1	9.2	10.5	12.5	9.3	10.6	12.6

These values permit an estimate of how likely any observed difference between two standard scores is to be a real one; there is no way of discovering, alas, what the actual *incidence* may be of such real differences and thus their abnormality. Woodcock–Johnson allows such an evaluation of the next order *cluster scores*. That between Basic Reading Skills (Letter–Word Identification and Word Attack) and Broad Reading (Letter–Word Identification and Passage Comprehension) is likely to be of interest but as the word-recognition test is common to both clusters, this blunt instrument is not quite what is needed.

Attainment in written number skills

Attainment in writing has been surveyed briefly under diagnostic tests of written language, with quality as well as productivity now a reasonably secure psychometric objective. There remains one further 'basic skill' which, though often overlooked and as much a Cinderella to spelling as spelling is to reading, is of enormous consequence to children's future: number.

Here let me at once say that number *concept* and *mental* arithmetic, in so far as these can be independent of bonds and table-learning, are *not* the main problem in dyslexia. The limited 'working memory' resources that research implicates in the common forms of learning disability restrict the capacity to hold in memory at one time all the elements of a task which is either highly sequenced or requires many simultaneous operations. As a result the basic skills of reading, writing and *arithmetic*, all of which make a considerable demand on working memory, are not easily acquired or are not well consolidated in automatic form. The results are most obvious in the difficulty otherwise intelligent pupils have with reading, spelling or memorisation of tables. We have already seen the devious heuristics invented by dyslexic people in order to avoid subtraction. In short it is *written calculation skills* or arithmetic that pose the familiar processing problems in relation to memory-intensive symbolic routines.

The common belief that written calculation skills are a problem only for some pupils, and that dyslexic people exist for whom number skills are *not* a problem, is not borne out by my own data, analysed in a subsequent chapter. On average, written number skills are *worse* in my clinical sample than are reading and spelling skills.

Once again, the comprehension element adds considerably to overall assessment times. The discretion to omit it enables written number skills to be measured rapidly and directly. In Britain the British Ability Scales Basic Number Skills Tests C, D or E are almost universally preferred. But again, the Differential Ability Scales revision has improved, in normative range (60 – 17;11) and in item diversity, on its prototype and older, more able pupils can estimate circumferences and rates of interest and yield accurate estimates of their calculation skills in short order.

WRAT-3 (Wilkinson, 1993) also improves upon WRAT-R Arithmetic in that 15 minutes, rather than 10, are now sacrificed to reliability. This useful, all-age test now boasts greater item diversity and depth of content. Compound interest and algebraic factors lie in wait for those, few of them dyslexic, whose perseverance survives the four rules.

This completes our survey of the main areas of attainment testing in relation to what seem to be the key issues for dyslexia assessment. Informal and semi-diagnostic procedures for categorising spelling errors or analysing 'miscues' in reading must remain unvisited. For the forseeable future these will not permit discussion in terms of validity and reliability. Exotic psychometric resources exist for the appraisal of achievement in science, social studies and humanities[14] that cast even the Richmond Tests' map-reading skills into the shade,[15] but such an excursion into the higher reaches of normality would constitute a frivolous detour.

Notes

1 Handedness, directionality, laterality, visual memory, fine motor control and so on.

2 This is true, too, of well-established published programmes: the secondary Distar literacy programmes *Corrective Reading* (Engelmann, Carnine and Johnson, 1988) and *Corrective Spelling Through Morphographs* (Dixon and Engelmann, 1979), both include simple placement tests to determine the point at which to begin teaching the child.

3 '. . . the Word Reading test is less accurate for high-achieving examinees' (Elliott, 1990, p. 303n).

4 After this passage of time comparable norms were not obtainable, so the BAS's Rasch resources were utilised for item scaling. A 'calibration sample' of 176 children in Years 3 and 5 was given both spelling and word-reading items and, following satisfactory goodness of fit of both tests to the Rasch model and to each other, 'alignment constants' were calculated. Ultimately 140 pupils took 69 items.

5 After an initial three points awarded for spelling first and last names.

6 See Notes 26–28 to Chapter 3 and the paragraphs to which they refer.

7 Median coefficient alphas are: reading *blue* 0.91; reading *tan* 0.91; reading combined 0.95; spelling *blue* 0.91; spelling *tan* 0.89; spelling combined 0.95. Stability coefficients are similar.

8 A jargon word used solely in educational testing, apparently derived from *closure*.

9 A female advantage has been claimed on Form 2, as well as lower difficulty for passage 6 than 5 (Stothard and Hulme, 1991); but this was not found in a subsequent study by Gregory and Gregory (1994), who report scores, for 63 children aged 5–8 and for a clinical sample of 30 children of all ages and abilities, some *nine months* lower on the Neale than BAS Word Reading. A stout defence of the test is provided in Halliwell and Feltham (1995).

10 A capacious review of comprehension processes in reading, together with a compendium of possible teaching approaches, all within a research-based framework, may be found in Carnine, Silbert and Kaneenui (1990, Part 3, pp. 273–409).

11 Average Neale intercorrelations for Rate are 0.62 with Comprehension and 0.71 with Accuracy (Manual, p. 57). A female advantage in Rate persists through all age-groups (ibid, p. 58). Test–retest reliability for Rate on Form 1 averages 0.69 across the age-group 6–10 years (ibid, p. 50). Data for internal reliability and standard error of measurement for Rate are omitted in the relevant Tables 13 and 14 (ibid, pp. 55–6).

12 I adhere to their older names, under which they are familiarly known.

13 Because of its accessibility to teachers, this test is discussed again in Chapter 9.

14 Tests 28, 29 and 30 in the Woodcock-Johnson Psycho-Educational Battery – Revised (Woodcock and Johnson, 1989, 1990).

15 Richmond Tests Of Basic Skills (RTBS), 2nd edn (Hieronymus, Lindquist and France, 1988).

Chapter 6
Structures for Reporting

Taking stock

We have now considered the three major phases of the individual assessment investigation: the general cognitive, the diagnostic and the attainment. In aggregate and in combination these measures afford all the estimations of different abilities, together with the distinctive contrasts among them, that are needed for a conclusive statement about the individual's dyslexia or other specific learning difficulty.

Here we run into a dilemma: though willingly enough discussed in public, all these considerations have so far been matters of technique and craft for the consulting psychologist. What may be communicated – and *how* – to an eager and well-motivated, but essentially *lay*, public?

In the distant future, perhaps, the consulting psychologist will be such a well-accepted, busy and authoritative member of the community that an illegible opinion scribbled on a half sheet of notepaper will suffice to *certify* someone as dyslexic. The kaleidoscope of behavioural tests will have given way to infallible indicators of unique markers for dyslexia of such sophistication that pleasant and secure occupation for psychologists is an assured necessity.[1]

In a sense this medical or general practitioner model is quite relevant to the diverse consulting practices of many psychologists. The technology involved is quite as arcane as that of barium meal and the cardiograph, the *dimensionality* of dyslexia is well-enough accepted at least to distinguish it from pregnancy,[2] and the treatment – specialist teaching – is specific. Already the expert status of practitioners is assured, or the clients desperate, enough that the migration of families with troubled children towards the latest syndrome or miracle remedy borders on the Gadarene. The absence of a critical or sceptical attitude among members of the consuming public makes the responsibility of the serious practitioner, who must advise tactfully on many of the fads that come and go, all the greater.

For the present the situation remains quite different. For one thing, the scientific procedures involved in dyslexia assessment remain new enough for established fellow professionals to react to their use still with unreasonable hostility, whilst the paying public is happy to accept experts at their own word. (Between these two dispositions a book such as this one seeks to pass.) Moreover, the climate of communication between all parties to the dyslexia predicament is highly democratic, with full explanations being sought and given. The enthusiasm of specialist teachers tends not to be daunted by the technical complexities of, say, neurology; whilst the commitment of parents to their children gives an exceptionally good boost to their understanding of the assessment process. The credulity of either will not be helped by any underestimate of their capacity for informed understanding.

Nevertheless the technicalities discussed in the foregoing chapters remain essentially beyond the reach of those who do not have the specialised background. The educational gap between specialist and client, however committed both parties are to the dialogue, can only grow wider, as newer methods and more sophisticated techniques become available. So perhaps the time has come for a parting of the ways. The assessing psychologist, as always, will want to deploy the most useful and informative procedures on the client's behalf, but the details of such procedures will largely remain 'under the bonnet' as far as the client is concerned.

Popular conceptions of dyslexia assessment can be retarding for the professional, in any case.[3] Public opinion in this area, as in others, tends to conservatism and simplicity. The reverse pitfall, the tendency of professionals to use secretive jargon and hierophantic rituals to distance and render captive the laity dependent on their services, needs equally to be restrained, for instance by competition.

The assessment crisis

A first responsibility for the consulting psychologist is to realise fully the contours of the family drama involved in the child coming for assessment. Often years of suffering have gradually built up a sense of misery that comes to affect the entire family, amid disparagement of the problem by those who should know better. Literacy failure is isolating. The advice of friends and neighbours somehow cannot be sought, as it can with other problems, because common sense loses heart where professional views are divided. The problem is still not really socially acceptable. Stigma attaches to it, and perhaps only someone similarly affected can truly understand.

So the problem is little discussed, the shame and misery surrounding it have grown and often the consultation is arranged as a result of a *straw* appearing – a magazine article, a phone number passed on by a chance acquaintance – to be *clutched at*. In this situation the pronouncements of the psychologist acquire an oracular status. Most individuals never receive a psychological assessment; most of those who do never receive a second one. It may therefore be a once-in-a-lifetime experience for those concerned. Counselling aspects of the assessment interview are quite as important as any other. The family must be handled with *sympathy*. Cheerfulness should not overbalance into levity. The tendency of all parents to blame themselves should not be heightened, for instance by the suggestion that there has been undue delay in seeking the assessment. They should be *listened to* and their concerns addressed in the assessment process. Particular questions can be answered by slight alterations of emphasis.[4] The child him- or herself has frequently needed persuasion, cajolery and several sorts of bribe even to *attend* the session. Making friends with the anxious child and securing trustful co-operation is a first ethical imperative.

The *crisis*-like nature of the *assessment*, therefore, has two balancing implications. On the one hand, the personal explanation and face-to-face debriefing assume a great importance. Many families of dyslexic individuals are not themselves overly literate and the personal interview matters more to them than a long report in the post.[5] On the other hand, emotional excitement and the cathartic aspects of the interview can lead to amnesia afterwards, in which case the report in the post will be studied very carefully. Other family members, sometimes fathers for instance, have not been able to attend the interview and must rely on reading the report. In any case reviewing matters in the aftermath of the interview may reveal aspects whose importance was lost sight of at the time.

These twofold implications apply to all communications, and equally to written and verbal communication. The face-to-face interview should cover all the ground that is important to the family, without omitting any technical matter the psychologist knows to be of strategic importance for the findings or ensuing actions to be based on them. The written report, as the sole trace for posterity[6] of the assessment encounter, should contain both details of outstanding interest at the time *and* a considered, longer-term statement about the child's development.

Multiple audiences

It is a matter of common observation that the psychological report passes through many hands and is much copied. Not that, in the first instance, the report is not a confidential document conveying vital information about the *family member who is its subject*.[7] If the family have commissioned and paid for the assessment, then the report is their private property, to be disclosed only at their discretion.

Nevertheless the report very often *is* disclosed; indeed, the parents sometimes ask specifically that suggestions helpful to this or that teacher be included, so that the report can be copied usefully to the child's school. Given that specialist teaching remains the most efficacious, and

perhaps only, appropriate intervention in dyslexia, any recommendations the psychologist makes have both interest and importance.

Beyond the child's class teacher or specialist tutor, multiple further
audiences open up. The headteacher of the child's school is likely, as a
courtesy at least, to receive a copy of the assessment report on the child
for whom he or she is responsible. This person performs administrative
duties on behalf of a great many children, including now the *staged*
assessment within school of special educational needs under the Code
of Practice.[8] Other professionals may be asked about the findings. The
child may become subject to formal assessment procedures. In this case,
the local education authority's statementing officer should receive a
copy, as should the authority's educational psychology service. In the
event of an appeal, the original report, often the single close and coherent account of the child as a recognisable individual, is circulated far and
wide. Lawyers may become involved and the psychologist's pronouncements, formed in the relative intimacy of the consultation with the
parent, are now angled for or against a particular objective in litigation.

By far the largest dilemma present even in the first, confidential context
of the family alone, but aggravated each time a wider audience is broached,
is the comprehensibility of technical detail. If for the present we cannot
expect (and would not wish) an unsubstantiated opinion to carry authority, then we are left with the need to marshal *evidence*, *argument* and
conclusions. This is familiar scientific terrain and the consulting psychologist will expect to be judged, ultimately, by the court of his or her peers.
Other psychologists are likely to read the report in due course, who are of
many different persuasions[9] and standpoints in relation to the apparently
simple question of the best educational interest of the child. So at one and
the same time a sophisticated and a lay audience must be satisfied.

This is what is meant by a parting of the ways. A single report must
anticipate and satisfy the many unfolding eventualities of a future case
history. The Dyslexia Institute has now moved to address the problem of
multiple audiences by means of a *tripartite report*. Essential findings
and recommendations are condensed into headed sections in a single-
page summary with which no lay person should have any difficulty. The
background, highlights and conclusions are discussed at greater length,
again in uncomplicated English, in a second section. Full technical
detail, presenting the testing procedures used, with statistical and
research background and publication sources, is included in the third
section, a technical appendix.

Communicating measurement to the lay person

The problems of communicating the results of sophisticated statistical
procedures, such as regression, to the lay person may be easier than
bypassing the common-sense account which is what the person thinks

he or she already knows. Thus 'How far is he behind?' or 'Will her IQ go up if she overcomes her problems?' or 'What should a student's reading age be?' are questions that, although of self-evident importance to a concerned parent, contain embedded misunderstandings. Nevertheless, between the lay, common-sense view of educational measurement and the specialist one, a direct, serviceable bridge can usually be built and there are few questions that are not worth answering or that cannot be answered.[10]

A series of comprehension difficulties for the lay person lurks in the question of uncertainty. Modern measurement instruments *are* of immense technical sophistication. Indeed, a great number of those who use them hardly appreciate how powerful they are. Yet there is a penumbra of doubt and uncertainty – or there should be – associated with every observation. Standard error is not a concept on which consultation time is wisely spent. Yet a reporting band of error is essential, at least with IQ, the most general statement of a person's abilities and the most reliable. From a network of fastidiously obtained and carefully evaluated test results, only broad and unambiguous contours can be interpreted with general confidence. This habit of care, systematic checking of effects and frequent employment of contrary arguments is alien to even the competent adult lacking a specifically *scientific* education.[11]

One way of communicating complex quantitative information with immediacy, yet without sacrificing either complexity or detail, is through the use of graphs. Many psychologists, in interviews with parents or teachers, make use of the simple graph outlines that appear on WISC and other record forms. Peaks and valleys are apparent; relationship to average levels for the age-group is obvious; internal contrasts, such as that between reading accuracy and comprehension, start to make immediate visual sense. Much parent and teacher feedback confirms that this holistic method of conveying *profile information* is appreciated. Because accurate measurement detail is preserved, a visual means of communicating complex information is satisfying to the professional also.

It is comparatively rare that parents or others have ideas about a child that are both fixed and unrealistic. On the whole the more accurate and realistic the profile of the child achieved by these objective, quantitative methods, the more likely the parent is to accept it as truthful. During the debriefing the psychologist may ask: 'Is this familiar? Is this the child you know? Is this right?' However, if a sophisticated assessment merely confirms, albeit with external authority and objectivity, what is already known, it has fulfilled only a modest purpose. Luckily, among the familiar truths there is usually some surprise, some unexpected finding, sufficient to alter the emphasis of tuition or the goals for family expectations and encouragement.

The choice of metric

The problem of *metric* remains to be solved, before any medium for expressing results is chosen. I have criticised previously[12] the habit prevalent even within the research community of describing attainment in terms of *age equivalents* – reading and spelling ages, for instance. This is much the commonest lay means for expressing the growth or retardation of achievement. Caution is in order in the face of such a firmly rooted usage. Two aspects of the age equivalent concept need to be understood and accepted, as it is quite certain that it will not fade away. First there is its intuitive immediacy.[13] Conceptions of differing ability and varying expectation levels play no part in the universal understanding that if an 8-year-old has a reading age of 6½, he is 18 months behind where he should be.[14]

The less obvious element of truth in the application of age equivalents to children's progress ensures its persistence among teachers. This is the element of *curriculum referencing*. In addition to the apparent normative reference of what other children, younger, older or the same age, might be expected to be doing, there is the fixed reference to the instructional sequence concerned. *All* readers have to progress through a reading age of 8 to a reading age of 10 – at whatever age. Primary teachers, moreover, may have a particularly rich idea of what is actually entailed in reading progression at these ages. To see the same reference system being used with comparable enthusiasm, one has only to look across the Atlantic, where pupils' *grade ages* or *grade equivalents* are universally used to describe attainment. Moreover the decimal system is enlisted to convey a spurious, but wholly pragmatic, sense of accuracy: G3.3 is meant to signify the level of an average pupil a third of the way through grade three.[15]

'It is better to be roughly right', said Maynard Keynes, 'than precisely wrong'. But when all possible honour for this venerable system has been scraped together, there remain intractable problems that effectively debar age equivalents from use in any serious measurement process. There are said to be 12 different ways of deriving them. Most test manuals, however, include a list of age equivalents of raw scores in perfunctory fashion, without bothering to say *how* they were derived. The two best known ways are:

- calculation of the average age of all individuals obtaining a given raw score;
- calculation of the average raw score of all individuals of a given age.

These two procedures produce intersecting lines of quite different slopes.

What is meant by *reading* alters subtly with the stage of progress that the individual is at (Chall, 1983; Turner, 1995b). Similarly, tests utilise methodologies of word recognition, sentence completion and passage comprehension, depending on what is appropriate at any age. It will not do, as the impatient journalist would wish, to assimilate quite different measurement procedures, in the belief that it is 'all reading'. Moreover grizzled adults are not amused to hear that their reading ages have shot up from 7;9 to 8;3.

The fundamental problem, however, is with the basic unit of measurement, the *month*. Nobody knows what this unit is: 30.4375 days, perhaps, or 4.3482 weeks. People compare 'months' of reading age with 'months' of schooling, vaguely aware that for many months children are not even *at* school. August, for instance, is not an auspicious month for reading and spelling ages.

Even assuming some sort of standard month uniform for the calendar and school year, the progress thus expressed is *different at different ages*. This may be readily seen in Figure 6.1.

Such a graphical presentation makes plain that a *month* of reading progress between the ages of 6 and 7 has quite a different value (steeper slope) to a *month* between the ages of 11 and 12. This is because at the

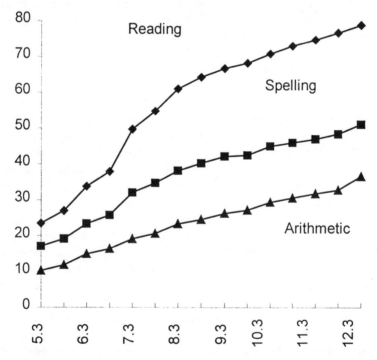

Figure 6.1. Mid-interval age equivalents for 15 norm groups of WRAT-R raw score means on tests of Reading, Spelling and Arithmetic, Levels 1 and 2. Source: Wilkinson (1983).

younger age children tend to be making rapid initial progress with reading in school, whereas such progress in single-word recognition at 10 or 12 is more a matter of vocabulary and word-meanings gradually acquired through continuing exposure to print.

It must be clear by now that the age equivalent metric, whether for reading, spelling or mentality, is subject to so many sources of error and distortion as to convey only the most impressionistic idea of anyone's development. It is unfit for any form of analysis, such as comparing status at two different times (progress) or comparing one individual with another (norm reference group).

What is it we wish to achieve with any educational measurement? Conceivably one might wish to chart the progress of individuals through a well-defined curricular sequence,[16] in which case one or more of different ages can be independently evaluated on the same tasks. For reasons weighed in Chapter 1, literacy skills do not fit very well in an invariant sequence though coherent teaching, which treats them as if they do, tends to be the most successful. Much of what is to be learned is arbitrary and its acquisition is not keyed in to specific child developments. Reading may be learned before the first birthday and after the 90th.

The foremost objective, surely, in seeking any assessment of a child's educational skills is *to compare the child with his or her contemporaries*. We wish to know, on the basis of comparison with other children of the same age, and especially with the *average* child of the same age, what this individual's development and progress are like. Normative testing thus forms the bedrock upon which we base even our sense of contrasts between one area and another *within* a child's development. This has many implications. One is that we will wish to use *contemporary* tests, regardless of where educational standards may have been heading during the postwar decades.[17] When we use the Holborn test we are comparing a 7-year-old today with a group of 7-year-olds in about 1947, individuals who are now well into their middle age. The interest of such information is remote.

Accordingly modern technology attempts to provide small, but very carefully selected and stratified samples for normative comparison purposes. If correct percentages sampled during test construction live in Aberdeen, or have parents earning 0.8 of median family income, or have forebears in Uttar Pradesh, this is so that the sample may be held fairly to reflect the *total* population composition of the community.[18] We wish to compare a child not with others in hospital, or in independent schools or in Easterhouse but with *all* others of the same age. The alternative to such liberal universalism is fragmentation into a multitude of special-interest groups, provincial identities, postcodes and *customer segments* already familiar to advertisers and producers of junk-mail.

Any standard score will contain information about the *distribution* of scores, as well as about the mean or median. This reflects the performance of the standardisation sample at the age in question: sharply ascending 7-year-olds, or lackadaisical 12-year-olds. Thus we may ascertain not just whether our individual is a bit above or a bit below the average for his or her age-group but *how far* above or below.[19] We can see, and explain, the consequences of a standstill, or of progress commensurate only with age, and the difficulties of any complete catching up. This way of measuring progress, after all, depends upon the activities of the peer group as well as the progress of our individual.

Essentially all standard scores work in the same way, though connoisseurs develop preferences among them. The *T-score*, for instance, is recommended for test construction by the American Psychological Association; the *stanine* is an enthusiasm of the US military but is scarcely met with in educational testing in Britain. Because such scores are standard, however, they need little explanation. They correspond to what a lay person's intuition expects them to mean. All necessary explanation can be couched in terms of the *percentage*, the world's favourite statistic.

Thus the *T*-score, the Wechsler scaled score, the standard quotient (mean 100, SD 15) and the *z*-score may all occur within the same assessment, because different instruments favour slightly different currencies. But all are directly comparable and facilitate the process of deriving meaningful answers to pressing questions.

The *percentile* is another form – the linear equivalent – of the standard score, this time telling the parent and teacher what they want to know in terms of the proportion of pupils above and below a given individual. This seems the best medium for talking about children's performances in relation to those of their contemporaries. There are minor sacrifices to be made: a percentile scale appears to equalise all intervals between percentile points whereas standard scores, based on standard deviations, preserve the distances among the various portions of the population. Herrnstein and Murray illustrate the compression of percentiles at the extremes, high and low, of a distribution as follows:

> Consider two people who are at the 50th and 55th centiles in height . . . their actual height difference is only half an inch. Consider another two people who are at the 94th and 99th centiles in height – the identical gap in terms of centiles. Their height difference is 3.1 inches, six times the height difference of those at the 50th and 55th centiles. The further out on the tail of the distribution you move, the more misleading centiles become. (Herrnstein and Murray, 1994, p. 559)

The Woodcock–Johnson (Revised), perhaps the world's most notable elaboration of psychometric technology, provides, on its record forms, for the many different metrics employed by its tests. By means of simple bars, which place standard scores and percentile equivalents alongside each other, scores are recorded in a way that makes their relationship transparent to the user (Figure 6.2).

Figure 6.2:Graphical illustration of the relationship between standard (upper) and percentile (lower line) scores, demonstrating the bunching of percentile scores towards either extreme of the distribution. Source: Woodcock–Johnson (Revised) Record Form; reproduced by permission.

The medium of *centiles* or *percentiles*, however, accomplishes the first purpose of the assessment exercise. The individual being assessed is compared precisely with his or her contemporaries, yet the comparison is expressed in such a way that the lay recipient of the assessment report can readily comprehend its findings. Moreover *all* results from well-normed tests can be reported in this way, for instance in graphical form.

The visual display of quantitative information

Having established, therefore, a particular metric which, with a degree of compromise, communicates scientific findings without absurdity or self-contradiction, we turn to another means of communication which involves no compromise at all: the *visual*. This is natural. All quantitative relationships originate in spatial judgements of observations. What could be more natural than to turn them back into schematised form to enable direct comparisons to be made with the aid of histograms, pie-charts and scatterplots?

This is not a matter of reflecting all the technical intricacies in the data. Error-banners, data labels and so on serve only to alarm the viewer with the threat of explanations to come, just as complex or visually aversive patternings in the bars themselves (in the case of bar-charts) can be distracting. The simplest metric of all, Ds or standard deviation units, are so intuitive as to need, fortunately, no explanation. Many psychologists will, through experiment, have found that the blank normal distribution graph supplied by publishers on the first page of test stationery is often an extremely useful aid in talking through the results of an assessment with a parent or teacher.[20]

Consequently the best visualisations of assessment data are often the simplest. Though a rough sketch on a blank sheet of paper may serve to anchor the main lines of enquiry, we are, for the most part, entering the world of the laptop computer. This is especially so when a graph is to be included as an appendix to a formal report. Psychologists do not always have access to the technology which, at the press of very few buttons, presents an admirable graph, but observation suggests that they may be less phobic than usual about using the machines in the first place. Certainly psychology undergraduates nowadays learn statistics directly from the screens of microcomputers.

Though there are infinite variations, many of them commendable, of the kinds of graphs that can be produced, in what follows I will concentrate on two. These, honed in long clinical trial-and-error, embody the conclusions reached so far about the *form* in which results are best reported, as well as the *intra-individual* nature of the assessment.

First to be considered is the *percentile graph*. This simply illustrates, by the height of the bars, the value in percentile terms of the individual's level of performance on a selection of tests. Though percentiles exaggerate the distances between bars, they have an intuitive meaning for most people. The origin of the bars can be zero.[21] This graphical presentation is suitable for displaying the results of a large number of tests in comparable form. If ability tests, with composites, are displayed to the left of the graph, with diagnostic and attainment data towards the right, the tendency, for dyslexic individuals, will be for the bars to decrease in height from left to right across the page. Given that each observation is the result of numerous accurate and technically scrupulous steps by test constructors and individual test administrators, the single-page graph of results represents a unique summary, without loss of technical detail, of a sophisticated assessment process.

Figure 6.3 is an example. Here it can be seen that JM, a 9-year-old boy, is of general ability, a little below the average, but that his General Conceptual Ability (GCA or IQ) comprises disparate *cluster scores*. In particular, like many dyslexic individuals, he shows unaccountable difficulty with the Matrices core test of ability.[22] This is not representative of his visuospatial ability in general and produces a discrepancy between non-verbal reasoning and spatial clusters that would be found in only 2% of individuals. As we move towards the right of the graph, we find the scores declining. This begins with the diagnostic tests of the DAS. The test of immediate verbal memory for digits, Recall of Digits, produces a lower score, though not one discrepant with the mean of JM's core tests. Speed of Information Processing is still lower, though again not significantly so. Of the two supplementary tests included from WISC-III, Digit Span confirms a difficulty with immediate verbal memory: this is at a level above only 2% of JM's contemporaries. All three attainment areas are depressed, though Word Reading unexceptionally and least of all. Only 2% of pupils of JM's age and ability would obtain a score this low on Basic Number Skills, and only 8–9% on Spelling. The three Woodcock Reading Mastery Tests used confirm the level of reading. The One

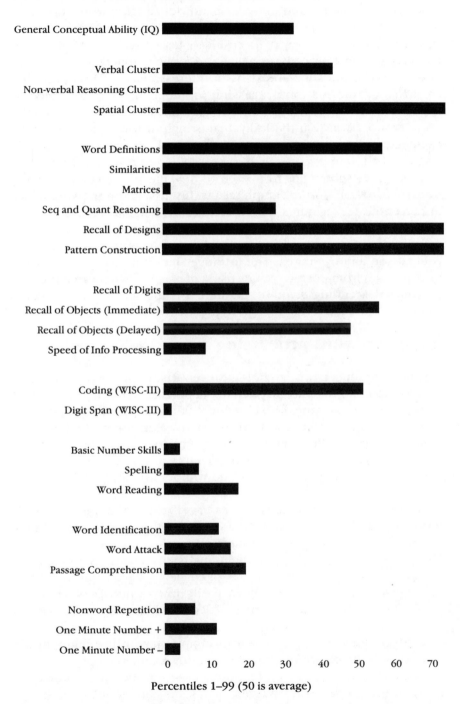

Differential ability scale: profile for JM (9:4)
core, diagnostic and supplementary tests

Percentiles 1–99 (50 is average)

Figure 6.3: Graphical display of psychometric information obtained for JM using the Differential Ability Scales with supplementary diagnostic and attainment tests

Minute Number Tests show low performance in both addition and subtraction, with the lower score for subtraction (relative to the norm group) that is often found in dyslexic individuals. Non-word repetition (CNRep), too, implicates a phonological difficulty.

After the general survey of *all* results of tests given (a total of 21, not counting informal procedures which cannot be graphed), a closer look at core and diagnostic subtests is of interest, because it is here that *cognitive* or information-processing problems may be presumed to appear. For this purpose one may disregard further comparison with the norm group, because if the individual is high or low in relation to his age-peers internal contrasts may be masked. By transforming JM's T-scores, first, into z-scores with a mean of 0 and a standard deviation (SD) of 1, then subtracting from each his *own* mean z-score and dividing by his *own* SD, an *ipsative* graph results. Just as a graph showing values in percentiles exaggerates the differences between scores, so a graph compiled in ipsative units will reduce such differences. This is because the subject's own standard deviation (high or low) is used as the basis of comparison among scores. The intuitive significance of such a visual display arises from positive values rising *above* his own mean and negative ones descending *below* it. Figure 6.4 is the second graph, which shows the score interrelationships in this way.

A note on word processing

For many producers of psychological reports, traditional methods of composition cannot easily be given up. Reports are written longhand, or dictated onto audio tape, for subsequent transcribing. The support of a secretary with a computer is seen as just an extension of the filing and typing that had, itself, sometimes made an appearance only lately as a result of management audits. Living memory has no difficulty with the psychology service as a one-man-band without *any* filing: this is recent history.

However, such office ministrations have, with subtle speed, become less menial and instrumental by the year, until their power to hold up a mirror to the service itself has had to be reluctantly acknowledged. Modern information methods, including client databases and spreadsheets to analyse multiple measures of efficiency, have contributed to a *management ethic* that has been easily intoxicated by such novel capabilities. The associated climate of accountability is held by many to be a prime cause of their woes.

A psychological assessment in principle may utilise many of the resources of the computer. Some species of commercial psychometric software have already been mentioned. The production of individual spreadsheets to perform favoured analyses is commonplace. Data are in any case best stored, analysed and charted by the use of

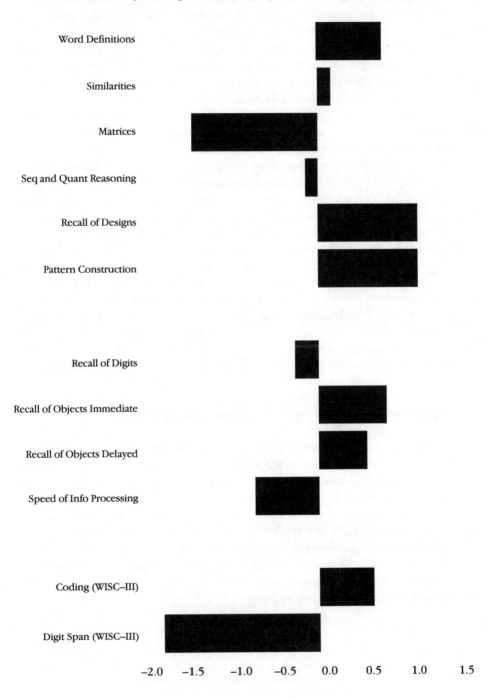

Differential ability scales: profile for JM (9:4) core and diagnostic subtests

Standard units - 0 = individual's own MEAN

Figure 6.4: Ipsative graph showing JM's core and diagnostic subtests, rescaled to his own mean and standard deviation, in SD units.

spreadsheets. Databases keep track of clients, colleagues and resources. In particular word processing software can make the production of a 3–4000 word report a routine matter. Gone are the days when a report that referred to Emily in the first few pages and Leroy thereafter was attributed to unbridled use of a word processor. This is now, rightly, seen as an instance of someone who is not using a word processor but *should be*.

Good word-processing software[23] will enable the accretion and accumulation of reporting methods over the years, with gradual but continuous incorporation of improvements and revisions to fine detail. The aim of automation of *writing* will probably remain a will-o'-the-wisp, as conscious management and mastery of detail cannot be abrogated. Actual composition, however, proceeds more freely when the many subroutines of *assembly* are taken care of. This does not mean that a great deal of what is said about each child who is the subject of an assessment will be the same: only that standard descriptions of, for example, tests do not need to be varied. Indeed it would be quite prohibitive to venture upon a psychological report of modern dimensions without automation of many subroutines. Most readers of such reports, including critical colleagues, accept that there are both *standard* and *unique* passages and the report is made up of both: the standard passages are assembled, the unique ones are composed. The tissues are the same each time; the sinews and tendons are different.

Sample psychological assessment report

Let us now gather together and express our conclusions in the form of a sample assessment report. We wish to convey a succinct summary in a single, photocopiable page; to detail full technical information in an appendix; and, in between the two, to give a narrative of the important findings of the assessment interview. In Figures 6.3 and 6.4 we saw in graphical form the main test results obtained in the assessment of JM. In addition to these two graphs, whose principal features will have been used to convey the main findings to the parents at interview, the analysis of results and drawing of conclusions, with implications for action, are contained in a full report, as follows:[24]

CONFIDENTIAL: PSYCHOLOGICAL REPORT

Name of child: JM

Date of interview: 17 06 95

Age: 9 years 4 months

SUMMARY OF FINDINGS

Abilities

JM is of average general ability (above that of 32% of individuals his own age) but only about 2% of individuals would show this level of discrepancy between non-verbal reasoning and spatial ability.

Pattern of relative strengths and weaknesses

JM has cognitive strengths in:

- spatial ability
- vocabulary

JM has cognitive weaknesses in:

- short-term auditory-verbal memory
- phonological processing
- non-verbal reasoning (verbal strategy)

Attainments

Following many remedial efforts, JM now reads at merely low levels but his spelling remains unexpectedly weak in relation to his age and ability and his number skills are his most intense focus of learning difficulty.

Conclusions

JM continues to show many signs of dyslexia, a specific learning difficulty.

Recommendations

He will need individual teaching from a trained specialist teacher, perhaps as a result of a special needs assessment. Some curricular suggestions are made.

[SIGNATURE AND DATE]

PSYCHOLOGICAL ASSESSMENT: HIGHLIGHTS
AND CONCLUSIONS

Background to this assessment (information from family)

JM is the older of two children in a family with some incidence of dyslexia, a specific learning difficulty.

JM's speech development was late and he suffered from ear infections. He took no interest in nursery rhymes. For several years he received speech therapy.

Initially JM was taught to read at school by the whole-word, flashcard method. But this was ineffective and before long he became frustrated and negative, even 'screaming at the sight of books'.

At school JM is said to lack concentration and to wander about the classroom. He is perceived as 'idle'. However, he 'is not on the school's special needs audit'.

Because of concerns about his progress JM was assessed by a consulting psychologist with the Dyslexia Institute in 1993. However, although JM's school took on board the finding that he was dyslexic, and though his dyslexia-trained private tutor has implemented a structured individual programme with him, JM is thought to have made little progress in the intervening two years – or in some areas to have gone downhill.

Behaviour during interview

JM co-operated willingly and worked well across a wide range of assessment activities. He chatted spontaneously at intervals and told me about his reading of *Swallows and Amazons* and of *Pigeon Post*. However, it turns out that these may have been audio books, without a printed page to follow.

General intellectual ability

JM is of average or below general ability (above that of 32% of other pupils his age). An explanation, however, of any lack of progress solely in terms of limited ability to understand and learn is implausible.

JM's IQ, lower than last time, rises seven points (to 100: exactly average) if the uniquely low Matrices result is omitted. On this test JM failed to engage fully with the task.

Cognitive style

JM shows some contrast between his development in language-based areas of thinking (ideas, concepts, words) and visual and spatial areas (shapes, patterns, relations), with the latter being better developed.

Spatial ability can be distinguished from non-verbal reasoning ability. The former is simultaneous and fairly language-free. The latter requires the application of a verbal strategy to visual materials. Reasoning is analytic and propositional and requires memory for the intervening steps in a sequence. This JM finds more difficult.

The internal contrasts in JM's cognitive profile may be seen in the first of the attached diagrams, which compares his development with that of others his age.

In the second diagram, JM's scores are adjusted to his own mean, so that strengths and weaknesses appear in relation to his own characteristic level of performance.

Core tests

JM shows inconsistent ability within one pair of tests: he obtained an unexpectedly low score on Matrices, a test of non-verbal reasoning. This may reflect poorly sustained attention or it may reflect difficulty naming shapes and features and applying a verbal strategy to visual materials.

All his other core test results are reasonably consistent.

Diagnostic tests

JM's average score on the four diagnostic tests is considerably below that on the six core tests. Recall of Digits is a test of verbal memory and on this he showed some weakness. On Speed of Information Processing, too, he showed a problem of slowness. Only on the pair of tests, Recall of Objects Immediate and Recall of Objects Delayed, did he achieve near-average performances.

Supplementary tests

This picture is confirmed on two extra tests from another system. On Coding (WISC-III) he showed average ability. But on Digit Span (WISC-III), another test of verbal memory, he showed again that this area, central to dyslexia, is an acute difficulty for him. He obtained his lowest score on this test.

On the Test of Auditory Analysis Skills JM showed some lack of the skills of phonological segmentation which are associated with reading and (especially) spelling in the early stages.

On the Children's Test of Nonword Repetition test, JM obtained a score that was very low in relation to others of his age. This suggests that he has some degree of difficulty in storing, analysing and reproducing speech sounds.

Attainment in written arithmetic

On Basic Number Skills JM's score was below expectation. Only 2% of pupils of JM's age and ability would obtain a score this low. This is highly exceptional.

On the One Minute Number Tests JM shows the marked weakness in subtraction, relative to addition, characteristic of many dyslexic individuals.

Attainment in spelling and writing

On Spelling JM's score was below expectation. Only 6–7% of pupils of JM's age and ability would obtain a score this low. This too is highly exceptional.

On the Test of Initial Literacy (TOIL) JM demonstrated his disorganised writing: he made numerous revisions and hesitations, as well as producing work that was hard to comprehend.

Attainment in reading

On Word Reading JM's score was below expectation. But though on the low side, this was not very exceptional in relation to age and ability.

On the One Minute Reading Test short, high- frequency words are used to minimise decoding time for unfamiliar words. JM read at an age equivalent of 9;0 years. This speed is comparatively fast, showing that his reading, at least, is now fairly well automated.

JM's reading speed was also measured using Aaron's lists of function and content words. Like many dyslexic individuals he read function words more slowly and inaccurately. Overall his reading speed was again quite fast.

On three tests from the Woodcock Reading Mastery Tests – Revised, JM performed variably: on Word Identification (single word reading), he achieved at a level above 13% of pupils his own age; on Word Attack above 16%; and on Passage Comprehension, above 21%. Dyslexic individuals' comprehension is typically better than their word recognition, as their recognition of words is better than their decoding of non-words. JM's reading, however, has now responded to remediation and his non-word reading (Word Attack) in particular is better than expected. But JM's level in all basic reading skills would be found in only 13% of pupils of his age and ability, according to another estimation.

Conclusions

JM shows the underachievement in spelling and number skills, with accompanying clinical features (verbal/non-verbal discrepancy, poor verbal memory, speed of information-processing and use of a verbal strategy), which together implicate dyslexia, a specific learning difficulty.

JM shows the limitation in working memory, especially phonological working memory, which research implicates in the common forms of learning disability. What is restricted is the capacity to hold in memory at one time all the elements of a task that is either highly sequenced or that requires many simultaneous operations. As a result the basic skills of reading, writing and arithmetic, all of which make a considerable demand on working memory, are not easily acquired or are not well consolidated in automatic form. The results are most obvious in the difficulty otherwise intelligent pupils have with reading, spelling or memorisation of tables. It is this group of children that is recognised to have dyslexia.

Recommendations

JM needs a range of specialist teaching, delivered individually by a qualified dyslexia specialist, which is able to suit his individual profile of abilities and difficulties, in particular, teaching to foster:

- simultaneous skills in reading, writing and spelling; effective recall in the use of these skills;
- numeracy skills, including the use of number language;
- development of sensitivity to the writing arm, hand and fingers, familiarity with the movement patterns of cursive writing, pleasure in fluency and control in writing;
- study and thinking skills development: the storage and representation of ideas and their expression in writing; habits of practice; reference and research skills; independent management of work projects.

Structured multisensory teaching aims to develop simultaneous skills in reading, writing and spelling so as to enhance effective recall in their use. Image, sound, movement memory (sky-writing) and touch are all employed to establish the sounds and shapes of letters, syllables and words. The most elaborate development of this specialist teaching programme is contained in: Walker, J, Brooks, L and others (1993) *Dyslexia Institute Literacy Programme*, 2 vols. Staines, Middlesex: The Dyslexia Institute. The published programme, however, is supplied only as courseware to teachers qualifying in the Institute's specialist postgraduate diploma, validated by Kingston University. A useful general source for teachers is: Thomson, M.E and Watkins, E.J. (1990). *Dyslexia: A Teaching Handbook*. London: Whurr.

Teaching Reading Through Spelling (the Kingston Programme) deserves its high reputation: this is a series of eight books, published by Mary Prince, Lucy Cowdery, Paula Morse and Sally Low, available from Frondeg Hall Technical Publishing, Aberoer, Wrexham, Clwyd LL14 4LG, 1992. The ACE (Aurally Coded English) Spelling Dictionary would be a valuable aid; and there is now a book of photocopiable masters of spelling worksheets in which word meanings are linked to structural patterns (both published by LDA).

Framework for action

Because of the poor outlook if his needs are not appropriately addressed in school, JM's parents should be aware that it is their right to request a statutory assessment under section 167 of the 1993 Education Act (Section 172(2) or 173(1); Code of Practice 3:17–3:21, pp. 42–3). Such a request should be addressed, in writing, to their chief education officer. A decision must be made within six weeks (Code of Practice 3:31, p. 47). 'Whatever the background, the LEA must take all parental requests seriously and take action immediately' (Code of Practice 3:18, p. 42). No more than 10 weeks may elapse between the decision to assess and the decision as to whether to make a statement (Code of Practice 3:30, p. 46).

It may be relevant to point out also that under Section 19 (4) of the 1988 Education Act a head teacher may make a 'special direction' to exempt a pupil from all or some of the National Curriculum, while consulting the LEA, the governing body of the school and the parent. It is clear from Regulation 5 that such an exemption, unless arrangements are specified to secure the return of the pupil to the National Curriculum, will be an indication that the pupil has special educational needs which should be assessed under Section 167 of the 1993 Education Act. A parent too may request such a direction under the 1988 Act and may appeal in the case of a refusal.

Any statement of special educational needs should identify all JM's needs and specify the quantity, and type, of appropriate specialist teaching that JM requires for each and every one of these needs.

I would suggest that 2–4 hours per week of individual or small-group teaching, of the kind described above, from someone not less well qualified than holders of a postgraduate diploma (or equivalent) in the teaching of students with dyslexia would be a minimum. Such teachers are highly trained and no substitute is likely to be effective.

Other sources of advice and information

Mr and Mrs M may want to be in touch with parents of other, similarly affected children. This often provides an informal network of advice, support and experience in dealing with the authorities. They should contact: British Dyslexia Association, 98 London Road, Reading, Berkshire, RG1 5AU; Tel: 01734 662677.

The Advisory Centre for Education is a valuable source of advice and guidance for parents and is at: 1b Aberdeen Studios, 22 Highbury Grove, London N5 2HA; Tel: 0171 354 8321. The *ACE Special Education Handbook*, 6th edn, a guide to the law on children with special needs, is an invaluable summary, useful to all. Further detailed advice on procedures and educational law may be found in Friel, J (1995) *Children With Special Needs: Assessment, Law and Practice – Caught In The Acts*, 3rd edn. London: Jessica Kingsley.

[SIGNATURE AND DATE]

TECHNICAL APPENDIX: TEST RESULTS

Differential Ability Scales (PsychologicalCorporation, 1990)

Summary measures

JM's performance is compared with that of all individuals of the same age. The results are expressed as *standard scores*, which have an average value of 100. Scores of 69 and below are Very Low; 70–79 are Low; 80–89 are Below Average; 90–109 are Average; 110–119 are Above Average; 120–129 are High; and 130 and above are Very High.

General conceptual ability (GCA or IQ): 93

JM is of average general ability (above that of 32% of his age-peers). This is necessarily a global measure of all-round ability and therefore penalises an individual who may have strengths offset by weaknesses. Because of errors inherent in the measurement process, it is best to say that that the true IQ probably lies within the range 88–99 (90% confidence).

Cluster scores:

Verbal Reasoning: 97
Non-verbal Reasoning: 78
Spatial Ability: 108

The contrasts between this level of GCA (IQ) and the cluster scores are significant and exceptional.

JM shows an unusual strength in the area of spatial ability. Only about 10% of pupils of this GCA (IQ) would have a level of spatial ability this high.

JM shows an unusual weakness in the area of non-verbal reasoning. Only about 6–7% of pupils of this GCA (IQ) would have a level of non-verbal reasoning this low.

Certain differences between these cluster scores are both statistically significant and exceptional.

JM shows some contrast between verbal and non-verbal reasoning. Only about 15% of individuals would show this level of discrepancy.

JM shows some contrast between non-verbal reasoning and spatial ability. Only about 2% of individuals would show this level of discrepancy.

Achievement scores:

Basic Number Skills: 73
Spelling: 79
Word Reading: 86

Certain achievement scores are unexpected in relation to JM's level of General Conceptual Ability (GCA or IQ). These are evaluated below in the section on Achievement in Basic Skills.

Subtest scores:

Details follow of the individual subtests that contribute to the summary measures. Results are reported in terms of *percentiles*: this is the percentage of children of this age who perform at or below JM's level of ability.

Verbal subtests

WORD DEFINITIONS

Percentile ... 54

This is a test of vocabulary or word-knowledge. The individual must demonstrate a precise understanding of the meanings of words.

SIMILARITIES

Percentile ... 34

Similarities involves the use of language to classify and define sets of items. Words, thoughts and ideas are all drawn upon in this test of verbal reasoning.

Non-verbal reasoning subtests.

MATRICES

Percentile ... 2

This requires the pupil to point out the design that successfully completes a pattern of shapes. It entails working through a sequence of steps in reasoning, naming shapes and verbalising features, silently if not out loud. This analytic task makes demands on working memory and on the ability to utilise a verbal strategy.

Only about 1% of individuals with his other scores would perform this poorly on this test.

SEQUENTIAL AND QUANTITATIVE REASONING

Percentile ... 27

This test requires realisation of a sequence, at first using shapes, later, with the older child, written numbers. The non-verbal relationship between pairs of numbers (half, triple, three-quarters) is perceived by a pupil who has internalised number concepts.

On this pair of tests, JM performed inconsistently: only about 12–13% of individuals would obtain scores so disparate.

Spatial subtests

RECALL OF DESIGNS

Percentile ... 69

This is a test of broad visual ability, with a memory component. Cards with simple abstract designs are exposed to the pupil for five seconds and then removed; the pupil reproduces the designs from memory using pencil and paper.

PATTERN CONSTRUCTION

Percentile ... 69

This requires the assembly of four or nine blocks to match patterns on a card. Such visuo-spatial ability utilises simultaneous processing, but requires analytic (part–whole) as well as synthetic strategies. The pupil does not need to remember the design, which remains present throughout.

Diagnostic subtests

RECALL OF DIGITS

Percentile ... 21

In this test, digits must be repeated, forwards only, after presentation at the rate of two per second. This low-level language task requires no transformation of the stimuli. But language memory capacity is vital for comprehension of speech and print.

RECALL OF OBJECTS IMMEDIATE

Percentile ... 54

and RECALL OF OBJECTS DELAYED

Percentile ... 46

More evidence of memory functioning is provided by these tests in which words and pictures are linked. A card with familiar objects is displayed for one minute while the objects are named. The card is then removed and the individual is asked to recall as many as he can. There are two further presentations followed by recall. After 10–15 minutes, a fourth, unexpected recall is attempted. This task, although a visual array, is also a verbal list. As a difficulty with naming is characteristic of many dyslexic individuals, and problems of retrieval are separated from problems of storage, the test is of clinical interest.

SPEED OF INFORMATION PROCESSING

Percentile ... 10

On this test the highest number in a row is marked repeatedly under timed conditions. In the case of the younger child, the circle containing the most squares in each row must be marked. This is a clerical checking task, requiring only threshold levels of arithmetical ability (place value).

Achievement in basic skills

BASIC NUMBER SKILLS

Percentile ... 4
Number age ... 7 years 7 months

This test requires recognition of printed numbers and performance of written calculations.

A score this low would be obtained by only 2% of other pupils of JM's age and general ability. It is highly exceptional.

SPELLING

Percentile ... 8
Spelling age ... 7 years 7 months

Writing of single words to dictation, with context supplied in short sentences.

A score this low would be obtained by only 8–9% of other pupils of JM's age and general ability. Whilst exceptional, this is not extreme.

WORD READING

Percentile ... 18
Reading age ... 7 years 10 months

Recognition of printed words singly and out of context.

Though on the low side, this is neither very exceptional, nor extreme.

Supplementary diagnostic tests

DIGIT SPAN

Percentile ... 2
Scaled score ... 4

Wechsler, D (1992) *Wechsler Intelligence Scale For Children – Third Edition UK* (WISC-III). New York: Harcourt Brace Jovanovitch/Psychological Corporation. Scaled scores range from 1 to 19, with 10 the average; two-thirds of scores fall between 7 and 13. This test is comparable to DAS Recall of Digits but digits are repeated forwards and backwards after a slower presentation time – one per second.

CODING

Percentile ... 50
Scaled score ... 10

Wechsler, D (1992) *Wechsler Intelligence Scale For Children – Third Edition UK* (WISC-III). New York: Harcourt Brace Jovanovitch/Psychological Corporation. Scaled scores range from 1 to 19, with 10 the average; two-thirds of scores fall between 7 and 13. This task requires the pupil to supply single digits with the symbols which accompany them in a model. The number correct within two minutes is credited. The test measures concentration, facility with printed symbols, rapid decision making and visual-motor speed.

TEST OF AUDITORY ANALYSIS SKILLS [TAAS]

From: Rosner, J (1993) *Helping Children Overcome Learning Difficulties*, 3rd edn. New York: Walker. This is a test of one of the skills of phonological analysis, phoneme deletion. The pupil is required to eliminate one of the sequence of sounds in a word ('Say *take*; say it again but don't say *t*'). JM obtained a score of 8, suggesting a level of development average for a child of about 6 years.

CHILDREN'S NONWORD REPETITION TEST [CNRep]

Gathercole, SE, Willis, CS, Baddeley, AD and Emslie, H (1994). The children's test of nonword repetition: a test of phonological working memory. *Memory*. This requires the child to repeat without error a number of non-words (which are, however, word-like) of 2, 3, 4 and 5 syllables (*perplisteronk*). JM was able to achieve a score of 26, at the level of less than 10% of his contemporaries.

Supplementary tests of attainment

ONE MINUTE NUMBER TEST

Westwood, ., Harris-Hughes, M, Lucas, G, Nolan, J and Scrymgeour, K (1974). One minute addition test – one minute subtraction test. *Remedial Education* 9(2), 71–2. This test consists of 30 single-digit addition sums (3 + 4 =) performed under timed conditions – the child is stopped after one minute. Similarly 30 simple subtraction sums are given, also within one minute. Results highlight any difficulties the child may have with simple, repetitive operations performed at speed. As number bonds or facts (6 + 9 = 15), like tables, may be learned by heart, more items will be achieved if recall is automatic. On the addition items, JM performed at a level above 12% of his contemporaries; on the subtraction items, JM performed at a level above only 3% of his contemporaries.

ONE MINUTE READING TEST

Transvaal Education Department, South Africa (April 1987). This test, normed for English-speaking children, requires the child to read out loud words of one syllable, row after row, for a duration of one minute. On this test JM scored at a level appropriate to an individual of 9:0 years. Overall he read at a speed of 0.86 seconds per word.

READING SPEED – FUNCTION AND CONTENT WORDS

From: Aaron, PG and Joshi, RM (1992) *Reading Problems: Consultation And Remediation*. New York: Guilford Press. Measures of reading speed are distorted by time taken over unfamiliar words. These two lists, of 20 words each, matched for frequency and number of syllables, offer a good alternative. The individual's reading of the words in each list is timed. Dyslexic readers make more errors on function words (*also, once ever*), as well as reading them more slowly than content words (*book, bird, gold*). JM read the content words in 15 seconds, making no errors; and the function words in 20 seconds, with 3 errors. Overall JM read at a speed of about 0.88 seconds per word. (A skilled adult reader reads silently at a speed of about 0.25 seconds per word or less.)

WORD IDENTIFICATION

Percentile ... 13
Age equivalent ... 8 years 0 months

Woodcock, RW (1987) *Woodcock Reading Mastery Tests – Revised* [WRMT-R]. Circle Pines, MN: American Guidance Service. This is a test of single- word decoding accuracy of a conventional kind. With 106 items, however, it is more than usually reliable.

WORD ATTACK

Percentile ... 16
Age equivalent ... 7 years 6 months

Woodcock, RW (187) *Woodcock Reading Mastery Tests – Revised* [WRMT-R]. Circle Pines, MN: American Guidance Service. On this test decoding skills are highlighted using made-up words (*bend, wrault*).

PASSAGE COMPREHENSION

Percentile ... 21
Age equivalent ... 8 years 3 months

Woodcock, RW (1987) *Woodcock Reading Mastery Tests – Revised* [WRMT-R]. Circle Pines, MN: American Guidance Service.

Comprehension is probed by questions about items ranging from simple pictures accompanied by short sentences, through longer sentences without pictures, to complex prose passages.

TEST OF INITIAL LITERACY

Kispal, A, Tate, A, Gorman, T and Whetton, C (1989) *Test Of Initial Literacy* [TOIL]. Windsor, Berks: NFER-Nelson. Exercise 9 is a test of free writing in which the pupil is asked to address and write a postcard to a friend. JM wrote 30 words in 2.5 minutes, a rate of 12 words per minute. Of these, 7 words were misspelt (29%).

Advocacy, representation and expert witness

Such a report claims to satisfy, as well as any can, the diverse requirements of many audiences, foreseen and unforeseen. It reconciles the expert and the lay accounts of dyslexia. It meets the demands of a possibly critical readership of professional peers. It presents evidence, advances argument and reaches conclusions. It makes recommendations in some detail without, however, presuming to know the specialist teacher's business or usurping teaching or case management decisions which must be made in the light of changing circumstances.

An assessment consultation is an important event which may have consequences for all concerned. Here let us touch briefly on the events that may ensue from a family's decision to use the statutory means available to contest the special education provision that the local education authority intends to make (or not to make). Over many years the pioneering role of independent experts, often working from an independent, charitable base outside the State education system, has led to important legal decisions. The separation of powers in a democracy means that the judiciary has been able impartially to consider and criticise decisions reached in the *command economy* of the State sector. In a series of such legal contests, the ultimate challenge has been to the *whole system*, represented in law by the Secretary of State.[24] Case law has been made and changes in guidance forced upon the education department, issued in due course in circulars. Ultimately the fruits of these historic struggles have been seen in subsequent, especially amending, legislation.

The role of the consulting psychologist is not usually a gladiatorial one. Indeed professionals who wish to avoid difficult experiences in courts of law are normally able to do so. In recent years the British Psychological Society has given space more frequently in its house journal, *The Psychologist*, to consideration of the pressures and demands on the *expert witness*. It may be thought that between the *métier* of science and that of a court of law there is much in common, for instance respect for rational argument and the rules of evidence. However, scientists do occasionally find themselves exposed to conflict with the legal process, the frequent result of which is to establish science as the court of higher authority! Whenever courts have chosen to disregard a body of scientific truth, as when this runs – as it sometimes does – counter to common sense, the effect has ultimately been to bring the law into disrepute. Time is on the side of the scientist, as is the ethic of claiming only 'piecemeal, provisional' truth.[25]

One certain way in which a psychologist can dissipate credibility, navigating as an expert witness in the difficult terrain of human behaviour and protected only by the banner of science, is to adhere to a single side of a disputed question. Necessarily, in an adversarial system, he or she must appear for one side or the other, but the value of any opinion expressed depends crucially upon impartiality. Yet even the scientist is human and so defensive haverings, too, will cause impatience among judges and lawyers and a loss of credibility.

The evidence of a psychologist carries enormous weight in any dispute involving identification of, and provision for, dyslexia. The mysterious psychometric rituals of the fledgeling science appear to impress people in all walks of life. All the more important, then, that truth be respected and the limitations to any evidence and line of argument made clear.[26]

Conclusions

The afterlife of an assessment and its documentary traces already take us beyond the scope of this chapter, which has set out the principles for devising written reports of assessment findings. We have attempted to address the needs of the technically expert and the innocent lay readers, keeping always uppermost the requirements of the parent who commissions and pays for the assessment[27] and whose right, in any case, not to disclose the report to anyone else may often be exercised.

Nevertheless a principal form of afterlife for an assessment, and one devoutly hoped for by most who write such reports, is the phase of practical teaching. This must ensue if learning difficulties, carefully detected by all the methods we have been discussing, are not to flourish unchecked. It is therefore to *specialist teaching* that we turn next.

Notes

1   Just how makeshift, in spite of everything, are our measures for detecting dyslexia was brought home to me by the enquiry of a PhD student who hypothesised that a small change in the diet of a clinical sample would, incidentally, bring about

a reduction in the dyslexic symptoms of some. What measures would I recommend to capture such an improvement in dyslexic disposition? Clearly such useful sensitivity remains largely beyond reach.

2 You either are or you aren't: see Shaywitz et al. (in press).

3 I should like to think that some specifics for successful private practice will be ignored. Always use the WISC (as unrevised as possible), add 10 points onto the IQ and don't blind the customer with science.

4 One parent wondered if it was true that that her son *had lots of good ideas* that were not realised on paper. The first part of this claim could be addressed by means of the little-used BAS Verbal Fluency scale, a simple test of creativity that utilises the most psychometrically stable aspect of creative thinking: productivity of alternative ideas.

5 A long, complicated document, received without benefit of a careful, responsive interpersonal explanation and collaborative discussion of findings, is rebarbative for families who have been unable to attend their child's assessment.

6 Some families treasure their child's psychological assessment report, handing it down as an heirloom; others, more careless, allow it to become dog-eared and tea-stained, eventually becoming submerged in the flotsam, jetsam and lagan of the household. Happily the former fate seems to be more common.

7 In the modern welfare bureaucracy, large meetings are convened that tend to discuss a child as if he or she scarcely belonged to the parents. It seems difficult, sometimes, for the welfare professional, paid by the State, to remember *whose the child actually is.*

8 Department for Education (May 1994).

9 In relation to dyslexia, professional differences can seem chronic; but as implied already, such differences may turn on deeply held attitudes rather than the points of *evidence, argument and conclusions* with which science would expect to do brisk business: 'The most striking feature of contemporary moral utterance is that so much of it is used to express disagreements; and the most striking feature of the debates in which these disagreements are expressed is their interminable character . . . There seems to be no rational way of securing moral agreement in our culture.' (MacIntyre, 1981, p. 6.)

10 The common basis which provides for effective transaction between expert and lay person is surely the position known as *common-sense realism.* 'I think very highly of common sense', writes Karl Popper (1953, 1974; reprinted in 1983, p. 105), distinguishing common-sense realism from the common-sense theory of knowledge or *bucket theory of the mind.* Realism is 'a conjecture to which no sensible alternative has ever been offered' (op. cit., p. 223).

11 However, the rehearsal of scientific attitudes can be a matter of mere *etiquette*, as for instance with the avoiding of certain words. Psychology graduates sometimes have grounds for complaint that they have been trained *never to reach conclusions*. Like distrust of theory this may be indicative of scientific immaturity.

12 Turner (1996).

13 George and Irina Tyk, in a summer holiday teaching mission on the rugged Mozart estate in North Paddington, filmed by Carlton television for a programme shown on ITV on 31 August 1995, tested and retested 27 children on the Holborn sentence-reading test at the beginning and end of the fortnight's course in reading. The children had made on average 13.5 months of gain in 10 working days. They were assembled and told publicly what their levels had been and what they were now. All showed delighted understanding!

14 The self-righteousness of common sense occasionally renders it militant. I

assessed a 30-year-old man accused of rape and found evidence of extremely low general intelligence. Pressed by solicitors to say what the *mental age* of the man might be, I forbore, on the grounds that I had not given him a child's test and so could not compare his abilities with those of children. I wished to avoid the implication that, if he had the mind of a child, he was not capable morally or emotionally of rape.

15 Here teachers habitually express *months* (0.083 of a year) as one or two digits *after a decimal point*: e.g. 8.9 instead of the unambiguous 8;9. This shows that accuracy is beside the point. With the advent of National Curriculum numerals for year groups (R, Y1, Y2, Y3 etc.), UK levels are now directly equivalent to internationally accepted *grades*.

16 Such as self-help skills in the pre-school years or for those following a developmental curriculum. The best examples of *criterion-referenced* assessment seem to be other such highly structured and elementary skill domains. An inventory or category-ticking approach is often all the measurement necessary. Issues arising from the choice among different basic models of assessment are well discussed in Dockrell and McShane (1993). The experiment of National Curriculum Assessment seems to have done much to discredit, perhaps irrevocably, the cause of criterion referencing.

17 See Turner (1996).

18 From international comparisons, including the WISC-III UK validation exercise, we know that there is little difference between one developed 'community' and another.

19 Until recently, specialist dyslexia teachers, uninformed about the wider spectrum of tests, relied upon the Aston Index (Thomson and Newton, 1982). I have regularly been brought 'profiles' to interpret. However the *age equivalent* concept has here roamed free: average levels are given for different primary ages on all its tests but *no standard deviations*, so that laboriously gathered data remain uninterpretable.

20 Whilst some morsels of technical information appear to be necessary to the consumer, others are not. I no longer attempt a formal explanation, with parents, of the *normal distribution*, finding instead that the concept of the *average* level of performance at this age, with distance above or below the mean, is quite sufficient. Similarly, teachers undergoing specialist training in dyslexia studies seem to need to know a *standard deviation*, including by seeing a worked example, but not a *correlation coefficient*.

21 *WISC-III Writer* provides a graph of scaled scores from 1 to 19, with the points only shown, each one extended in both directions by bands of standard error. This graph can be printed out, indeed incorporated into another report with suitable acknowledgement. However, though exemplary from a measurement point of view, the graph is limited aesthetically by the constraints of the ASCII file format.

22 See the discussion in Chapter 3; also Turner (1994c).

23 This was written with Microsoft Word 6.

24 The anonymous child may be represented by *Regina*. The point is that, no matter how apparently sympathetic any individual Secretary of State may appear, he or she is the prisoner of the department concerned, albeit a temporary, even fugitive, one. Any parent caught up in a conflict with the machinery of government will glimpse how different are the interests of elected politicians from those of their settled departments, as the latter are from those of a quickly maturing child.

25 Popper.

26 Temptation to trade on one's authority is not lacking. When asked to give an opinion on the essentially *undecidable* question of whether trauma could have induced a case of dyslexia as to whose inheritance evidence was unobtainable, I pointed out the limits to scientific certainty. Back came the request, 'Yes, but where in your opinion does the *balance of probabilities* lie?'

27 Most reports, however, are still commissioned by public education authorities, corporate employers in Britain of the majority of educational psychologists. The requirements of LEAs should, for exactly the same reasons, be preserved and respected in the writing of their reports.

Chapter 7
Recommendations for specialist teaching

Specialist teaching – a craft skills tradition

Can there be any useful discussion of teaching, its methods, materials and effectiveness? Teachers in Britain have long had 'a notoriously low professional reputation' (Wooldridge, 1994, p. 154) and psychologists, too, may have 'suffered for their connections with individual children' (ibid, p. 154):

> . . . acutely conscious that their regular contact with the messy world of children and teachers reduced their status in the eyes of their scientific colleagues . . . As they moved up the professional hierarchy, they tended to abandon their contacts with children and teachers and transform themselves into pure academics (ibid, p. 158)

The awkward growth of educational psychology, a new profession largely the creature of the Welfare State, continues but the former privileges of the university department are vanished, as the *accountability ethic* meshes with the obligation to teach the proportion, rising almost to a third, of all youngsters destined to enter higher education. Nowadays, psychological researchers in Britain's ivory laboratories, in a competitive climate compelled by external markers of productivity, remain, if not pure, then certainly frugal.

Authenticity, meanwhile, arises from those 'messy' children. Demand for the professional services of educational psychologists is one of the few constants in the changing world of a service economy. Even if today's psychologist does not side, as one hopes he or she would, with ordinary human suffering and its existential claim, the close-range study of children and schools can be a proving-ground of theories and the matrix of new insights and interventions. If teaching is an admixture of art and science, then we should not forget that, as Picasso once said, works of art are produced as princes beget heirs: by way of shepherdesses.

Times have changed, too, from when pioneers such as Ballard, Adams and Nunn sought to place teaching and the training of teachers on a scientific research basis.[1] As recently as the 1970s the question of teaching *effectiveness* may have been dismissed as a vain attempt to pin down the ineffable, to discuss the undiscussable. The effective teacher had a specially *charismatic personality* and, though certain ways of operating could be learned,[2] what was needed in essence, and what every trainee soon came to feel he or she lacked, was a similarly charismatic personality. Now there is very little to be done if, like many trainee teachers, you seem to have the *wrong personality*, so such a message from the training institutions was essentially a counsel of despair. But, patiently and modestly, research has continued to make, through successive provisional attempts, considerable inroads into such attitudes. Effective teaching can be identified, talked about, made explicit; more important, its principles and techniques can be communicated and, largely regardless of personality, learned and mastered.

In this context of the *demystification* of teaching, then, we need to look at one area in which knowledge and technical competence have developed within a tradition that has never lacked for respect: the form of specialised teaching for dyslexics known as *multisensory* teaching.[3] Is this categorically distinct from the ordinary teaching of literacy? If it is, why does such teaching seem to benefit non-special children? Though no doubt practice and experience informed by results ('feedback') contribute greatly to what are thought of as the *art* aspects of specialist, as of all, teaching, to what extent is the *craft* aspect – the tradition of techniques and lore – informed by, or at least compatible with, research?

These are questions that will accompany our examination of specialist dyslexia teaching. Though this chapter will attempt a brief survey of published materials and resources, such products may be of little use without an appropriate background of training and experience in specialised methods. To consider these, therefore, we need to look at three areas:

- curriculum design;
- analysis of communicative interactions (teaching methods);
- effective teaching.

Design of the work

Visitors to children's primary classrooms soon learn that there are two questions worth asking of any individual child. First, 'What is your work?' If a satisfactory answer can be given to this question, there is a second one: 'What is your next work?' Where children are able to specify what they are doing and what they expect to do, the chances are that some curriculum design has taken place and that it has been successfully communicated to at least some of the children in the class. Of course, this presupposes that whole-class teaching is not in progress. If it is not, as normally in Britain, then such an interrogation is not a breach of good manners towards the teacher. If it is, as normally in France, then the visitor can hardly engage individual children in conversation.[4]

Curriculum analysis and design – the objectification of the curriculum – has been the subject of the prolonged experiment of the National Curriculum in Britain, now reined in (Dearing, 1993a, 1993b). This has encouraged the view, as has the tactical positioning of government and teachers, that *what is to be taught* is fundamentally a separate matter from *how it is to be taught*. This is by no means an isolated view. Reviewing Somerville and Leach's (1988) evaluative study of a Direct Instruction programme, Pumfrey and Reason (1991) comment:

> The study does not make clear whether it is the direct instruction principles of teaching or the programme content that is responsible for the success. It can be argued that such a distinction is analogous to considering which constituent in a cocktail determines the cocktail's unique effect on taste-buds. (p. 120)

Yet whilst some parties to the successful teaching transaction, such as parents, may be merely pleased with the outcome, others will undoubtedly have a concern for the spectrum of taste. The Direct Instruction methodology, in any case, specifically relates the 'analysis of cognitive learning' to the three spheres of:

- within-child psychological variables (abilities and difficulties in learning);
- teaching communications;
- design of *the work*:

This explicit linking aims to redress the separation in more usual analyses. Successful learning does not just depend upon the individual's cognitive efficiency in learning, the traditional preoccupation of those concerned with dyslexia. It also depends upon the effective design and preparation of the *content* of the lesson, together with its unambiguous communication: effective teaching.

Though often marginalised as relevant only to early learning situations or to the teaching of basic skills, Direct Instruction principles represent an area within the professional domain of teaching in which experimental methods have made important, if initial, progress. It has done this by largely ignoring the rhetorical and philosophical issues which educators find so beguiling and instead concentrating upon what happens in the teaching interaction. The result, a large empirical literature that bears on the practical questions of instructional, including curriculum, design, is properly the subject for another book.[5] Here we will merely sample some of the main features that bear on the specialist teaching of dyslexic pupils.

General features of good curriculum design, though well accepted, are critical for dyslexics. Thus objectives should be carefully specified in realisable form, which is susceptible to evaluation of whether they have been achieved or not. Strategies, which may be learned informally by non-dyslexic pupils, must be devised and explicitly taught (e.g. *sounding out*). Presentation formats must be constructed ahead of time so that each skill is separately taught. Appropriate examples must be selected. Skills must be ordered in a teaching sequence. Opportunities for practice must be generously provided (Carnine et al., 1990).

The design of skills sequences is especially important in dyslexia teaching and is the reason such teaching is known as *cumulative*. There are five principles:[6]

1. Components of a strategy are taught before the strategy. For instance, before teaching the *silent* E or CVCe rule, names of vowels must be known.
2. Examples that support the rule must be taught before any exceptions (*take* before *done*).
3. More useful skills should be taught before less useful ones (*was* before *heir*, in the case of irregular words).
4. Easier proficiencies are taught before harder ones (easier-to-pronounce sounds, *a* and *m*, should appear before harder ones, *l* and *e*).
5. Elements likely to be confused should not be introduced together (*b* and *d*, *were* and *where*).

Research evidence tends to favour these principles of curriculum design. Initial readers who were taught a strategy (sounding-out) identified significantly more new regular and irregular words than did others who memorised the training words without the strategy (Carnine, 1977). Of two groups taught CVCe words, the group who received *discrimination* (*cap*, *sit*) as well as *introductory* examples (*cape*, *site*) identified significantly more new CVCe words on a post-test (Carnine and Kameenui, 1978). Explicit step-by-step strategies have been developed and field-tested for teaching pupils to:

•   draw inferences from reading scheme materials (Carnine, Kameenui and Woolfson, 1982);
•   solve arithmetical problems expressed in words (Darch, Carnine and Gersten, 1984);
•   learn basic legal concepts (Fielding, Kameenui and Gersten, 1983).[7]

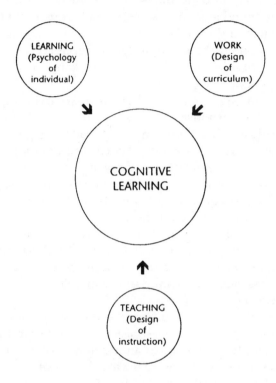

Figure 7.1: Equal influence upon learning of curriculum design, teaching technique and child's learning abilities. Source: after Engelmann and Carnine (1982, p. 1).

Practice in letter–sound correspondences to the point of *overlearning* or *mastery learning* enabled children to achieve 79% correct identifications, as opposed to the 28% achieved by another group who received only 50 practice trials (Carnine, 1976).

Techniques and methods of teaching

Pupils with difficulties learn best when teachers follow a consistent practice of demonstration, guided practice and feedback (Rosenshine and

Stevens, 1984). In addition, recent highlights in a mainly empirical literature[8] have been the establishment of the following principles:

- adult supervision contributes to pupil involvement; pupils working alone spend less time on task; small-group instruction is more efficient than individual instruction;
- active responding helps pupils learn; pupils accustomed to failure are reluctant to respond and are more likely to do so when others are responding;
- use of hand signals to elicit group responses improves pupil attention and response;
- the speed of teacher presentation (pacing) significantly affects pupils' attentiveness and rate of correct responding;
- where pupils' responses are actively monitored, their learning and application of new knowledge can be evaluated; this may include increased eye contact with pupils, walking round the room, displaying graphs of pupils' performance;
- instruction with correction of errors is more effective than without, especially when correction is immediate, accompanied by the right answer (not just the information about whether the pupil's answer was right or wrong) and responded to by the pupil, for instance by tallying errors;
- the use of praise significantly increases on-task studying behaviour, especially where praise is *precise* rather than vague and generalised; belittling and shaming of pupils and use of sarcasm are all associated with low-achieving classrooms;
- these various attributes of effective instruction also have a combined effect, one associated with a high level of implementation of such techniques; their combined effect can be measured in terms of on-task behaviour and correct responding;
- highly structured, direct teaching régimes also significantly increase enquiry skill, creativity and self-esteem.

Teaching effectiveness

As with schools effectiveness,[9] the study of what makes for effective teaching has burgeoned in recent years, to the point where influential reviews are beginning to make sense of a scattered literature. O'Neill (1988) in particular will be drawn upon in what follows.

The 20 most promising factors in effective teaching to have emerged from the many empirical studies that now cluster around these questions are addressed by O'Neill under three headings:

- the *preactive* phase refers to the planning and organisation that takes place before contact with the pupils;

- the *interactive* phase refers to the contact or active teaching phase;
- the *postactive* phase refers to the teacher's responses, though these are not, of course, separated in time but occur during active teaching.

The following is a summary of these variables and an indication of the findings:

Preactive

1. Learning environment (architecture, arrangement of space): pupils do better in traditional, self-contained settings.
2. Teacher knowledge (subject-matter specialisation): an important prerequisite to effective teaching – but this has received too little research attention.
3. Teacher organisation (materials, teaching strategies, pre-selected learning objectives, long-range planning, an instructional agenda implemented through each school day):'well-organised teachers are the most effective . . .'
4. Curricular materials (learning resources interesting, varied, geared to the right level): some pupil choice recommended , 'seat-work' should not be abused – mere busywork.

Interactive

5. Teacher expectations (achievement demands on individual pupils by the teacher, the conveying of explicit performance standards): this has 'immense impact on a child's academic record' if expectations are realistic but high achievers are frequently given more attention.
6. Teacher enthusiasm (contact with the teacher is 'energising'): there are consistent positive associations between teacher enthusiasm and pupil achievement.
7. Classroom climate (global attitudes, interpersonal ethos): an effective climate is 'supportive', 'warm', 'pleasant', 'fair', 'democratic', 'personal', 'congenial' and 'understanding'.
8. Classroom management (maintenance of work-habits and routines): well-managed classrooms are strong determiners of pupil learning; the teacher is in control, pupil responsibilities are emphasised, there is a minimum of disruption, problems are nipped in the bud, transitions are smooth.
9. Teacher clarity (few vagueness terms ['uh'], false starts, word tangles; instead there is emphasis on content and clear transitions): there is a positive relationship with pupil achievement, especially in maths and science.
10. Advance organisers ('cognitive scaffolding' to bridge the gap to new material to be learned, for example by introductory

activities): advance organisers facilitate learning, retention and transfer in maths, sciences and social sciences.

11. Instructional mode (for example individual, small group, large group): whole-class instruction is favoured in maths and primary reading.

12. Questioning level (higher-order divergent versus lower-order convergent styles of questioning): there is either little difference or some support for a convergent style (knowledge, fact or product questions).

13. Direct instruction (teacher-directed instruction): that this is highly associated with increased learning gains among primary children is the 'almost universal conclusion of recent research'.

14. Time on task (academic learning time): the amount of time spent on a task powerfully predicts pupil achievement.

15. Variability (diversity of teaching behaviours between expository, discovery and experimental formats): this is not well researched.

16. Monitoring and pacing (momentum of any particular lesson, as determined through checking of pupils' work): effective teachers continually monitor learning experiences and adjust the pace (generally rapid, brisk).

17. Teacher flexibility (ability to meet the demands of the moment): there is too little research to support this.

Postactive

18. Feedback (simple impartial teacher response to pupil success or failure): this is most effective if it is regular, systematic, immediate, prompt, specific and clear, corrective and academically focused.

19. Teacher praise (specific detailed information about the value of a pupil's behaviour): praise has to relate to the topic under consideration, be genuine and credible and judiciously used (it seems to be less effective with high-SES,[10] high-ability pupils).

20. Teacher criticism (negative personal response, going beyond mere feedback): this has a consistent negative correlation with achievement (shouting, shaming, sarcasm, ridicule), especially with low-SES, low-ability pupils; infrequent but justified criticism helps high-SES, high-ability pupils in primary education.

Some curriculum specifics

There is no question, then, that the techniques of effective teaching can be taught and learned. No necessity for a special or charismatic personality is claimed but a penchant for self-discipline does not go amiss. Professionalism is as daunting a path for the teacher as for any other professional.

Particular training options exist for the would-be specialist teacher, such as, in Britain, the Dyslexia Institute Postgraduate Diploma with

Kingston University, the Royal Society of Arts Diploma, the Hornsby and Helen Arkell Diplomas and other related qualifications. Increasingly these courses of training are winning the respect and interest of a formerly sceptical and hostile world; some now yield academically recognised credits towards higher degrees.

In the main, dyslexia training courses employ the principles of structure, organisation and planning enunciated. In addition, however, they rightly concentrate on the cognitive characteristics of dyslexic pupils, and what contemporary science can tell us about them, as well as how they may best be assessed and provided for.

It remains to review some of the more useful curricular resources available for both teacher and parent to use. Of course a knowledgeable teacher will supplement or even supplant such commercially available materials, often preferring custom-built alternatives, just as a parent with the confidence of pragmatic instinct will know what is working, or not, with her or his particular child. In all that follows prior knowledge is assumed to be beneficial rather than harmful. However, one does not wish to erect a professional barrier round anything that is not altogether arcane and about which common sense might reasonably hold an opinion. This is especially true for the novice or inexperienced teacher, who wishes to develop skills without discouragement from those who already have them.

Accordingly, let us now visit in turn some of the major categories of interest to teachers of dyslexic individuals. Descriptions will be given of some of the principal methods and resources that have been found helpful in the special education of the learning-impaired child.

Motor and fine motor control

The learning-impaired child may benefit from some activities to develop motor control and motor planning, as research indicates that this can be boosted in the early years. Two books may be recommended for this purpose:

Russell, JP (1988) Graded Activities for Children with Motor Difficulties. Cambridge: Cambridge University Press;
Nash-Wortham M, Hunt, J (1990) Take Time. 2nd edn. Stourbridge, W. Midlands: Robinswood Press.

In addition, there are, in the classroom situation, many organised games and activities that are designed to promote the movement skills of children with co-ordination problems. These are described in detail in:

Brown A (1987) Active Games For Children With Movement Problems. London: Paul Chapman.

Handwriting

Much useful guidance on handwriting is to be found in the recent publications by Rosemary Sassoon and Jean Alston. Cursive writing, between four lines, with approach-strokes and open *p*s and *b*s, and loops below but not above the line, is very advantageous and can be taught early: as well as in word recognition there are gains in attention-control, phonic awareness and learning of spelling sequences. A movement skill is more easily acquired than any other and provides a kinaesthetic anchor for the literacy skills.

Handwriting (as well as most aspects of literacy and spelling: see next section) is well dealt with in one of the series of eight books called *Teaching Reading Through Spelling* (the Kingston Programme) by Mary Prince, Lucy Cowdery, Paula Morse and Sally Low, available from Frondeg Hall Technical Publishing, Aberoer, Wrexham, Clwyd LL14 4LG, 1992. Spelling, a principal cause of aversion to writing, is dealt with separately below – and further under 'spelling checkers' and 'group interventions'.

Writing is sometimes a problem independent of spelling. A separation of composition from execution aspects of writing makes sense and is in line with multisensory principles. The mechanical aspects of writing can in turn be disaggregated into finite, manageable tasks. Sets of three words can be given for which the pupil must compose short sentences. Later the instruction may be varied to composing sentences *with a comma in the middle*. These tasks can be timed and reducing times recorded to aid motivation.

In relation to *letter-formation*, the lowest – foundation – level in the cumulation of writing skills, a publication of interest is Melvyn Ramsden's *Putting Pen To Paper: A New Approach To Handwriting*, which combines a scholarly integration of the several aspects of literacy with many practical ideas for teaching. It is published by Southgate Publishers, Glebe House, Church Street, Crediton, Devon EX17 2AF. (Ramsden's companion volume on spelling is discussed below.)

Further details of some of these publications are:

Alston J (1993) Assessing And Promoting Writing Skills. Stafford: NASEN.
Sassoon RA (1983) Practical Guide To Children's Handwriting. London: Thames & Hudson.
Sassoon RA (1990) Handwriting: A New Perspective. London: Stanley Thornes.
Ramsden M (1992) Putting Pen To Paper. Crediton, Devon: Southgate.

Teaching of literacy: general

Structured multisensory teaching aims to develop simultaneous skills in reading, writing and spelling so as to enhance effective recall in their use. Image, sound, movement memory (sky-writing) and touch are all employed to establish the sounds and shapes of letters, syllables and words. The most elaborate development of this specialist teaching programme is contained in: Walker J, Brooks L et al. (1993). Dyslexia Institute Literacy Programme. 2 vols. Staines, Middlesex: Dyslexia Institute.

The published programme, however, is supplied only as courseware to teachers qualifying in the Institute's specialist postgraduate diploma, validated by Kingston University.

The following titles represent a variety of approaches within a range of agreement as to the utility of this approach:

Augur J, Briggs S (Eds) (1992) The Hickey Multisensory Language Course, 2nd edn. London: Whurr Publishers.
Hornsby B, Shear F (1980) Alpha To Omega: The A–Z of Teaching Reading, Writing and Spelling. 3rd edn. London: Heinemann.
Thomson, ME, Watkins EJ (1992) Dyslexia: A Teaching Handbook. London: Whurr Publishers.
Miles E (1992) The Bangor Dyslexia Teaching System, 2nd edn. London: Whurr Publishers.

With all basic skills the learning-impaired child needs a carefully designed individual learning programme, structured in small steps – to permit success – through a sequence of specified objectives. Teaching should be given a little every day, avoiding too long intervals, and on an individual or pair basis. A reading programme, for instance, should start with a series of letter-sounds, learned in isolation, four at a time. Letters should not be vocalised (b = *buh*) but whispered. It is then much easier to blend, first, regular vowel–consonant words (*on, at, if*) and, then, consonant–vowel–consonant words (*but, can, dot*). Phonically irregular but high-frequency words (*one, water, friend*) can be added later when the child's grasp of the simple regularities is secure. About half the alphabet – 13 letters – generates by a factor of three around 39 regular two- and three-letter words. A child who can read 39 words is well and truly launched. In addition observation suggests that phonically taught children are far better spellers later.

Teaching of literacy: specific interventions

Letterland (author Lyn Wendon) is a particularly friendly and well-ordered system which integrates multisensory approaches to letter sounds, handwriting, spelling patterns and language enrichment. It is based on the motivating power of animation (the letters are characters) and the mnemonic power of stories (the letters interact in instructive ways). Children who normally have difficulty remembering things may have trouble forgetting *Letterland*. In addition *Letterland* emphasises the visual forms of letters which are important in the early stages of learning to read, when adults tend to overestimate the linguistic aspects of reading. Materials and catalogue are available from: Letterland Ltd, Barton, Cambridge, CB3 7AY. Tel: 01223 262675.

Letter Box is an inexpensive and useful aid in the early teaching of reading. Words and sentences, which the child can make up, are assembled and displayed from individual letters on cards. These are plastic and wear well. Little shelves provide a firm grip, making the *Letter Box* unlikely to spill if knocked over. Red vowels can be used for those which 'say their name' (*i* in *tiny*). *Letter Box* is obtainable from: Contour School Supplies, Forum House, Stirling Road, Chichester, PO19 2EH. Phone 01243 378305.

Few reading schemes reflect the early sequence of learning objectives structure by structure. If this were done, children would learn much more comprehensively and swiftly, and be free sooner of the necessity to read within a scheme at all. Only one such linguistically informed scheme has been produced, to my knowledge: Language In Action (Dr Joyce Morris). Though this is no longer in print, copies of some individual titles are available from Language In Action, Glenshee Lodge, 261 Trinity Road, London SW18 3SN. Three titles remain from Level 1, 6 from Level 2 and 7 from Level 3.

A well-researched arrangement of words for early readers is to be found in: *The Morris-Montessori Word List* (Dr Joyce Morris), London Montessori Centre Ltd, 18 Balderton Street, London W1Y 1TG. Tel: 0171 493 0165.

Building on a successful research project which demonstrated that teaching letters and words in conjunction with sounds achieves greater success than teaching either words or sounds (phonology) alone, Peter Hatcher's *Sound Linkage* introduces the learner to words and syllables and their phonemic constituents:

Hatcher PJ (1994) Sound Linkage: An Integrated Programme For Overcoming Reading Difficulties. London: Whurr Publishers.

A series of seven books, *Finger Phonics*, and a wall frieze from Jolly Learning, developed from Sue Lloyd's *Phonics Handbook* (see below), are highly suitable for the initial teaching of reading in a multisensory way. Similarly to the Dyslexia Institute Language Programme, a selection of six consonants and vowels is taught first with strong visual, tactile and auditory reinforcement. Other sounds and blends soon follow. A total of 42 letters and blends is covered, with more extensive word-lists in use by Book 7.

Lloyd S, Wernham S (1994) Finger Phonics, Books 1–7. Chigwell, Essex: Jolly Learning Ltd.

An introduction to written language which assumes nothing is Pippin Products' *My Reading And Spelling Box*. In the Pippin format of little cards in 22 sections of a box, this introduces the whole alphabet in lower-case letters, whose sounds are learned first (with pictures on the reverse of the cards), and shapes next (with arrow movement indicators). Regular CVC words come next, introducing one vowel at a time (in the order *a*, *o*, *i*, *e* and *u*).

During this stage the *look–cover–write–check* method adds a dimension of written spelling. The terms *vowels, consonants, syllable, digraph, hard, soft* support the rule-teaching that follows. Consonant digraphs arrive late in the day and, after affixing (*marries* in 19e is mistakenly referred to as a plural), written forms of capital letters come last. At this stage transfer to My English Box is within reach. The rationale is dependably phonic, though the accompanying guidance makes reference to 'several methods' and urges memory for the 'shapes' of words. Suitable for ages '4-Adult', the self-testing format allows for independent progress but the non-reader will need the instructions read out and explained. *My Reading And Spelling Box* is available from Pippin Products, Clifton, Shefford, Bedfordshire SG17 5ET. Tel: 01462 811485.

An enjoyably structured approach to many of the elements of formal written English is *My English Box*, also from Pippin Products at the above address. This too consists in sections of little cards, arranged in order to be self-monitoring, with questions on the front and answers on the back. There is guidance for adult supervision but as progress develops it can remain under the control of the learner.

Units of Sound is a structured, cumulative audiovisual reading, spelling and comprehension programme, for ages nine and above, developed within the Dyslexia Institute over 20 years. It is now offered as teaching materials (Stage 1, RA 5;6–8;0; Stage 2, RA 8;0–10;0; Stage 3, RA 10;0–12;6), with a 70-page teacher's manual and 10 hours of audio-cassette recordings at each stage. Ten-hour training courses for teachers in the use of these materials is provided nationwide; a case study, a practical assignment and private study are requirements.

Number skills teaching

Some useful sources for teachers on the teaching of number skills to the dyslexic learner are:

Ashlock RB, Johnson ML, Wilson JW, Jones WL (1983). Guiding Each Child's Learning Of Mathematics. A Diagnostic Approach To Instruction. Columbus, OH: Charles E. Merrill.
Chinn SJ, Ashcroft JR (1983) Mathematics For Dyslexics: A Teaching Handbook. London: Whurr Publishers
Chinn SJ (1996) What To Do When You Can't Learn The Times Tables.

Mark College, Highbridge, Somerset: MarkCo Publishing.

El-Naggar O (1996) Specific Learning Difficulties in Mathematics – a Classroom Approach. Amington, Tamworth, Staffs: NASEN Publications.

Henderson A (1989) Maths And Dyslexics. Llandudno: St David's College.

Hughes M (1986) Children And Number – Difficulties In Learning Mathematics. Oxford: Blackwell.

Miles TR, Miles E (Eds) (1992) Dyslexia And Mathematics. London: Routledge.

Thomson, M.E. (1991). Mathematics and dyslexia. In Durkin K, Shire B (Eds) Language In Mathematical Education: Research And Practice. Milton Keynes: Open University Press.

Number concepts are also a matter of verbal labels for sets or numerals and should not be neglected in favour of literacy skills. In addition to *My English Box*, Pippin Products now offer *My Maths Box* from 41 Church Street, Shefford, Bedfordshire SG17 5ET. Tel: 01462 811485.

The frequent experience of dyslexics is that no alternative method for memorising times tables is effective for long. But one such alternative, using visual and story cues, is:

McDougall S (1990) Table Time: The Exciting New Way To Learn Multiplication Tables. London: Harrap.

Then:

Chinn SJ (1996) What To Do When You Can't Learn The Times Tables. Mark College, Highbridge, Somerset TA9 4NP: MarkCo Publishing.

This is a shorter, more focused version for parents and teachers of Chinn SJ, Ashcroft JR (1993) *Mathematics For Dyslexics: A Teaching Handbook*. London: Whurr Publishers. Further, a 90-minute *'Video Class Times Tables* that uses rap, rock'n'roll and singing and dancing to make learning tables easy and fun' is advertised by Innovations (Tel: 01793 514666). A well produced pack, *My Tables Box*, is available from Pippin Products, Clifton, Shefford, Bedfordshire SG17 5ET. Tel: 01462 811485. This enables each product (e.g. 7 x 9) to be presented one at a time with the answer on the reverse; a set for each table is supplied on cards also, with divisions on the back. This does not, however, present any new teaching method, merely attractive materials for conventional learning. Finally, a *Musical Times Tables* tape, in which the learning of tables is enhanced by another medium – music, is sold in Early Learning Centres. The 2 to 10 times tables are included, with counting multiples, in a form suitable for 5–8-year-olds at least.

For children stuck in the early, infant stages, there are two Direct Instruction offerings. Engelmann S, Carnine D (1992) *Connecting Math Concepts*. Chicago: Macmillan/McGraw-Hill (SRA), is available in the UK from Science Research Associates (address below). Level A (120 lessons) assumes only that children can count to 10 and can count nine objects. It reaches two-digit addition and subtraction. Level B adds another 120 lessons and takes in time, money, three-digit addition and subtraction with decomposition, some geometry and use of signs (> = <).

Distar Arithmetic II (Engelmann S, Carnine D (1976) *Distar Arithmetic II: An Instructional System*. Chicago: Macmillan/McGraw-Hill [SRA]) is also available in the UK from Science Research Associates (address below) and covers much the same ground. Any child who successfully completes the programme will be able to give the answer to 60 addition facts, 20 algebra-addition facts and 43 subtraction facts, without counting fingers or lines; solve a variety of fraction problems; solve negative-number problems; and solve many word problems using language such as *find, lose, get more, not small*. The 160 lessons take the child to counting in threes (3, 6, 9, 12) and counting backwards (19–5).

Further elaboration on the four functions is provided in: Engelmann S, Carnine D, Silbert J (1981) *Corrective Mathematics*. Chicago: Macmillan/McGraw-Hill [SRA]. There are about 60 lessons each in separate modules: Addition, Subtraction, Multiplication and Division. The work is suitable for pupils of secondary age and includes much practice at solving problems of various kinds expressed in words. This Direct Instruction programme too is available in the UK from Science Research Associates at McGraw-Hill Book Co Europe, Shoppenhangers Road, Maidenhead, Berks SL6 2QL. Tel: 01628 502518.

Spelling

With spelling, it is necessary to teach word-specific knowledge (*quiet, answer*), phonemic (*skillet, splashing*) and morphemic (*adherence, undesirable*) skills. *Spelling Mastery* (2nd edn, 1990, by Robert Dixon and Siegfried Engelmann) is organised in six levels, for children aged 6–11, and *morphographs* (meaningful units: bases and affixes) are introduced at the third level. Pupils are taught in homogeneous groups, following a simple placement test, and receive about 120 short (15–20 minutes) lessons a school year. The sheer multiplication effect – two bases and five affixes generate upward of 25 spellable words – makes this the only efficient way to teach English spelling. The aim of the programme is that pupils learn to make generalisations and the design ensures that knowledge is both regularly reviewed and transferred to

free writing. Like other DISTAR programmes, *Spelling Mastery* is
published by Science Research Associates (address above).

The *ACE (Aurally Coded English) Spelling Dictionary* is a valuable
aid; and there is now a book of photocopiable masters of spelling worksheets in which word meanings are linked to structural patterns:

Moseley D, Singleton G (1993) ACE [Aurally Coded English] Spelling
　　Activities For Use With ACE Spelling Dictionary. Cambridge, UK: LDA.

Recently published, too, is a new edition of the dictation exercises by
Margaret Peters, which many teachers have found useful, together with a
systematic account of methods of teaching spelling:

Peters M, Smith B (1993) *Spelling In Context: Strategies For Teachers
　　And Learners*. Windsor, Berkshire: NFER-Nelson.

Another recent resource for the teacher of spelling is Melvyn Ramsden's
Rescuing Spelling. This draws on the contribution that etymology makes
to word-forms and integrates, in a scholarly but readable way, the mutual
influences of phonology, orthography and morphology. It is published
by Southgate Publishers, Glebe House, Church Street, Crediton, Devon
EX17 2AF. (Ramsden's companion volume on handwriting is discussed
in that section above.)

Spelling checkers

The spelling checker is now as valuable and universal as the pocket
calculator – and of similar size. Children and adults with persistent
spelling difficulties report that the check-and-select process renews the
process of learning spelling. If a difficult word is looked up before writing, the resulting certainty about how it is spelled conveys increased
confidence towards the whole writing task. To make satisfactory use of
spelling checkers pupils need to be able to select the correctly spelled
word from a list of plausible alternatives.

For children and disabled learners Franklin now market the *Elementary Spellmaster*. This has a QWERTY capitals keyboard and performs an
ingenious phonic search. Spelling lists can be customised and games
played. For definitions each word is given a page reference to the *Oxford
Children's Dictionary*, which is included with the *Spellmaster*.
Franklin's Pocket Spellmaster, Credit Card Spellmaster and Wordmaster
are available from Innovations (Tel: 01793 514666). These and other
models are now available from W.H. Smith and high street office equipment shops, an advance on mail-order.

A word processor and spelling-checker specially designed for dyslexic learners, which can be adjusted to the individual's pattern of errors (visual sequencing, phonological) has been developed at Dundee University for IBM PC-compatible machines. PAL and PALSTAR can be ordered from Scetlander Ltd, 74 Victoria Crescent Road, Glasgow G12 9JN. Tel: 0141 357 1659.

The fast-changing use of information technology is a subject in its own right. However, three good programs may be mentioned:

- Northern Micromedia advertise a program, *The Complete Speller*, for all ages and all makes of micro in school use. It is graded in order of grapheme difficulty and cumulative in design. A game rewards accuracy and fluency. This is available from: Northern Micromedia Resources Centre, Coach Lane Campus, Coach Lane, Newcastle-upon-Tyne, NE7 7XA. Tel: 0191 270 0424.
- *Hi-Spell 1* is an ambitious series whose development continues. A suite of programs for the BBC micro, these come on five disks with a single manual, and comprise: *Keyboard Trainer* and *Letter Recognition, Word Maze* (short vowel program), *Sentence Pumper, Boxes* and *Word Scroller*. The series addresses multiple aspects of literacy and is distinguished by its ingenuity, attractive use of colour and use of high screen resolution. It is available from: Xavier Educational Software (Mr Lane), Psychology Department, University College of North Wales, Bangor, Gwynedd, LL57 2DG. Tel: 01248.351151, ext. 2616.
- *Word Attack Strategies* is a set of programs for the BBC Master and RM Nimbus micros which addresses 90 different features of words (in reading and spelling) through screen presentations of each phonic rule followed by a sentence completion task. It is available from Pholio Publications, 34 Essex Road, Standish, Wigan WN1 2TH.

An important extension of creative possibilities for dyslexics is Thinksheet by Richard Marriott of Fisher-Marriott Software, 3 Grove Road, Ansty, Coventry, Warwickshire. This enables a series of computer screens to receive, develop, link and organise concepts as keywords and phrases. (The process of composing sentences, which is where problems reside for dyslexics, is left to the end, when it can receive attention in its own right.) This useful piece of software exists in versions for all main types of machine.

Finally, typing is itself a most useful skill to learn young. Learning to touch-type can now be accomplished by tutorial software. There are many varieties of such software but a free-standing portable keyboard suitable for children is Type-right from Systema, of Video Technology

Hong Kong (HKVTEL; 1985), available from retail outlets. Lessons are organised in levels with games and there is immediate feedback. It may be helpful during practice to stick letters onto the child's fingernails.

Group teaching

Spelling Mastery, mentioned above, is a group intervention. For small groups of children left behind at an early stage in reading there is Direct Instruction: *Reading Mastery Fast Cycle I/II*, published by Science Research Associates (address above). Once bought, the programme may be reused, at small subsequent cost, with generations of children. The reading programme is sequenced, structured, phonic and highly effective: it is the best researched of all reading interventions. Groups of eight children receive daily sessions of no more than 20–30 minutes. If it is desired that learning-impaired children should received structured teaching in a small group, the DISTAR programmes are exemplary.

For small groups of secondary-aged pupils the equivalent programme is Direct Instruction: *Corrective Reading (Decoding A, B1, B2 and C)*, from the same publisher. Group intervention is an efficient use of resources and requires that children be grouped by attainment. Equating with the upper levels of *Spelling Mastery* is *Corrective Spelling Through Morphographs*, another member of the DISTAR (direct instruction) family of tightly structured and scripted interventions, developed from extensive field trials, and published by Science Research Associates (address above). Spelling is seen as a matter of word forms; patterns are learned as base units with affixing; and written English is treated as comprising morpho-phonemic, not just phonic, structures. The sequence of 140 lessons may be completed in one school year or less. Initially the student learns 12 morphographs (meaningful structural units), and from these can spell over 75 words. By mid-programme, after only 252 morphographs, the student can spell over 3000 words.

Higher reading skills

Dyslexics who have progressed successfully through a structured literacy programme may still have greater than expected difficulties mastering aspects of grammar, such as the compounding of words. They may also acquire a reading vocabulary more slowly than would be expected.

•   *Megawords* is a series that teaches compound words for reading and spelling. Word lists build sequentially on structural elements

(Johnson K, Bayrd P (1982-88) *Megawords* Books 1–8. Cambridge, MA: Educators Publishing Service Inc).

- *Wordly Wise* is a series of vocabulary-building workbooks from the same publisher and develops a precise use of word meanings (Hodkinson K, Ornato JG (n.d.) *Wordly Wise: Vocabulary Builder Workbooks For Grades 4–12*. Cambridge, MA: Educators Publishing Service Inc).

- *Reading Comprehension In Varied Subject Matter* by Jane Ervin improves upon the conventional comprehension exercise by highlighting main idea and facts, going beyond the facts, arranging statements in narrative or logical order and building up vocabulary through words and meanings. A thinking approach is combined with an emphasis on accurate reading and writers' styles are analysed (Ervin J (n.d.) *Reading Comprehension In Varied Subject Matter*. Cambridge, MA: Educators Publishing Service Inc).

- *Find The Missing Word* by Hilda King similarly aims to develop a grasp of grammar through practice of parts of speech. Published by Hilda King Education Services, these and similar materials may be obtained through Better Books and Software, 3 Paganel Drive, Dudley, West Midlands DY1 4AZ. Tel: 01384 254276.

Thinking skills teaching

It is possible that learning and thinking skills can be addressed directly by teaching. An approach such as that of Feuerstein's *Instrumental Enrichment* or the *Somerset Thinking Skills* may well be helpful. The latter can be purchased from Simon & Schuster Customer Services Division, Campus 400, Maylands Avenue, Hemel Hempstead, Herts HP2 7EZ. Tel: 01442 882211. These materials are ready for the teacher to use, but training is advisable. Nigel Blagg Associates (Tel: 01823 336204) conduct regular courses.

Resources for students and young adults

An effective framework for teaching spelling and writing to students and adults is *A Resource Pack For Tutors Of Students With Specific Learning Difficulties* by Marion Walker and may be obtained from the author at 14 Weston Close, Dorridge, Solihull, West Midlands B93 8BL, UK. In addition, many useful suggestions and resources for literacy in adult and later school life are contained in:

Bramley W (1993) Developing Literacy For Study And Work. Staines, Middlesex: Dyslexia Institute (ISBN 0 9503915 5 7).

A pioneering work that holds its place is:

Klein C (1993) Diagnosing Dyslexia: A Guide To The Assessment Of Adults With Specific Learning Difficulties. London: Adult Literacy and Basic Skills Unit.

Managing interpersonal skills

The best aid to social development and adjustment in the learning impaired child is the experience of mastery of essential skills; the worst experience is that of persistent failure. The complex development and management of social and interpersonal skills are well described in several books:

Kronick D (1981) Social Development Of Learning Disabled Persons. San Francisco: Jossey-Bass.
Osman BB (1982) No One To Play With: The Social Side of Learning Disabilities. Novato, CA: Academic Therapy Publications.
Silver LB (n.d.) The Misunderstood Child: A Guide For Parents of Learning Disabled Children. New York: McGraw Hill.

Home learning programmes for parents

There are now at least six helpful, phonic-based programmes of initial reading instruction which can be used by parents:

- A comprehensive home teaching programme of reading instruction, based on Direct Instruction, a method whose effectiveness is renowned in world research, is: Engelmann S, Haddox P, Bruner E (1983) *Teach Your Child To Read In 100 Easy Lessons*. London: Simon & Schuster.
- A basic 91-day programme suitable for parents who want to teach their child to read using a phonic method is contained in *Step By Step* by Mona McNee, available from the author at: 2 Keats Avenue, Whiston, Merseyside L35 2XR.
- More comprehensive is *Alpha-Phonics: A Primer For Beginning Readers* by Samuel L Blumenfeld (1983; reprinted February 1991), available from The Paradigm Company, Box 45161, Boise, Idaho 83711, USA. Tel 00 208 322 4440

Recently published, too, are:

- Sue Lloyd's *Phonics Handbook*, available from Jolly Learning Ltd, Tailours House, High Road, Chigwell, Essex IG7 6DL;
- Annis Garfield's (1992) *Teach Your Child To Read*. London: Vermilion. The latter combines letter teaching, word families, graded animal stories and traditional nursery rhymes.
- The very successful Butterfly Project, by means of which 93 unselected retarded readers from north London made on average a year of gain in reading age in three weeks, has been published as *The Butterfly Book: A Reading And Writing Course* by Irina Tyk, Butterfly Books, 55 Elmfield Road, Potters Bar, Herts EN6 2JL, ISBN 0 9521410 0 0.

For those who learn more easily from video, and who do not mind a genial Australian style of presentation, there are series of easily understood videocassetes and booklets for *English Made Easy* and *Maths Made Easy*. English comes in five levels, ranging from punctuation and parts of speech to essay writing; spelling is taught at all levels. Maths comes in five levels, but with 5–7 volumes at each level, ranging from addition and subtraction to circle geometry and calculus. The programme includes teacher assessment and support, including by telephone. The Home Study Video series originates from Gosford, New South Wales, and is distributed by the Student Support Centre (UK) Ltd, 46 Church Avenue, Beckenham, Kent BR3 1DT. Tel: 0181 289 9504. Fax: 0181 289 9506.

Notes

1 See Wooldridge (1994, Ch. 3).
2 Or, like spelling, 'caught': see Peters (1985). Such examples of mysticism, once popular in teacher training, already have a period flavour.
3 The only serious alternative to multisensory teaching for dyslexics deliberately styles itself unisensory teaching. This entails the linking of morphemic elements in written words with mnemonic icons. To date it is described only in Brown (1990).
4 In Britain, the progressive education movement has gone much further than in the USA or other European countries. Overseas visitors are regularly surprised by the *laissez-faire* regime in our primary classrooms. Apparently without the help of costly social experiments they are able to see that choice and discovery spell the end of real education; the pain and pleasure principles see to that. Only through being compelled to learn what is valuable but difficult, and relinquish what is frivolous but gratifying, do ordinary hedonists achieve anything worthwhile.
5 A separate working, if necessarily incomplete, bibliography of the Direct Instruction literature is given in Appendix 2.

6   After Carnine, Silbert and Kameenui (1990, pp. 14–15).
7   All these examples entail application of Direct Instruction principles to domains where the skills to be learned are far from basic.
8   Conveniently summarised by Craig Darch in Ch. 3 of Carnine, Silbert and Kameenui (1990), where full references may be found.
9   See, for example, Chubb and Moe (1990).
10 Socioeconomic status.

Chapter 8
Analysis of a casework sample

The scope of independence

We have now followed the process of the psychological assessment of dyslexia from its logical beginnings in a changing theoretical context, through methodology and test repertoire, by way of reporting format to recommendations for specialist teaching. Given the empirical emphasis so far, perhaps we may now ask what *actual characteristics* are shown by the population of those children of school age[1] who seek such an assessment.

The Dyslexia Institute is a national charity established in 1972 to develop and provide professional services in the cause of dyslexia. So successfully has it grown in 24 years that more than 200 teachers a year now acquire its postgraduate diploma in dyslexia studies, the premier UK specialist teaching qualification. About 3000 children and adults at any time receive individual specialist teaching in 23 centres and 120 outposts throughout Britain. Upwards of 6000 individuals a year are provided with individual psychological assessments which, since January 1995, have been quality controlled according to published criteria.

Assuming a school-age population in Britain of about 6.5 million and a (modest) incidence rate of 3.5%, does it follow that nearly a third of *all* dyslexic children in Britain are seeking and receiving an independent consultation and paying a fee to a charity unsupported by government money? This extraordinary possibility is eloquent testimony to the negative outlook on dyslexia that has prevailed in local education authorities. However, the figures do not bear quite this interpretation, as we shall see, because as many as a third[2] of those seeking an independent psychological assessment do not, in fact, meet the principal criterion for dyslexia, though they may have other problems and virtually always have *some* learning difficulty. A few families travel from overseas to seek such a psychological assessment; others return for a review of progress. Nevertheless a massive share of SEN services, supposedly secured free of charge by statute for those who need them, is being provided by the families of those concerned at their own expense. Dyslexia, let it be remembered, is probably the largest single category of special educational need, the commonest and best defined *specific learning difficulty*.

The clinical sample

Since January 1993, I have systematically collected psychometric data on *all* individuals assessed by me at the Dyslexia Institute using the Differential Ability Scales (DAS), some 100 cases each year. Because of the especially high quality of the DAS data, the accumulation is of considerable interest. No large clinical dataset in this field has been examined since Miles's pioneering *Dyslexia: The Pattern Of Difficulties*, now in its second edition (Miles, 1993). The size of the collection enables us to ask, and answer, some questions of general interest and broad implications.

This is, however, a *clinical* population and one self-selected both by ability to pay and by the particular reputation and expertise of the Institute. In recent years the Institute's specialised assessment has increasingly done duty as a *general purpose cognitive assessment*, as more clients have sought an opinion on a wide range of presenting problems. Modest personality and vocational components have been added to the basic assessment at the request of some. Though sociological data[3] have not been sought or collected, the aggregate IQ of children thus assessed has long hovered around the 100 mark, suggesting that in this respect at least there is nothing to distinguish them from a random sample. However, it is my impression, though one which cannot be convincingly supported, that there are fewer non-intact families than would be expected. It perhaps requires some level of determination and coherence to take and sustain independent action, beginning with the psychological assessment, on behalf of a child with suspected learning difficulties. This is easier for those with stable marriages than for those who experience divorce or remarriage.

Basic dimensions

Initially the dataset consists in 298 individuals whose mean age at assessment is 11.20 decimal years (SD 3.5) and whose mean GCA (IQ) is 103.2 (SD 15.9). Of these children, 65 are girls, some 28%. This accords with the ratios of 3–5:1 in favour of boys that are commonly reported. The average age seems surprisingly high; we shall look shortly at the distribution of ages.

Are all these children dyslexic? By no means. The two main criteria, already discussed, are:

•   discrepancy between general ability and attainment in one or more area of basic skill (reading, spelling, number);

- positive signs of difficulty in information-processing (immediate verbal memory, speed of processing).

These can be applied to the entire collection so as to differentiate dyslexics from non-dyslexics (those who do not meet *both* main criteria) and to illustrate degrees of severity among the dyslexics. First, however, they must be operationalised.

The easier and more usual way of applying a discrepancy criterion is to calculate sheer psychometric distance between the measure of ability (for instance GCA) and of attainment (for instance, reading), the method of so-called simple difference. As already discussed in Chapter 3, however, this method is unfair with regard to children of lower ability, as at least half of the children in the present dataset would have to be described. Accordingly the full regression method is applied to all children in the set, as it has been already in each individual assessment, the parent consultation that followed, and the detailed report written at the time. The distance is calculated between the *expected* and *observed* attainment scores (Basic Number Skills, Spelling, Word Reading) in each case where the relevant test has been given.[4] Taking GCA or IQ as the principal index of psychometric intelligence or general conceptual ability, and the *average of all three* discrepancy values as the general index of achievement, the dataset is ranked according to underachievement, operationalised in this way.

This gives an index, expressed in Ds or standard deviation units, of discrepancy between general ability and general achievement. Figure 8.1 shows the results of this exercise. It will be observed that the distribution of underachievement approximates to the normal, though the cases are far from being a random sample. Moreover in this analysis fully a third of the children in the dataset are *not* significantly underachieving.

Seven degrees of underachievement

One possibility that arises from this analysis is the quantification of degrees of severity of underachievement. There appear to be seven degrees of underachievement, corresponding to the degrees, quantified in half-SD units, to which the criterion of general underachievement applies. Table 8.1 gives the expectations, for each of these categories, of their occurrence in the population as a whole.

Table 8.1: General underachievement in class intervals showing observed frequencies in sample and expected frequencies in population

SD units	0.0:0.4	0.5:0.9	1.0:1.4	1.5:1.9	2.0:2.4	>2.5
Frequencies	48	71	62	27	33	9
% of sample	16.4	24.3	21.2	9.2	11.3	3.1
Expected frequency in population (%)	>25	10–25	5–10	1–5	<1	<<1

Frequencies of underachieving children by class intervals

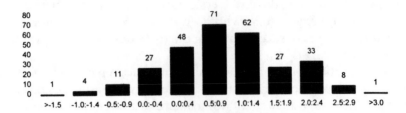

Degrees of over- and under-achievement: Standard deviation units (Ds)

Figure 8.1: 298 children are ranked by degree of underachievement (average of expected minus observed scores in number, spelling, reading) in relation to general ability by half-SD units. Negative values indicate over-achievement.

Applying a literacy-only criterion

But this analysis is of *general* under-achievement. Arithmetical skills have been included in the description of each child's learning difficulty. One feature of this dataset is the general poverty of written calculation skills in the children, quite as bad as spelling skills. Whilst this procedure reveals a degree of retardation in all basic skills, it differs in important respects from the narrower, more powerful definition of dyslexia as primarily affecting literacy skills. Verbal sequences and routines dominate the early, arithmetical stages of mathematical learning. Some individuals' excellent number skills contrast sharply with their poor literacy skills. Correspondingly, some children show a particular focus of difficulty in the learning of number work, whilst their literacy skills, effectively remediated perhaps, are much less problematic. The discrepancy of fully 17% of pupils in the dataset changes by 0.5 SD points or more if number skills are left out of account and the narrower definition is adopted.

Figure 8.2 shows the same exercise repeated for all children in the set, but this time a criterion of retardation in reading and spelling, averaged together, is applied. Now a less normal distribution appears. Those children overachieving to any extent are many fewer. The majority clearly have difficulties specifically with literacy skills; the written number skills were a confounding element. Severity increases continuously from a highly populated middle ground of not-very-exceptional literacy retardation. After literacy skills fall about one standard deviation below expectation, dyslexia seems to become a more particular matter.

This is important theoretically as a severity continuum may make unnecessary such categorical accounts of reading acquisition as dual-route theory (Snowling, 1994). The search for further dyslexia genes, too, continues after discovery of the first (Cardon et al., 1994) since more genes are needed to code for the often-observed phenomenon of differing degrees of severity.

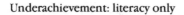
Underachievement: literacy only

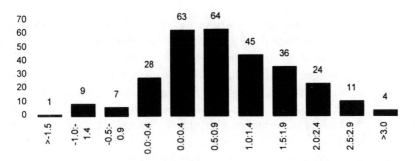

Degrees of over- and under-achievement: Standard deviation units (Ds)

Figure 8.2: 292 children are ranked by degree of underachievement in literacy (average of expected minus observed scores in spelling and reading) in relation to general ability by half-SD units. Negative values indicate overachievement

Seven degrees of dyslexia

The first four columns in the bar chart may be discarded from further analysis. Overachievement takes the individuals concerned beyond the reach of this description of dyslexia, though clinically there may be valid reasons for concern. The difficulties of younger children are not adequately identified by this regression approach, skilled teaching can bring literacy scores back into line with expectations, a strong family heredity may produce cognitive deficits without underachievement, and so on.

Repeating the analysis in terms of class-intervals, we can see that there are seven degrees of dyslexia, now acceptably distinct from general underachievement. Table 8.2 gives the class intervals, frequencies, percentages in the sample and expected frequencies in the population.

Table 8.2: Literacy underachievement in class intervals showing observed frequencies in sample and expected frequencies in population

SD units	0.0:0.4	0.5:0.9	1.0:1.4	1.5:1.9	2.0:2.4	2.5:2.9	>3.0
Frequencies	63	64	45	36	24	11	4
% of sample	21.6	21.9	15.4	12.3	8.2	3.8	1.4
Expected frequency in population (%)	>25	10–25	5–10	1–5	<1	<<1	<<<1

These data selected according to a literacy criterion make better sense of why these children were referred for an assessment in the first place. Although only six more children are described by a 1.5 SD cut-off, the gradient of severity seems much plainer.

Qualitative descriptions

Literacy failure is common enough, sadly, and of the seven degrees thus described only that found in 5% or fewer of the population can be unequivocally classified as dyslexic. From those in three of the seven categories, therefore, the dyslexia label, using the normally conservative criteria, is withheld. Such a cautious approach to diagnosing dyslexia has brought credibility to the dyslexia movement over 25 years. However, such classification is ultimately an arbitrary process, though sometimes one with major administrative implications, and other considerations, notably those of cognitive profiling, enter into the picture.

0.0 to 0.4 SDs	Clinically the first of these seven degrees might be denied the appellation *dyslexic*, as this level of literacy under-achievement is commonly found in the general population. Such a discrepancy already established in a young child (6–7 years) would be taken as a warning feature, however. Parents and teachers of children with this degree of retardation will not in any case want to wait for a clinical category: this is distinctly on the low side and progress will be sought through focused teaching.
0.5 to 0.9 SDs	This now approaches a more serious degree of literacy retardation though still without being very exceptional: perhaps 15–25% of individuals show just such a discrepancy between ability and literacy achievement.
1.0 to 1.4 SDs	From 1.0 SD onwards we are looking within the most extreme 5–10% of the child population. These are the children the reality of whose problems is least likely to be argued about. However, unless there are cognitive or case history features to implicate dyslexia, the causes may be ones other than dyslexia.
1.5 to 1.9 SDs	Few would argue that the literacy problems within the extreme 1–5% of the spectrum are severe and complex. Together with the distinctive profile of phonological and memory impairments they implicate dyslexia, a specific learning difficulty.
2.0 to 2.4 SDs	Sometimes in older pupils, especially those untreated and those diagnosed late, there is a tendency for the

achievement gap to widen with the years, thus providing members of a more extreme category; others are simply severely dyslexic to begin with.

2.5 to 2.9 SDs   A more extreme category still. Such children show only disappointing progress after the investment of much teaching effort. Separate specialist provision, especially in the secondary years, is always a serious consideration.

3.0 SDs or above   Though only 1–2% of even a highly selected, clinical sample, these most extreme individuals of all need equally extreme efforts in planning and resourceful teaching. Because the main effects of dyslexia are seldom much mitigated even so, the transition to adult life and to the economic sphere are as pressing a consideration, as their parents realise early, as any during the school years.

Collective characteristics of dyslexics

These, then, are the degrees of literacy learning difficulty with which children are referred to the Dyslexia Institute. To be as inclusive as possible, however, and to maintain numbers and variety, we shall apply only a mild definition of dyslexia to the pupils in this dataset: that of being at least 0.5 SD below expectation in reading and spelling. This reduces the dataset by a third and leaves only children with pronounced problems in literacy, many of whom meet stringent criteria for dyslexia. The average age has shifted upwards slightly to 11.95 decimal years but the average IQ has moved downwards to 102.8.[5]

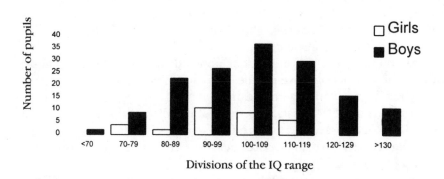

Figure 8.3: Numbers of boys and girls in literacy-retarded subset by IQ.

Figure 8.3 shows the new distribution by sex and also by IQ band. The boys are apparently normally distributed across IQ levels, including extremes of high and low. The girls, on the other hand, though fewer, tend, as one would expect, to be less extreme but also to cluster about a lower overall IQ level of 98.4. Perhaps to be referred for an assessment a dyslexic girl must show additional, more general learning problems, just as boys of low IQ are more likely to be selected for special education if their behaviour, too, is a problem. Table 8.3 gives the corresponding information in tabular form.

Table 8.3: Numbers of boys and girls in 10-point categories of IQ

IQ BAND	<70	70–79	80–89	90–99	100–109	110–119	120–129	>130	Totals
SEX									
Girls	0	4	2	11	9	6	0	0	32
Boys	2	9	23	27	37	30	16	11	155
All	2	13	25	38	46	36	16	11	187

Diagnostic profile features

So far we have been considering literacy under-achievement on its own, as perhaps, with all its imperfections, the major criterion for dyslexia. However, there is a second diagnostic determinant: that of anomaly in cognitive processing, observed by means of the cognitive profile. As we saw in Chapter 4, this is the scientifically more interesting realm where description ventures into explanation. Profile information, however, has not thus far been isolated sufficiently well to serve reliably as sole criterion, which ideally it should be able to do. Nor are characteristic dyslexic features always shown by the individuals who ought to show them. A multitude of constraining factors intervene – compensatory strategies, effort, effects of tuition and so on. Dyslexia diagnosis in this area is still a matter of *average* shortfalls across numerous tests thought to have diagnostic significance.

What, then, do the children in our now reduced and selected dataset show in the way of cognitive profiles? An idea of how these 187 children look when aggregated together can be seen in Figure 8.4. All six core and four diagnostic DAS tests, together with Coding and Digit Span from WISC-III, are expressed in z or standard score form, with values above 0 indicating scores above, and scores below 0 below, the population mean for the age-group.

There are many features here of interest. First, though all the dyslexic[6] pupils are, in the main, of average ability this is not evenly distributed across factors. Verbal and spatial factors[7] tend to be better

Dyslexics' group profile on DAS cognitive tests (with Ns)

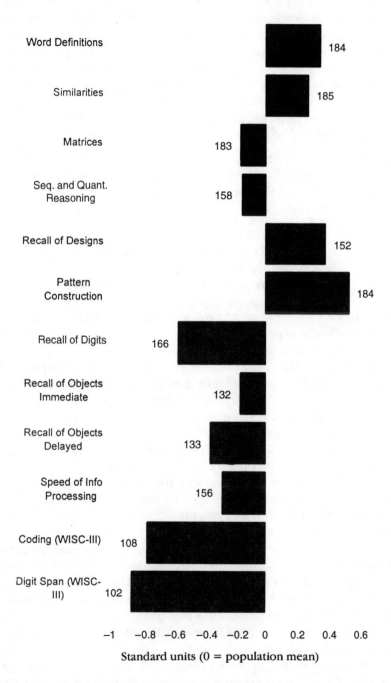

Figure 8.4: Group means (with varying Ns) of dyslexic subset on six core and six diagnostic tests.

than average but non-verbal reasoning, discussed at length in Chapter 3, is clearly an area of weakness.

Throughout the history of the development of psychometric tests, the nemesis of test developers' much criticised empiricism, or freedom from theory, has been the tendency of the tests to develop a life of their own and behave in an unexplained diagnostic fashion! This was especially true of Coding and Digit Span from the WISC. Could it be the same for Matrices in the BAS/DAS, a test which, on the face of it, is no more than an innocuous yearling from the stable of Progressive Matrices? However, the association with Sequential and Quantitative Reasoning (SQR) is clear: the *control of sequential schemata*[8] or quantitative ability itself (see Chapter 3) or the

> ability dynamically to manage a large set of problem-solving goals in working memory (Carpenter, Just and Shell, 1990, p. 404; cited in Carroll, 1993, p. 696)

or (finally) some frontal-lobe-like planning and set-maintenance function is consistently proving a weak point with a large number of dyslexics. An intelligence-measuring test is behaving, in part, like a diagnostic test.[9] Moreover its pair in the non-verbal reasoning cluster, Sequential and Quantitative Reasoning, proves to have a persistent relationship in factor analyses with the WISC Arithmetic subtest, which, in turn, is notorious for measuring verbal memory better than it does number concept.

Turning to the diagnostic tests, four from the DAS and two supplementaries from WISC-III, we find, first, that all six are depressed. The least 'diagnostic' (the one dyslexics are best at) is Recall of Objects Immediate but this, as we shall see in Chapter 10, is much the most powerful diagnostic test for children younger than six. The present population is on average aged 11–12. The Delayed version of the test, which requires consolidation of verbal information in intermediate-term memory, is found more difficult by these children.

Speed of Information Processing has been independently found to have high convergent and divergent validity and to measure *speed of apprehension* (RT) well and *movement time* (MT) not at all (Buckhalt and Jensen, 1989). Collectively the dyslexic children in the present data set do not have major difficulties with it. But there is some evidence that the test is a good indicator of severity of dyslexia. When criteria of severity are adopted, children with greater difficulties are more likely to perform poorly on this test, which begins to show an unexpected relationship with spelling (Rack, 1995).

Recall of Digits, not unexpectedly, is a strong indicator of dyslexics' characteristic difficulty with immediate verbal memory. Indeed some sort of distance test between Pattern Construction (block design) and Recall of Digits might serve as a quick discrepancy indicator. The test, discussed in Chapter 4, functions in an unambiguous way, with digits presented at half-second intervals to be repeated forwards only. Digit span tests are beloved of designers of psychometric test batteries, not least because of their high reliability.

But the two subtests from WISC-III are by far the best indicators in this collection and are included as supplementary tests for just that reason. Coding, though a poor measure of *g* and an ambiguous mixture of hand–eye co-ordination, mental and motor speed, memory and verbalisation, seems perhaps for this very reason to press against dyslexics' processing difficulties at many points.

Digit Span (WISC-III) remains the most powerful dyslexia indicator of all. Theories about this abound and received some discussion in Chapter 4. It seems to this one observer that decay time of the slower administration may have more to do with this than the challenge of repeating digits backwards.

The two WISC subtests, however, do not register as difficult for dyslexics solely for cognitive reasons. The Wechsler 19-point scale is comparatively rigid,[10] with each score split within its own distribution. Thus if pupils score at about half a standard deviation below the population mean, as they typically do on Recall of Digits, they obtain a WISC scaled score of 8, though this should be about half way between 8 and 9.

Intercorrelation of core, diagnostic and attainment tests[11]

Table 8.4 shows the values reached by performing an intercorrelation analysis on all six core, four diagnostic and three DAS attainment tests, with age included as a further variable.

Table 8.4: Intercorrelation matrix of 183 pupils on age, six core, four diagnostic and three achievement tests from school-age DAS; decimal points omitted. For abbreviations, see Appendix 1

	AGE	WDef	SIM	MAT	SQR	RDes	PCon	RDig	ROI	ROD	SIP
AGE	1										
WDef	27	1									
SIM	31	66	1								
MAT	29	54	49	1							
SQR	32	59	58	66	1						
RDes	36	45	47	48	47	1					
PCon	33	39	40	52	61	52	1				
RDig	36	43	44	28	41	31	25	1			
ROI	28	31	30	21	33	39	28	38	1		
ROD	32	26	26	22	27	38	26	38	70	1	
SIP	08	37	20	40	37	23	34	22	40	33	1
BNS	17	46	35	47	53	22	38	31	24	15	55
Spel	07	48	30	41	47	18	21	30	20	15	44
Read	03	59	41	42	47	25	21	37	18	16	32

In general these intercorrelations are high. There is also a higher-than-expected level of background correlation of test data with age, given that standard scores express status in relation to age. It is plain some general factor, no doubt g, must account for a great deal of the variance. Most expected relationships are confirmed. Each core test correlates best with its pair in the cluster, with the exception that Pattern Construction (block design) shows a higher correlation with SQR than with Recall of Designs. Recall of Digits clearly behaves in this battery like a linguistic test and shows an expected relationship with Similarities and Word Definitions. The two Recall of Objects tests relate mainly to each other, whilst Speed of Information Processing shows a tendency to vary with two tests of attainment, Spelling (see above) and Basic Number Skills.

In the overall pattern of intercorrelations, SQR lives up to its reputation as the most highly g-loaded test with an average intercorrelation with all other tests of 0.506. The next most highly intercorrelated test is Word Definitions, with 0.446.

Fine-tuning the second criterion

Pursuing our interest in tests classified as diagnostic, let us take the safest way forward, given that no single test performs as a dyslexia indicator in all circumstances. What happens if we group the four DAS and two selected WISC-III diagnostic tests together as an indicator, at least, of generally impaired processing of temporary information? We have seen that all six tests fall below the population mean for the 300 or so pupils aggregated together. Similarly the DAS verbal and spatial clusters (but not the non-verbal reasoning clusters) rise above the mean. Could not this separation of *all* diagnostic from *all* core tests act as a dyslexia criterion on a par with the principal literacy underachievement one?

If this analysis is done and quantified in SD units or z-scores for each child in the dataset, then another very normal distribution results, as shown in Figure 8.5.

Again, frequencies of children falling within discrepancy bands are shown separately for the sexes. Again girls are skewed slightly towards less serious symptomatology, though this no doubt partly reflects female strengths in verbal memory and clerical, fine motor speed. Girls this time, however, are not underrepresented at the extremes of the distribution.

On the face of it, then, a *cognitive profile criterion* produces an analogous partition of the clinical sample as the *literacy under-achievement criterion*, though we do not know to what extent different children are selected this time. Wanting as before to discard equivocal children, whose cognitive processing deficits are less discrepant from their general ability range, we select only those where at least 0.5 SD separates the two.

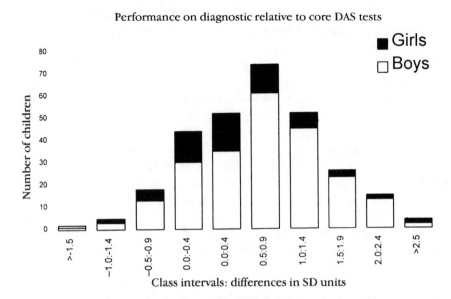

Figure 8.5: Children reclassified in half-SD intervals according to how far their mean scores on six diagnostic tests fall below their mean scores on six core tests. Negative values signify diagnostic scores rising above general ability scores.

The range of other diagnostic measures

Numerous other diagnostic procedures have been introduced and described in this book (Chapter 4). They consist equally of psychometrically developed, fully normed tests and informal diagnostic procedures. Scores produced by each kind can be treated differently. How valid are these procedures and how well do they serve as diagnostic indicators?

The supplementary and experimental measures are theory based and are mainly of four kinds:

- the *subtraction* deficit apparent on the One Minute Number Tests, in which elementary addition and subtraction tasks are performed at speed;
- the *linguistic* preference apparent in the reading of content over function words (Aaron and Joshi, 1992; Aaron, 1994), where error and reading speed data may be combined;
- deficits observable on at least three tests of *phonological processing*: Rosner's phoneme deletion task (Rosner, 1993), Gathercole's non-word repetition task (Gathercole et al., 1994)[12] and the Sound Blending task from the Woodcock–Johnson battery (Woodcock and Johnson, 1989, 1990), where it appears as a fully normed test of verbal ability;
- the *non-word reading deficit* is commonly taken as the best

indicator of a phonological and hence dyslexic reading difficulty: word and non-word reading may be contrasted, especially if taken from the same psychometric battery (Turner, 1995b).

Such candidate tests for diagnostic use are best validated against established ones. Though this is the conventional way to approach concurrent validity, and is especially useful in the case of intelligence-measuring tests (such as Jensen, 1984), we can hope in the case of dyslexia-sensitive tests to do little more than weigh the unknown against the uncertain.

Nevertheless the opportunity should not be foregone to evaluate putative diagnostic tests in the light of well-constructed and well-established measures. The present data set enables us to do just this, although on a small scale, crudely and with a limited clinical sample. Where possible the invention of composite measures improves reliability; other indexes must be constructed. In all cases data may be averaged across the same class intervals as for the DAS Core-Diagnostic discrepancies.

Data from the One Minute Number Tests are the number of addition and subtraction items correct within one minute, a measure of speeded performance. Raw scores on subtraction may be subtracted from raw scores on addition items. When this is done and averaged across diagnostic categories, the distribution in Figure 8.6 appears.

Subtraction deficit on one minute number tests by category of
Core-Diagnostic deficit on DAS (with Ns)

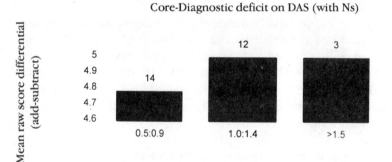

Core-diagnostic DAS deficit (SD units)

Figure 8.6: Deficit in speeded performance on easy subtraction versus easy addition items on the One Minute Number Tests (Westwood et al., 1974), by category of DAS Core-Diagnostic deficit.

Here the numbers of children relatively poorer on diagnostic tests are fewer at the more extreme levels. Nevertheless the One Minute Number Tests do appear to function as a useful diagnostic procedure at discrepancy levels of 1 SD or greater, though the margin of group differences is small, 0.214 points of raw score.

In the case of Aaron's wholly informal lists of function and content words, an index must be constructed. As it is hypothesised that dyslexics read function words both more slowly and more erroneously, it is possible to combine reading speed times with error counts. This may be done by means of the formula:

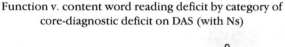

$$(F_t - C_t) + (F_e - C_e)$$

where t = time in seconds for each set of 20 words and e = number of errors made per list; the two differentials are first calculated, function minus content, then added together.

When this is done the resulting scores may be averaged across the DAS class intervals, as in Figure 8:7.

Function v. content word reading deficit by category of
core-diagnostic deficit on DAS (with Ns)

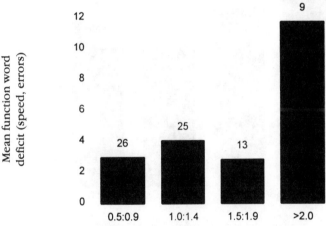

Figure 8.7: Reading preference for content over function words, expressed in a measure derived from speed and accuracy raw scores (see text), by category of DAS core-diagnostic deficit.

Here the measure appears to act as a diagnostic indicator of severity, coming into its own when the skills assessed by DAS diagnostic tests are separated by more than 2 SDs from the level of general ability. Though higher this time, the numbers in the more extreme categories remain small enough to warrant cautious interpretation.

Next we shall examine the measures of phonological ability. The WJ-R Sound Blending test is fully developed and standard scores are available drawing on recent US norms. However, for present purposes raw score totals are used, to indicate actual numbers of items children are able to do. The highest raw score observed was 21. Raw scores are also available, for the Rosner (maximum total possible: 13) and Gathercole (maximum total possible: 40) tests. Children have often been given two, but not three, of these tests. By applying approximately equal weighting to all three scores, as in the formula

$$(3R + 2SB + G) / 3$$

where R = Rosner, G = Gathercole and SB = Sound Blending, a composite raw score was obtained for each child. Averaging the resulting scores across the DAS categories, we find the distribution in Figure 8.8.

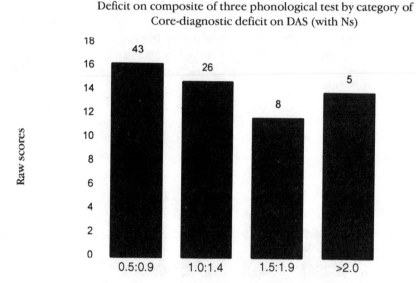

Deficit on composite of three phonological test by category of Core-diagnostic deficit on DAS (with Ns)

Core-diagnostic DAS deficit (SD units)

Figure 8.8: Weighted raw scores on phonological tests of sound blending, non-word repetition and phoneme deletion, by category of DAS core-diagnostic deficit.

Here no diagnostic advantage appears, the level of performance remaining, on this combined measure of phonological skill at least, rather constant across levels of severity as measured by the DAS.

The data from the Gathercole test of non-word repetition (CNRep) are worth looking at in a little more detail. If a conventional literacy achievement discrepancy analysis is performed on the whole dataset, and then again those pupils who have a literacy score less than 0.5 SD below their GCA (IQ) are eliminated, this leaves a total of 65 children who might be dyslexic in the sense of our first criterion. The children may then be ranked by age and averaged within each year-group (wider bands for older children), as in Table 8.5.

Table 8.5: Raw score means on Non-word Repetition test of 65 children by age-band and degree of dyslexia, defined by ability/achievement (literacy) and expressed in SD units

				Raw scores on CNRep of dyslexic groups at different ages			
Age-band	6;0–6;11	7;0–7;11	8;0–8;11	9;0–9;11	10;0–11;11	12;0–13;11	14;0–15;11
Discrepancy	1.2	1.3	1.3	1.5	1.5	2.1	1.9
n	8	7	13	12	14	5	6
Raw score	19.3	24.1	28.5	25.3	27.0	27.4	30.8

Here it may be seen that all the children have significant non-word repetition difficulties relative to the ages at which the unimpaired norm group achieve these raw scores.

There remains the non-word reading deficit. Concurrent scores from within a single battery that included word and non-word measures (e.g. Woodcock, 1987; Woodcock and Johnson, 1989, 1990) were not always available. Results using fully developed psychometric tests, however, could be drawn upon. Consequently the mean standard score for each individual on all concurrent measures of reading, principally DAS Word Reading or Word Basic Reading, was contrasted with his or her Word Attack (non-word reading) standard score. The latter was subtracted from the former and expressed in SD units. The results appear in Figure 8.9.

Non-word reading deficit by category of core-diagnostic deficit on DAS (with Ns)

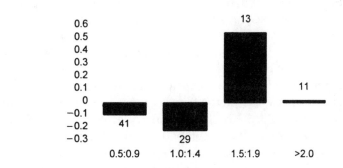

Core-diagnostic DAS deficit (SD units)

Figure 8.9: Word minus non-word reading standard scores, by category of DAS Core-Diagnostic deficit

Once again it appears that a sizeable non-word reading deficit (0.5 SD or more) appears only for one category of more disabled dyslexic individuals, those with a core-diagnostic discrepancy above 1.5 but below 2.0 SDs.

This, it will be remembered, was the level of severity suggested as the minimum applying to ability/achievement in order to diagnose dyslexia without equivocation. However, the non-word reading deficit appears in the main, from these data, to be distributed somewhat indifferently across the severity spectrum.

Girls

Our data permit us to take a critical look at a venerable and widely held, if little supported, hypothesis concerning dyslexia in girls. There are clearly fewer girls with dyslexia, even if we take seriously a predisposing bias in some of the better-known diagnostic measures (see Chapter 4). Reasons adduced for this are innate in character and biological in conception. Evidence just reviewed suggests, in addition, that girls referred for independent psychological assessment may be marginally lower in ability and freer from diagnostic symptomatology.

Perhaps female dyslexics are less frequently identified for reasons other than their lower incidence in the population, though the latter is not in doubt. In particular, cognitive sex differences (or preferences), though of little significance in the normal population, may be critical at the margin, for example in learning-impaired individuals. Girls' language skills may be more advanced at all ages, like their skills of manual dexterity. By contrast girls yield, in adolescence especially, to the advantage in spatial skills shown by boys. The hypothesis arises that though girls present less often with catastrophic levels of reading failure, accompanied by weak verbal memory and poor fine motor planning or control, they may have equally severe problems with spelling, number skills, aspects of organisation and applications of spatial ability such as map-reading. Just as the speed at which planets recede may be identified by a *red shift*, so there may be some sort of *cognitive shift* between male and female profiles of dyslexia.

Our data permit us to test the principal element in this hypothesis by asking the question: are girls in the data set more likely to have particular problems of spatial ability? The DAS is particularly useful in addressing this question. Not only is spatial ability defined more purely than in the WISC, for instance, but a reliable composite, the Spatial Cluster, may be compared with GCA (IQ or overall ability). Moreover, significance and frequency levels are specified at which GCA/spatial discrepancies may be evaluated. A difference of 10 points of standard score would be expected in only 25% of the population, one of 13 in only 15%, one of 15 in only 10% and one of 17 in 5% or fewer. We are thus well placed to interpret any such differences as may be observed between boys and girls.

Looking first at the direct test of the hypothesis, a GCA/spatial discrepancy in the direction of spatial *weakness*, we find the numbers of boys and girls distributed as shown in Figure 8.10.

Pupils with significant and unusual spatial difficulties

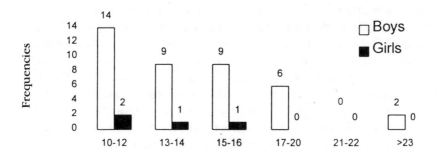

DAS GCA-Spatial Cluster: points of standard score

Figure 8.10: Frequencies of boys and girls with given levels of weakness in spatial ability relative to general ability.

Clearly, there are very few girls here with any significant degree at all of weakness in spatial ability: only four out of a full sample of 262 – just 1.5%.[13] Not very impressive evidence in favour of a female dyslexic cognitive profile.

The values given above are for two-tailed tests, however. That is, the given number of points between GCA and Spatial Cluster refers to a discrepancy in either direction – strength or weakness. What is the position if we ask how many individuals of each sex have a *weakness or strength* in spatial ability? Dyslexics are sometimes thought of as showing compensating gifts in language-free zones of wholistic and three-dimensional visual perception. Figure 8.11 shows the resulting distribution.

Expected and observed numbers of boys and girls with relative spatial strengths or weaknesses

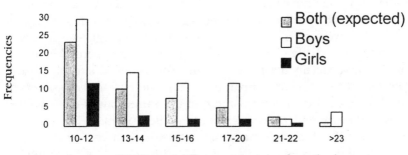

GCA/Spatial differences (points of standard score)

Figure 8.11: Frequencies of boys and girls falling into the categories of spatial strength or weakness found in fewer than 25% of the population. Also shown: numbers of boys and girls together expected in a collection this size.

Boys are, once again, supernumerary at the extremes of this particular distribution, especially in the most extreme category of all where two boys have a weakness of more than 23 points and two a strength of the same proportion, eight times the number expected. Even in the lowest category of frequency, a spatial strength or weakness of 10–12 points, the number of boys is 2.5 times that expected and these boys are as likely to have a weakness as a strength. But a chi-square analysis shows that the numbers of girls falling into the various categories of spatial deficit or strength is very close to the numbers expected ($P = 0.38$).[14]

We are entitled, then, to draw a conclusion from evidence taken from nearly 300 pupils seeking a psychological assessment of their learning problems over a three-year period, 30% of them girls. This is that there is no evidence that girls are more likely to have *a different kind* of dyslexia, one with an enhanced role for visuo-spatial difficulties. On the contrary, girls are less likely to show such difficulties and the evidence suggests that dyslexia in girls is of exactly the same kind – based in a linguistic, and especially phonological, deficit – as in boys.

Personality

Finally, we may wish to ask about personality characteristics of children seeking an assessment for dyslexia. Over the period the Eysenck Personality Questionnaire – Junior (EPQ) (Eysenck and Eysenck, 1975) was offered as an optional extra to those parents who wished it. It was of interest but not necessarily related to the cognitive assessment.[15] Parents of 42 children accepted. What are the main personality characteristics of these children, as described by the Eysenck test?

For the EPQ the child answers 'Yes' or 'No' to 81 simple questions, constructed so as to yield scores on the three empirical dimensions of personality: Psychoticism, Extraversion and Neuroticism. (These are best communicated as Tough-mindedness, Emotionality and Extraversion.) Psychoticism reflects the capacity to act heedlessly and without too much concern for others; Neuroticism manifests a tendency towards anxiety and worry; and Extraversion measures how outgoing and gregarious a person is. In addition a Lie-scale (Complaisance) registers how prone the person is to answer in a socially desirable way: this shows a desire to please and gain approval. Children are compared on these dimensions with others of the same age and sex, thus furnishing, in the same way as on cognitive tests, scores that are high or low in relation to their peers.

The subsample of 42 children (representative, with an average age of 11.20 years, of the larger set) may be divided by means of the criterion already applied. Those with literacy achievement discrepancies with general ability of less than 0.5 SD may be considered less dyslexic; those with a discrepancy of 0.5 or greater more dyslexic. Results may be seen in Figure 8.12:

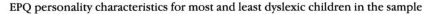

EPQ personality characteristics for most and least dyslexic children in the sample

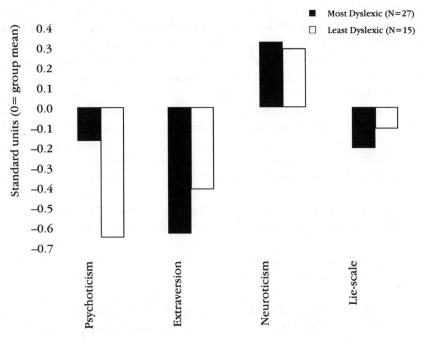

Four factorial dimensions (see text)

Figure 8.12: Scores on the four EPQ factor dimensions of personality for the groups of children with larger (more dyslexic) or smaller (less dyslexic) GCA>Reading, Spelling discrepancies.

Here it may be seen that *all* children in the sample share some characteristics though they are not, in these respects, noticeably different from a random sample of the population. They all tend to have higher levels of anxiety, perhaps in connection with their school work, and higher introversion, with Lie-scale scores ('complaisance') close to or a little below average for their age.

Where the more and less dyslexic children differ is on the first two factors. It is the *less* dyslexic children, perhaps surprisingly, who show greater 'tender-mindedness' (lower *psychoticism*) and presumably the reduced capacity for self-defence that goes with it. However, the *more* dyslexic group does seem still to be more introverted than the others.

Conclusions

Manifestly there are innumerable further ways of interrogating a data set such as this and the best ways may not yet have been found. Though some findings are clearer than others, these basic analyses are all of interest, given the novelty of the exercise. Nevertheless the limitations in size, selectivity and diagnostic coarseness do make conclusions some-what tentative.

The Differential Ability Scales (DAS) yield descriptive assessment data of unparalleled quality and their 10 tests behave in analyses much as they ought to do. In particular, the battery's estimations of intelligence (of three main kinds) seems highly reliable. The total data set of nearly 300 school-age pupils is a collection of children under-achieving in all major areas of basic skill but, within this categorisation, there is a major tendency for literacy under-achievement to be more severe. The intellec-tual range is remarkably normal, though the subset of girls is many fewer and perhaps of lower ability. A clear cognitive profile emerges even on core (intelligence-measuring) tests with the pair of non-verbal reasoning tests depressed in relation to verbal and spatial abilities. All four diagnostic tests appear to capture information-processing difficulties, especially if two subtests from the WISC-III are used in supplementary fashion. On diagnostic tests girls appear to show fewer such information-processing difficulties overall. Of the additional tests given for their diagnostic interest, some (One Minute Number Tests, Aaron's Function versus Content word lists) appear sensitive to dyslexia severity, whereas others (phonological tests, measures of non-word reading deficit) disclose comparable difficulties across the range of severity. Spatial strengths as well as weaknesses are an unexpectedly prominent feature in boys but are entirely unexceptional in girls. Personality measures show referred children to be more thin-skinned, anxious and introverted than would be expected.

Notes

1   Groups of individuals younger than six years will be examined in the chapter on assessing preschool children, and those 18 years or older in that on adults.
2   Children with literacy skills at least half a standard deviation below expectation based on ability. On a more stringent criterion the proportion will rise.
3   For instance on parental occupation, income, educational level, race or ethnic background.
4   Cases are eliminated when, for some reason, *no* DAS achievement tests have been given.
5   There appears to be, therefore, no population of less bright, middle-class children, in search of a *dyslexia* excuse for poor achievement, who fail to meet discrepancy criteria.
6   Henceforth so-called for convenience, notwithstanding diagnostic rigour.
7   Groups of abilities; empirically, those which tend to go together (constellate as factors).
8   Dr Harry Chasty's phrase.
9   This is clear, also, from the tendency of Matrices to associate equally with Full Scale IQ and the third, distractibility factor on the WISC-R, at least for older children (14- and 15-year-olds: see Elliott, 1990, p. 228, and the fuller discussion in Chapter 3 of the present book).
10 Though happily reused in new tests such as KAIT (Kaufman and Kaufman, 1993) and WRAML (Sheslow and Adams, 1990).

11 I am indebted to Dr John Rack for this analysis.

12 CNRep is published by the Psychological Corporation early in 1996.

13 Or 6.7% of the girls.

14 Expected numbers refer to boys and girls *combined*; the numbers of boys alone, or girls alone, therefore, must be doubled before it is compared with the number expected. Figures expected for the sexes separately, which would be most useful, do not exist.

15 Parents do occasionally request a personality assessment and, because to get the child to complete the questionnaire during an already lengthy assessment would be an unnecessary burden, all parents are offered the opportunity of bringing the completed form to interview.

Chapter 9
Testing For Teachers[1]

The requirements of teachers

There is now a larger constituency among teachers for good quality tests, and guidance as to how to use them, than there has ever been. Anyone actively involved in training teachers to be dyslexia specialists will be aware of how keen is the interest in psychological methods and techniques. However, levels of experience with assessment vary enormously. Although this book will not help inexperienced teachers to grasp basic psychometrics, it should attempt to satisfy legitimate curiosity as to how skilled teachers may follow its principles and implement some of its methods.

I hope it will have become apparent by now that *measurement* is the heart of the dyslexia assessment process. On the whole the teachers who make the most capable assessors are those who object least to numbers. Little that goes on 'under the bonnet' of tests need concern them, but they will prefer a good test – a test that measures well – to a bad one, a modern test to an antique, an efficient test to a long-winded one. They will communicate in percentiles and stoop only reluctantly to age-equivalents. They will administer tests to children with a sly combination of *bonhomie* and detachment, restraining primitive urges to *teach* the moment a child hesitates. They will provide good quality accounts of their findings, which are of far from temporary interest, in writing to parents and others.

Many children will never see a psychologist for an individual assessment of the kind that has been occupying us. Others who do may still benefit from a skilled preliminary look at their functioning by the teacher who may have the first opportunity to give it. It is fallacious to suppose that a different assessment model must be devised for a teacher's assessment, though such an accommodation, which of course patronises teachers, has many a precedent.[2] No: concern for the highest quality assessment procedures admits of no compromise on grounds so dubious.

The context

Testing is now accepted as integral to good teaching beyond the confines of the dyslexia world. Teaching is associated with instruction, putting information *in*; assessment with drawing evidence of skills *out* of pupils. However, just as there is an important confidence-building aspect to conventional testing, so evaluation makes a vigilant and rational activity of teaching. Yet during the 1980s, technical development in testing advanced while unrealistic notions about reading, including an aversion to testing, enjoyed some popularity. The latter may now be waning, whilst a revival of interest in objective assessment methods is observed by sales directors.

Among tests of more recent origin, however, may be detected attempts to enshrine redefinitions of reading. Learning to read is a sequential process, whose top-down, linguistic and contextual aspects have been grossly exaggerated. Progress is from lower, visual discrimination levels, through whole-word identification and lexical decision, to higher levels of sentence parsing, text modelling, comprehension and interpretation. No developmental research calls this sequence into doubt.

Early in 1990 some colleagues and I asked a number of schools in a south London borough to describe by questionnaire their approach to the teaching of reading. Out of a selection of 12 general statements about the teaching of reading, schools were asked to choose the three that most closely approximated to their own approach. More than 30 primary schools responded, and 60% of the 'votes' went on just three statements:

In an environment with print children develop reading skills as active learners. [22%]

Free choice of absorbing reading material is the best guarantee of lifelong positive attitudes. [20%]

If parents share books with their children this will be the main influence on their progress in reading. [18%]

This does illustrate, fairly I believe, that in the 'debate' at the time about which method of teaching reading is best, by far the most widespread of all the possibilities was no method at all. Things may have improved.

Four more statements accounted for a further 33% of the votes:[3]

Children's reading develops naturally from an interest in stories. [10%]

Reading is managed for the most part within the context of the school's reading scheme(s). [10%]

Parents should be involved in their children's learning by hearing them read from books or sets of words. [7%]

Familiarisation with letters and letter-sounds is the key to getting started with reading. [6%]*

The remaining 7% of votes went on just three statements:

Direct instruction is the most important factor in early reading. [3%] *

Children can recognise and remember whole words if these are presented systematically (lists, flashcards). [2%]

Some kind of literacy work should be tackled for an hour every day. [2%]

Of course, participation in a dyslexia specialist training course virtually guarantees, and even partly assumes, a knowledge about literacy teaching which has clearly been far eroded in the mainstream teaching world. The dyslexia organisations, only now venturing out of isolation, have for years been quasi-monastic reservoirs of traditional teaching knowledge. One has only to see what facile materials appear on the literacy booklists of teacher-training colleges[4] to witness what a cultural distance has grown between the two.

Testing, also, seen as a central feature of education by all except educators, had almost fallen into desuetude before concern about standards and the agenda of reform swept it briskly again into their laps. The kinds of concerns which have led us this far in this book inform specialist testing also: accuracy, rigour, precision, reliability.

Without compromise, then, we approach the challenge of a serviceable assessment for skilled specialist teachers with an eye to its foremost component: good quality instruments. Ultimately, it will be argued, interpretation of such tests is a matter of conversance with statistical, psychometric and developmental fields that belong within a postgraduate education rather than in a single chapter. But the production of good quality measurements usually contributes valuable information, and only a few misunderstandings, to the practical management of the child with difficulties, and so this is what we shall attempt to enhance.

A review of tests

It may be useful to review tests of reading, writing, spelling and cognition that are available, useful and current, and which address most purposes and ages of pupil. The task of reviewing reading tests has been performed at book length by Vincent et al. (1983) and Pumfrey (1985).

The former is useful for what it reviews but has not been revised for an updated addition. The latter was updated for a second edition but is currently out of print. For the American scene, and comprehensive coverage of assessment issues generally, see Sattler (1988).

Pre-reading skills

The partial development of literacy skills in young or learning-disabled children who are unable to score on reading tests is diagnostic territory. But *readiness* is a concept which has not stood the test of time. Many reading tests have a diagnostic apparatus associated with them: Neale (Neale, 1989), Daniels and Diack (Daniels and Diack, 1958). There is in addition an abundance of materials with an inventory approach: Ted Ames' Macmillan Diagnostic Reading Pack (Ames, 1980) and the Barking Reading Project (Trickey, 1983) materials deserve mention, as does a useful source, Chall and Curtis (1990). In the United States, the Slingerland Pre-Reading Screening Procedures (revised edition, Slingerland, 1977) offer un-normed tests of visual memory, letter knowledge and phonemic awareness, all well-established predictors of literacy, in convenient form; these are quite widely used. An upward extension for school-age children of six to 10 is also available: the Slingerland Tests for Identifying Children with Specific Language Disability (revised edition, Slingerland, 1974).

A disappointing but salvageable production is the Test of Initial Literacy (TOIL; Kispal et al., 1989), developed in tandem with the Reading Ability Series (Kispal, Gorman and Whetton, 1989; see below). Whilst consistently underestimating, in spite of the representations of teachers, the proportion of pupils with serious reading difficulties, the NFER team gave this series of 10 exercises to 1512 7–12-year-olds with reading problems. (This enabled them to discover, for instance, that 92% of children punctuated below an acceptable level.) There are no meaningful norms and marking is fairly subjective. However, the exercises are of diagnostic value in experienced hands and several incorporate good ideas. Free writing, for instance, is elicited by asking the pupil to write the address and a message on a postcard.

Word Recognition

Much scorn has been poured on traditional word recognition tests. On the whole this point of view is misconceived and ill-informed and should be resisted.

Words come and go in popularity (Shearer and Apps, 1975). Few are really new and the obsolescence of certain words is, like the irregularity of English spelling, an index of present-day ignorance. The vocabulary range of words in school textbooks has been shrinking steadily since the

1920s. There are obvious fluctuations in use of fashion and technology words, Professor Cox instances *frock* and *wireless*; my secretary knew *scullery* only because her grandfather had one. I find it astonishing that 11-year-olds in the 1950s should have been expected to know the word *contumely*, which occurs in NFER Test NS6 and also in Hamlet. From a technical point of view the difficulty values of items, like bias, can be calculated and taken into account if necessary. Usage, however, changes and *Has a cat legs?* (Daniels and Diack Reading Test) is nowadays an unfamiliar locution.

For theoretical reasons the rapid, accurate identification of single words out of context forms a vital component – perhaps the most vital – in the acquisition of reading. The central role of automaticity has been recognised since the work of LaBerge and Samuels (1974) and the ability to recognise words out of context is what discriminates between skilled and unskilled readers (Lovett, 1986).

Burt (Burt, 1921) and Schonell (Schonell and Schonell, 1950) both designed simple word recognition tests in the 1930s which have been popular ever since, enjoying various revisions and restandardisations. The words in the tests are not problematic. Provided the original norms are not used – specifically, the procedure of adding up the number of words correctly read, dividing by 10 and adding 5 to obtain an age equivalent – the tests are perfectly acceptable today. British norms dating from the 1970s are readily available and are no less satisfactory than the US norms of the same period that have been widely accepted for the WISC-R. Burt's reading test was given a Scottish standardisation in 1954 (Vernon, 1969) and again for a 1974 revision (SCRE, 1976). In 1973 the test was given to 27 000 children aged 6;6 to 7;7 in the West Riding of Yorkshire. Schonell's was given to 10 000 Salford children in 1971. Both the Burt and Schonell tests were given to a representative sample of Cheshire children in 1972. Norms, therefore, from the period 1971–74 are available for both tests in the form of technical papers published by NFER but now out of print.

There is a single modern addition to the family of British word recognition tests: the Macmillan Graded Word Recognition Test (Macmillan Test Unit, 1985a). This is experienced as harder – the child may be able to do less of it – but this is no reflection on the efficiency of the test and a shorter test is in general to be preferred to a longer one. Note the instructions for administration of the test. The Macmillan tests often require procedures that differ in important respects from similar tests. In particular the tester must not prompt or encourage. The GWRT offers two parallel forms.

There is a very useful 1993 edition of a standard US test used all over the world, the Wide Range Achievement Test Third Edition – the WRAT-3 (Wilkinson, 1993). This includes a test of word recognition. As norms extend from 5 to 75 years old, it solves several problems at once, including how to assess older pupils and adults (see below). In the newer edition, different age-levels are replaced by all-level parallel forms so that retesting at intervals is feasible. American spellings have vanished. With this test comes an equally versatile spelling test and a test of basic number skills. Apart from the substitution of £s for $s, little Anglicisation of the latter is needed. But, unlike the well-known British Ability Scales test of written arithmetic, Basic Number Skills tests D and E, WRAT-3 includes more challenging items, such as logarithms and square roots. The US norms, from 1992–93, are recent.

The Boder Test (see below) utilises regular and irregular words and therefore was well ahead of the research enterprise when it was published in 1982. This test, however, has off-putting features which include over-complex instructions and ratio quotients.[5] It has never become very popular though a handful of loyal devotees persist with it.

One quickly administered reading-age test whose virtues may have been overlooked is the Salford Sentence Reading Test (Bookbinder, 1976). Akin to word recognition, the stimulus items are in the form of sentences, rather than single words, but are read aloud. There are three parallel forms, A, B and C, and administration is very quick. Norms date from 1974 and 1975. The test is derived from the older Holborn (Watts, 1948), which it replaces. Reading ages above about 10 cannot be obtained and so the test is unreliable in certain conditions.

Lastly, one new test claims to discriminate finely among poor readers. By definition, therefore, it should be sensitive to gains made by them. This is Word Search (Godfrey Thomson Unit, 1986). Pupils aged from 7;0 to 12;0 may be given the test. Instead of norms, criterion performances are offered; raw scores from 33 to 56 give reading ages of 7;6 to 9;7. The test discriminates well, in other words, within this range. The task requires the child to select the word, from a choice of several words printed in a box, that fits each gap in two passages of connected prose (matching cloze). The word must be copied in writing, however. The test is timed (30 minutes).

Sentence Completion Tests

This is the commonest form of group-administered test, designed to monitor progress in large groups of children and to screen for remedial intervention, usually at age seven. Apparent progress on these tests may be disappointing, but an individual administration greatly enhances the reliability. The Suffolk test (Hagley, 1987) is perhaps technically the best of the newer group tests and is timed (20 minutes). Sentence completion requires the child to work through a series of similar items in which a gap in a sentence must be filled from a choice of several alternative words. The selection is by underlining or circling, so the measurement of reading is not contaminated by the measurement of writing (a child may be poor at one and good at the other). Parallel forms enable progress to be measured – or cheating avoided! – through the whole primary age range.

The Macmillan Group Reading Test (Macmillan Test Unit, 1985b) is another good recent group test of the sentence-completion type for infants. The earlier items are enhanced, for younger children, by picture cues (as in paired associate learning). Reading ages may be achieved from 6:3 to 13:3. Another test of this type which is short and useful is SPAR (Young, 1976; Spelling and Reading) from Dennis Young. This is better known as a spelling test (see below) but a group reading test comes with the package. As with the hardy perennial, the Group Reading Test (Young, 1969), the more difficult items are straight vocabulary choices. Presumably, if children are equally well able to decode all the items, the test discriminates among them on the grounds of word knowledge (reading experience).

During the 1970s the National Foundation for Educational Research (NFER) developed a number of sentence-completion reading tests which, today, seem less used but which have a solid, no-frills appeal. Reading Test A (NFER, 1970) consists of 38 items suitable for 7-year-olds, is untimed (but can be done in under half an hour) and provides norms from 6:09 to 8:09. Reading Tests BD (NFER, 1971) and AD (NFER, 1978) are roughly equivalent junior-age tests. AD has 35 items and age-norms from 8:0 to 10:7; BD has 44 items and age-norms from 7:0 to 11:04. The manual for AD – the more recent test – states that it is easier and more appropriate for younger, less-able children. Reading Tests SR-A and SR-B (Pritchard, 1971) are a pair of tests of greater scope, with age-norms that run from 7:06 to 11:11 (Key Stage 2). SR-A and SR-B are equivalent forms, with 48 items each; they are timed tests which take 20 minutes. The NFER's Reading Comprehension Test DE (NFER, 1976) is an excellent test of passage comprehension for pupils aged from 10:00 to 12:10. Eight texts, one of them from *The Rime of the Ancient Mariner*, are presented. Multiple-choice questions, mostly convergent but in some cases open-ended, must be answered. The test is untimed but according to the manual takes less than 50 minutes.

A welcome development is a 9–14 extension of the Macmillan Group Reading Test (Macmillan Test Unit, 1990). This reports reading age levels from 8:0 to 15:3 for children aged 8:3 and above. There are equivalent forms, X and Y, for retesting. But in addition to the usual sentence completion task there is a context comprehension test. Four complete passages are provided, so that a context effect may be built up. This enables children, once past the early stages of learning to read, to demonstrate a more sophisticated grasp of low-content words, for instance prepositions. Apparently obvious words do not, when examined, fit the context; instead, words like *then* or *between* must be selected. The task demands more in the way of a grasp of syntax and narrative form. The tests are untimed but should not take more than 30 minutes.

The GAP Reading Comprehension Test (McLeod and Unwin, 1970) still lingers in schools. This uses a form of cloze (the child writes in the missing word) with connected prose passages and reports reading ages (only) from 7:8 to 12:6 for 30 items. This test, named after an Australian primary school, is rather old now and compares unfavourably with others mentioned. However, its stablemate, GAPADOL (McLeod and Anderson, 1973), which also uses cloze, offers mean values for 50 items for ages from 8:8 to 16:10, as well as cut-off points for the top and bottom 10% of pupils. Any description of a distribution is preferable to (non-linear) reading ages and GAPADOL retains its niche as a test of comprehension for older children. No doubt its norms do not flatter them.

Higher reading standards in Scotland are more than just Scottish propaganda. Evidence lurks in the norm tables of the Edinburgh Reading Tests (Godfrey Thomson Unit, 1972–77). These appeared from 1972 onwards from the Godfrey Thomson Unit and revisions continue. Effective group reading tests are offered for four stages throughout the age range 7:0 to 16:0. Their hallmark is methodological innovativeness. For instance at Stage 1 (7:0–9:0), for word recognition there are nine pictorial items followed by 11 sentence-completion items. Syntax is then assessed by items in which single words are deleted on the basis of syntactical superfluity (*Here is the ball if you lost*), passage cloze with words supplied or questions and answers (*Alice, who was tired, carried her mother's coat*: was the owner of the coat tired?). Further subtests assess knowledge of word order and verbal reasoning. The intent is clearly to pass beyond word recognition to the thinking skills that reading makes possible.

Almost alone among published tests the Edinburgh at this age offers separate norms for the sexes, desirable if specific learning difficulties in girls are not to be under-detected. At Stages 2 to 3, reading comprehension, fluency and retention skills are surveyed by means of further ingenious procedures. The children who decode but do not comprehend, about whom secondary teachers complain, can thus be identified by profiling at Key Stage 2. At nearly two hours, though, this will seem a little elaborate for many teachers. But at Stage 4, pupils in years 8 to 11 (ages 12:0 to 16:0), in just one hour, may be assessed on En2 (reading) at levels 2 to 9! (The contrast with National Curriculum Assessment is plain.) Though literary texts do not play a part, attributions of points of view are delightfully sophisticated.

There is evidence (Wiliam, 1992) that the National Curriculum's 10-level structure may have underestimated the rate of spread of attainment. A corrective for psychometric inefficiency may be found in the Shortened Edinburgh Reading Test, which offers a selection of 75 items from all four stages and thus brings maximum psychometric firepower to bear on the widest age-span. Because of its subtest structure, experienced users will find this series offers scope for the individual administration of selected subtests for diagnostic purposes, including the assessment of reading speed in the older reader.

Integrated passage reading

Tests of word recognition and sentence completion provide reliable, though incomplete, information about reading skill. For assessing levels of skill development, even the shortest and most rudimentary test is likely to correlate highly with something much more elaborate, detailed and time-consuming. A word recognition test, short though it is, releases a large amount of behavioural information for the observer. This type of test requires the child to look at each word and scrutinise it closely for phonemic and orthographic (letter sequence) cues. Even a careless, hasty reader is forced to attend to the internal detail of words. However, the same reader may obtain markedly lower (or higher) levels of score on a passage of connected prose read aloud. In passage reading the task demands an integration of word recognition, sentence structure and cumulative meaning to achieve the fluency necessary for comprehension. Like miscue analysis, this exercise opens a window onto the child's reading system.

The Revised Neale Analysis of Reading Ability (Neale, 1989) provides two equivalent forms, each with six graded passages. Instructions for administration are detailed. The harder norms at the bottom end of the test are more likely to be the result of limitations in the original (late 1940s) standardisation than of any rise in reading standards, though over 40 years the latter should not be ruled out. This test is the Rolls Royce of individual reading testing: norms for the primary age range are provided separately for speed, accuracy and comprehension. Results for dyslexic children are especially interesting, given the ingenuity of compensatory strategies in high-ability learning-impaired children. The limitation of the test is the ceiling: a reading age in excess of 13 years cannot be achieved.

The New Macmillan Reading Ability (NMRA) Test (Vincent and de la Mare, 1985) is preferred by some. Similar graded passages are provided but scores are provided in bands that are usually so wide as to defeat the intentions of the tester. No fluency (speed) score is obtained. The test contains a hidden Rasch scale as an alternative means of administration. By scoring only certain words which occur in the passages, an equivalent result is given. This may make test administration quicker and simpler, without compromising reliability. However, I have yet to meet anyone who actually uses the test in this way.

Many dyslexic children have great difficulty scoring on such tests; in particular guessing and prediction strategies play havoc with accuracy. For the child with minimal text integration skills, Macmillan have produced the Macmillan Individual Reading Analysis (MIRA; Vincent and de la Mare, 1990), which gives three equivalent forms, each with five graded passages. The first four pages of Form X have on average 6.5 words each, below large attractive pictures. Reading ages of up to 10;5 to 10;10 years may be obtained for accuracy and comprehension; there are no standard scores[6] or measures of fluency. There is an emphasis on a sight vocabulary of high-frequency words; a child with good decoding strategies but poor consolidation will not score well.

One group test should be mentioned: the Hunter-Grundin Literacy Profiles (Hunter-Grundin, 1980) contain Reading for Meaning tests at five levels, extending through the primary ability range and beyond. The profile includes vague measures of free writing and spoken language; there are attitude scales for which children select from five faces ranging from happy to sad; and the provision of spelling tests is said not necessarily to imply an undue emphasis on correct spelling. Reading uses cloze procedure and provides connected prose passages with four words supplied for each deletion. Spelling likewise draws the words to be spelled from sentences of connected prose, the only test to do so. Contrasting norms are offered for areas of different socio-economic status and for Scotland, as well as for the UK as a whole. The Scottish children prove to be very much better at spelling. However, the virtue of the group reading tests is that, without loss of reliability, they require only 10 minutes to administer.

Reading ability in older, more capable pupils

The problem of assessing higher order reading abilities is a challenge. Many pupils make satisfactory progress but remain, for their age and ability, comparatively slow and laborious readers or poor spellers. Their general level of attainment, nevertheless, may be very high. Prior to GCSE, for instance, for which they may need special arrangements, how is one to assess their speed of comprehension under exam-like conditions?

The Macmillan Group Reading Tests 9–14 (Sentence Completion and Context Comprehension) have already been mentioned. In Form X of the latter, 21 points of raw score give 57 points of standard score (70–127) for pupils aged 15 years and 3 completed months. This is quite a useful degree of discrimination. The Richmond Tests of Basic Skills (Hieronymus, Lindquist and France, 1988) offer a range of possibilities, some of which will be discussed later. The Reading Comprehension test requires multiple-choice (no writing) responses to comprehension questions about several complex passages. At 15:8 years 57 points of raw score give 60 points (70–130) of standard score, an even finer power of discrimination. However, the test at Level 6 occupies nine pages of the pupil booklet, and 55 minutes of testing time is somewhat luxurious.

We have already seen that the testing of simple word recognition is performed very efficiently at higher ages by the WRAT-3 Reading test. Sentence completion, with its combination of fluency, accuracy and (limited) comprehension is also a possibility. Of considerable interest therefore are NFER Reading Tests EH1 and EH2 (1975), which address respectively the vocabulary element, always prominent in sentence-completion tasks, and comprehension. The latter is tackled by requiring multiple-choice responses, mainly through underlining, though with four instances of copying, to questions on seven varied passages. The tests are untimed, though 25 minutes ought to be sufficient and EH1 (vocabulary) was standardised with a 25-minute time-limit. The norms range from 11:0 to 15:11, making this the most efficient and powerful instrument in its class for the more able secondary-age reader.

Disappointing, by comparison, is the more recent Reading Ability series from NFER, based on the 1979–83 work of the Assessment of Performance Unit in national language monitoring (DES, 1988). Pupils aged from 7:0 to 13:11 are asked to read from one booklet and write in another, in two sessions of 45 minutes each, separated by from one to seven days. (7–9-year-olds may be tested on Level A in one session of one hour). The test, though less psychometrically puny than the TOIL, mentioned above, is nevertheless enormously inefficient and conflates reading with writing in order to gain a single, global measure of literacy.[7]

New possibilities for the assessment of the school leaver and young adult are contained in the Basic Skills Tests (Smith and Whetton, 1988) of the NFER-Nelson Occupational Test Series. Here are two short and manageable tests which, in spite of an over-statistical presentation, with too many accompanying pieces of paper, seem an efficient way to assess the functional literacy and numeracy of school leavers and young adults. Literacy requires information to be extracted from the *Shelley Gazette*, a mock-up of a local free newspaper, in 20 minutes. In a second part, taking 15 minutes, answers must be written and scored for grammar, spelling, handwriting, clarity and relevance. Many more skills than reading are required: one question, answered correctly by only 47% of the normative sample, requires the reconciling of a bus timetable with a street map. A comparable numeracy test takes 25 minutes, with timed sections. Items are grouped into calculations, approximations and problems. Norms are supplied for final-year comprehensive pupils, who are presumed to be unselected and therefore representative of the adult population; and for YTS groups, who tend to obtain lower scores. Other relevant occupational and training groups obtain scores which are reported in case studies. We learn that trainee electricians obtain higher numeracy scores than other trainees in the construction industry.

An all-purpose reading test

Most of the categories employed thus far are irrelevant to the Woodcock Reading Mastery Tests – Revised (WRMT-R) (Woodcock, 1987), which includes tests of word and non-word recognition, word-level and passage comprehension and early learning skills including letter recognition. It also offers norms for all ages, including students and other adults. It therefore presents as the best single test of the many processes and facets of reading for most purposes (Turner, 1995b; see also Turner, 1996, and test reviews in that volume). Aside from measures that entail reading aloud, such as the Neale test, which are of interest for the reader's management of emphasis and interpretive prosody, or which offer, measures of speed if desired, there is not a single test discussed hitherto that is necessary to someone who has the Woodcock. As the components of this battery have already been described in Chapter 5, the reader is referred to the discussion there.

Spelling

Spelling is easy to test. A graded list of words is dictated; the answers are right or wrong. There are several important spelling tests, whose domains overlap but whose strengths lie in addressing slightly different populations. One must first mention a traditional test whose use can no longer be recommended: the Schonell (Tests A and B; Schonell, 1932). Evidence has accumulated over 15 years – see Vernon's and Young's comments in the manuals for their respective tests – that Schonell's spelling standards have either slipped most remarkably or his test construction methodology, nowhere described, leaves a lot to be desired – or both. This is not to impugn the validity of the test. All spelling tests correlate extremely highly – typically 0.9 or above (see Turner, 1991a) – and measure incremental spelling ability simply and directly. The norms given by Schonell are quite inappropriate today, however, and possibly always were. In the secondary years the spelling ages obtained on the Schonell and Vernon (Vernon, 1977) tests come adrift by a year at age 11 and 2.5 years at nearly 16. Tests from three different decades chart the erosion of this important ability (Turner, op. cit.). Both Vernon and Young in their manuals accept a decline in spelling standards over many years. The conclusions of the recent NFER study (Brooks, Gorman and Kendall, 1993) of spelling standards between 1979 and 1983, which measured errors in the self-chosen vocabulary of 15-year-olds writing down for younger readers, must be questioned.

The WRAT-3 Spelling test is much the most versatile, recently normed and technically robust of the tests available. With only 40 items it is efficient. Norms cover the full age range (5–75). There are no US spellings.

The best general-purpose spelling test developed in Britain would seem to be the SPAR (Young, 1976), mentioned already. Young had it in mind to develop a spelling test on the bank principle, with banks of parallel items to permit repeated administration. The SPAR tests are effective for the whole primary range, though norms for the first edition extend right up to 15:11. However, a nearly full score at this age yields a standard score of 90: one is only discriminating among the bottom 25% of the population. The second edition of the test, the only one now obtainable, contains 40 items; the first edition was content with only 30.

An outgrowth of the same development work is the author's Parallel Spelling Tests (Young, 1983). The same principle is retained, that of banks of alternative items for retesting. In Test A, 34 words are given to infants and 40–46 to juniors. Age-norms range from 6:4 to 9:11, possible spelling ages from 5:11 to 13:8. In Test B 44–50 words, depending on age, are given to junior pupils aged from 9:0 to 12:11, who may obtain spelling ages from 6:8 to 15:0. There is a slight ceiling effect from the ages of 11:2 to 12:11 but the test continues to discriminate well.

This leaves us with the problem of the older, better speller. For this individual one needs the Vernon Spelling Test (Vernon, 1977). Vernon's 80 items do provide suitable material for children aged from 6:0 to 17:6, and it is not envisaged that one would give more than a subset of items to any particular child. However, one gives a larger number of items than with the Young tests and so the Vernon comes into its own with the more competent speller who can do all the SPAR items and who needs to be stretched.

Evidence already mentioned (Turner, 1991a) suggests that even the Vernon test, normed in the 1970s, is already too hard for contemporary students: 120 pupils, who were on average at the 75th percentile rank (standard score 110) on tests of general ability were able to score only at an age-appropriate level (percentile 50, standard score 100) on the Vernon test. We may thus erroneously attribute a low standard of spelling ability to a pupil when in fact this level of spelling is average. The WRAT-3 Spelling test remains the only test of spelling that is free from the problems mentioned.

Is there any special value in more elaborate or diagnostic tests of spelling? The otherwise inadequate Daniels and Diack Spelling Test provides (in list D) irregular words which implicate the phonological or surface form of dyslexia. The TOIL test of 12 dictated homonyms (exercise 6) would show up the ('dyseidetic') dyslexic with poor visual skills. Indeed the Boder Test (Boder and Jarrico, 1982) offers a purely reading/spelling methodology for identifying three subtypes of dyslexia. The main drawback of this kind of analysis of spelling error patterns is that it nowhere deals with the hypothesis that spelling ability is an indirect product of the methodology (and thoroughness) with which the individual was taught to read in the first place, sometimes many years earlier.

Spelling ability is taken to include orthographic sensitivity, like reading competence generally, perceptual skill in discriminating letters and letter-like forms, and to some extent vocabulary itself . One should not diagnose spelling behaviour in isolation, even though doing so may have implications for teaching

The Vincent and Claydon Diagnostic Spelling Test (Vincent and Claydon, 1982) is based on the work of Margaret Peters and the hypothesis, which has lost ground in the 1980s and 1990s, that spelling is a visual skill. Of the six subtests involved, therefore, at least one (Test 4, which links *fruit* and *ruin, watch* and *catching, saucer* and *because*) may be deemed perverse; and a global score for a child requires the administration of all subtests. However, other of the subtests show considerable ingenuity. One for instance (Test 5), requires the child to make a judgement about subtle patterns in English morphology: which is most like an English word out of *naviksi, munsur, cajvik, ingillent*? (Familiarity with Slavic or Turkic languages is a handicap here.) Another requires the timed use of dictionary skills. Two equivalent forms are provided with age-norms in the range 7:8–11:8, though at the upper end the best 25% of spellers would be restricted by the test's ceiling. Such a test has undoubted benefits for teaching but, as always, these must be weighed against the time taken in administration (60 minutes).

If dictating a list of words to be spelled still seems the most revealing and economical strategy, one can ask the pupil to do more than merely make errors. The TOIL asks the child to find nine spelling mistakes in a letter of 57 words, but as we have seen the test in effect has no norms. The Diagnostic Spelling Test (Test 3) asks the child to identify and correct an unidentified number of errors (five) in a passage of 52 words. However, the Richmond Tests, as usual, go one better in this direction. The pupil is asked to identify, in lists of four words, which if any is wrongly spelled. The fifth alternative, that there are no errors, is always an option. Skill in this kind of proof-reading or error-detection is predictive of progress. Norms, as we have seen, are good for this test.

From literacy to English?

With both reading and writing, there is the gradual requirement for the pupil to integrate different skills into a harmonious ensemble. Good tests exist which measure gradually higher levels of text comprehension and interpretation. Such an integration of writing activities is more usually thought of as English. What useful measures are there?

The National Foundation for Educational Research (NFER) produced, from 1959 onwards, a series of English Progress Tests (A2, NFER, 1966; B2, NFER, 1959; C2, NFER, 1961; C3, NFER, 1970a; D2, NFER, 1971; D3, NFER, 1970b; E2, NFER, 1963; F2, Henchman and Hendry, 1963) that move steadily through the junior and secondary age ranges, and through

English writing skills, with a sense of structure which could surely do with revival. Rhymes, plural and interrogative forms, tenses, punctuation, sentence expansion, ordering of sentences, use of pronouns and prepositions, active and passive voice, adjective/adverb contrasts, even explication of proverbs are all addressed, as well as reading, comprehension and vocabulary tasks of the kinds already touched upon. As creative and open-ended tasks are not neglected, others involving accurate analysis should not be disparaged as 'Latinate grammar' (Cox, 1991).

The Richmond Tests of Basic Skills (Hieronymus, Lindquist and France, 1988) offer in compact form several useful measures which can be given on their own. Reading comprehension and spelling have already been mentioned. Use of Capital Letters is perhaps limited, a matter of two or three rules. Punctuation potentially involves the whole articulation of sentence structure. Usage requires the pupil to discriminate between standard and non-standard English; there are, after all, correct grammatical forms. However, none of these tasks entails actual writing: the demand characteristics of the Richmond Tests are consistently those of a machine-markable multiple-choice format. Norms, as has been noted already, enable accurate discrimination of pupils up to the age of 15:8.

Writing

The Assessment of Performance Unit has made inroads into the inherent intractability of the objective assessment of writing proficiency (DES/APU, 1988). Holistic approaches to quality of pupils' writing govern the judgements of experienced examiners at A level and above. The writing of pupils exhibiting a lesser degree of integration, however, tends to be viewed in terms of spelling, script legibility, punctuation and sentence structure, all as separate facets.

No useful tests of writing under standard conditions exist. The best that can be done is to ask pupils to write on an agreed topic, or in response to a stimulus, for a set length of time. There is some pioneering work (notably Dutton, 1991) which samples across the secondary age range writing speed, sentence length, incidence of polysyllabic words and the extent to which productive effort can be sustained over time. A useful recent summary of her own work and the work of Dutton and others is given in Alston (1994). A structured exercise (sentence-completion writing task) for eliciting reliable estimations of writing productivity now exists in Hedderly (1995). But concentration upon such measurable variables in free writing will always stumble against the fact that a pupil, by taking time to think, may eke out one or two sentences of immaculate quality in a much longer time, perhaps, like WB Yeats, with words misspelled, like Robert Lowell with haphazard command of the conventions, or like William Wordsworth in illegible script. The problem of quality is inescapable.

Repeated testing

Testing for the purpose of measuring progress following specialist teaching is desirable but difficult. The parent and lay person wants to see steady progress measured in reading age, the established convention for expressing gains in reading ability. This is not unreasonable. However, (minor) difficulties of measurement occur, as well as (major) difficulties of being unable to demonstrate latent learning: foundations may be secure though no house is yet visible. Four principles should be borne in mind:

(1)   Reading skill should always be retested on the same instrument. Different measures correlate well, but not perfectly, with each other. Composites, scores combined from different tests, are more stable and reliable.
(2)   A pupil receiving intensive teaching over a long period should at least annually receive a full-passage reading test (see below) of the kind that integrates the many concurrent operations of reading.
(3)   At least two different measures of reading should be used, for instance word recognition and passage reading.
(4)   Progress should be estimated termly or at least once every six months.

There are many instruments suitable for repeated testing that should be considered, in addition to the obvious word recognition tests. Sentence-completion tests (see above) integrate accuracy, fluency (the tests are usually timed) and comprehension. These may be given to children in groups or, with enhanced reliability, to individuals. The pupil's response is silent and therefore will not disturb or cue others in the room. Parallel (same norm-table) or equivalent (alternative norm-table) forms are a usual feature of the tests. Progress is observed, first in terms of raw score, second in terms of reading age or standard score.

Number Skills

One good all-age test of written calculation skills has already been mentioned: WRAT-3 (Wilkinson, 1993). Timed in this edition to 15 minutes, this provides a reliable check on the kinds of skills that are most evidently impaired in dyslexics. Number concept and, after the arithmetic stage, more abstract mathematics do not seem to give the same trouble to the dyslexic learner.

Two simple tests that identify difficulties with both concepts and operations that still seem to be in regular use are the Basic Number Screening Test (Gillham and Hesse, 1976), suitable for the early stages of number learning or Key Stage 1; and the Nottingham Number Test (Gillham and Hesse, 1973), suitable for junior or Key Stage 2 pupils.

Cognitive ability

Should teachers give tests of intelligence? The conventional answer to this has been, in the main, no. As a result, powerful individual tests of general cognitive ability have remained restricted to those with a postgraduate qualification in a relevant branch of psychology. These tests, however, disclose in specific detail what someone's intellectual make-up actually is. Another question concerns the use of intellectual tests as a screening device, to *rule out* general learning difficulty as a possible explanation for retarded achievements. This question, much less commonly put, is: How can one reliably distinguish dyslexia from illiteracy?

Dyslexia, to be sure, is a special case of illiteracy but a cardinal feature for most practitioners is that these two are not always the same. If one wishes to believe they are always the same, or to ignore the question that cannot be answered, then so be it. A more honest response is to tackle the problem I have called the *general cognitive survey*, however difficult this may turn out to be.

Of course, there are problems inherent in a teacher's attempt to assess the general ability of a child or adult. The commonest such test in use by teachers, Raven's Progressive Matrices, is central to a psychometric view of what general intelligence actually is, though we may have concerns about unexpected challenges that it presents to some dyslexics (Carpenter, Just and Shell, 1990, p. 406). A majority of individuals who are given this test rejoice at being asked to perform at something they *can* do. Nevertheless an important minority of individuals has verbal abilities significantly different from the kinds of visuo-spatial abilities engaged by the Raven tests. If this measure of non-verbal reasoning is taken as a proxy for general intellectual ability, then an injustice will be done. It is expecting too much of even a well-qualified teacher to analyse different groups of abilities by means of tests.

Nevertheless, the market already supplies many good quality tests of general ability – mostly group tests designed for schools – and has done so for a long time. There are no means of preventing the intrepid teacher from administering such tests even if it were desired to do so. The aim of a good postgraduate training course for specialist teachers must be to guide and inform the use of such tests for the benefit of clients of all ages.

Some principles may be borne in mind.

(1)   IQ *estimates* are permissible if they do not imply that a reliable individual test of cognitive ability has been administered by an appropriately qualified professional. Such estimates are best

produced by combining two or more results from tests of one kind or another of general ability. Such *composites*, as they are known, though more reliable and stable, carry the pitfall that regression will carry them towards the mean (standard score of 100) and below 90 or above 110 this will mean a difference larger than the standard error of most tests. Half the population will be affected. This applies to any second or subsequent test result for an individual. Such a regression effect can be counteracted by means of the table of normal distribution values given in Appendix 3. For single results columns 1–5 give equivalents among some of the various types of scores available. For two or more results in combination, however, such as a composite obtained by averaging several results together, the same scores in columns 5–8 should be selected. A test result from, say, column 4 (a standard score with mean 100, SD 15) behaves like a score from column 6 if used in combination with others. The same statistical principle applies to combinations of attainment test results.

(2)   Another principle is that tests are actually more reliable if used in combination. A good rule of thumb is that tests should be used in *pairs* and the results expressed as composites. Thus a pair of tests of verbal or non-verbal or word recognition ability gives excellent results. However, teachers may feel that duplication of tests is not always possible in the time available.

(3)   A third principle, being applied in this chapter, is that a few good quality tests are preferable to a multitude of ones of indifferent quality.

To facilitate the application of this last principle, let us look more closely at some specific tests that are in use and accessible to teachers.

An individual teacher-usable test of intelligence

Postgraduate-level training in educational measurement includes the better validated courses for specialist dyslexia teachers, for which the Kaufman Brief Intelligence Test (K-BIT) (Kaufman and Kaufman, 1990) may be purchased and used. Of recent American provenance, this consists in a non-verbal reasoning component, Matrices, and two verbal components, Definitions and Expressive Vocabulary. The latter are combined into a single vocabulary score, which in turn is combined with the non-verbal score into an IQ composite.

This Matrices test is a welcome addition to its class (for Raven and others, see below). However, it is more than another variation on a traditional theme, as its earlier items (K-BIT norms range from 5 to 90) are *pictorial* and only gradually become abstract. Thus the individual is presented, for example, with a picture of a *fish* and the task is to select which one of four or five accompanying illustrations it goes with (such as the person with a rod on a river bank). Retest reliability values given in the manual are all 0.80 or above. Mean internal consistency is 0.85 for ages 4–19 and 0.94 for 20–90.

Definitions, unfortunately, uses the KAIT format of using as stimuli words printed in capital letters with letters missing and a clue. An (invented) example might be:

SI_G carol

A non-dyslexic subject might very well answer *sing*. However, not only does this format shamelessly impose a literacy criterion for verbal ability – it also uses US spellings (*plow* etc.).[8] It can hardly, therefore, be recommended for British dyslexics. Its companion, Expressive Vocabulary, is a creation much more sympathetic to a British audience. The format requires naming of single pictures. Though word-finding may be a problem for some dyslexics, the test is untimed and only concrete objects are pictured. Little loss of precision should result, with a vocabulary test of this conventional type, from doubling the resulting score before combining it into a composite with Matrices. In this way Definitions may be omitted. The vocabulary composite, which of course *includes* Definitions, achieves very high split-half reliability coefficients of 0.91 (ages 4–19) and 0.97 (ages 20–90), as is usual with tests of this type.

Internal consistency for the IQ composite is high (0.92 at ages 4–19, 0.97 at ages 20–90) and concurrent validity satisfactory (WISC-R, 0.80, $n = 35$, ages 6–15; WAIS-R, 0.75, $n = 64$, ages 16–47).[9] Because the norms are all-age and administration time is likely to be in the region of 20 minutes, this test is a uniquely valuable contribution to the work of the specialist teacher with learning-impaired individuals of all ages.

General verbal ability

First some tests which nowadays one can afford to pass by. The Raven tests include ill-normed measures of vocabulary (Crichton, Mill Hill; Raven, Court and Raven, 1978) which are probably best avoided. There are some verbal tests in the recent Verbal Reasoning tests (Hagues and Courtenay, 1993) but my preference would be to avoid these with dyslexics as they seem to be biased towards letter-coding skills. Many alternatives are available and can be recommended without reservation.

Passive or receptive vocabulary is measured across a wide age-range (3–18) by the British Picture Vocabulary Scale (BPVS) (Dunn et al., 1982). As this test requires only a pointing response it is particularly useful with a shy child or one whose first language is not English.[10] The short form is a little too short and the long form too long, perhaps, but the added reliability associated with the longer form makes it preferable if time and patience are not at a premium.

There are four useful pencil-and-paper verbal tests in the Children's Abilities Test (CAT) (Thorndike, Hagen and France, 1986), whose norms range from 8–15. As with the non-verbal tests in this battery (see next section), these can stand alone and therefore should be selected among for reliability. The manual gives adequate detail to permit this.

Another good choice is Vocabulary in the Richmond Tests of Basic Skills, 2nd edn (RTBS) (Hieronymus, Lindquist and France, 1988). Although designed for testing groups of pupils, this can be adapted and given on its own. Its synonym-type items can be read aloud to reading-disabled pupils.

General non-verbal ability

All the traditional Raven tests (Raven, 1947, 1956, 1958, 1962; Raven, Court and Raven, 1978; Raven and Court, 1989) continue in use. If the user is not forgiving of their antiquity, they can be shortened (Turner, 1994c). The Advanced Progressive Matrices are a strategic asset with adults, for whom generally very little exists. However, all Raven materials are sold in labyrinthine and expensive packages, which test distributors themselves seem hardly to understand. Moreover they are engulfed in controversy over a new edition whose norms have failed to win the confidence of the professionals who use them (see Gudjonnson, 1995a, 1995b; Raven, 1995).

A better bet for the 5–16 or school-age population is the short form of the Matrix Analogies Test (Naglieri, 1985). This offers a standard 33-item set[11] for all ages. Instructions are simple and clear; the manual is slim yet eloquent and a specimen set has always been reasonably priced.

There are four useful pencil-and-paper non-verbal tests in the Children's Abilities Test (CAT) (Thorndike, Hagen and France, 1986). Again they can be used selectively with an eye to subtest reliability.

Finally the new Non-verbal Reasoning tests (Smith and Hagues, 1993) are innovative and excellent. Like their Verbal Reasoning companions they are stepped with respect to age-group, so involve a larger purchase if a complete stock is required. But their item types have probably received more thought and care than other comparable tests.

Diagnostic tests

Psychologists, as we have seen in Chapter 4, rely largely on their main cognitive batteries (WISC, BAS/DAS and others) for tests of *diagnostic* relevance. But a considerable number of other diagnostic procedures discussed there may be used by teachers.

The Test of Auditory Analysis Skills (TAAS) (in Rosner, 1993), a short phoneme deletion procedure, is of particular relevance up to about 8 years and is informative with learning-impaired children thereafter.

The Children's Test Of Non-word Repetition (CNRep); (in Gathercole et al., 1994 and to be published by the Psychological Corporation in 1996) presents norms from large administrations for ages 4–10 and constitutes one of the most potent additions to the diagnostic repertoire in recent years.

Non-word reading, as we have seen, is a particularly effective probe of phonological reading skill. Already mentioned and published, unre-stricted, in the USA, the Woodcock Reading Mastery Tests – Revised (WRMT-R) (Woodcock, 1987) contain a well-developed and well -normed test, Word Attack. My Nonword Decoding Test (NWDT; Turner, 1994d) is unnormed but revealing of guessing, lexicalisation and other strategies associated with a phonological reading deficit.

WISC Digit Span norms for the average number of digits recited correctly forwards and backwards are in the public domain (see Carroll, 1993, p. 265) and seem from the new standardisation not to have changed with time. In principle this version of Digit Span can be adapted for teacher use without either infringing copyright or incurring unac-ceptable loss of precision. The selection of digits and the order in which they appear in the WISC tests are copyright but in principle, apart from the avoidance of zeros and repeated digits, both are random.

Rhyming and Non-rhyming Sentences (Turner, 1995c) are offered with indicative primary norms.

The Phonological Awareness Test 1 (Appendix 3 in Aaron and Joshi, 1992) consists in 10 procedures, taken from Stanovich, Cunningham and Cramer (1984), the first four normed for 6-year-olds.

The Bangor Dyslexia Test (Miles, 1982) and Aston Index (Thomson and Newton, 1982) may be used selectively. Effectiveness in their use seems to accrue with experience.

Perin's spoonerism task (Perin, 1983) is useful for older pupils and there are indicative norms for the 14-year-old age-group. A spoonerism procedure is the centrepiece of University College's *Phonological Assessment Battery* (PhAB) (Brook and Dalton, 1995), for a commercial development of which plans are afoot.

The Auditory Discrimination Test (Reynolds, 1987) is a revision of the better-known Wepman test (Wepman, 1973) and involves presenting minimally different pairs of words with the request to say if they are the *same* or *different*. Another useful, but longer and unnormed, set of auditory discrimination procedures is given as an appendix to Hornsby (1989).

Finally, Hatcher's Test of Phonological Awareness (Hatcher, 1994, 1996) directly serves the teaching programme of which it is a part. Taking no more than 15 minutes to administer, it includes syllable blend-ing, phoneme blending, rhyme, phoneme segmentation, phoneme deletion and phoneme transposition tasks. Moreover, data derived from its administration in 1995 to a stratified sample of 229 Carlisle children aged 4;8 to 8;8 yield estimates of concurrent and predictive relationship to WORD (Rust, Golombok and Trickey, 1993) and Burt[12] word recognition tests of about 0.60. Reliability and validity are excellent (Hatcher, 1996). Standard scores are provided for this age-group plus an apparatus to evaluate, given observed scores on the tests of reading and phonological awareness (PA), whether the observed PA score falls below that expected, in which case:

> there is some support for the hypothesis that poor phonological awareness is a factor contributing to [the child's] delayed reading ability. If other factors have also been considered, we might consider providing such a child with phonological awareness training that is very carefully linked to a profile of [his or her] reading strengths and weaknesses (Hatcher, 1996, p. 19)

Note that another discrepancy methodology, of the kind discussed at length in this book and of which IQ/achievement scores is only one example, is here being advanced without any necessity, within its rationale, for extraneous clinical investigations.[13]

Conclusion

This completes this brief survey of ability, diagnostic and attainment tests currently available for the use of teachers. Just as important as the actual selection of tests for review is the basis for comparison and evaluation, which I have tried to make explicit wherever possible. The coverage is mainstream: there may well be more recondite tests for the connoisseur. But the reason for any important omissions lies in my own ignorance.

Further details of tests mentioned

Publication details of tests are given wherever possible, as for books, in the References section. The following list of publishers and distributors may provide additional help to those wishing to pursue items mentioned:

NFER-Nelson publish or distribute the following materials:[14]

> Basic Skills Tests (Occupational Test Series, available from ASE, a division of the company)
> Diagnostic Spelling Test
> Macmillan Graded Word Reading Test (came originally from the Macmillan Test Unit)
> Macmillan Group Reading Test 9–14 (came originally from the Macmillan Test Unit)

Macmillan Individual Reading Analysis (came originally from the
   Macmillan Test Unit)
Neale Analysis of Reading Ability (Revised British Edition, 1989).
New Macmillan Reading Analysis (came originally from the
   Macmillan Test Unit)
English Progress Tests are published as a series (Tests A2, B2, C2,
   C3, D2, D3, E2 and F2)
Reading Comprehension Test DE
Reading Tests A, AD, BD, SR-A/B
Reading Tests EH1 and 2
Reading Ability Series
Richmond Test of Basic Skills
Test of Initial Literacy (TOIL)

The Psychological Corporation, a division of Harcourt Brace Jovanovich,
publishes or distributes the following materials in the UK:[15]

Boder Test of Reading-Spelling Patterns
Matrix Analogies Test

Hodder and Stoughton publish or distribute the following materials in
the UK:[16]
   Edinburgh Reading Tests. Stage 4 is available to LEA order only
   Parallel Spelling Tests
   Salford Sentence Reading Test
   SPAR (Spelling and Reading) Tests
   Vernon Spelling Test
   Word Search

Heinemann publish or distribute the following materials:[17]
   GAP
   GAPADOL

The Dyslexia Institute distributes the following:[18]
   Kaufman Brief Intelligence Test (K-BIT)
   Wide Range Achievement Test – Third Edition (WRAT-3)
   Woodcock Reading Mastery Tests – Revised (WRMT-R)

Hunter-Grundin Literacy Profiles are published by The Test Agency.[19]
There is neither specimen set nor general guide.
   Slingerland Revised Pre-Reading Screening Procedures and Screening
Tests For Identifying Children With Specific Language Disability are
obtainable from Educators Publishing Service Inc.[20]

Barking Reading Project materials are now available from their principal author, Geoff Trickey.[21]

Notes

1 I am indebted to Mick Archer, editor of *Special Children* in which it originally appeared as Turner (1993), for permission to republish some of the material in this chapter.
2 Such as the alternative to the scientific methodology that has been devised for teachers studying for research degrees, on the grounds, presumably, that what is good enough for everyone else must be too good for teachers.
3 The statements asterisked are the ones with actual research support.
4 Analysed first by Gorman (1989), subsequently by others.
5 Including *mental age*, for instance.
6 However for users of Form Z, Sawyer and Potter (1994) have helpfully provided standard score equivalents of raw scores, based on a large administration in Dorset.
7 For the connoisseur, both the RAS and TOIL enshrine examples of the determined multiculturalism and appropriacy which have been part of the effort to redefine English.
8 Though specific item content seems less abrasively monocultural than that of KAIT.
9 But compare the 12-minute pencil-and-paper Wonderlic Personnel Test (Wonderlic and Hovland, 1937–95), a highly g-loaded measure whose total score correlated, for 30 adults, 0.96 with WAIS-R IQ.
10 This is, though, precisely a reason to want to give a test of English *comprehension*.
11 Forty-five to 60 minutes and 60 items, as in Raven's Standard Progressive Matrices, are unnecessary to measure non-verbal reasoning.
12 Burt remains a useful test for a research exercise of this kind since it includes 110 words, about twice as many as WORD, and additional points of raw score allow variation more scope.
13 Though 'other factors' will have 'been considered'.
14 Address: NFER-Nelson, Darville House, 2 Oxford Road East, Windsor, Berkshire, United Kingdom, SL4 1DF. Tel: 01753 858600.
15 Address: Harcourt Brace Jovanovich (The Psychological Corporation), Foots Cray High Street, Sidcup, Kent DA14 4BR. Tel: 0181 300 3322.
16 Address: Hodder and Stoughton, Mill Road, Dunton Green, Sevenoaks, Kent TN13 2YA. Tel: 01732 450111.
17 Address: Heinemann Educational, Halley Court, Jordan Hill, Oxford OX2 8EJ. Tel: 01865 311366.
18 Address: The Dyslexia Institute, 133 Gresham Road, Staines, Middlesex TW18 2AJ. Tel: 01784 463851.
19 Address: The Test Agency Ltd, Cournswood House, North Dean, High Wycombe, Bucks HP14 4NW. Tel: 01494 563384.
20 Address: Educators Published Service Inc., 75 Moulton Street, Cambridge, Massachusetts 02238, USA.
21 At: Psychological Consultancy Ltd, Victoria House, Grover Street, Tunbridge Wells, Kent TN1 2QB. Tel: 01892 547500.

Chapter 10
Assessment of the Younger Child

The move to earlier assessment

Over several years attention has moved towards the earlier assessment of the dyslexic child. This has occurred for many reasons. The general benefit of early intervention is hardly to be doubted[1] but as the dyslexia movement matures, there is an increasing number of young parents who, diagnosed themselves at a late age, now have concerns about their own children for whom they want earlier advice. Since the experience of their parents' generation was of diagnosis as adults or not at all, the average age for dyslexia detection would seem to be moving gradually downwards. Such families have in the recent past sought professional assistance and advice for their young children – and been turned away.

Alas, common practice has been to cling to the primary criterion for dyslexia, underachievement – (see Chapter 3) and to refuse to address a child's developmental problems until he or she was old enough to fail on a reading test. While this enabled regression-based statements to be made about 8-year-olds with due scientific confidence, for the child it meant lost time, lost self-esteem and irreversible experience of classroom failure. As a consequence interest has been drawn to checklists and developmental inventories furnished by parents and the mills of folklore.

Early identification initiatives

In Britain the British Dyslexia Association, a national charitable network for families, has promoted early identification with some success. Both an information booklet (Brereton and Cann, 1993) and a video (British Dyslexia Association, 1995) have been produced. The former, an edited volume, draws together distinguished contributors.[2] Above all the hope has been that an early detection screening system could be applied to all children at an early age, before or just after the start of schooling, so that children likely to become dyslexic could be *caught early*. We shall need to look in general at the mechanics of such systems for mass screening in order to see what the challenges and pitfalls really are, but first let us note that even a successful dyslexia screening exercise creates assurance and alarm in about equal proportions. The assured are all those families who receive realistic professional advice about their children at an early stage, so that, even if the news is bad, at least the worst can be prevented. The alarmed are all those who must bring additional resources to bear.

Research initiatives

In the last few years two university-based research initiatives to develop just such a screening measure have won publicity and given encouraging hope of success. Both deserve a closer look.

Within the University of Hull Psychology Department Dr Chris Singleton and his colleagues, taking a pragmatic approach, have turned their attention to the development of diagnostic software that could prove useful in the infant departments of schools (Singleton, Thomas and Leedale, 1995). To date, their resulting software suite, CoPS or Cognitive Profiling System, a set of games-format tests with which the young child interacts directly through a keyboard, has been brought into use within eight local educational authorities (LEAs).[3]

The rationale for this development accepts that 'cognitive precursors of dyslexia' include aspects of 'memory, sequential information processing, phonological awareness and, in some cases, visual-perceptual difficulties' (p.1).[4] The interpretation that this supposes 'two broad subtypes . . . *auditory dyslexia* and *visual dyslexia*' (p. 5; original emphasis) is encouraged.

There are nine tests whose methodology is based on a pragmatic sense of the processes that might be of significance in the development of dyslexia. Thus one test, Rabbits, in which one or more rabbits at the entrance to various burrows situated around the screen disappears, requires the child to remember in the correct order where each was seen. This might be expected to involve spatial ability and to fall somewhere at the extreme non-linguistic end of the ability spectrum; as such, it provides a useful contrast with the abilities usually impaired in dyslexia. But no, this is defined as *sequential memory (spatial/temporal)* and is included on equal terms with tests of rhyme awareness and *sequential memory (names)*.

No matter that this might seem a trifle naïve:

> the information gleaned from the statistical analysis was the primary factor in determining the composition of the final suite of software. (Singleton, Thomas and Leedale, 1995, p. 6)

Let us therefore inquire into the empirical findings. Beyond the summary that '80% of children [thus identified were] subsequently found to be dyslexic' (op. cit., p. 6), such information remains in short supply. However, figures given at a recent symposium are more explicit (Singleton, 1995). During development a sample of 380 children aged 5 years was obtained from 24 participating schools. These were followed up over three years using a variety of psychometric measures. The BAS Word Reading test given during the first 18 months of the project was found to be more closely related to CoPS scores than the Neale integrated passage reading test given at age 8, whether because of the shorter interval or the different nature of the reading task is not known. The outcome frequencies are reported in Table 10.1.

Table 10.1: Proportions of children classified as pre-dyslexic or not at 5 years and found to be dyslexic or not at 8 years

		Predicted (%)	
		Dyslexic	Not dyslexic
Actual	Dyslexic ($n = 16$)	75	25
	Not dyslexic ($n = 38$)	18	82

These data permit an analysis along the lines of Bayes' theorem, in which outcomes are evaluated in the light of *antecedent probabilities*. Thus, accepting a low estimate for unambiguous dyslexia of some 2–4%, by deeming the whole population of 5-year-olds to be not dyslexic one will be right more than 96% of the time. This, of course, is a hard target on which to improve.

That Bayesian criteria are indeed the ones by which screening packages must be evaluated is made clear by publishers' increasing use of such statistics to win professional credibility, just as Cronbach's Alpha and measures of test–retest reliability are quoted in support of claims made for new tests. For instance a recent computerised continuous performance test for diagnosis of attention deficit (hyperactivity) disorder, the Test of Variables of Attention (TOVA), appears in the 1996 clinical catalogue of American Guidance Service. The accompanying description reads, in part, as follows:

> Discriminant analysis of TOVA and 10-item Conners Parent–Teacher Questionnaire of hyperactive children with ADD and matched (age, sex) normals correctly classified 87% of normal and 90% of the ADHD subjects with 13% false positives and 10% false negatives. A similar study of children without hyperactivity correctly classified 83% of normals and 97% of children with ADD.

Numbers of subjects are not reported, nor the time interval, if any, but clearly CoPS has some leeway to make up, with a quarter of all dyslexics being incorrectly classified and a false positive rate (normals incorrectly predicted as dyslexic) of nearly a fifth. More information on this small study would be welcome, since nearly a third of children included are dyslexic. Information about detection base rates for a full population cannot at present be inferred. Moreover it is unknown to what extent this predictive accuracy rate could be improved by fine adjustments (incorporation of some developmental discrepancy, for instance) or use of concurrent questionnaire data.

A parallel development has been the work of Angela Fawcett and Rod Nicolson at Sheffield University Psychology Department (Fawcett, Pickering and Nicolson, 1992). This proceeds squarely from their well-known theoretical perspective that an automatisation deficit, originating in cerebellar dysfunction, impedes the learning of basic skills in dyslexia, as well as primitive motor skills such as balance (Nicolson and Fawcett, 1990, 1995). A great deal of experimental evidence is presented for this view and has been added to over half a decade, so these studies have the inestimable merit of being *brittle*, that is, capable of being proved wrong.

Their Dyslexia Early Screening Test (DEST) is soon to be published[5] and though neither Bayesian nor other predictive validity data are yet available, the test is normed for children aged 4;6 to 6;5. Requiring pencil and paper only and a minimum of equipment, the DEST is capable of being administered to a child in just half an hour. It comprises 10 subtests, the nature of which arises directly from dyslexia research:

1. rapid automatised naming of pictures of common objects
2. bead threading
3. phonological discrimination (minimal word pairs)
4. postural stability
5. rhyme detection and alliteration
6. forward digit span
7. naming of printed digits
8. naming of printed letters
9. sound order (temporal auditory integration: which came first, the duck or the mouse?)
10. shape copying.

Bead threading and postural stability reflect Nicolson's and Fawcett's experimental claims rather than any consensus.

Firm performance criteria are specified, as are clear procedures for deriving an *at risk quotient*. Clearly this is a *test* and will be judged by conventional psychometric criteria.

The challenge of screening

Together with the elegant, phonologically focused and teaching programme-related Test of Phonological Awareness (Hatcher, 1994,

1996) mentioned briefly in the last chapter, these two imaginative contributions will yield lessons that are bound to carry forward the efforts being made to identify early, and ameliorate, dyslexia. We need next to enquire more closely into the methodological issues in assessing young children, but first we should note the inherent difficulties of delivering an effective screening service.

Recent adverse publicity given to *false positive* detection of breast cancer shows that uncertainty is not confined to the behavioural domain. Concerns about anxiety needlessly aroused through measurement error also affect the provision of health services. An influential study by Sweden's Office of Health Care Technology Assessment of 40 000 women aged from 40 to 64 found that about 2.4% were identified, three-quarters of them falsely, by mammography. Subsequent investigation, including invasive biopsies, could take up to two years and cost about £6000 per false positive with an unquantifiable cost in terror. Those aged under 50 who *had* breast cancer went on to die from the disease at the same rate as those in the unscreened group.

Some medical screening programmes are worth undertaking: thyroid malfunction and phenylketonuria in newborn infants, treated early, need not lead to mental retardation but others, such as annual screening for cervical cancer, seem driven by consumer emotion, often fanned by media story-telling. With any measure repeated often, the chances of a false positive eventually occurring are high. Other examples of medical screening include conditions where treatments are risky or of dubious value, such as for prostate cancer, or have no effects on total mortality, such as for high blood cholesterol. The demand for screening and associated treatments is high, however, and tends to acquire a momentum of its own with consequences in the political sphere. Increasingly, genetic discoveries intensify this situation, with expensive searches in prospect for genes for conditions, such as cystic fibrosis, whose course is anyway unpredictable.

The dilemmas of screening are highlighted in conditions that are hard to put right and do not do much harm. While this is not a good description of dyslexia, the pressures – and the base rates – are undoubtedly similar to some of the medical conditions mentioned. Moreover we will do well to note the prime lesson from the experience of medical researchers: that most practical problems will arise in relation to those individuals falsely identified as positive for dyslexia.

What are *not* signs of dyslexia?

We have seen that folklore has much to say about the development of dyslexia. Many are the parents who, sitting in a waiting room or reading a magazine article, have mentally compared their child with a published checklist of signs. The result invariably is: 'It could be my James (or

Jane)!' There is a response bias operating here. No attempt is made to identify all the points James or Jane has in common with non-dyslexic children or does *not* have in common with dyslexic ones. There is no critical shift. All conclusions must lead in one direction.

This reporting or response bias is reinforced by the presence in the checklists of many features which, though unusual, are present in a great many children and have no known connection with dyslexia. Many dyslexic and non-dyslexic children have difficulty tying shoelaces, for instance, or copying geometric forms. In educational terms these features may be important, just as any teacher will want to take account of a child's left- or mixed-handedness. They may coexist with dyslexia; they may interact with, compound and confuse the symptoms of dyslexia. But either, like the relationship between handedness and reading, they 'lack predictive ability' or, like letter reversals (*b*s and *d*s), they are 'not a marker for dyslexia' (Aaron and Joshi, 1992, p. 248). They are likely to proceed from a different origin from the dyslexia; there is a tendency for children with one developmental difficulty[6] to have others.

Informal procedures for investigating lateral preference (hand, foot, eye) continue in use but from an extensive and controversy-riven literature:

> . . . a clear picture does not emerge . . . [If there is] . . . a link between handedness and specific childhood disorders...there is certainly no direct relationship . . . [and] . . . none of the scientists studying these questions venture views on the practical implications. (Henderson and Sugden, 1992, pp. 233–4)

It should be borne in mind that when the McCarthy Scales (McCarthy, 1972), which include a test of this kind, were standardised prior to 1972, 40% of the population was found to be 'cross-lateral' and that inconsistent preferences are found in about one-third of the population (Annett, 1985). If such common developmental aberrations are included in checklists for dyslexia, the result, not surprisingly, will be that numerous children will be wrongly recruited as victims.

Three kinds of evidence to be sought

Though early screening efforts are taking shape and parents are encouraged to look for 'signs' at an ever earlier age, the psychologist's individual cognitive assessment remains at this age, as at others, the canonical account of whether the young child actually is dyslexic. So what are the features of dyslexia that appear first in a child who will later have a difficulty with literacy?

It may be helpful, given the scope for confusion, to identify three distinct classes of signs or early warnings of dyslexia. First, there are *constant features* of dyslexia that are the same in the pre-school child as in the late adolescent. Second, there are *precursors* or features that fore-shadow dyslexia. Third, there are *concomitants* or indirect features that may accompany the disorder at any given stage. Moreover the evaluation of all of these in an individual assessment must remain an *audit of risk factors*, more or less numerous in any case, rather than a definitive statement about a child's dyslexia. Given the largely descriptive nature of dyslexia diagnosis at all ages, and the continuing centrality in it of observed literacy failure, the assessment of the younger child must remain a provisional matter, tentative rather than categorical.

Concomitants of dyslexia

In suitably dyslexic fashion, let us take these categories in reverse order. It has often been said that the best indicator of dyslexia in young children is the performance of the father on a reading test. As 80% of cases [7] may be identified in this way, it would compare favourably with more elaborate screening exercises! Though to my knowledge nobody has been brave enough to implement such a investigation,[8] the rationale for doing so is clear enough, as indicated in Table 10.2.

Table 10.2: Degrees of risk associated with parent–child relationships. From Vogler, DeFries and Decker (1985)

	Affected (%)	
Risk to	Mother	Father
Son	35	40
Daughter	15	20
	Mother	Father
Son	7	6
Daughter	2	2

That elements of literacy may be treated as components with different associated heritability is also clear, as can be seen from Table 10.3.

Table 10.3: Differential heritability of components of word reading. From Olson et al. (1989, 1991).

	h^2_g (%)
Word reading	46
Phonological decoding	65
Orthographic knowledge	23

More recent unpublished work by the same team, reported at conferences, tends to show rising heritability values for orthographic knowledge. Because orthography depends, directly or indirectly, upon phonology, this development runs in accordance with, rather than against, expectations.

If a positive family incidence is the first major risk factor, then impairment of aspects of memory is the second. Whether for reasons of word-finding (lexical access: see next section) or articulation speed, young children's immediate verbal memory difficulties may be demonstrated easily. Because of their known covariance with literacy skills, these may be conveniently regarded as concomitant rather than constant features, though they seldom disappear.

Another little researched concomitant deserves to be mentioned. Children who have learned and played happily prior to formal schooling, who have shown no undue difficulties with separating from their mothers, sometimes start to show unexpected *unhappiness* soon after starting school. They become reluctant to go to school and reluctant to separate. This may the first indication that something is wrong. This case has, in the UK, been argued best by Gerald Hales (for example Hales, 1994).

Precursors of dyslexia

Precursors are developmental features of the pre-literate (and hence pre-dyslexic) child that fade as learning and maturation take place. Speech delay and word-finding difficulties are good examples. Children who present as dyslexic aged 8 or 10 were:

- frequently late developing speech initially;
- either weeks or months later than their first birthday in producing their first words;
- later than 18 months in producing words in combination or in producing 'thousands [of syntactic types] before the third birthday' (Pinker, 1995, p. 269).

They may, of course, exhibit all three. Though research does not unequivocally implicate language delay as a precursor of dyslexia, it must be regarded as a risk factor.

Deficits in rapid automatised naming are well attested in dyslexic children of all ages (Denckla and Rudel, 1976). These are normally theorised, within lexical access accounts of dyslexia, as word-finding difficulties. As we shall see, tests of immediate memory for lists of names, which without context must be stored largely by phonological structure, are especially good indicators at this age of unusual difficulty in verbal learning.

Children in the preschool years tend to pick up recognition of letters[9] and numbers spontaneously, whether or not they attend playgroups, nurseries and preschool. Parents of dyslexic children, however, frequently report an *absence of interest* in books and a lack of facility with letters and numbers, even when these *have* been introduced in a semi-formal learning environment.

The non-response of children to such teaching once they begin at school, or after a longish period in both preschool and school combined, furnishes a further precursor, because test norms assume nothing about length of opportunities provided. For their *age* some children of 5–6 are normal enough, but not when ability and exposure to early instruction are considered.

Constant features of dyslexia

Language control difficulties, notably in segmental phonology, are a relatively constant sign, whether in spontaneous spoonerisms at age 4 or difficulty in producing spoonerisms to order at age 17.

The useful generic term for these is disturbance in phonological processing or the ability to hear, store, reproduce and manipulate the *sounds* of speech, such as the sequence of syllables in *car park* or *barbecue* (rather than *par cark* and *cubeybar*). *Phonology* is a term used in many ways and no putative restriction is proposed, just as no view is implied as to whether a store or just a process is a sufficient explanation of the phenomena observed. Parents frequently report mix-ups in *syllable* and occasionally word order in the speech of developing children who later are confirmed to have dyslexia. Other aspects of language, including phonology, are more conveniently regarded as precursors, as we have seen.

A small-scale study

There is now a quite extensive literature identifying the precursors of literacy. It is well summarised in Adams (1990), though subsequent studies, applying sophisticated path analyses, have added considerably to the picture given there (for example Muter, Snowling and Taylor, 1994).

During the period 1990–93 I conducted, with two south London maintained primary schools, a small investigation into what was subsequently to become known as *added value*. A number of measures were taken of 49 children in their first week at school aged 4–5 years.[10] Three years later, 29 children were given group attainment measures (reading, arithmetic, non-verbal reasoning, spelling). As well as providing information useful to schools and parents at both stages, the exercise permitted an analysis of which entry level measures best predicted which outcomes.

Five baseline measures were employed:

•   Verbal ability: the long form of the *British Picture Vocabulary Scale* (BPVS) (Dunn et al., 1982).

- Non-verbal or visuo-spatial ability: Raven's *Coloured Progressive Matrices*.
- Number recognition: ability to find a number from an array when it was named (total correct out of 10: 0–9).
- Knowledge of letter sounds: *Daniels and Diack Test 5* (Daniels and Diack, 1958) (total correct out of 21).
- Knowledge of lower-case letter names: ability to pick these out of an array when named (total correct out of 26).

The outcome measures when the children were in Year 2 (summer term)[11] were as follows:

- Form F of the British Ability Scales *Matrices* test, a measure of non-verbal reasoning in the Raven tradition (Elliott, Murray and Pearson, 1979, 1983).
- Form D of *Basic Number Skills*, the test of written arithmetic from the British Ability Scales (Elliott, Murray and Pearson, 1979, 1983).
- The *Suffolk Group Reading Test* of sentence completion (Hagley, 1987).
- The *Wide Range Achievement Test* (Revised) (WRAT-R) of *spelling* (Jastak and Wilkinson, 1984).

Pearson's *r* correlation coefficients were computed between the two sets of measures. Results[12] are presented in Table 10.4.

Table 10.4: Correlations between ability and achievement measures at 4–5 and 6–7 years ($n = 29$):*$p < 0.05$; **$p < 0.01$; ***$p < 0.001$.

	Age 4–5 measures			
	Suffolk Reading	WRAT Spelling	BAS Matrices	BAS Arithmetic
Age 6–7 measures				
BPVS vocabulary	0.69***	0.36	–0.09	–0.03
Raven's CPM	0.44*	0.33	0.27	0.40*
Numbers 0–9	0.67***	0.48**	0.07	0.23
Letter sounds	0.32	–0.06	0.39	–0.16

Age 7 Suffolk reading scores were highly correlated with age 4 BPVS vocabulary, as with age 4 Raven's Coloured Matrices. This suggests a larger role for general ability than is often found in similar studies. However, later reading was also highly correlated with earlier number recognition ability. Scores for the latter were raw and not standardised for chronological age. There was, though, a near-zero correlation between number recognition score and age, suggesting that the former

was not a mere surrogate for age. Age 4 number recognition was also significantly associated with age 7 spelling ability. Non-verbal ability at age 4 predicted later arithmetical ability (BAS Basic Number Skills) better than it did later non-verbal reasoning (BAS Matrices).

Because there were three significant age 4 correlates of later reading, a stepwise regression analysis was conducted to discover whether there were multiple independent predictors of later reading ability. BPVS vocabulary and number recognition were significant independent predictors of reading. The multiple R was 0.78: i.e. 57.3% (multiple R^2) of the reliable variance in reading test scores at age 6–7 was accounted for by vocabulary and number recognition at age 4–5.

While this finding assigns an important place to general linguistic ability at least, it confirms as a precursor of reading the kind of digital, code-oriented skills that were described in Chapter 2 as 'perceptual and pattern recognition skills'. The acquisition or non-acquisition of facility with numbers and letters may, as mentioned above, already be significant when provision of opportunities to learn is taken into account.

A preschool casework sample

The Differential Ability Scales (DAS), as described in Chapter 3, includes excellent tests for the 2–6 year age-group. Indeed this preschool module is distinct and overlaps with the school-age module (6–18) only at a few points (Pattern Construction, Digit Span, Immediate and Delayed Visual Recall), though school-age tests are also normed downwards and preschool ones upwards to permit additional overlap if needed.

During the years 1993–95 data using the pre-school DAS were collected for a clinical sample of 40 children, whose mean age was 5.19 decimal years (SD 0.67). All these children had been brought by their parents to the Dyslexia Institute for an independent psychological assessment for the variety of reasons already alluded to and probably best summed up as anxiety about their general development. The children thus referred were not assigned labels (*dyslexic, non-dyslexic*) but were given as detailed a cognitive-developmental assessment as time, tolerance and availability of suitable test materials would permit. Results were discussed and reported in terms of *predisposing risk factors* for dyslexia or other learning difficulties.

This data collection permits a special further analysis along the lines conducted in Chapter 8. However, this sample, though again a clinical one, is very different. Much smaller, it does not permit easy extrapolation even to the plurality of pre-school dyslexic children, even though of interest in its own right. These children are in the main, presumably, still not causing their parents, oblivious of what lies ahead, any major concerns. The children in the sample, however, *have* caused concern to the extent of inducing their parents to seek external specialised professional help, a very considerable step to take with children of this age.

Let us look first at the distribution of ages of these children (Table 10.5).

Table 10.5: Frequencies of ages of pre-school sample by sex in half-year intervals

	3:5–3:9	4:0–4:4	4:5–4:9	5:0–5:4	5:5–5:9	Total
Girls	1	1	2	3	11	18
Boys	2	3	4	6	7	22
Both	3	4	6	9	18	40

Girls were referred in more equal numbers at these ages than in the school-age sample discussed in Chapter 8. Older children, too, were more numerous among those referred.

Next let us look at the cognitive characteristics of this sample in aggregate: for this purpose the three DAS composites provided at this age, and shown in Figure 10.1, are most useful.

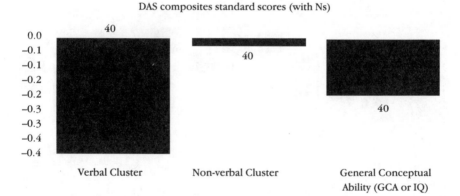

Figure 10.1: Average composite DAS abilities of 40 children in the preschool sample.

This figure shows clearly that we are no longer dealing with a normal distribution of cognitive ability. Only the non-verbal abilities of these children are close to the average. The summary measure of General Conceptual Ability or IQ is depressed by the poor language abilities of the children in the sample.

Next, therefore, we need to investigate how the profiles of these children are composed. If there is one salient feature of these children as a group, apparent in Figure 10.2, it is their poorly developed linguistic abilities. Note how Picture Similarities behaves like a linguistic test here. Perhaps the conceptualisation required, though no doubt in part *fluid*, arising from number patterns and visual forms, otherwise draws largely upon *verbal strategy* (in Chapter 4's terms), the application of naming and other strategies to diverse task materials.

Indeed these children justify their parents' concerns. One generalisation about them that will hold pertains to the skills that are *not* impaired. Three test bars rise above the line: Pattern Construction, Copying and Matching Letter-like Forms. These are all unambiguously visuo-spatial. Interestingly in respect of children whose parents think they may be dyslexic, these ones are *not* poor at copying geometric forms, *or* at resolving the rotation and orientation of abstract shapes! Indeed, like the large samples of learning-impaired school-age children described in the DAS manual (Elliott, 1990, pp. 258–62), their non-verbal and spatial abilities are their highest scores.[13]

These children's language skills, on the contrary, are uniformly poor for their age. Indeed it begins to become apparent why the assessment was sought. Linguistic skills are prominent and carry a vital social premium even at this age. Their children's developmental disadvantage had become obvious enough in relation to the development of others for the parents to seek help.

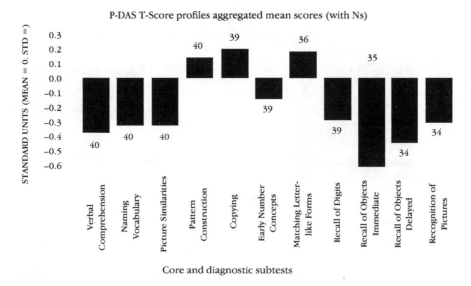

Figure 10.2: Aggregate DAS ability T-score profiles of 40 children in the preschool sample

One finding that deserves particular note is the tendency for Immediate Visual Recall to highlight learning and memory difficulties in many cases. This test, which utilises a conventional verbal learning paradigm, is described in Chapter 3. The child views a card with 20 coloured objects, which are named for him or her; he or she then must recall as many as possible within a minute. Two further similar trials follow, with another unannounced one after 15–20 minutes. The average of the first three trials gives an Immediate result, which may be compared with the norm group. The two results, on Immediate and Delayed trials, may be compared statistically. This test seems to be a peculiarly effective test with younger children. Since we consider that word-finding, lexical access and phonologically coded memory may be dyslexia precursors or concomitants, this test nicely captures early dyslexic learning behaviour.

But are these children dyslexic or pre-dyslexic? It is tempting to generalise the finding that rotations, reversals and fine motor control form no part of the diagnostic picture in young children! However the data are too limited to permit this. The sample is clearly biased towards children with linguistic impairment that is unusual in young dyslexics.

With the literacy criterion unavailable, however, we can apply the second, *cognitive profile* criterion, using the same cut-off procedure as before. If we do this on an individual (not aggregate) basis, we find the situation shown in Figure 10.3.

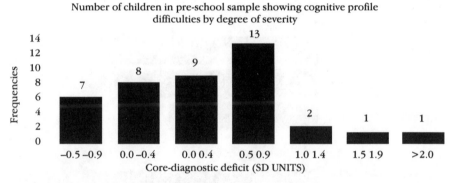

Figure 10.3: Numbers of children in the preschool sample (girls and boys combined) with various degrees of severity of information-processing difficulties (P-DAS Core-Diagnostic deficit in D units).

The approximate balance between halves of a normal distribution we met with in Figure 8.5 is not reproduced here. Numbers are smaller, of course, and the 0.5:0.9 interval is still the most populous, but 60% of this group now show core-diagnostic deficits smaller than half a standard deviation. Of course, the absence of cognitive profile is a function of lower than expected core test scores. As linguistic difficulties reduce children's ability to perform on general tests, so evidence of a specific cognitive deficit disappears.

Too few children remain to pursue an analysis of concomitants of severity similar to that in Chapter 8. Non-word repetition (CNRep) and Rosner (phoneme deletion) scores are available for many of the sample, and standardised Sound Blending (WJ-R) scores for some, and these in the main confirm the pattern of generalised language difficulties. But otherwise a variety of supplementary diagnostic tests is spread too thinly across a small sample to justify more ambitious analysis.

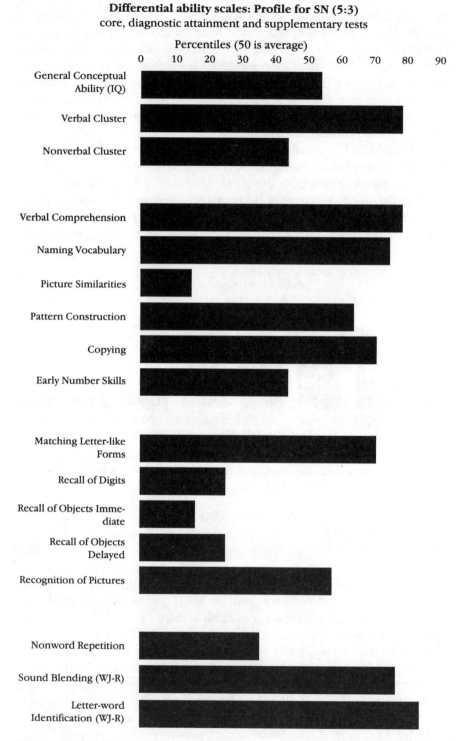

Figure 10.4: All DAS and other cognitive assessment results for SN (5:3) in percentile form.

Perhaps then we must conclude, agnostically, that it is impossible to decide of what population these children constitute a sample. General cognitive-linguistic difficulties untypical of dyslexic children have driven their families to seek an assessment, and often more than one. A general-purpose psychological assessment can contribute usefully to understanding and planning educationally for such children as they prepare to start at school but it seems unwise to draw any firm conclusions from this about the early development of dyslexia.

An illustrative report

Finally, then, let us consider an actual case, neither typical of those considered in aggregate, nor very different from them either. This illustrates the kinds of dilemma posed to the assessing psychologist, together with some of the possible responses in terms of test choice, hypothesis construction and individual consideration, that characterise work with the younger child.

SN is a self-possessed 5-year-old girl who nevertheless clearly shows a profile of difficulties with information skills, including those of memory, verbal strategy and phonology, in spite of mainly excellent language skills. The report which follows is self-explanatory and will end this chapter. First, however, let us view her profile of cognitive skills just as her parents did, in two graphs. These are shown in Figure 10.4, which, just as with JM, the 9-year-old boy whose report appeared in Chapter 6, portrays all her scores on normed tests in percentile form; and Figure 10.5, which displays core and diagnostic tests only in *ipsative* form to highlight internal contrasts in her profile.

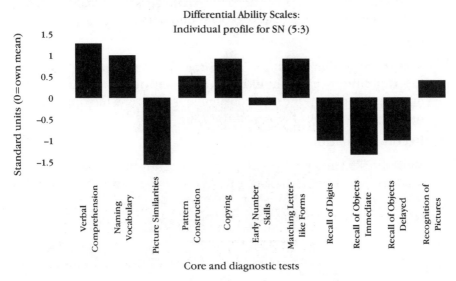

Figure 10.5: SN's DAS Core and Diagnostic test results adjusted to her own mean and SD (ipsative profile).

CONFIDENTIAL: PSYCHOLOGICAL REPORT

Name of child: Sara N
Age: 5 years 3 months

SUMMARY OF FINDINGS

Abilities

Sara is of average general ability (above that of 55% of individuals her own age); but only about 25% of individuals would show this level of discrepancy between general and language abilities.

Pattern of relative strengths and weaknesses

Sara has cognitive strengths in:

*   development of higher language abilities (naming, vocabulary, comprehension)
*   artistic and visual abilities

Sara has cognitive weaknesses in:

*   all verbal memory areas
*   phonological (speech sound) processing

Attainments

Sara has good letter knowledge and already attains well in reading, though her comprehension is evidently much better than her decoding; nevertheless her decoding *strategy* is well established. Sara shows something of a block with numbers.

Conclusions

Sara shows a number of risk factors for dyslexia, a specific learning difficulty, which should be taken seriously. She is well motivated and responds to a challenge, so there is the opportunity for successful early intervention.

Recommendations

Sara's present and past teaching has apparently been on the right lines and is already paying off. Additional supportive work, including direct tuition, should be considered to secure basic techniques and to insure against later failure.

[SIGNATURE AND DATE]

PSYCHOLOGICAL ASSESSMENT:
HIGHLIGHTS AND CONCLUSIONS

Background to this assessment

(information from family and school)

Sara is the younger of two children in a family with a possible incidence of dyslexia, a specific learning difficulty. Her birth and early development were normal and, after grommet insertion at 2, her hearing has remained good. She continues to be 'very articulate' and to demonstrate a 'good vocabulary'.

At 3 years and 2 months Sara began to attend Nursery and a teacher from the United States observed to Mr and Mrs N that Sara showed certain difficulties. She was frustrated in her attempts at board games by an inability to count. At four she moved on to a reception class but around this time began to have temper tantrums and other behaviour difficulties at home. After two terms she transferred to her present school and, in September 1995, moved into Year 1. At a little over five, then, she has received nearly seven terms of education, four of them in more formal settings.

Difficulties continue with literacy and 'pre-phonics'. Sara wants to progress to more 'grown-up' books but needs print skills for promotion. Her artistic abilities are obvious and she has a 'vivid imagination'. She excels at sport and games. Consciously she likes school but is reluctant to go. She is sensitive to being 'bossed' and 'told off' and having to do 'too many take-aways'.

At school Sara is perceived as average in ability and all attainment areas but is sometimes distractible and slow to complete tasks. There are concerns about her listening skills and concentration.

Behaviour during interview

In spite of initial tension Sara decided the interview situation was all right and proceeded to have fun and enjoy herself. Her co-operativeness was exemplary. Finally, though, she was allowed to do what she had been longing to do: show me her drawings and paintings! These were indeed breathtaking and were also duly admired in the office next door.

General intellectual ability

Sara is of average general ability (above that of 55% of her age-peers); there can therefore be no explanation for her lack of progress in terms of limited ability to understand and learn. Indeed, because she was getting over flu, her true abilities may be higher. A single inconsistent result (Picture Similarities) lowers the IQ somewhat and it may be more sensible to ignore it.

Ability profile

Sara shows some contrast between her development in language-based areas of thinking (ideas, concepts, words) and visual and spatial areas (shapes, patterns, relations), with the former being better developed.

The internal contrasts in Sara's cognitive profile may be seen in the first of the attached diagrams, which compares her development with that of others her age.

In the second diagram, Sara's scores are adjusted to her own mean, so that strengths and weaknesses appear in relation to her own characteristic level of performance.

Core tests

On all of these Sara showed higher than average ability, especially marked in language areas, which are rightly perceived to be her strength. The single discordant result, Picture Similarities, has already been mentioned and suggests no particular interpretation: it may be a somewhat accidental result.

However, Sara does show an interpretable shortfall in her next lowest result, that for Early Number Concepts. Though not statistically exceptional, this below-average score does suggest some difficulty with both written numbers and number concepts. It also makes reading more likely to be a difficult area.

Diagnostic subtests

On two tests involving a significant *visual* component (Matching Letter-like Forms and Recognition of Pictures) Sara performed at her characteristic (above-average) level. However on three tests whose character is principally that of *verbal memory*, it is a very different picture. On Recall of Digits Sara obtained a score low in relation to her other abilities. Sara thus shows the marked deficiency in short-term or immediate working memory of the kind associated with dyslexia, a specific learning difficulty. And on Recall of Objects she obtained scores at comparably low levels.

These three test results are not low in an absolute sense, nor are they significantly discrepant from Sara's other scores. They merely form a pattern whose consistency is diagnostically worrying.

Supplementary tests

On the Woodcock–Johnson test of Sound Blending, Sara

performed well and in accordance with her strong language abilities generally.

On the Children's Test of Non-word Repetition, however, Sara obtained a score which was low in relation to others of her age. This suggests that she has some degree of difficulty in storing, analysing and reproducing speech sounds. This, too, is central to a dyslexia diagnosis.

Attainment in reading

Sara attempted two tests of reading from the Woodcock–Johnson repertoire.

On the first, Letter–Word Identification, she had to name nine letters, all of which she did successfully, and recognise some words. Of the latter she could manage only *in* and *his*. However, she was doing much silent or subvocal decoding, so evidence of her technique is reassuring. For instance she read *was* as *saw*, *as* as *ass* and *when* as *win*; she read *must* as *much*. All these errors are closely related to the target words.

On the second test, Passage Comprehension, matters are, from the dyslexic's point of view, easier. Simple sentences and passages must be completed using picture cues and sentence prediction, as well as knowledge of the world. Sara obtained a much higher score, one which puts in context concerns about her decoding.

Conclusions

Sara is a charming and vivid young person of at least average abilities and, in particular, excellent language skills. Her sporting and artistic abilities are well attested. Nevertheless there are persistent concerns about how well she learns some of the specific academic skills which are expected at school in the early years.

Although one cannot definitively diagnose or predict dyslexia at Sara's age, one can evaluate known risk factors and be specific about the degree of risk she shows of following a dyslexic developmental path.

Broadly the most important risk factors are as follows:

- A family pattern of literacy difficulty, especially in one or both parents. Here Sara shows a degree of risk, for memory tasks and mathematics if not so much for literacy learning.
- A history of speech delay or abnormal development. Sara's language development, in spite of glue-ear, has been excellent.
- Difficulties with the sounds of words, as in rhymes, sequencing of syllables, auditory memory or imitation. Sara does have unexpected phonological difficulties.

- Failure to learn, already in the early years, those academic skills which others of similar age and ability are able to learn. This is a complaint made about Sara, in spite of her youth, because of much unsuccessful exposure to letter- and number-learning. However, effort has paid off, in the sense that her reading skills are already considerable.
- Difficulty with naming of pictures or objects; finding the right or obvious word. Again, her language skills are excellent.
- Assimilation of information visually when this entails attaching words to things in a verbal strategy. The two tests which pinpoint this ability do show Sara performing at levels low for her.
- Unhappiness at school from the beginning, where this is hard to explain on grounds of immaturity or dependence noticeable before the start of school. Sara has manifested disappointment, frustration, behaviour difficulties (at home) and reluctance to attend which do implicate this as a problem.

In short, Sara shows too many of these warning signs to allow for complacency about the possibility of an inherited dyslexia. Nevertheless her progress thus far in literacy, though more apparent in linguistic aspects of the printed word than code aspects, should not be overlooked. She is already past some of the hurdles to literacy which keep back dyslexics much older than her.

But Sara shows the limitation in working memory capacity, especially phonological memory capacity, which research implicates in the common forms of learning disability. What is restricted is the capacity to hold in memory at one time all the elements of a task that is either highly sequenced or that requires many simultaneous operations. As a result the basic skills of reading, writing and arithmetic, all of which make a considerable demand on working memory, are not easily acquired or are not well consolidated in automatic form. The results are most obvious in the difficulty otherwise intelligent pupils have with reading, spelling or memorisation of tables. It is this group of children which is recognised to have dyslexia, a specific learning difficulty.

Recommendations

In order to *consolidate foundations*, therefore, without waiting for this to happen by itself, Sara needs an experience of specialist teaching as an *early intervention*, in particular to foster:

- skill in recognising shapes and sounds consistently;
- language skills development, competences in finding words and *identifying the components of speech-sounds*, within a range of sentence structures;

- structured multisensory teaching to develop simultaneous skills in reading, writing and spelling; effective recall in the use of these skills;
- a similar approach to numeracy skills, including the use of number language;
- development of sensitivity to the writing arm, hand and fingers, familiarity with the movement patterns of cursive writing, pleasure in fluency and control in writing.

Structured multisensory teaching aims to develop simultaneous skills in reading, writing and spelling so as to enhance effective recall in their use. Image, sound, movement memory (sky-writing) and touch are all employed to establish the sounds and shapes of letters, syllables and words. The most elaborate development of this specialist teaching programme is contained in:

- Walker, J, Brooks, L and others (1993) *Dyslexia Institute Literacy Programme*, 2 vols. Staines, Middlesex: Dyslexia Institute.

The published programme, however, is supplied only as courseware to teachers qualifying in the Institute's specialist postgraduate diploma,validated by Kingston University.

A useful general source for teachers is:

- Thomson, ME and Watkins, EJ (1990) *Dyslexia: A Teaching Handbook*. London: Whurr.

Letterland (author Lyn Wendon) is a particularly friendly and well-ordered system which integrates multisensory approaches to letter sounds and shapes, handwriting, spelling patterns and language enrichment. It is based on the motivating power of animation (the letters are characters) and the mnemonic power of stories (the letters interact in instructive ways). It enhances learning most in the initial stages of learning to read, but is also effective with older pupils. Children who have trouble remembering things may have difficulty forgetting *Letterland*. In addition Letterland emphasises the visual forms of letters which are important in the early stages of learning to read, when adults tend to overestimate the linguistic aspects of reading. Materials and catalogue are available from:

- Letterland Ltd, Barton, Cambridge, CB3 7AY. Tel: 01223 262675.

[SIGNATURE AND DATE]

TECHNICAL APPENDIX: TEST RESULTS

Differential Ability Scales
(Psychological Corporation, 1990)

Summary measures

Sara's performance is compared with that of all individuals of the same age. The results are expressed as *standard scores*, which have an average value of 100. Scores of 69 and below are Very Low; 70–79 are Low; 80–89 are Below Average; 90–109 are Average; 110–119 are Above Average; 120–129 are High; and 130 and above are Very High.

General conceptual ability

(GCA or IQ): 102

Sara is of average general ability (above that of 55% of her age-peers). This is necessarily a global measure of all-round ability and therefore penalises an individual who may have strengths offset by weaknesses. Because of error inherent in the measurement process, it is best to say that that the true IQ probably lies within the range 96–108 (90% confidence).

Cluster scores

Verbal Cluster: 112
Non-verbal Cluster: 97

The contrast between this level of GCA (IQ) and one of the cluster scores is significant and exceptional. Sara shows an unusual strength in the area of verbal reasoning. Only about 25% of pupils of this GCA (IQ) would have a level of verbal reasoning this high.

The difference, also, between these cluster scores is both statistically significant and exceptional. Sara shows a contrast between verbal and non-verbal reasoning which would be expected in only about 25% of individuals.

Subtest scores

Details follow of the individual subtests which contribute to the summary measures. Results are reported in terms of *percentiles*: this is the percentage of children of this age who perform at or below Sara's level of ability.

Verbal cluster

VERBAL COMPREHENSION

Percentile: 79

Receptive language; understanding of oral instructions involving basic language concepts.

NAMING VOCABULARY

Percentile: 73

Expressive language; knowledge of names.

Non-verbal cluster

PICTURE SIMILARITIES

Percentile: 14

Non-verbal reasoning shown by matching pictures that have a common element or concept.
Only about 10% of individuals with her other scores would perform this poorly on this test.

PATTERN CONSTRUCTION

Percentile: 62

Arranging coloured tiles or blocks to copy a demonstration pattern, with higher marks awarded for speed.

COPYING

Percentile: 69

Visual matching and fine visual–motor coordination in copying line drawings.

Within the non-verbal cluster, Sara performed inconsistently: only about 15% of individuals would obtain scores so disparate on Picture Similarities and Copying; only about 20% of individuals would obtain scores so disparate on Picture Similarities and Pattern Construction.

Other core subtests

EARLY NUMBER CONCEPTS

Percentile: 42

Knowledge of pre-numerical and numerical concepts.

Diagnostic subtests

MATCHING LETTER-LIKE FORMS

Percentile: 69

Visual discrimination among similar shapes.

RECALL OF DIGITS

Percentile: 24

Short-term auditory memory and recall of number sequences of increasing length.

RECALL OF OBJECTS IMMEDIATE

Percentile: 16

Immediate recall of information in which words and pictures are linked.

RECALL OF OBJECTS DELAYED

Percentile: 24

Intermediate-term recall of information in which words and pictures are linked.

RECOGNITION OF PICTURES

Percentile: 58

Short-term visual memory measured through recognition of familiar objects.

Supplementary diagnostic tests

CHILDREN'S TEST OF NON-WORD REPETITION

Percentile: 35
Age equivalent: 4–5 years

Gathercole, SE, Willis, CS, Baddeley, AD and Emslie, H (1994) The children's test of nonword repetition: a test of phonological working memory. *Memory* 2: 103–28. This requires the child to repeat without error a number of non-words (which are however word-like) of 2, 3, 4 and 5 syllables (*perplisteronk*).

SOUND BLENDING

Percentile: 77
Age equivalent: 6 years 3 months

Woodcock, RW and Johnson, MB (1989, 1990) *Woodcock-John-*

son Psycho-Educational Battery – Revised [Test 11]. Allen, TX: DLM. Segments of words are pronounced in isolation at one-second intervals (*b...oat*). The child must identify the words by imagining the sounds combined.

LETTER–WORD IDENTIFICATION

Percentile: 81
Age equivalent: 6 years 4 months

Woodcock, RW and Johnson, MB (1989, 1990) *Woodcock–Johnson Psycho-Educational Battery – Revised* [Test 22]. Allen, TX: DLM. Of the 57 items in this test, the first four require identification of *rebuses* (picture-signs) and the next nine naming of capital and lower-case letters. Thereafter 44 word recognition items make up a word recognition test of the familiar kind.

PASSAGE COMPREHENSION

Percentile: 94
Age equivalent: 6 years 3 months

Woodcock, RW and Johnson, MB (1989, 1990) *Woodcock–Johnson Psycho-Educational Battery – Revised* [Test 23]. Allen, TX: DLM. Comprehension is probed by questions about items ranging from simple pictures accompanied by short sentences, through longer sentences without pictures, to complex prose passages.

BROAD READING

Percentile: 91
Age equivalent: 6 years 3 months

Woodcock, RW and Johnson, MB (1989, 1990) *Woodcock–Johnson Psycho-Educational Battery – Revised*. Allen, TX: DLM. This cluster score is made up of two test results which reflect components of reading, Letter–Word Identification and Passage Comprehension, to give a higher level, summary score.

Notes

1   For figures on the diminishing returns of specialist intervention in reading problems with the age of the pupil generally, see Taylor and Taylor (1983).
2   However, amongst the many excellent suggestions to facilitate early recognition lurk the nuggets of make-believe. Even as a baby, we are told, the dyslexic 'did not crawl – he was a bottom shuffler'. This is a ludicrous but ancient tradition which, I believe, can be traced back at least to the 1940s.
3   The software suite is distributed by Lucid Systems, 26 Tunis Street, Sculcoates Lane, Hull HU5 1EZ.
4   Page numbers refer to an eight-page summary of Singleton, Thomas and

Leedale (1995), entitled: Cognitive Profiling System for the Diagnosis of Dyslexia and Assessment of Special Educational Needs.

5   Early in 1996 by The Psychological Corporation UK (Harcourt Brace Jovanovich) at 24–28 Oval Road, London NW1 7DX. Tel: 0171 267 4466. A school-age Dyslexia Screening Test (DST), which includes innovative tests of speeded reading and spelling and 'nonsense passage reading', will follow.

6   Such as non-dyslexic gneral reading backwardness.

7   Some would say 100%. However quantitative risk assessments support only conclusions very much less cavalier than these.

8   Many fathers of children brought for a dyslexia assessment refer, if at all, to their own past difficulties in learning literacy only at the end of a long consultation, with their hand already upon the door handle.

9   Naming, for instance, letters in capitals from their name.

10 Mean age 4.52 years (SD 0.28).

11 Mean age 7.21 years (SD 0.31).

12 I am indebted to Dr Ian Deary, University of Edinburgh Department of Psychology, for the analyses which follow.

13 The mean spatial cluster for 136 DAS-defined reading-disabled school-age children is 100.5 (Elliott, 1990, Table 9.54, p. 260).

Chapter 11
Assessment of the dyslexic adult

The historical position of dyslexic adults

Only recently has the methodology for the assessment of dyslexic adults been accorded the same inventive interest as that for children. Undoubtedly this has reflected the poverty of assessment materials for the post-school population. This position has gradually begun to change as social awareness and acceptance of dyslexia have improved. In effect there is a longitudinal structure of the dyslexic population defined by strata of public awareness.

As mentioned in the previous chapter in relation to the characteristics of pre-school children for whom assessments are sought, the experience of dyslexia is now markedly different for people of different ages. Reasons why younger children may be brought for an assessment are in a sense over-determined; prevention and pre-emption are to the fore. Young adults, recently out of school, however, tell a very different story. In some cases their learning difficulties had attracted no specialist notice and attention throughout their 11 years of statutory schooling. Only the advice or example of a friend, or a chance meeting with a college counsellor, had brought them to seek advice.

Universities give the impression, to what extent well founded is hard to establish, of having been sympathetic to the needs of dyslexic students for many years. More recently colleges of further and higher education, released from local authority governance, have set about doing the right thing by dyslexics without the hang-ups and institutional baggage of the maintained school environment. Consequently it is impressive to see how alert and resourceful colleges and their often single-handed 'co-ordinators' have been in responding to the needs of dyslexic students. Sometimes this is the first constructive response such dyslexic individuals have encountered.

Matters are different again for the over-30s. In the main their schooling has predated the dyslexia movement altogether. After internalising concepts of themselves as *thick* (though not lazy) they have discovered, to their amazement, that the world of work has been very much more charitable than the world of school. They have taken like ducks to water to jobs where their skills can come into their own: design, draughtsmanship, engineering, catering, retailing, horticulture, manufacturing. With chagrin they have observed a younger generation being accorded a special status as dyslexics and have wondered if this was, all along, their own problem. Prompted by the unfolding stories of their own children, or by the career pressure of a *paper ceiling*,[1] they seek an assessment for themselves.

Assessment methodology and repertoire

The IQ/achievement discrepancy, even fine-tuned by the use of regression, may be only descriptive, not explanatory, and IQ as a measure may attract opprobrium, much of it no doubt directed at intelligence itself. But in special education we are not greatly concerned with these larger conversations which, though interesting, are also interminable. We simply hold that *dyslexia is a contrast*, as emphasised throughout earlier chapters and that it is identified not by a measure but by the distance between two measures. IQ and achievement merely provide the most obvious of these contrasts, others of which include, for instance, word and non-word reading, reading accuracy and comprehension, reading and listening comprehension. We will undoubtedly wish to move beyond this most obvious contrast, but we will not wish to move back from it.

There seems to be no reason to depart from this basic rationale in assessing dyslexia, whether it is a psychologist or specialist teacher doing the assessing, whether the dyslexia is embryonic or fully developed, whether it is being assessed in schoolchildren or adults. As we turn to adults we look for different tools, to be sure, just as we take account of the very different social circumstances generated by our subjects. But dyslexia is still a contrast, a distance between two measures, and we refine our techniques in the light of this unvarying principle.

Obliged by necessity to administer to bemused middle-aged clients the quiz-like and sensorimotor subtests of the Wechsler Adult Intelligence Scale – Revised (WAIS-R) (Wechsler, 1981) the consulting psychologist may well feel ashamed. The adult client may already suspect that he or she is about to make a precipitous return to the humiliation of the classroom. The intellectual level of this most venerable of the Wechsler tests, with comic strips, jigsaws and questions about geography, will serve only to confirm this fear.

The WAIS is due for a revision, which cannot come soon enough. However WAIS-III will present new challenges to factorists and there will be inevitable delays while the profession digests altered item content and diagnostic dimensions. WAIS-R may be the most shoddy and old-fashioned member of the Wechsler family, the shuffling grandfather, but several telling points must nevertheless be made in its favour.

First is its research investiture. In common with all Wechsler family members of all generations, the test is surrounded – encrusted – with a wealth of research findings that have accumulated over many years. Moreover these are ably summated in a book devoted exclusively to the test, *Assessing Adolescent And Adult Intelligence* (Kaufman, 1990), perhaps the best of the three Kaufman books about the Wechsler tests.

Second, the WAIS measures intelligence extremely well, appearances to the contrary notwithstanding. Of its 11 subtests[2] fully seven load on an unrotated first factor (the *g* component) at 0.70 or above, five at 0.75 or above. Only *g*-loadings on Digit Span, Picture Arrangement, Object Assembly and Digit Symbol (as Coding is called in this battery) hover around the 0.60 mark; nothing falls below 0.59 (Digit Symbol). When median loadings for the 9 WAIS-R and the 11 WISC-R standardisation groups are compared, a mean of 0.71 is obtained for WAIS-R, compared with one of only 0.64 for WISC-R (Kaufman, 1990, p. 253). In effect the same or very similar tests acquire, once they are used with adults, remarkable *g*-saturation.

Third, research analyses, especially three- and four-factor ones, can be brought to bear on the 11 subtest results for any individual to give great diagnostic penetration. We shall look more closely at such *cluster analyses* and other enhancements in a moment. A further consequence is that short forms of the WAIS, though sacrificing the profile information that comes from a full administration, preserve unusually high validity and reliability while offering significant economy.

An alternative to the WAIS-R

First let us look at an alternative, for there is one. The Kaufman Adolescent and Adult Intelligence Test (KAIT) (Kaufman and Kaufman, 1993) is a modern, innovative, sophisticated test battery which yields measures of Fluid and Crystallised Intelligence (as well as a composite, IQ) and is normed downwards to 11 years as well as upwards to 85+. It thus complements its stablemate, the Kaufman Assessment Battery For Children, a primary age test of ability (Kaufman and Kaufman, 1983).

The theoretical rationale used in the development of the KAIT is a concept of intelligence appropriate to adolescence and adult maturity. That is, Piaget's concept of *formal operational thinking* is drawn upon, as are Luria's (Luria–Golden's) definition of *planning ability* and, most important, the Horn–Cattell theory of *fluid* and *crystallised* abilities. So effectively is this done that the first sensation the user has is one of relief: at last some *reasoning* is being demanded by a test, departing from the tradition of relatively trivial tasks and questions exemplified by the Wechsler children's tests. Just as the concept of creativity in psychological research has often seemed to embody a distinct lack of creativity, so the concept of intelligence has stood in need of some elevation. The KAIT at last attempts a proper engagement of intellectual activity. The test was standardised between April 1988 and October 1991 on a national US sample of 2000 subjects appropriately stratified by age, sex, region, level of education, race or ethnic group and combinations of these variables. Subjects were drawn in 14 age-groups, mainly in five-year intervals. A robust two-factor structure was determined after collection of these data. The principal Horn–Cattell theoretical axis, Fluid versus Crystallised ability, emerged 'clearly' and 'easily' from the analyses (Kaufman and Kaufman 1993 Manual, pp. 67–8). Three subtests each comprise the Fluid and Crystallised scales and are scored, Wechsler-fashion, with a mean of 10 and a standard deviation of 3. In addition there is a 'spare' subtest for each scale which can be used as a substitute, and two optional delayed administrations of previously administered scales which can be interpreted in terms of consolidation of learning. A supplementary Mental Status subtest of alertness or confusion requires the subject to know the answers to 10 questions, such as what day it is.

A considerable apparatus is provided, as one would expect, for the interpretation of profiles, on the basis of statistical significance and exceptionality. Easy-to-use scoring software adds some simple but cautious narrative. Split-half reliabilities for the six core tests are all at or above 0.87, averaged across all age-groups; Fluid and Crystallised IQs are each 0.90; Composite IQ is 0.97. Test–retest reliabilities for core subtests range from 0.72 to 0.95 and for the composites from 0.87 to 0.94.[3] The highest SE_m for any core test is 1.1 points of scaled score. Fluid IQ, as one would expect, declines by nearly 2 SDs between 24 and 85 years (this reduces by some 4 points if one adjusts for years of education); Crystallised IQ does so by only about 1 SD (reduced by 5 points if adjusted for education).[4] Five of the six core tests load at 0.70 or above on the first unrotated principal factor (g-loading), the three obviously 'verbal' tests at 0.79–0.82. The exploratory oblimin principal factor loadings are more ambiguous and dip as low as 0.55 in the case of one core fluid subtest, Rebus Learning, but the fluid and crystallised dimensions are just as apparent from the nature of the items and tests as from internal and external correlation patterns. Separation of the two dimensions is at least complete. Joint analyses for 118 subjects with KAIT and WISC-R show gratifying contrast between Performance tests on the WISC-R and Fluid tests of the KAIT. The third, *fluid* factor attracts only Arithmetic and Coding on the WISC-R, while the second, PO factor on the WISC-R attracts only the most obviously spatial of the KAIT Fluid tests, the fourth, substitute test (Memory for Block Designs). The same holds true for concurrent performances on KAIT and WAIS-R, though this time Digit Span, whose fluid aspects have been discussed earlier, now loads 0.29 on the Fluid factor. Confirmatory factor analyses show higher loadings on the relevant factors, varying from 0.80 to 0.85 for the core Crystallised subtests, and from 0.74 to 0.77 for the Fluid subtests.

Construct validity analyses were conducted with WISC-R (118 subjects), WAIS-R (343 subjects), K-ABC (124 subjects) and SB-IV (79 subjects). As barely a decade had transpired since the standardisation of WAIS-R,[5] gains in mean Full Scale IQ (Composite Intelligence) larger than those observed, 3.0 points averaged across four age-groups, were not to be expected. For a sample of 461 subjects Full Scale (WAIS-R) and Composite (KAIT) IQs correlated 0.84. Similarly close relationships were observed with the Stanford-Binet. (Lesser relationships with K-ABC scores for 124 subjects of 11–12 years perhaps reflect the different structure of the tests[6] as well as the K-ABC's lower g-loadings.) Concurrent validity, then, must be adjudged good.

Sadly a decision was taken at the production stage to drop from KAIT two tests of 'functional' reading and mathematics which would have provided a co-normed basis for regression evaluation. However, these have now been published as the Kaufman Functional Academic Skills Test (K-FAST)(Kaufman and Kaufman, 1994). Both tests are highly g-loaded, to an extent which remains surprising to anyone who expects ability and achievement to differ in all ways. Arithmetic comprises 25 items, Reading 29. Both would need minor Anglicisations, for instance with currency items, pictorial and text, to be used in Britain. The tests are *functional* in that they draw from the environment the challenges that are typical of daily life: Reading deals with signs, abbreviations, medicine and cooking instructions; Arithmetic with maps, bar-charts, recipe quantities, time and prices.

As the KAIT is manifestly an exemplary modern test in a field – that of assessment of adolescents and adults – in which it is badly needed, what obstacles might there be to prevent an assessing psychologist from simply switching to it from WAIS-R?

There are two and unfortunately they are considerable. First the concept of *crystallised* ability virtually guarantees an overloading of items culturally specific to North America. This is conspicuously so on Famous Faces, a supplementary test in which American sportsmen and newscasters feature, but such items are scattered across many of the tests. As always, some ingenuity will overcome minor problems quite easily, but many instances defy mere ingenuity. One wonders whether crystallised items could have been devised which would *export* a little more smoothly, or whether (by contrast, for instance, with the DAS) no care at all was taken to avoid blatantly American content.

The second obstacle concerns the nature of two crystallised subtests, Word Definitions and Double Meanings. Both involve reading *printed words* and making decisions as to filling in blanks based on clues, written as well as spoken. This flagrantly imposes a literacy criterion upon verbal intelligence, of little consequence with the fortunate majority but a fatal limitation in the assessment of dyslexia. In their manual, Kaufman and Kaufman (1993, p. 107) actually comment, with a convincing degree of surprise,[7] on the lower Crystallised than Fluid IQ scores obtained by 14 reading-disabled adolescents: there is a difference of half a standard deviation. Yet this is surely because they cannot read!

Salvaging a brilliant test for use with British dyslexics may require that the Fluid scale be given in isolation, perhaps with the supplementary subtest, Memory for Block Designs, as a stabilising addition, though its psychometric properties are imperfect. In fact this short-form IQ may be the most fair assessment of unimpaired intelligence that can be obtained for dyslexic subjects aged 18 and over. But such a procedure, in spite of its attractions, offers no insight into the contrasts among different groups of cognitive skills. For this *profiling* we turn back to the WAIS. First, though, let us see a live example of an assessment report in which referral issues are addressed directly by means of the KAIT technology.

CONFIDENTIAL: PSYCHOLOGICAL REPORT

Name of individual: AA

Age: 16 years 7 months

SUMMARY OF FINDINGS

Abilities

AA is of above-average general ability (above that of 87% of individuals his own age).

Pattern of relative strengths and weaknesses

AA has strengths in:

- logical, non-verbal reasoning.

AA has weaknesses in:

- immediate verbal memory;
- speed of information processing, especially written.

Attainments

AA reads and comprehends very well; this has never been a problem. However, his spelling remains especially weak, his writing slow and unproductive, and his written calculation skills very poor.

Conclusions

AA continues to show dyslexic-type difficulties in the processing of low-level information, while he shows better than ever his high general problem-solving abilities.

Recommendations

AA would benefit from individual tuition in mathematical, especially arithmetical, skills. He will need extra time in timed, written, public exams if he is to compete on equal terms.

(SIGNATURE AND DATE)

PSYCHOLOGICAL ASSESSMENT: HIGHLIGHTS AND
CONCLUSIONS

Background to this assessment (information from family)

I first assessed AA in June 1993, when he was just 14. In a report dated 14 June 1993 I commented on this assessment as follows:

AA is the younger of two children in a family with some incidence of specific learning difficulties (dyslexia). His older sister, Sara, 16, has always had good phonological skills . . . His official ambition is to be an accountant (but as we shall see he has a major obstacle in his number skills). However, 'My uncle's a mechanic' and I felt AA rather hankers after something skilled but practical.

AA is of high general ability (above that of 81% of his age-peers). On Speed of Information Processing . . . AA was initially hasty, but as his accuracy increased his speed fell away, demonstrating a trade-off between the two . . . AA's capacity to recall number facts and common sequences is of interest. He can say the days of the week forwards and backwards (a challenge to working memory) but could say the months of the year only with difficulty (forwards) and with the help of his fingers (backwards). He could say the letters of the alphabet, but his doubt about the order of the letters increased towards the end of the sequence. When asked for products out of sequence from the multiplication tables, AA was able to supply only 3× and some 4× without difficulty. For 4 × 7 he worked through the sequence 7, 14, 21, 28. He solved 6 ×8 as (5 ×8) + 8; and 7 ×9 as (10 ×7) − 7.

AA shows the severe underachievement in spelling and number (though not reading) skills, with accompanying clinical features (verbal/non-verbal discrepancy, poor verbal memory and speed of information-processing), which together implicate specific learning difficulties (dyslexia) . . . AA needs a wide range of specialist teaching which is able to suit his individual profile of abilities and difficulties. In particular his number skills have proved to be remarkably weak, in addition to his known weak spelling skills.

The full background is contained in the earlier report and I shall not rehearse it here. Since the earlier visit, AA has been fortunate to receive specialist teaching from a qualified dyslexia teacher, with noticeable benefits. At GCSE he achieved five passes at grades A to C, including Cs in English Language and Literature and a B in Maths. He obtained eight passes in all. Now at college he is studying Maths, Business and Chemistry at A level. He still hopes to be an accountant but is finding difficulty with the maths: 'Everything I do seems to be wrong.'

Behaviour during interview

AA cooperated willingly and worked well across a wide range of assessment activities. Pleasant good humour remains his most immediate characteristic; and, in addition, he discussed his learning difficulties and academic experiences in a mature and helpful way.

General intellectual ability

AA is of above-average general ability (above that of 87% of other pupils his age). Consistency among the scores on which the Composite Scale IQ is based makes for confidence in the reliability of this assessment.

Cognitive style

AA shows some contrast between his development in *fluid* (general reasoning) and *crystallised* (culture-specific) ability, with the former being better developed. In general this favours the kind of mathematical work he is attempting, as fluid ability comprises high-level logical reasoning, domain-free transfer of problem-solving strategies and non-verbal intelligence. He has a strength in all these areas, and his Fluid IQ places him above 93% of his age-group, a level which ought to be adequate for A level.

The internal contrasts in AA's cognitive profile may be seen in the first diagram, which compares his development with that of others his age.

In the second diagram, AA's scores are adjusted to his own

mean, so that strengths and weaknesses appear in relation to his own characteristic level of performance.

Supplementary diagnostic tests

Supplementary tests give an insight into AA's continuing vagaries with information processing. On a measure of speed, Coding (WISC-III), which has motor, clerical and linguistic elements, he obtained a low score; and on Digit Span (WISC-III), a test of immediate verbal memory, he obtained a score merely average for his age.

Both results have implications for classroom learning. AA will have much more difficulty than his fellow A-level students, with whom he is otherwise intellectually comparable, in memorising information in the short term and will perform written work much more slowly.

Achievement in basic skills

On three tests from the Woodcock–Johnson battery, AA produced contrasting performances. On Letter Word Identification (single-word reading) and Passage Comprehension he showed his continuing high achievement in these chief aspects of reading skill; on Word Attack, however, he achieved significantly less well, showing his former underlying difficulty with phonological aspects of reading. Although none of these scores is at a worrying level, and AA has not now, nor did he ever have, a reading *problem*, this profile is characteristic of dyslexics, whose recognition of words is better than their decoding of non-words.

AA's reading speed was measured using Aaron's lists of function and content words. Though he did not read function words more slowly or inaccurately, his reading speed seemed somewhat slow.

On the Kirklees Reading Assessment Schedule, AA again obtained a high score on this measure of integrated reading for meaning. He performed the test within a 10 minute time limit, suggesting that low speed of reading is not a great problem.

On the Wide Range Achievement Test (WRAT-3) of Spelling AA scored at a level above only 30% of individuals his own age. This score was highly unexpected: perhaps only 10% of pupils of his age and ability would obtain a score this low. Spelling remains a markedly weak area.

On the Woodcock–Johnson test of Writing Fluency AA obtained one of his lowest scores, above only 18% of his contemporaries, showing that writing productivity is at the heart of his continuing problems. Similarly on the Wide Range Achievement Test (WRAT-3)of Arithmetic AA scored at a level above only 25%

of individuals his own age. This score, too, was highly unexpected: perhaps only 4% of pupils of his age and ability would obtain a score this low. He solved 33 –17 as 26 and was unable to express 0.42 as a percentage. He avoided altogether 823×96.

Conclusions

AA is a pleasant and understanding young man whose ability to undertake demanding A levels should probably not be doubted. But he shows continuing dyslexic-type information-processing difficulties which may have a major impact on his achievement. Most notable are: poor short-term verbal memory, low clerical speed, weak spelling, unproductive writing and a very poor level of written calculation skills.

AA is aware that a B grade in GCSE maths is no guarantee of ability to manage the very different A-level maths course; nor does a high grade at GCSE say anything about arithmetical skills without a calculator. Whether with his difficulties with arithmetic he can still expect to handle higher level and abstract mathematical problems is a question that is beyond my competence, but it would be valuable if his present tutors considered the implications of AA's persistent low-level information problems in combination with his adequate underlying mathematical abilities.

Recommendations

It would be helpful if individual tutoring, not necessarily from a dyslexia specialist, could be arranged to focus on AA's arithmetic skills, especially if this were as effective as his previous literacy tuition.

Meanwhile further elaboration in the 'four functions' is provided in:
* Engelmann S, Carnine D, Silbert J (1981) *Corrective Mathematics*. Chicago: MacMillan/McGraw-Hill [SRA].

There are about 60 lessons each in separate modules: Addition, Subtraction, Multiplication and Division. The work is suitable for pupils of secondary age and includes much practice at solving problems expressed in words. This Direct Instruction programme is available in the UK, from:

* McGraw-Hill Book Co Europe, Shoppenhangers Road, Maidenhead, Berks SL6 2QL. Tel: 01628 502518.

Systematic practice in the routine operations of number may be achieved in a structured way by participation in the Kumon home learning programme. This Japanese franchise operates in Britain through regional centres which parents attend with their children. However, the work is mainly done at home under parental supervision. Completion of worksheets is at the heart of the method and much practice leads to fluency and success. Kumon may be contacted at:

• Kumon International UK, Elscot House, Arcadia Avenue, London N3. Tel: 0181 343 3990; Fax 0181 343 2857.

In addition AA would benefit from special tuition in study skills. These should include:

• the use of mnemonics in memory training;
• strategies for organising thoughts and planning activities;
• pacing in exams and general management of time;
• forming of objectives with appropriate schemes of study; and
• the building of confidence that accompanies the successful and effective use of such strategies.

With AA's spelling and writing in mind, many useful suggestions and resources for literacy in adult and later school life are contained in:

• Bramley W (1993) *Developing Literacy For Study And Work.* Staines, Middlesex: The Dyslexia Institute (ISBN 0 9503915 5 7).

Special arrangements at GCE/GCSE

The examination boards now accept that the following special arrangements may be required for pupils to demonstrate their attainment in examination conditions:

• extra time for timed written papers;
• access to word-processor with later printing where this is the candidate's normal method of working (possible abuse of memory features for unfair advantage must be ruled out).

AA's need for these special arrangements should be represented to the relevant examination boards in good time by his examination centre. Examiners should be made aware at the moderation stage that the scripts they read were produced by an individual with dyslexia. This enables assessment of knowledge and work to become distinct from a survey of clerical skills.

It is probably not desirable to request exemption from the new spelling rule as only 5% of marks are at stake and GCE/GCSE examination certificates must then be endorsed.

(Signature)

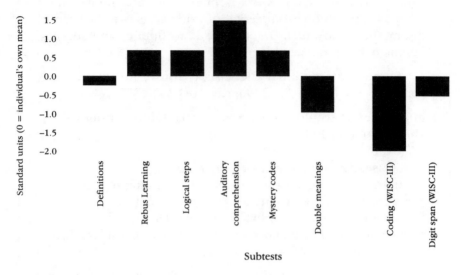

Figure 11.1 KAIT: Strengths and Weaknesses for AA (16:7)

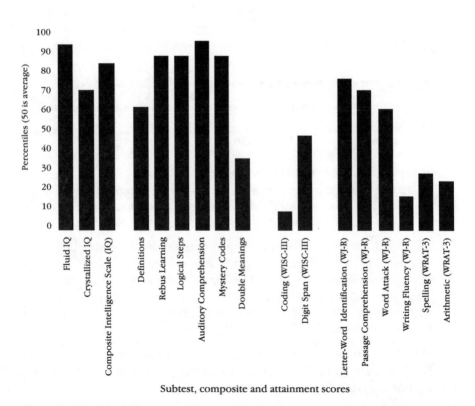

Figure 11.2 Kaufman adolescent and adult intelligence test cognitive profile for AA (16:7)

TECHNICAL APPENDIX: TEST RESULTS

Kaufman Adolescent and Adult Intelligence Test

Kaufman AS, Kaufman NL (1993) *Kaufman Adolescent and Adult Intelligence Test [KAIT]*. Circle Pines, MN: American Guidance Service. The Kaufman Adolescent and Adult Intelligence Test is an individually administered measure of general intelligence for people aged 11 to 85+ years. It is composed of separate Fluid and Crystallised Scales.

Summary measures

AA's performance is compared with that of all individuals of the same age. The results are expressed as standard scores, which have an average value of 100. Scores of 69 and below are Very Low; 70–79 are Low; 80–89 are Below Average; 90–109 are Average; 110–119 are Above Average; 120–129 are High; and 130 and above are Very High.

Crystallised IQ: 109

The Crystallised Scale measures the ability to solve problems that are dependent on schooling and cultural learning for success. AA's score places him above 72% of the population of others the same age.

Fluid IQ: 122

The Fluid Scale measures the ability to solve new problems. AA's score places him above 93% of the population of others the same age.

Composite Intelligence Scale: 117

The Composite Scale is made up of both Fluid and Crystallised abilities and corresponds to a general IQ. AA is of above-average general ability; his IQ places him above 87% of the population of others the same age. Because of error inherent in the measurement process, it is best to say that that the true IQ probably lies within the range 113–121 (90% confidence).

Internal contrasts between the scales

The contrast between Fluid and Crystallised Scales is significant but not very exceptional. About 25% of individuals would show such a discrepancy between Fluid and Crystallised Ability. In AA's case, Fluid is a relatively strong, and Crystallised a relatively weak, area of ability.

Subtest scatter

Among the Crystallised subtests, AA showed a difference of 7 points between his highest and lowest scaled scores. This difference is unusual, being shown by only about 5% of the population.

SUBTEST SCORES

Details follow of the individual subtests which contribute to the summary measures. Results are reported both in terms of *scaled scores* and *percentiles*. *Scaled scores* have an average value of 10. Half the population will obtain scores between 7 and 13 on any subtest. *Percentiles* indicate the percentage of individuals of this age who perform at or below this level of ability.

Crystallised Scale

DEFINITIONS
Scaled score: 11
Percentile: 63

A test of written-word comprehension with clues as to meaning (synonyms or short phrases) and word length (blank spaces for letters).

AUDITORY COMPREHENSION
Scaled score: 98
Percentile: 16

Some news items are read, headlines or stories. Questions about detail or general meaning follow.

DOUBLE MEANINGS
Scaled score: 37
Percentile: 9

Another written word problem of *homonyms*: two sets of clue words must converge on a related word which belongs to both sets (for example *pool* is both a puddle of water and a billiard-like game).

Fluid Scale

REBUS LEARNING
Scaled score: 91
Percentile: 14

Symbols which correspond to words are first taught and then sentences containing them must be 'read' correctly.

LOGICAL STEPS
Scaled score: 91
Percentile: 14

Rules must be applied to solve problems, shown in diagrams, of the type: *If Bill sits two places to Anne's right and Linda one place to her left, how far is Bill from Linda?*

MYSTERY CODES
Scaled score: 91
Percentile: 14

Aspects of simple pictures such as shape and length are coded by stars, dots and other means. The right code must be found for a new shape, consistent with the rule.

Supplementary diagnostic tests

DIGIT SPAN

Percentile: 50
Scaled score: 10

Wechsler D (1992) *Wechsler Intelligence Scale For Children – Third Edition UK* (WISC-III). New York: Harcourt Brace Jovanovitch, The Psychological Corporation. Scaled scores range from 1 to 19, with 10 the average; two-thirds of scores fall between 7 and 13. This test is comparable to DAS Recall of Digits but digits are repeated forwards and backwards after a slower presentation time – one per second.

CODING

Percentile: 9
Scaled score: 6

Wechsler D (1992) *Wechsler Intelligence Scale For Children – Third Edition UK* (WISC-III). New York: Harcourt Brace Jovanovitch, The Psychological Corporation. Scaled scores range from 1 to 19, with 10 the average; two-thirds of scores fall between 7 and 13. This task requires the pupil to supply single digits with the symbols which accompany them in a model. The number correct within two minutes is credited. The test measures concentration, facility with printed symbols, rapid decision-making and visual-motor speed.

Tests of attainment

LETTER–WORD IDENTIFICATION

Percentile: 77
Age equivalent: 21 years

Woodcock RW, Johnson MB (1989, 1990) *Woodcock-Johnson Psycho-Educational Battery – Revised (Test 22). Allen, TX: DLM. Of the 57 items in this test, the first four require identification of* rebuses (picture-signs) and the next nine naming of capital and lower-case letters. Thereafter 44 word recognition items make up a word recognition test of the familiar kind.

WORD ATTACK

Percentile: 62
Age equivalent: 15 years 0 months

Woodcock RW, Johnson MB (1989, 1990) *Woodcock-Johnson Psycho-Educational Battery – Revised* (Test 31). Allen, TX: DLM. On this test decoding skills are highlighted using made-up words (*gusp, knoink*). AA's score on this test is so different from his score on Letter–Word Identification that the discrepancy has only a 5% chance of being random variation.

PASSAGE COMPREHENSION

Percentile: 69
Age equivalent: 19 years

Woodcock RW, Johnson MB (1989, 1990) *Woodcock-Johnson Psycho-Educational Battery – Revised* (Test 23). Allen, TX: DLM. Comprehension is probed by questions about items ranging from simple pictures accompanied by short sentences, through longer sentences without pictures, to complex prose passages.

BROAD READING

Percentile: 72
Age equivalent: 20 years

Woodcock RW, Johnson MB (1989, 1990) *Woodcock-Johnson Psycho-Educational Battery – Revised*. Allen, TX: DLM. This cluster score is made up of two test results which reflect components of reading, Letter–Word Identification and Passage Comprehension, to give a higher level, summary score.

BASIC READING SKILLS

Percentile: 62
Age equivalent: 19 years

Woodcock RW, Johnson MB (1989, 1990) *Woodcock-Johnson Psycho-Educational Battery – Revised*. Allen, TX: DLM. This cluster score is made up of two test results which reflect more basic components of reading, Letter–Word Identification and Word

Attack, to give a higher level, summary score which describes the individual's mastery of elementary reading skills.

READING SPEED – FUNCTION AND CONTENT WORDS

Ffrom Aaron PG, Joshi RM (1992) *Reading Problems: Consultation and Remediation*. New York: Guilford Press. Measures of reading speed are distorted by time taken over unfamiliar words. These two lists, of 20 words each, matched for frequency and number of syllables, offer a good alternative. The individual's reading of the words in each list is timed. Dyslexic readers make more errors on function words (*also, once, ever*), as well as reading them more slowly than content words (*book, bird, gold*). AA read the content words in 16 seconds, making no errors; and the function words in 15 seconds, with 1 error. Overall AA read at a speed of about 0.78 seconds per word. (A skilled adult reader reads silently at a speed of about 0.25 seconds per word or less.)

KIRKLEES READING ASSESSMENT SCHEDULE

Percentile: 90

Hedderly R (1993–94) Huddersfield: Kirklees Education Authority. In this reading comprehension test, originally devised by Valerie Warden and Philip Vernon at the London Institute of Education in 1955, 42 sentences must be completed by the underlining of one of a choice of words supplied (for example Ducks swim in a . . . *bucket, pond, yard, cage, garden*). Recent administration of the test to individuals aged from eight to adult in Kirklees enables the performance of a pupil to be compared with the level achieved by others of the same age.

Attainment in written arithmetic

ARITHMETIC

Percentile: 25

Wilkinson GS(1993) *The Wide Range Achievement Test*, 3rd edn (WRAT-3). Wilmington, DE: Wide Range. Basic written arithmetic problems extending into algebra.

A score this low would be obtained by only 4% of other pupils of AA's age and general ability. It is highly exceptional.

Attainment in spelling and writing

SPELLING

Percentile: 30

Wilkinson GS (1993) *The Wide Range Achievement Test*, 3rd edn

(WRAT-3). Wilmington, DE: Wide Range. Individual words are written to dictation in the context of sentences.

A score this low would be obtained by only 10% of other pupils of AA's age and general ability. While exceptional, this is not extreme.

WRITING FLUENCY

Percentile: 18
Age equivalent: 12 years 1 month

Woodcock RW, Johnson MB (1989, 1990) *Woodcock-Johnson Psycho-Educational Battery – Revised*. Allen, TX: DLM. In this task the individual has to form short sentences out of sets of three words. Spelling, grammar and punctuation are not marked down, though the sentences must be grammatically complete and the words themselves must not be changed. This timed, seven-minute task is a good measure of writing productivity.

Research-based profiling on the WAIS

The factor structure of the WAIS-R is quite as clear as that for WISC-R and, like the latter test, it performs the diagnostic function (for which it was not designed) with ease and efficiency, but let us digress briefly to consider, first, one adaptation of the WAIS which sacrifices such information, that of the *short form*.

The literature on short forms for all the Wechsler tests is considerable. Kaufman (1990) devotes a full chapter to the subject (Chapter 5); Sattler (1988) provides all information – weights, constants and equations – necessary to achieve any such adaptation of the WAIS.[8] None of this material need therefore be reproduced here. Essentially the method used is the Tellegen and Briggs (1967) formula for 'grouping Wechsler subtests into new scales' and involves obtaining the sums of the age-corrected scaled scores for selected subtests, multiplying this by a factor and adding a constant. Factor and constant are selected according to age-group. Sattler (1988, p. 138) gives a clear account, with a worked example. Different subtests have different validity coefficients (Sattler, Table C-34, p. 849), with pentads higher than tetrads, and tetrads higher than triads. Different subtests, of course, suit different purposes. Information, Arithmetic and Coding would probably disappear from a dyslexia assessment; Object Assembly might be rejected out of consideration for what a mobile psychologist is likely to want to carry round in a briefcase.

I would suggest a *tetrad* consisting of Vocabulary, Similarities, Picture Completion and Block Design (two subtests from each scale); this has a validity coefficient of 0.93. These four subtests provide six intercorrelations at nine different age-levels; they are needed to derive the weighting factor in the Tellegen and Briggs calculation. However, for this tetrad the factor is 1.5 at all ages except two: between 18 and 24 it is 1.6. This clears the way. To obtain a short-form IQ sum the age-corrected scaled scores for these four subtests, multiply by 1.5 (or 1.6 if the subject is aged between 18 and 24), and add 40 (36 if the subject is aged between 18 and 24). The resulting IQ carries a 90% confidence band of +/–6.4 points of standard score. This gives a rapid and serviceable estimation procedure for IQ and of course Coding and Digit Span can be given as free-standing extras if dyslexia is the quarry.

The WAIS and WAIS-R have received a greater weight of attention, perhaps, than any other psychometric tests in history. WAIS-R has been elaborately criticised and endlessly reviewed and there is little point in beginning the task again here. Interested readers will find a useful summary and adjudication based on the work of three analysts at the end of Chapter 8 of Kaufman (1990), 'Evaluation of the WAIS-R' (pp. 257–61). The following are excerpts:

> It is my opinion that the WAIS-R is probably the best standardized test designed for individual administration which the science and profession of psychology has produced to date. (Matarazzo, 1985; quoted in Kaufman, 1990, p. 261)
>
> The WAIS-R is the standard against which all other measures of adult ability are compared. The paragon of intelligence tests, it is used in a wide variety of settings requiring an accurate assessment of a person's abilities. (Spruill, 1984; quoted in Kaufman, 1990, p. 261)[9]

However, the psychometric shortcomings of WAIS-R are acknowledged[10] and one in particular should be mentioned: the use of a reference group (ages 20–34) to determine the scaled scores of all examinees is 'indefensible' (Kaufman, 1990, p. 260). This arrangement impairs profile interpretation at ages outside this age-band. With co-normed achievement measures lacking, the production of an IQ is of much less significance in any dyslexia assessment, though to be sure psychometric distance between different measures can be evaluated even if subjectively. Thus the use of WAIS-R is likely to be mainly for profile interpretation purposes. How are we to get round these shortcomings?

In effect the sums of scaled scores are standardised for each of the nine age-groups to produce Verbal, Performance and Full Scale IQs, because scaled score equivalents of raw scores are obtained by reference only to individuals aged 20–34. A scaled score of 10 may or may not be average at any given age. Given the non-comparability of scaled scores at various ages, bypassing them to get straight to IQs may seem no great loss, if also revealing of the importance that was assigned to IQ on its own 20 years ago. However, profile information is in fact supplied for each age (Manual, Appendix D, Table 21), though surrounded by caveats about using this to compute IQs.

In view of the importance that such 'age-corrected' or 'age-adjusted' scaled scores acquire in any normative profiling process, these alone will be referred to in what follows. Age-scaled scores are in fact the kind of scores that are provided routinely with any new test and are what one expects them to be: 10 is the mean for the particular age-group, 3 is the SD for that age-group. They differ significantly at times from scaled scores obtained from the age 20–34 reference group and used to compute IQs. It is inconceivable that this major structural limitation in WAIS-R will not be removed in any future edition.

To see what the aggregated group profile looks like of a sample of adults referred to the Dyslexia Institute, consider Figure 11.3, in which age-scaled score means are displayed for varying ns, together with achievement scores on WRAT-R and WRAT-3. This is only a small sample of heterogeneous adults referred for many different reasons, but some features deserve comment. First, the abilities of these adults, like their school-age counterparts, depart little from the average for their age, though as the composite scores show (VIQ, IQ, FSIQ) they are a little below. Second, Comprehension is the sole notable strength though, as it has been given to fewer individuals, this is harder to interpret. Third, Digit Symbol is quite as potent a diagnostic test for the WAIS-R with this population as Coding (WISC-III) typically is with school-age children. In all, with uniformly depressed attainment scores, the profile is as strongly descriptive of dyslexia as we have come to expect. The small numbers do not warrant further analysis.

Age-scaled scores permit not only cognitive profiling of the kind we have met with already but some evaluation of personality and learning characteristics over and above IQ. There is good agreement that WAIS-R is able to encompass them (Matarazzo, 1985; Spruill, 1984). We shall consider these different applications in due course. But first let us turn to conventional cluster analyses.

Factor-based clusters

The members of the ACID quaternity behave differently within the WAIS-R standardisation sample. Information, for instance, never loads on the third, FD, factor above 0.46. Digit Symbol (Coding) rises to 0.59 only for males aged 16–19.[11] The two main components of the *learning difficulty* factor, therefore, are Arithmetic (whose loadings range from 0.48 to 0.71) and Digit Span (also 0.48–0.71). Both are, in effect, behaving like tests of immediate verbal memory.

Wechsler Adult Intelligence Test-revised (WAIS-R): aggregated data with Ns

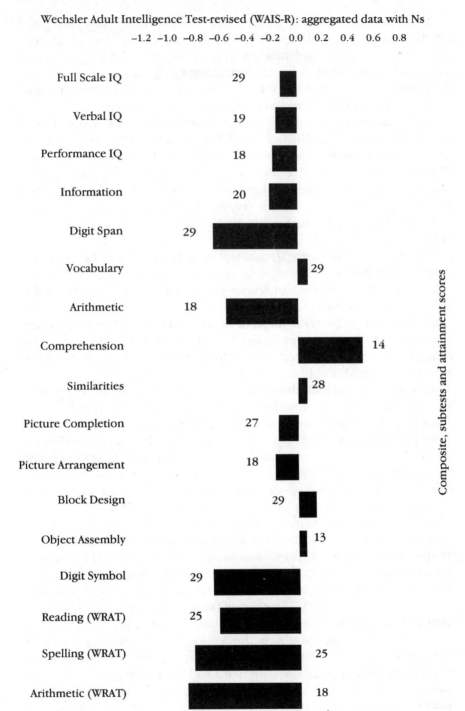

Figure 11.3: Group profile of a sample of adults: Composite IQs, age-scaled score and WRAT achievement scores are given in comparable SD units.

The composition of the Verbal Comprehension (VC) and Perceptual Organisation (PO) factors is more straightforward. Only Picture Arrangement fails to load strongly or consistently on any factor at any age and perhaps should be dropped altogether in a revision. Picture Completion is the weakest of the non-verbal tests, but three of these, and four verbal tests, remain to contribute to factor scores.

The compilation of factor scores still seems the best summation of performance for all individuals on WISC-R and WAIS-R. The resulting levels and inconsistencies can be graphed, evaluated and explained. They have both intuitive meaning and scientific interpretability. Moreover, alternative clusterings tend to confirm the patterns that emerge in this first three-factor profile analysis. Bannatyne and Horn analyses, though, add further dimensions and we shall consider these below.

The method for deriving factor scores from 11 WAIS-R subtest age-scaled scores is detailed in full in worksheets given in Chapter 13 of Kaufman (1990, pp. 460–8). Precise significance values may be applied to determine strengths and weaknesses at the individual subtest level by evaluating each subtest's deviation from the mean of its own scale. (Population base rates should be applied to significant Verbal/Performance discrepancies, computed using scaled scores derived from the reference group, to determine how unusual, and hence clinically significant, these are.)

Factor scores are calculated as follows. The VC score is obtained by adding age-scaled scores for *four* verbal subtests (Information, Vocabulary, Comprehension and Similarities), multiplying by 1.4 and adding a constant, 44. The PO score is obtained by adding age-scaled scores on the *three* performance subtests (Picture Completion, Block Design and Object Assembly), multiplying by 2.0 and adding a constant, 40. The FD score is obtained by adding age-scaled scores on the *two* subtests, Digit Span and Arithmetic, multiplying by 2.8 and adding a constant, 44.

Sadly the immense literature seems not to extend to a table of population frequencies of the three-way discrepancies of VC, PO and FD, as has been done for WISC-R by Clampit, Adair and Strenio (1983; reproduced in Sattler, 1988, Table 8.2, p. 174). But at least each factor score's deviation in either direction from the mean of all three can be evaluated at the 5% significance level (VC 7 points, PO and FD 9 points each, for individuals aged 20–74). Often results are so striking one need look no further.

Bannatyne's clusterings are the longest established and have a continuing utility. The Information subtest transfers to a fourth factor, Acquired Knowledge, as do Arithmetic and Vocabulary, both of which contribute also to their main Verbal Conceptualisation and Sequential factors. The same three subtests contribute to Bannatyne's Spatial as to Kaufman's PO factor. For weightings, constants and evaluation criteria see Kaufman (1990, pp. 464–5), who has developed these applications of others' as well as his own work.

Third, Horn's development of his own and Cattell's theory of intelligence is well known. WAIS-R dimensions for Fluid, Crystallised and Retention factors may also be determined. All Performance subtests (minus Picture Arrangement) contribute, with Digit Span and Similarities, to Fluid Intelligence: the sum of these scaled scores is multiplied by 1.1 and the product added to 34. Information, Vocabulary, Comprehension and Similarities (again) are added, multiplied by 1.4 and the product added to 44 to give Crystallised Intelligence. Retention is obtained by adding together the age-scaled scores for Information (again), Digit Span (again) and Arithmetic, multiplying the result by 2.0 and adding the product to 40. Differences of 6–7 points (ages 20–74) are significant at the 5% level and may be interpreted.

Dimensions of personality and learning

Another approach, much more obviously *clinical*, is the Jastak Cluster Analysis (Jastak and Jastak, 1979). This has been touched on before in relation to the WISC-R.[12] Essentially age-scaled scores for all 11 WAIS-R subtests are combined with scaled score equivalents for all three WRAT-3 tests (Reading, Spelling, Arithmetic) and numerous higher order learning and personality measures are derived. The rationale for this is based on the authors' empirical and clinical work, published references to which are given in the manual. Clinical experience, however, has contributed as much as empirical factoring. Clinical experience, let it said though, tends to confirm the reliability and accuracy of Jastak Cluster Analyses at individual case level.

The workings are quite complicated and Jastak Corporation apparently expects users not to devise spreadsheets to lessen the load. Scoring software, however, is not being revised to take account of new editions of tests. There are four sets of parallel procedures. Male and Female profiles are generated at each of two levels: Child (WISC) and Adult (WAIS). WRAT is given at all ages. This is one of the few psychometric procedures to take account of cognitive sex differences which, as we have seen, may be important at the margin, for instance in the diagnosis of learning disability. In summary, the 14 age-scaled scores are used and subjected to a further adjustment for sex. A regression constant is then applied and the regressed scores are evaluated for each of 10 dimensions, ranging from Lexigraphics, a global proxy for literacy, to Depression (based on scores for the 'social' subtests, Comprehension and Picture Arrangement). In each case tendencies in the data to fall above or below the subject's own mean are exaggerated by a treatment which adds or subtracts a specified value accordingly. Fourteen first-order scores disappear and 10 derived scores take their place.

Two illustrative case studies

All these clusterings clearly have much in common, as they should, given their common research base in factor analyses of Wechsler datasets. They often tell the same story. To see such an analysis in action, let us consider two contrasting actual cases, PF and JB.

PF was a prisoner serving a long term for a serious offence at the time of his assessment. His solicitor sought the assessment on his behalf and this activism was resented by the prison authorities. However, they were welcoming to the visiting psychologist. Several difficult circumstances attended this assessment. A bare minimum of background information, such as educational history, was available, most of it only from PF himself. PF was felt to be 'swinging the lead' and it was suggested there was a danger of shamming. A positive dyslexia diagnosis might favour a decision to transfer him to another prison in a lesser category of security because specialist teaching was available there, a considerable dilemma for the authorities. PF was equable and co-operative, but the timetable for prisoners and staff allowed little time for the assessment and there were several prompts to finish. Finally, an immediate yes/no decision on PF's dyslexia was sought (but not given).

Here, an edited version of PF's assessment report is given, followed by *four* profile graphs (Figures 11.4–11.7; for abbreviations see Appendix 1). The latter illustrate the major features of cognitive assessment discussed thus far.

CONFIDENTIAL: PSYCHOLOGICAL REPORT

Name of individual: PF
Age: 30 years 0 months

WECHSLER ADULT INTELLIGENCE SCALE
(REVISED UK EDITION)

IQs
The following standard scores relate PF's performance to that of individuals of the same age and have an average value of 100. Scores of 69 and below are Very Low; 70–79 are Low; 80–89 are Below Average; 90–109 are Average; 110–119 are Above Average; 120–129 are High; and 130 and above are Very High.

Verbal: 70 – above 1–3% of his contemporaries
Performance: 74 – above 3–5% of his contemporaries
Full Scale: 71 – above 2–3% of his contemporaries

SUBTEST SCORES
The following standard scores have an average value of 10. Two-thirds of individuals fall between 7 and 13. Only about 5% of individuals fall below 4 and above 16.

VERBAL SUBTESTS
Information: 1
Digit Span: 3
Vocabulary: 5
Arithmetic: 6
Comprehension: 8
Similarities: 4

PERFORMANCE OR NON-VERBAL SUBTESTS
Picture Completion: 1
Picture Arrangement: 8
Block Design: 6
Object Assembly: 9
Digit Symbol: 5

SUBTEST RESULTS IN DETAIL
Results are now reported in terms of *percentiles*, that is, the percentage of individuals of this age who perform at or below this level of ability. Percentiles of 1–2 are Very Low; 3–8 are Low; 9–24 are Below Average; 25–74 are Average; 75–90 are Above Average; 91–97 are High; and 98–99 are Very High.

Verbal

INFORMATION
Percentile: <1
Spoken answers to general knowledge questions.

DIGIT SPAN
Percentile: 1
Number lists are repeated, backwards and forwards.

VOCABULARY
Percentile: 5
Giving the meanings of words.

ARITHMETIC
Percentile: 9
Spoken answers to mental arithmetic questions.

COMPREHENSION
Percentile: 25
Spoken answers to questions requiring common sense or knowledge about society.

SIMILARITIES
Percentile: 2
Saying why two items belong to the same category.

Performance

PICTURE COMPLETION
Percentile: <1
Spoken responses to say what important part of a picture is missing.

PICTURE ARRANGEMENT
Percentile: 25
Silent rearrangement of picture cards so that their order makes sense of the story.

BLOCK DESIGN
Percentile: 9
Silent arrangement of coloured blocks at speed to reproduce the pattern on a card.

OBJECT ASSEMBLY
Percentile: 36
Silent arrangement of pieces of a jigsaw within time limits.

DIGIT SYMBOL
Percentile: 5
Timed matching and copying of symbols to go with numbers.

FACTORIAL SCORES (CLUSTERS)
The subtest scores of the WAIS-R make more clinical sense if they are related, first, to the individual's own age-group (age-corrected scores) and, second, grouped in at least three different ways. All are described in detail in Kaufman AS (1990) *Assessing Adolescent and Adult Intelligence*. Boston: Allyn and Bacon.

The main analysis (Kaufman's) is in terms of **Verbal Comprehension** (higher level language skills), **Perceptual Organisation** (ability to manage and interpret sensorimotor stimuli) and **Freedom from Distractibility** (attention control and short-term memory).

Another analysis is in terms of the Bannatyne categories:

Verbal Conceptualisation (language skills), **Spatial** ability (non-verbal ability), **Sequential** ability (working memory, symbolic routines) and **Acquired Knowledge** (general knowledge, vocabulary and arithmetic).

A third analysis is in terms of the Cattell–Horn theory of intelligence, which distinguishes between **Fluid Intelligence** (relatively culture-free), **Crystallised Intelligence** (acquired through and applied in education) and **Retention** (immediate memory).

Like IQs all these scores are standard scores and have an average value of 100.

PF obtained the following cluster scores:

Verbal Comprehension:	69
Perceptual Organisation:	72
Freedom from Distractibility:	69
Verbal Conceptualisation:	75
Spatial ability:	72
Sequential ability:	66
Acquired Knowledge:	66
Fluid Intelligence:	68
Crystallised Intelligence:	69
Retention:	60

Other tests
Wide Range Achievement Test – Third Edition (WRAT-3)
Reading
Percentile: <0.02

Using as a guide regression equations based on the child population, fewer than one individual in 100 of PF's age would obtain a score of this extreme lowness. It corresponds to a reading age of below 5 years 0 months.

Spelling
Percentile: <0.02

Using as a guide regression equations based on the child population, fewer than one individual in about 100 of PF's age would obtain a score of this extreme lowness. It corresponds to a spelling age of about 6 years 2 months.

Arithmetic
Percentile: 1

Using as a guide regression equations based on the child population, fewer than one individual in 16–17 would obtain a score of this lowness. It corresponds to a number age of about 9 years 9 months.

Jastak Cluster Analysis
Jastak JF, Jastak S (1979) Meanings And Measures Of Mental Tests [Manual: Jastak Cluster Analysis]. Wilmington, DE: Jastak Associates. This is based on further analysis of all 11 WAIS-R and three WRAT-3 subtest scores. Results are in the form of standard scores as for IQs and cluster scores and have an average value of 100.

Lexigraphics:	84 – proficiency in learning language codes.
Linguistics:	85 – verbal communication skills.
Semantic:	113 – comprehension of meaning from language.
Reality:	108 – alertness to environmental stimuli.
Motivation:	93 – will to persist and persevere.
Psychomotor:	110 – harmony between mind and muscles.
Elation:*	82 – mood reaction to praise and success.
Depression:*	120 – mood reaction to criticism and failure.
Judgement:	112 – independent and decisive behaviour.
Reasoning:	105 – logical, systematic thinking.

* NB 'In the Affect/Mood clusters (elation and depression), it is necessary to understand that the higher the cluster score the less the person reveals that emotional trait; the lower the score, the more the person manifests that emotional trait.' (Jastak, op. cit., p. 23.)

Pattern of relative strengths and weaknesses
PF has strengths in:

• verbal comprehension;
• perceptual and spatial ability.

PF has weaknesses in:

• acquiring and retaining information;
• sequential reasoning.

Background to this assessment
(information from PF in interview and from authorities at the prison)

PF, a Negro man of 30, is serving a 10 year prison sentence. He has complained that, being dyslexic, he should not receive 'foundation' course teaching in basic skills, suitable for prisoners with literacy skills greater than his own, but instead should receive one-to-one teaching from a dyslexia specialist. As this might mean, administratively, a transfer to another, more open prison, this line of campaign is viewed with suspicion by the authorities at the prison. However, he has enlisted the services of a solicitor, who has pressed to have this question determined.

PF is the fourth of seven children – and the youngest boy. His parents separated when he was young but later reunited and are now retired in Jamaica. When PF was 7–8 he was taken to Jamaica for the first time; there, at a private school, he was 'rude' and truanted from lessons. Then at age 14 he returned to London and attended secondary school where, placed in a 'lower grade', he was 'ashamed about that'. After school he attended college to do retailing, someone else having filled out the application form for him; but within 2–3 weeks his illiteracy was discovered and 'that was a total drop out for me'. Then he tried panel beating and spraying but 'couldn't read the labels on paint tins'.

PF is the father of two children aged 12 and 7. The long prison term, his first, resulted from charges of [...]. The precise origin of the difficult relationship at the bottom of the major episode was described for me: PF characterised the circumstances as 'purely domestic'. However, this word occurred later in a test of vocabulary and he defined it as 'problems at home, fighting with common law wife or mistresses'; so one should not presume from his occasional verbal fluency that he is aware of the ordinary meanings of words.

Behaviour during interview

PF came late but exuberantly into the hospital wing to meet me. It is felt that he shams or exaggerates some of his illiteracy, as an instance of his manipulativeness. Indeed I occasionally felt that he was doing this with me. So I announced early on to him that dyslexics were very bad at some tests but good at others, thus suggesting that he should not be uniformly bad at everything.

In fact the assessment activities both interested and made him anxious. He occasionally laughed, as when asked to define a sentence: 'I'm doing a sentence – this is funny!' He became thoughtfully absorbed on non-verbal activities, concentrating well. On verbal items he suffered agonies, because he lacks the most elementary information. He could not say what a thermometer was, for instance.

However, by contrast he showed much higher comprehension abilities. If he was the first to discover a fire in a cinema, he would 'alert the authorities'. And when the long-suffering member of staff in the medical wing, due to go off duty, put his head round the door to ask if I had finished by the time promised, and I pleaded for quarter of an hour more, PF turned to me and said: 'I don't think this should be rushed, do you?'

FINDINGS AND IMPLICATIONS OF THIS ASSESSMENT

General intellectual ability

PF is of extremely low general ability (above that of only 2–3% of his age-peers). There are contrasting highs and lows in his cognitive profile but appearances rather belie this general difficulty in learning: if PF were a school pupil, he would need to be considered for special education on the grounds of moderate learning difficulties.

His low overall ability, with the possibility of his shamming and the explicit request by the authorities for a clear Yes/No decision (not always possible) with regard to the question of dyslexia, all combined to present a challenge but, however unpropitious the circumstances, the question can in fact be decided, in the usual way, by reference to:

(1) the discrepancy between expected and observed levels of attainment in relation to IQ; and
(2) evidence of specific information-processing difficulties within PF's cognitive profile.

Ability differences in different modes

PF shows little contrast between his development in language-based areas of thinking (ideas, concepts, words) and visual and spatial areas (shapes, patterns, relations), with neither being better developed. This level of Verbal/Performance discrepancy is not exceptional.

The internal contrasts in PF's cognitive profile may be seen in the **first** of the attached diagrams, which compares his development with that of others his age. It will be observed that only on one subtest does PF fall anywhere near the average range; on only three out of 11 subtests does he rise above the lowest 10%; and on six out of the 11 he falls within the bottom 5% of the population.

In the **second** diagram, PF's scores are adjusted to his own mean, so that strengths and weaknesses appear in relation to his own characteristic level of performance.

In the **third** diagram, the clusters derived by means of the Jastak Cluster Analysis are given, also in variations about PF's own mean. This analysis brings out convincingly the personality dimension to PF's general functioning. Lexigraphics and Linguistics are notable weaknesses, including reading and spelling with impoverished vocabulary, but his reality orientation, his judgement and reasoning, his grasp of social meanings, his abundant cheerfulness and lack of depression are all confirmed.

In the **fourth** diagram, the factorial scores computed from Kaufman (Verbal Comprehension, Perceptual Organisation, Freedom from Distractibility), Bannatyne (Verbal Conceptualisation, Spatial, Sequential, Acquired Knowledge) and Horn (Fluid Intelligence, Crystallised Intelligence, Retention) are displayed in variations about PF's own mean. Here again, PF's high verbal comprehension is apparent, while his dyslexic features – poor sequencing and acquired knowledge, and dismal memory operations – are clearly illustrated.

Attainment in reading

On the Wide Range Achievement Test (WRAT-3) of **Reading** PF scored at a level above fewer than 0.02% of individuals his own age and obtained a reading age of below 5 years. A score this low would be expected in fewer than 1% of individuals of PF's Full Scale IQ. Because of how far this result is contrary to expectation, PF meets the principal criterion for dyslexia. Even if PF was exaggerating his word-reading difficulties (his teacher said he could read the word *church*), this is unlikely to alter the result sufficiently to disturb this conclusion.

On the Woodcock–Johnson test of **Word Attack** skills, which uses orthographically plausible non-words, PF scored at a level appropriate for an individual of 6 years 7 months, but he read only two words (*tiff* and *lish*) and showed the greatest discomfort with this activity. He knows letter names but not sounds, and blends sounds in the familiar letter-patterns of English only with extreme hesitation.

Because of PF's extremely limited decoding skills no more complex test of reading was possible.

Attainment in written arithmetic

Written arithmetic is highly sequenced and draws continually upon working memory, both for names of numbers, rehearsed auditorily, and for spatial position and direction. It therefore presents a multitude of challenges for the learning-impaired individual. On the Wide Range Achievement Test (WRAT-3) of **Arithmetic**, PF scored at a level above 1% of individuals his own age and obtained a number age of 9 years 9 months. A score this low would be expected in only one individual in 16–17 (6%) of PF's Full Scale IQ. Use of regression methods is not possible but it is likely that this result, while low, is *not* very exceptional.

Attainment in spelling

On the Wide Range Achievement Test (WRAT-3) of **Spelling** PF scored at a level above 0.02% of individuals his own age and obtained a spelling age of about 6 years 2 months. A score this low would be expected in fewer than 1% of individuals with PF's Full Scale IQ. Because of how far this result is contrary to expectation, PF meets the principal criterion for dyslexia in spelling as well as reading.

PF wrote letters from spoken letter-names correctly. But the only writing he can do with some ease is his own name. *And* he wrote with difficulty as *eram*.

Conclusions

In spite of the difficulties mentioned, a satisfactory answer emerges to the question of PF's putative dyslexia. He does indeed meet the criteria for dyslexia on two grounds:

- his literacy attainment, even in the context of very low general abilities, is so severely low as to be statistically unexpected; and
- PF shows the distinctive pattern of impaired information-processing in language and working memory areas, while showing relatively robust performance in areas demanding visuo-motor control and organisation, spatial ability and verbal comprehension.

(A recommendations section follows but is omitted here.)

[SIGNATURE AND DATE]

Wechsler Adult Intelligence Scale profile for PF (30:0)

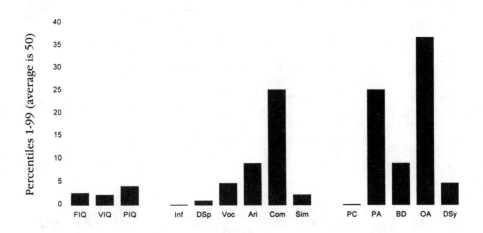

Figure 11.4: Normative graph for PF, showing WAIS-R composite and subtest scores on a percentile scale.

Relative strengths and weaknesses WAIS-R profile for PF (30:0)

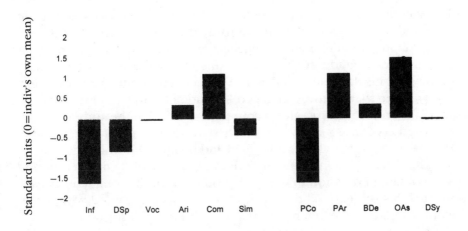

Figure 11.5: Ipsative graph for PF, showing WAIS-R subtests rescaled to his own mean and SD in SD units.

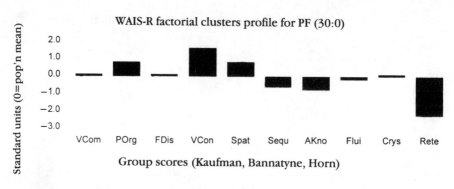

Figure 11.6: Factor graph for PF, showing second-order WAIS-R clusters (Kaufman, Bannatyne, Horn) in ipsative form in SD units.

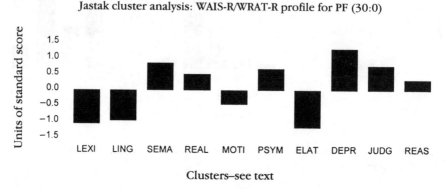

Figure 11.7: Factor graph for PF, showing second-order Jastak clusters (WAIS-R/WRAT-3) in ipsative form in SD units.

The second case chosen to illustrate many of the methods and techniques of adult assessment is that of JB, a businessman aged 50 years. An alert, adaptive man of high intelligence, his history exemplifies many of the comments made at the start of this chapter. Attending parents' evenings at his daughter's college, he observed how enjoyable it was for her and her friends to be engaged in academic study and decided to enrol in an A-level sociology course himself. This he duly did and returned to formal study for the first time in a great many years. However, the terminal exams loomed and he knew he would be unable to write without the information technology he had grown to rely upon. So to obtain permission to use his laptop in exams he sought an assessment of his dyslexia. The latter had always been accepted within the family as a fact of life, but had not previously been investigated.

As before, the complete report on JB is reproduced, followed by the four graphs which convey, as for PF, the relationships among the first-order and derived scores (Figures 11.8–11.11; for abbreviations see Appendix 1).

CONFIDENTIAL: PSYCHOLOGICAL REPORT

Name of individual: JB

Age: 50 years 9 months

SUMMARY OF FINDINGS

Abilities

JB is of high general ability (above that of 96% of individuals his own age).

Pattern of relative strengths and weaknesses

JB has cognitive strengths in:

- verbal conceptualisation;
- visuo-spatial ability.

JB has cognitive weaknesses in:

- immediate verbal memory;
- clerical speed.

Attainments

JB now attains in literacy (reading and spelling) at levels commensurate with his ability; arithmetic skills are lower. However, his reading is slow and he often loses his place; and without word-processing his writing remains a focus of difficulty – slow and illegible.

Conclusions

JB is unmistakably dyslexic and he continues to show distinctive signs of linguistic information-processing difficulties.

Recommendations

Specialised individual tuition would still enable JB to overcome remaining difficulties in basic skills. He will need special arrangements in order to compete on equal terms in timed, written public examinations.

[SIGNATURE AND DATE]

PSYCHOLOGICAL ASSESSMENT: HIGHLIGHTS AND CONCLUSIONS

Background to this assessment (information from JB)

JB is the second of four children in a family with no apparent incidence of dyslexia, a specific learning difficulty. From the age of 5–6 he showed specific learning difficulties and, partly as a result, attended six different schools, including schools in the Republic of Ireland.[13] He never received appropriate assessment or specialist teaching. Recently he has learned to use word-processing technology to great effect, such that he now produces creative reports with little of the former struggle. He claims that the use of spell-checker and the thesaurus has indirectly improved his literacy skills, after many years of poor functioning and no improvement. In the different climate that prevails today he is able to return to formal study (A-level sociology), have his dyslexic difficulties evaluated and seek fairer examination conditions which take account of his dependence upon information technology.

General intellectual ability

On the Wechsler Adult Intelligence Scale – Revised (WAIS-R), JB obtained scores which place him above 96% of the population of his age-group in terms of general ability.

Cognitive style

JB shows little contrast between his development in language-based areas of thinking (ideas, concepts, words) and visual and spatial areas (shapes, patterns, relations), with neither being better developed.

The internal contrasts in JB's cognitive profile may be seen in the first of the attached diagrams, which compares his development with that of others his age.

In the second diagram, JB's scores are adjusted to his own mean so that strengths and weaknesses appear in relation to his own characteristic level of performance.

Other ability groupings

Grouping JB's subtest scores together in various ways, including with attainment results in reading, spelling and arithmetic from the **Wide Range Achievement Test** Third Edition (WRAT-3), enables a more powerful analysis of his cognitive strengths and weaknesses to be made.

- *Verbal Comprehension*: this summarises the ability to comprehend and use words effectively.

- *Verbal Conceptualisation*: an outline of verbal reasoning and concept formation abilities.
- *Crystallised Intelligence*: problem solving and factual learning that are dependent on formal schooling and cultural experience.

JB has significant **strengths** in these groups of abilities.

- *Freedom from Distractibility*: this is a measure of attentiveness and memory.
- *Sequential*: this identifies how well information is processed in series or sequences.
- *Retention*: aspects of learning ability in which memory is the main component.

JB has significant **weaknesses** in these groups of abilities.

In the third diagram, these groupings are displayed in variations about the population mean.

A further grouping uses the **Jastak Cluster Analysis** to identify 10 notable areas of ability and difficulty.

- *Linguistics* describes verbal communication skills.
- *Semantic* describes comprehension of meaning from language.
- *Judgement* describes independent and decisive behaviour.

JB has significant **strengths** in these areas.

- *Lexigraphics* describes proficiency in learning language codes.
- *Motivation* describes the will to persist and persevere.
- *Reasoning* describes logical, systematic thinking.

JB has significant **weaknesses** in these areas.

The clusters derived by means of the **Jastak Cluster Analysis** are given, also in variations about the population mean, in the fourth diagram.

Pattern of performance on diagnostic tests

In **Digit Span** digits are repeated forwards and backwards after a presentation time of one per second. On this test he obtained a score which would place him above only 25% of the population. JB shows the marked deficiency in short-term or immediate working memory of the kind associated with dyslexia, a specific learning difficulty. Poor verbal memory is perhaps the most obvious feature, indicating difficulties in phonological processing.

Digit Symbol requires the individual systematically to substitute for single digits the symbols which go with them in a model. This test is performed under timed conditions: the number correct within one-and-a-half minutes is credited. The test measures concentration, substitution of written symbols, rapid decision making and fine motor control of hand and pencil. Difficulty is likely to be related to the manipulation of symbols in memory as well as executive speed with a pencil. On this test he obtained a score which would place him above only 50% of the population.

Pattern of performance on other diagnostic measures

On **Perin's spoonerism task**, JB performed reasonably well, but achieved at a level which is comparable to those individuals who have some difficulties with spelling.

On **Townend's Perception of Syllables**, JB showed considerable difficulty in separating and comparing syllables.

Achievement in basic skills

On the Wide Range Achievement Test (WRAT-3) of **Reading** JB scored at a level above 68% of individuals his own age. This score was close to expectation.

JB's reading speed was measured using Aaron's lists of **function and content** words. Like many dyslexics he read function words more inaccurately. Overall his reading speed seemed somewhat slow.

On three tests from the Woodcock Reading Mastery Tests – Revised, JB performed as follows. On **Letter-Word Identification** (single-word reading), he achieved at a level above 75% of pupils his own age; on **Word Attack** above 67%; and on **Passage Comprehension**, above 95%. This profile is characteristic of dyslexics, whose comprehension is typically better than their word recognition, and whose recognition of words is better than their decoding of non-words. These tests provide a further analysis of how expected or unexpected a given level of reading is in relation to IQ or verbal ability. JB's present level of basic reading skills would be found in about 30% of pupils of his age and ability. This is not exceptional.

On the Wide Range Achievement Test (WRAT-3) of **Spelling** JB scored at a level above 70% of individuals his own age. This score was not exceptional.

On the Woodcock–Johnson test of **Writing Fluency**, JB showed serious underachievement, falling within the lowest 30% of his age-group. This low result suggests a degree of difficulty that must seriously prejudice his performance in written examinations.

On the Wide Range Achievement Test (WRAT-3) of **Arithmetic** JB scored at a level above only 47% of individuals his own age. This score was below expectation.

Conclusions

JB is unmistakably dyslexic, though now cognitive or information-processing anomalies remain more evident than do difficulties with reading and spelling. The latter have responded over the years to much diligent self-help, including more recently with the use of information technology.

JB shows the limitation in working, especially phonological, memory which research implicates in the common forms of learning disability. What is restricted is the capacity to hold in memory at one time all the elements of a task that is either highly sequenced or that requires many simultaneous operations. As a result the basic skills of reading, writing and arithmetic, all of which make a considerable demand on working memory, are not easily acquired or are not well consolidated in automatic form. The results are most obvious in the difficulty otherwise intelligent individuals have with reading, spelling or memorisation of tables. It is this group of individuals that is recognised to have dyslexia, a specific learning difficulty.

Recommendations

An effective framework for teaching spelling and writing to students and adults is *A Resource Pack For Tutors Of Students With Specific Learning Difficulties* by Marion Walker and may be obtained from the author at 14 Weston Close, Dorridge, Solihull, West Midlands B93 8BL, UK. In addition, many useful suggestions and resources for literacy in adult and later school life are contained in:

- Bramley W (1993) *Developing Literacy For Study And Work*. Staines, Middlesex: Dyslexia Institute (ISBN 0 9503915 5 7).

Special arrangements at GCSE

The examination boards now accept that the following special arrangements may be required for students to demonstrate their attainment in examination conditions:

- extra time for timed written papers;
- access to word-processor with later printing where this is the candidate's normal method of working (possible abuse of memory features for unfair advantage must be ruled out).

JB's need for these special arrangements should be represented to the relevant examination boards in good time by his examination centre. Examiners should be made aware at the moderation stage that the scripts they read were produced by an individual with dyslexia. This enables assessment of knowledge and work to become distinct from a survey of clerical skills.

It is probably not desirable to request exemption from the new spelling rule as only 5% of marks are at stake and GCSE examination certificates must then be endorsed.

[SIGNATURE AND DATE]

TECHNICAL APPENDIX: TEST RESULTS

WECHSLER ADULT INTELLIGENCE SCALE (REVISED UK EDITION)

IQs

The following standard scores relate JB's performance to that of individuals of the same age and have an average value of 100. Scores of 69 and below are Very Low; 70–79 are Low; 80–89 are Below Average; 90–109 are Average; 110–119 are Above Average; 120–129 are High; and 130 and above are Very High.

Verbal IQ: 121 – this places him above 92% of his contemporaries.

Performance IQ: 124 – this places him above 95% of his contemporaries.

Full Scale IQ: 126 – this places him above 96% of his contemporaries.

IQ is necessarily a global measure of all-round ability and therefore penalises an individual who may have strengths offset by weaknesses. Because of error inherent in the measurement process, it is best to say that that the true Full Scale IQ probably lies within the range 122–130 (90% confidence).

SUBTEST RESULTS IN DETAIL

Results are reported first in terms of *scaled scores*, then in terms of *percentiles*. *Scaled scores* have an average value of 10. Half the population will obtain scores between 7 and 13 on any subtest; scores of 6 and below are low; scores of 14 and above are high. For this purpose *age-corrected scaled scores*, which more nearly relate JB to his contemporaries, are used. *Percentile* indicates the percentage of individuals of this age who perform at or below this level of ability.

Verbal

INFORMATION

Percentile: 75
Scaled score: 12

Spoken answers to general knowledge questions.

DIGIT SPAN

Percentile: 25
Scaled score: 8

Number lists are repeated, backwards and forwards.

VOCABULARY

Percentile: 99
Scaled score: 19

Giving the meanings of words.

ARITHMETIC

Percentile: 50
Scaled score: 10

Spoken answers to mental arithmetic questions.

COMPREHENSION

Percentile: 95
Scaled score: 15

Spoken answers to questions requiring common sense or knowledge about society.

SIMILARITIES

Percentile: 95
Scaled score: 15

Saying why two items belong to the same category.

Performance

PICTURE COMPLETION

Percentile: 95
Scaled score: 15

Spoken responses to say which important part of a picture is missing.

PICTURE ARRANGEMENT

Percentile: 91
Scaled score: 14

Silent rearrangement of picture cards so that their order makes sense of the story.

BLOCK DESIGN

Percentile: 95
Scaled score: 15

Silent arrangement of coloured blocks at speed to reproduce the pattern on a card.

OBJECT ASSEMBLY

Percentile: 84
Scaled score: 13

Silent arrangement of pieces of a jigsaw within time limits.

DIGIT SYMBOL

Percentile: 50
Scaled score: 10

Timed matching and copying of symbols to go with numbers.

Factorial scores (clusters)

The subtest scores of the WAIS-R make more clinical sense if they are related, first, to the individual's own age-group (age-corrected scores) and, second, grouped together in different ways. This method is described in detail in: Kaufman AS (1990) *Assessing Adolescent and Adult Intelligence*. Boston: Allyn and Bacon.

The main analysis (Kaufman's) is in terms of *Verbal Comprehension* (higher level language skills), *Perceptual Organisation* (ability to manage and interpret visuospatial stimuli) and *Freedom from Distractibility* (attention control and short-term memory).

Another analysis is in terms of Bannatyne's categories: *Verbal Conceptualisation* (language skills), *Spatial ability* (non-verbal ability), *Sequential ability* (working memory, symbolic routines) and *Acquired Knowledge* (general knowledge, vocabulary and arithmetic).

A third analysis is in terms of the Cattell-Horn theory of intelligence, which distinguishes between *Fluid Intelligence* (relatively culture-free reasoning), **Crystallised Intelligence** (abilities acquired through and applied within a cultural context) and **Retention** (immediate memory).

Like IQs all these scores are standard scores and have an average value of 100. Scores of 69 and below are Very Low; 70–79 are Low; 80–89 are Below Average; 90–109 are Average; 110–119 are Above Average; 120–129 are High; and 130 and above are Very High.

JB obtained the following cluster scores:

- Verbal Comprehension: 129
- Perceptual Organisation: 126
- Freedom from Distractibility: 94
- Verbal Conceptualisation: 136
- Spatial ability: 126
- Sequential ability: 96
- Acquired Knowledge: 121
- Fluid Intelligence: 122
- Crystallised Intelligence: 129
- Retention: 100

JASTAK CLUSTER ANALYSIS
Jastak JF, Jastak S (1979) *Meanings and Measures of Mental Tests* [Manual: Jastak Cluster Analysis]. Wilmington, DE: Jastak Associates. This is based on further analysis of all 11 WAIS-R and three WRAT-3 subtest scores. Results are in the form of standard scores as for IQs and cluster scores and have an average value of 100. Scores of 69 and below are Very Low; 70–79 are Low; 80–89 are Low Average; 90–109 are Average; 110–119 are High Average; 120–129 are High; and 130 and above are Very High.

LEXIGRAPHICS: 89
Proficiency in learning language codes.

LINGUISTICS :   116
Verbal communication skills.

SEMANTIC: 119
Comprehension of meaning from language.

REALITY: 114
Alertness to environmental stimuli.

MOTIVATION: 59
Will to persist and persevere.

PSYCHOMOTOR: 95
Harmony between mind and muscles.

ELATION:* 86

Mood reaction to praise and success.

DEPRESSION:*   120

Mood reaction to criticism and failure.

JUDGEMENT: 120

Independent and decisive behaviour.

REASONING: 85

Logical, systematic thinking.

*NB 'In the Affect/Mood clusters (elation and depression), it is necessary to understand that the higher the cluster score the less the person reveals that emotional trait; the lower the score, the more the person manifests that emotional trait.' (Jastak, op. cit., p. 23.)

Other diagnostic procedures

PERIN SPOONERISM TASK

Perin D (1983) Phonemic segmentation and spelling. British Journal of Psychology 74: 129–144. This is a harder phonological processing task, suitable for older individuals. The individual must produce spoonerisms from the names of singers (Bob Marley becomes Mob Barley). Difficulty with this task is associated with weak spelling but not with weak reading. On this task, JB performed fairly quickly and confidently, achieving at a level which is comparable with individuals who have some difficulties with spelling.

PERCEPTION OF SYLLABLES TASK – experimental version

Townend J (1994) unpublished. Words and non-words are presented, partly orally, partly on the page, in which the individual must count the numbers of syllables or isolate the stressed syllable. On this task JB showed considerable difficulty in separating and comparing syllables. He was able to number correctly syllables within 2–4 syllable words only 71% of the time; with identification of accented syllables he was even less successful: 67% correct.

Attainment in written arithmetic

WIDE RANGE ACHIEVEMENT TEST - THIRD EDITION (WRAT-3)

Arithmetic
Percentile: 47

A score this low would be expected in only one individual in six (16–17%) of JB's Full Scale IQ. This is somewhat exceptional.

Attainment in spelling and writing

WIDE RANGE ACHIEVEMENT TEST – THIRD EDITION (WRAT-3)

Spelling

Percentile: 70

A score this low would be expected in one individual in three of JB's Full Scale IQ. It is not exceptional.

WRITING FLUENCY

Percentile: 30

Age equivalent: 11 years 7 months

Woodcock RW, Johnson MB (1989, 1990 *Woodcock–Johnson Psycho-Educational Battery – Revised*. Allen, TX: DLM. In this task the individual has to form short sentences out of sets of three words. Spelling, grammar and punctuation are not marked down, though the sentences must be grammatically complete and the words themselves must not be changed. This timed, seven-minute task is a good measure of writing productivity.

Attainment in reading

WIDE RANGE ACHIEVEMENT TEST – THIRD EDITION (WRAT-3)

Reading

Percentile: 68

A score this low would be expected in one individual in three of JB's Full Scale IQ. It is not exceptional.

NATIONAL ADULT READING TEST

Nelson HE (1982) *National Adult Reading Test*. Windsor, Berks: NFER-Nelson. This is a list of irregular words which predicts adult intelligence. JB made 16 errors, a score which would predict a Full Scale WAIS-R IQ of 111; he actually obtained a WAIS-R IQ of 126; a discrepancy of this many points (15) of standard score would be expected in one individual in 25 (4%). This level of reading, therefore, *is* highly exceptional.

READING SPEED – FUNCTION AND CONTENT WORDS

From Aaron PG, Joshi RM (1992) *Reading Problems: Consultation And Remediation*. New York: Guilford Press. Measures of reading speed are distorted by time taken over unfamiliar words.

These two lists, of 20 words each, matched for frequency and number of syllables, offer a good alternative. The individual's reading of the words in each list is timed. Dyslexic readers make more errors on function words (*also, once, ever*), as well as reading them more slowly than content words (*book, bird, gold*). JB read the content words in 15 seconds, making no errors and the function words in 14 seconds, with one error. Overall JB read at a speed of about 0.73 seconds per word. (A skilled adult reader reads silently at a speed of about 0.25–0.50 seconds per word or less.)

WORD IDENTIFICATION

Percentile: 75

Woodcock RW (1987) Woodcock Reading Mastery Tests – Revised [WRMT-R]. Circle Pines, MN: American Guidance Service. This is a test of single-word decoding accuracy of a conventional kind. With 106 items, however, it is more than usually reliable.

WORD ATTACK

Percentile: 67

Woodcock RW (1987) Woodcock Reading Mastery Tests – Revised [WRMT-R]. Circle Pines, MN: American Guidance Service. On this test decoding skills are highlighted using made-up words (*bend, wrault*).

PASSAGE COMPREHENSION

Percentile: 95

Woodcock RW (1987) Woodcock Reading Mastery Tests – Revised [WRMT-R]. Circle Pines, MN: American Guidance Service. Comprehension is probed by questions about items ranging from simple pictures accompanied by short sentences, through longer sentences without pictures, to complex prose passages.

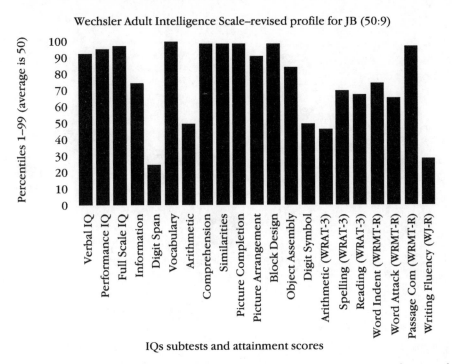

Figure 11.8: Normative graph for JB, showing WAIS-R composite, subtest and attainment scores on a percentile scale.

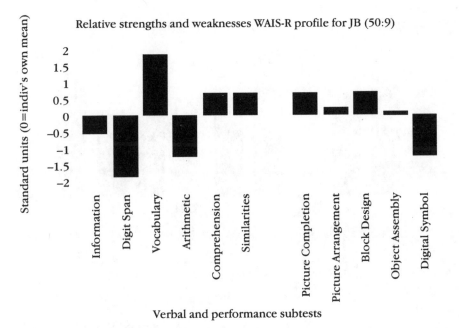

Figure 11.9: Ipsative graph for JB, showing WAIS-R subtests rescaled to his own mean and SD in SD units.

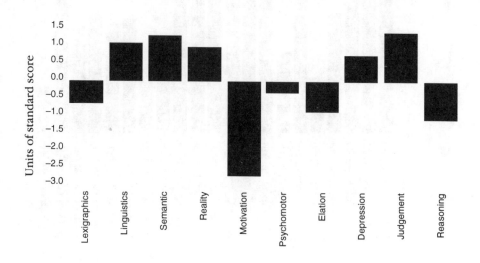

Figure 11.10: Factor graph for JB, showing second-order WAIS-R clusters (Kaufman, Bannatyne, Horn) in ipsative form in SD units.

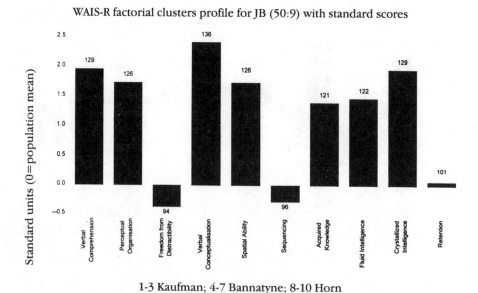

1-3 Kaufman; 4-7 Bannatyne; 8-10 Horn

Figure 11.11: Factor graph for JB, showing second-order JASTAK clusters (WAIS-R/WRAT-3) in ipsative form in SD units.

These two adult cases are reported in detail because of the way they encapsulate clinical and technical challenges. The case of PF, especially, demanded the categorical resolution of the question of whether he is dyslexic or not,[14] in circumstances cramped for time and fraught with extraneous pressures. A particular dilemma for the clinician is: how can the question of dyslexia be resolved in cases of very low general ability?

The solution presented in the form of PF's assessment narrative may not be accepted by all, but the argument is at least given in enough detail to be contested:

- Regression[15] shows underachievement to be conspicuous in literacy (but not number skills), even when ability and achievement are both at marginally low levels.
- Cluster scores show a focus of difficulties with literacy-related skills (Jastak's Lexigraphics and Linguistics).
- Factorial scores show evidence of a cognitive profile of learning difficulty, especially Bannatyne (Sequencing, Acquired Knowledge) and Horn (Retention).

JB, on the other hand, is much more straightforward, largely because his abilities are high. His cognitive profile is as plain as could be wished and is of a conventionally dyslexic kind. All three factor scores (Kaufman, Bannatyne, Horn) show up his learning difficulty. The Jastak analysis enables us to see his low motivation for the WAIS tasks and the three WJ-R literacy tests display the familiar within-reading profile:

comprehension > word reading > non-word reading

Compensation strategies

There is some question of whether the dyslexia cognitive profile attenuates with maturity to the point where it is of diminished diagnostic significance. Evidence for this does exist (for example Nicolson, Fawcett and Baddeley, 1992). However, equivocal cases exist at all ages and clear-cut examples of adults, such as JB, still with marked diagnostic features, abound.

It seems most likely that compensation strategies, discussed in Chapter 4 in relation to children of higher ability, increase in use with age. Digits backwards, for instance, known to be more highly g-loaded than digits forwards, are more easily performed by brighter and older individuals. As dyslexic individuals go through life, they learn to cope with the challenges of school and work by evolving strategies, sometimes called *metacognitive*, to make the best of their abilities. These may be as straightforward as mnemonics or leaving written messages to oneself around the house.[16]

A regression resource for adults

JB does illustrate one further available technique which has not been mentioned. There *is* a reading regression method available for adults: the National Adult Reading Test (NART)(Nelson, 1982).[17] Devised as a proxy test of premorbid intelligence, for instance where a patient has suffered brain injury and no historical record exists of abilities prior to the accident, the test requires the reading of 50 capitalised exception words (*aisle, demesne*) in isolation. The rationale is that, as these words do not respond to rule-governed sound-symbol translation, they must, if known, have been acquired singly by acts of verbal enquiry and memory and must therefore be a good guide to the patient's former intellectual level.

A regression apparatus is provided with WAIS-R (Verbal, Performance and Full Scale IQs), such that a given number of NART errors predicts level of WAIS-R ability. However, this serves dyslexia assessment purposes quite well too, albeit in reverse. An *observed* level of WAIS-R intelligence may be greater than an expected level, based on NART errors. The difference between the two, if greater than chance, may be interpreted in the usual way, with frequencies of such discrepancies given in the manual. The words, though, will all be quite difficult for many dyslexics. Even where this method comes into its own, as with JB, it should be used in combination with other investigations.

Counselling aspects

The first aspect of assessment work mentioned by those who work with adults is the interpersonal. Children, let it be said, enjoy tests and have none of the hang-ups sometimes attributed to them in anti-psychometric propaganda. This is not true of adults, who are usually circumspect and understand fully the implications of the tests being given. The infantile nature of many tests does not help.

Above all, adults want to talk. Though talk may be a diversion from testing and is costly in time, the assessing psychologist will also want to talk. An assessment will proceed very fruitfully if the preliminary talking has been effective.

A mainly communicative approach to young adults, especially, has been understandably successful (Klein, 1993). In terms of therapeutic orientation and the ability to deal successfully, often in groups, with clients' feelings left over from years of problematic schooling, this approach is inspiring. In other aspects, it is less certain. Antipathy to psychological testing, itself left over from an ILEA tradition,[18] excludes any precise comparison of individuals' features and any distinction between dyslexia and illiteracy. The rejection of multisensory phonics, similarly, although a reasonable response to histories of poor and ineffective phonic teaching, shies at the principal hurdle to literacy such young adults face.[19]

Background information is obtainable directly from dyslexic individuals by means of the Adult Dyslexia Checklist. This originated in the Dyslexia Institute but is now pragmatically named by users in honour of its reviser, Dr Michael Vinegrad, lately of Goldsmiths College. This consists of 20 questions (*Is your spelling poor? Do you mix up bus numbers like 95 and 59?*) which may be answered 'yes' or 'no'. This simple questionnaire has recently been given to 679 adults aged 18 to 68, 79% of whom were students. Thirty-two students in the group had also been assessed as dyslexic and a comparison was therefore enabled between dyslexic (12.7 'yes' responses on average) and non-dyslexic (mean 'yes' responses 4.4). In all, 90% of the total sample gave eight or fewer 'yes' responses. Twelve questions were especially good indicators of dyslexia, discriminant function analysis revealed, including *Do you find difficulty in telling left from right?* (Vinegrad, 1994). It is hard to see how the screening needs of further and higher education institutions could be met more cheaply and effectively than by means of this 'Vinegrad Checklist'.

Socioemotional aspects of dyslexia are poorly served in a literature with a mainly cognitive emphasis. It was not always so, and an older literature often took personality dimensions very seriously (Klasen, 1972). Books for parents and teachers are now obtainable, often from the United States (Osman, 1982; Silver, 1984). In Britain, too, there are the beginnings of valuable enquiry (Dodds, 1994, 1995; Edwards, 1994; Hales, 1994). In relation to adults, the first-hand experience, dictated to the wife of a conference organiser, of a gifted mathematician with a long, troubled history of severe dyslexia is of particular interest (Jansons, 1988).

Notes

1 Just as women and minorities are sometimes said to experience a glass ceiling beyond which, for no good reason, they cannot seem to get promoted, so the dyslexic, in order to enter the ranks of management, must sit down at a desk and write. Faced with such letter- and report-writing, many even prefer to avoid well-earned promotion.

2 I except Mazes, which is in a class of its own (normally 0.40– 0.50) for lack of relationship to intelligence.

3 Gain scores are presented for all results in three different age-groups, an appreciable innovation as Kaufman has done much to bring gain effects upon retesting to the attention of clinicians. Between the ages of 11 and 54, for instance, there is a mean gain of 7.8 points of standard score on the Fluid Scale.

4 All such scores are of course standardised separately for each group, so the decline is concealed; an IQ of 100 is considered average in relation to a subject's contemporaries. Perhaps the best discussion of ageing effects upon psychometric intelligence is to be found in Chapter 7 of Kaufman (1990).

5 WAIS-R was standardised on 1880 individuals between May 1976 and May 1980.

6   The K-ABC attempts to capture *sequential* and *simultaneous* processes, as well as *achievement*.

7   It is described as an 'interesting trend'.

8   See especially Appendix C, Tables C-25 to C-40, pp. 840–54, for information relevant to the WAIS-R.

9   In Britain there is the particular advantage, not of a UK standardisation, contrary to what many appear to believe, but an *Anglicisation*, a lesser exercise in which 12% of verbal items were rewritten, trialled with a stratified sample of 174 subjects for item difficulty equivalence and reliability, and reordered as necessary. See Lea (1986, pp. 3-10).

10 Poor teenage norms, several subtest 'floors' not low enough, low subtest reliability at ages 16–17, non-uniformity of range of scaled scores of different subtests, manual uninformative on a number of counts.

11 The symbols are more abstract and less susceptible to verbalisation.

12 A revision of the procedure and accompanying software to take account of WISC-III is 'not a priority' for Jastak at present.

13 The Christian Brothers, his parents believed, would *beat* some knowledge into him.

14 Contrary to perception, the sheep-and-goats categorisation of people as dyslexic is not usually a main concern. The clinician is not an administrator and however categorical dyslexia may turn out to be in theory, it is dimensional in practice, as the criterion-based sorting in Chapter 8 made clear.

15 Actually, though the normal distribution may be used in this case to quantify discrepancy distance, because actual regression values based on co-norming are unavailable, DAS and WISC/WORD tables predict much higher levels of literacy attainment than those observed and have been used as a guide.

16 I once worked with a senior official of a London embassy who, unable to remember the codes, passed through numerous electronically coded security gates by recalling the spatial layout and serial order of the buttons to be pressed.

17 I am grateful to Dr Hazel Dewart for bringing this test to my attention.

18 The Inner London Education Authority was, until it was abolished in 1988, an exemplar of publicly financed egalitarian innovations. Its traditions live on.

19 Dyslexia Institute experience is that people of all ages can be successfully taught phonic-based reading and spelling technique.

Chapter 12
Severity: the case for resources

The end of the story?

Thus far we have looked carefully, within the psychological assessment of dyslexia, at the heart of the technology, the construction of certain statistical arguments, and more broadly at the research context within which modes of professional communication have come to be accepted. Adults and preschool children have offered opportunities for special applications of the method, and the teaching that awaits the person identified as dyslexic has demonstrated an impressive range of interest and ingenuity. An assessment repertoire for teachers has been proposed, bearing in mind that there are perhaps 300 teachers for every educational psychologist and that a dyslexic pupil is more likely to meet an interested teacher than a psychologist. Finally we have examined observed patterns of ability and difficulty in a mainly dyslexic clinical sample referred for learning difficulties.

Identification may mark the limit of technical interest. However, there remain enormous questions concerning the implementation of assessment findings, recommendations for action and negotiation of altered educational circumstances for each individual. Indeed for most families the scientific legerdemain of assessment, however fascinating, is empty until it culminates, brightly, in the Tolstoyan question: *What is to be done?*

The implications of the dyslexia assessment begin with teaching, carry through to pre-statutory and statutory special needs administration and for most dyslexic children return at examination time. Even in the further and higher education sectors there are resources, for instance laptop computers, which may be awarded to dyslexic students on the basis of a psychological assessment. Administrative regulations and procedures change. Even the statutory framework with its attendant nomenclature, though apparently stable, is revised by Act of Parliament with surprising frequency as public understandings and expectations change.[1] But the educational issues, by contrast, are as constant as the laws of the Medes and Persians. As we shall see, the best guiding principle to help all parties, parents as well as administrators, through what is often a combat zone may be respect for the principle of *severity*.

In this final chapter it will be best, then, to follow the logical course of examining each of these implementation issues in turn. Psychological assessment may have surprisingly exact implications for teaching, for planning provision and for accommodating the individual within mainstream education. However, the onus of *effective communication* falls squarely upon the consulting psychologist if the definition of the problem, the explanation of the learning difficulties, the detailed plan of action and the objective basis for resolving disputes are to prove useful to the many parties to the child's education. Many psychologists will not even have met with some of these professional groups before. For instance, the experience of providing expert testimony and appearing as an expert witness in a legal dispute remains beyond the horizon for many professionals. There may be some fear and reluctance to get involved.

Experience is the germ of confidence. The standard and objective nature of the enterprise makes the findings especially valuable to the lay person in whatever role. The principles of assessment can be conveyed in clear, non-technical fashion (we have already examined alternative reporting devices for statistics). And practice in covering the main ground, whether with parents or teachers, gradually makes the professional a seasoned explainer.

Issues in teaching

We have already encountered many of the teaching options available in Chapter 7. What needs to be added to the account given there is that specialist teaching is the provision of choice in dyslexia, and that further issues mainly resolve themselves into those of quantity and quality. To elaborate: *if* an individual is positively identified as dyslexic, *then* specialist teaching is largely the appropriate, if not the sole, remedy. Performance-enhancing drugs may, in time, alter this situation. Even if they do, an enhanced capacity to learn – for instance in the teaching situation – will be one obvious benefit.

Teaching remains the road to progress for the dyslexic learner. Independent learning, especially through reading practice and 'exposure to print', becomes more important as that progress continues. As we know, however, it is in the difficult early stages that problems are concentrated for the dyslexic pupil.

This, then, is the issue of quality. Only specialist teaching from a fully qualified person is likely to make a decisive difference. Conventional remedial instruction or 'diagnostic-prescriptive remediation' constitutes, for most individuals, only *more of the same* teaching with which they have already failed to learn the skills of literacy. Individuals qualified to the level of a postgraduate diploma (or equivalent) will not only make reference to a fully articulated programme of reading and spelling but employ radically different, so-called multisensory, teaching methods. Many struggles to obtain better provision centre on the level of qualification of the specialist teacher.

Quantity issues are those to do with *how much* extra teaching is made available. Short, frequent sessions are generally held to be more useful than long, infrequent ones because of the memory characteristics of dyslexic people. More teaching, in terms of hours per week, is felt necessary the greater the *severity* of the dyslexia. Naturally, with dyslexia now acknowledged as 'the most common and best defined learning disability' (Orton Dyslexia Society, 1994), there are more people pressing legitimately for scarce resources than can be accommodated. The battles for publicly funded provision are discussed further below.

Another set of issues links assessment with teaching. In the dyslexia-teaching world, faith in psychometric assessment methods has never weakened. Accordingly there are some surprisingly literal-minded beliefs in the significance for teaching subtest scores on the WISC.[2] As we have seen, diagnostic profiling must ride the stormy waters of test unreliability. Three-quarters of the population have scaled score ranges – distances between highest and lowest subtest scores – on 10 subtests of the WISC-R of at least 6 points, or two standard deviations (Kaufman, 1979, p. 197). Nevertheless, the majority of specialist teachers retain an unshakeable conviction that a good psychological assessment has detailed implications for the way a dyslexic individual must be taught.

Is this true? How is this issue of *prescriptive precision* best understood? What are the main implications for the teacher in the sort of assessment outlined so far?

The important items of information seem to be as follows:

- What age is this individual?
- Is he or she dyslexic or not?
- If so, is the dyslexia mild, moderate or severe?
- Are the individual's general abilities average, above average or below average?
- Should reading, spelling or number be addressed first?
- How emotionally damaged by recurrent failure is this individual?

These considerations will rightly be seen as very general. Perhaps only the latter three points need a psychological assessment in order to be addressed satisfactorily. Nevertheless they are the essential co-ordinates of an adaptive understanding of the candidate for teaching. To summarise the main arguments:

- Age is the first piece of information needed to set about tuning provision to the individual.
- A dyslexia diagnosis carries certain very specific implications for the kind of teaching which is needed. Although many cases are borderline or ambiguous, such teaching is simply not needed by the non-dyslexic individual.
- Severity is the dimension which stands proxy for much detailed diagnostic information. Severely dyslexic people, for instance, are likely to have major phonological difficulties with the pronunciation of words, as well as much more pervasive difficulties with immediate memory.
- IQ is the second most important piece of information for broadband tuning of teaching to the learning capacity and style of the individual. More-able and less-able individuals are taught in largely different ways.
- Reading carries the emotional weight in intervention and is much more likely than spelling or number to have been addressed already; consequently main choice of focus for teaching is an important early decision.
- Even if negatively motivated, the damaged individual is likely to respond favourably to the initial sessions of specialist teaching. However, counselling and interpersonal sensitivity aspects of the teaching situation may loom large and should form part of the planning.

Are these very broad-band implications, even if the most immediate and important, the *only* ones? No, probably not. The next most important considerations when planning teaching are those of the pupil's *strategies*, and the psychological assessment can certainly help with these. By strategies is meant, especially, reading strategies and these seem to be largely a matter of instructional history. The child introduced to reading by means of big books on the classroom floor, stories meaningfully shared and pictures canvassed for 'cues' is likely to think for the rest of its life that reading is a matter of guesswork. Such attitudes are remarkably hard to shift. Another child, taught that reading is a matter of the sounds of *letters*, perhaps at first not encountered in books at all, is likely to be attentive, constructive and reluctant to guess and may not need to be taught much about spelling.

There is undoubtedly an interaction between instructional method and dyslexic propensities in the pupil. Dyslexic readers are *anyway* more likely to look to visual and non-print sources of help, such as pictures, as it is with the alphabetic coding that they have constitutional difficulties,[3] but whole-word and whole-language teaching methods do seem to raise the dyslexia casualty rate. This is something that parents may feel very strongly about. A mother who brought her child to the

Dyslexia Institute for an assessment wrote:

> [He is] what we would call illiterate, whatever the school stan-
> dards suggest . . . I believe the school so-called system has
> contributed to and/or helped mask his difficulties. For a long time
> I believed it was entirely responsible (real books, emergent
> writing, child centred, play-way, non-competitive and wet as the
> weather forecast, with ultra-thick teachers in his first two years
> and refusal to acknowledge under-achievement).

In particular, the way the child approaches text may reflect the way he or
she was *taught* to read. In the main, hasty guesswork, low inspection
times, premature lexical decision, giving up or paying attention to
pictures or an adult's face represent maladaptive strategies, all of them
important targets for intervention.

Though many expert teachers feel comfortable about undertaking
memory work, with the explicit aim of improving 'learning skills',
psychologists tend to be more pessimistic about altering the underlying
structure of an individual's abilities. The most complete environmental
intervention – adoption into a stimulating, caring, educating home –
adds only about 6 points onto IQ (Herrnstein and Murray, 1994, p. 411),
and other intervention studies, even successful ones, tend to show a
wash-out effect over time. Scepticism is therefore well advised when it
comes to trying to raise abilities.

All abilities are not alike, however, and it may be that *crystallised* or
culture-specific abilities are more amenable to influence than *fluid* ones
rooted in age and current physiological functioning. There are well-
established programmes, for instance, for teaching vocabulary.[4] Moreover single case studies show remarkable changes in verbal memory
capacity following the adoption of mnemonic strategies (Ericsson and
Oliver, 1989, pp. 198–202). One does not want to discourage teachers
from attempting to improve, by practice and metacognitive strategies,
skills that may demonstrate the truth of the folk theory that abilities are
like muscles – they improve with use.

One final aspect of teaching, not addressed in Chapter 7, is that of
evaluation. So rare is any evaluation of teaching, specialist or otherwise,
that one wonders why.[5] Part of the answer lies in the pressures which
swirl in the that world of scarce resource. Parents, teachers and children
are far too busy trying, against the clock, to establish the skills that
fundamentally affect life-chances. Research can seem a leisured luxury.
Nevertheless the keeping of evaluative data, especially test data independent of teaching, can be accommodated within the routines of regular
teaching. Not to attempt evaluation is to lay teaching open to charges of
irresponsibility and unaccountability. The independent psychological
assessment is one effective vehicle for in-depth evaluation of changes –
in strategy, confidence and technique – which skilled teaching may have

brought about. Such changes are often most evident in measures of non-word reading and reading rate (Bodien, 1996).

Accommodating the individual within the main-stream

In May 1994, to implement changes in practice advised by the 1993 Education Act, the Department for Education issued a Code of Practice (Department for Education, 1994). This had been compiled largely by the National Children's Bureau, in consultation with many local educa-tion authorities and schools. It managed to enshrine existing 'good practice' in ways which schools have nevertheless found difficult to implement. The exact status of the Code – whether statutory or non-statutory – remains in dispute. Like all recent education reforms, this one seems to animate a lurking spirit of bureaucracy and to result in much new form-filling by people who lack the time to do it. Moreover, local authority experience of 'stages' of assessment suggests that the real objective is *demand management*: concerned parents may be told that they cannot have whatever they are asking for – usually testing, specialist teaching or a statement of special needs – because their child is 'only at stage one'. For the child who is not even at stage one, placing him or her on the school's register appears to constitute action; forms will be filled and records kept. Early indications are that stages of assessment, together with Appeals Tribunals, are proving successful in limiting access of dyslexic children to special educational services.

Nevertheless, from a dyslexia point of view there is much in the Code that amounts to explicit recognition of dyslexia and the place of psycho-logical testing and specialist teaching. Its appearance was greeted with dismay by establishment voices and cries of hope from organisations representative of parents.

Most parents of dyslexic children must look to the State system to identify and provide appropriately for the learning difficulty, as is its duty. What is wanted is a detailed and comprehensive psychological assessment to establish the problem, followed by expert tuition, individ-ually or in a small group, from an appropriately qualified specialist teacher. If this can be provided successfully and early, there is little attraction in a statement. However, parents soon learn that *only* a state-ment of special need, legally enforceable on authorities, will secure a bare minimum of provision. Consequently they are little interested in 'stages' of assessment within school, seeing these, rightly, as an adminis-trative device.

The following is a summary of what is meant by Stages 1–5.

Stage 1
Identification of possible problem by teacher, parent, health or social

services professional. Teacher informs SEN co-ordinator, who registers child's SEN. Teacher gathers information, makes an initial assessment and informs parents. Teacher works closely with the child in the normal classroom context, and monitors and reviews the child's progress.

Possible outcomes:

- Child no longer a cause for concern, removed from SEN register.
- Child stays at stage 1 with new targets set.
- Child moves to stage 2.

Stage 2

Following discussions about an initial concern with parents, teachers and SEN co-ordinator it is considered that early intensive action is necessary, a child may go direct to stage 2. SEN co-ordinator, with teacher, reviews available information and obtains information from outside agencies. SEN co-ordinator and teacher draw up individual educational plan (IEP), and inform parents and head teacher. IEP implemented. Progress is reviewed with parental involvement.

Possible outcomes:

- Child reverts to stage 1 or no longer needs special help.
- Child stays at stage 2 with revised IEP.
- Child moves to stage 3.

Stage 3

Following discussions about an initial concern with parents, teachers and SEN co-ordinator it is considered that early intensive action is necessary, in consultation with the head teacher a child may go direct to stage 3. SEN co-ordinator, teacher and outside support services draw up IEP, and inform parents. IEP implemented. Progress is reviewed, preferably in the presence of parents.

Possible outcomes:

- Child reverts to stage 2 or stage 1.
- Child stays at stage 3, SEN co-ordinator, teacher and support services draw up revised IEP.
- Refer to head teacher and responsible person. Head teacher requests statutory assessment.

Stage 4

The Local Education Authority (LEA) consider the need for a statutory assessment and, if appropriate, make a multidisciplinary assessment within specified time limits.

Stage 5

In light of the information obtained from the multidisciplinary assessment, the LEA considers the need for a statement of special educational needs and, if appropriate, makes a statement and arranges, monitors and reviews provision.

This is a framework within which effective action by all concerned could be organised and communicated. However, it neither describes nor guarantees anything of substance.

There is a tendency within the mainstream sector to see the National Curriculum as a duty rather than an entitlement, a good thing devised by those who know what is good for the rest of us, to be introduced forcibly. In keeping with this ethic, *withdrawal* for individual tuition, for instance multisensory teaching, is viewed with disapproval. The fact that a child can neither read nor write, and finds a modern foreign language constitutionally arduous, does not alter the requirement to have him or her physically present during lessons. True, the child may lack what are onerously called the *skills of access* to the National Curriculum, but the law must be obeyed. Let the child be prevented, by enforced attendance upon the materials to be read, from acquiring the skills with which to read them.

Manoeuvring with incomprehension in a milieu of such absurdity, many parents feel forced to have recourse to the law. Let their child receive, then, the individual tuition as a result of the law; let her or him be exempted from the foreign language under provisions of the 1988 Education Act.

Entry into this world of activism is, for many parents, the beginning of a new career, of distorting mirrors, blandness and nuance, of statement and counter-statement, ring-binders and box files, of rising telephone bills and legal fees: a loss of innocence from which there is no turning back. The motivation to pursue matters is simple: it is *one's own child* whose well-being is at stake and whose life is passing rapidly by while the bureaucracy performs its callisthenics.

Detailed guidance to the convolutions of the fight to secure appropriate provision for the dyslexic child within the state sector is beyond the scope of this book. The 1993 Act's innovation, the system of regional Appeals Tribunals independent to a significant extent of the local education authorities, is daily sailing into uncharted waters. A pattern of decisions, some of them apparently contradictory, is only just taking shape. An authoritative account cannot perhaps yet be written. Fortunately there are two publications which offer high-quality guidance to those who may need it. The Advisory Centre for Education publishes a *Special Education Handbook* whose seventh edition (ACE, 1996) includes the text of the relevant Acts, summaries of procedure, advice on action, even draft letters to the authorities. Legal penetration, however, is afforded by Friel (1995), in the latest edition of a book revised and reissued to reappraise rapid developments, and which offers a compelling and thoughtful examination of the key issues.

The following is therefore merely a summary of some of the main points confronting parents at the beginning of the statutory process, illustrated by reference to official documents.

1993 EDUCATION ACT:
Guidance relevant to an assessment under section 167

Reference is made to: Department for Education, Code Of Practice On The Identification And Assessment Of Special Educational Needs, London: Central Office of Information, May 1994.

Assessment arrangements, including criteria for deciding to assess 'specific learning difficulties (for example dyslexia)'.

LEAs must identify and make a statutory assessment of those children who have special educational needs and who probably need a statement. (Sections 165 and 167; Code of Practice 3:1–3:121, pp. 38–78.)

Parents may ask the LEA to conduct a statutory assessment. (Section 172(2) or 173(1); Code of Practice 3:17–3:21, pp. 42–43.) A decision must be made within six weeks. (Code of Practice 3:31, p. 47.) 'Whatever the background, the LEA must *take all parental requests seriously* and take action immediately.' (Code of Practice 3:18, p. 42.) No more than ten weeks must elapse between the decision to assess and the decision as to whether to make a statement. (Code of Practice 3:30, p. 46.)

An LEA is responsible for a pupil at an *independent school* if he or she lives in their area and . . . has been brought to the LEA's attention as having or probably having special educational needs. (Section 165(3) of the 1993 Education Act.)

The views of an *educational psychologist* are essential in fully assessing a child's special educational needs and in planning for any future provision. (Code of Practice 3:113, p. 76.) The educational psychologist from whom the LEA seeks advice *must consult*, and record any advice received from, any other psychologist, such as a clinical or occupational psychologist, whom he or she believes to have relevant knowledge of or information about the child. The LEA must consider any advice from a *fully qualified educational psychologist commissioned independently* and submitted by the parents. (Code of Practice 3:115, p. 76.)

The facts of academic *attainment* . . . must always be understood in the context of . . . *expectations* of the child's performance. Apparently satisfactory attainment may . . . fall far short of the performance expected of the child as assessed by . . . educational psychologists . . . and . . . by *standardised tests*. (Code of Practice 3:50, p. 53.)

Academic attainment is the essential evidential starting point. LEAs...should be alert . . . to *significant discrepancies* between . . . a child's attainments . . . and the performance expected . . . supported by such *standardised tests* as can reliably be administered.' (Code of Practice 3:51, p. 53.)

Some children may have *significant difficulties* in reading, writing, spelling or manipulating number, which are *not typical of their general level of performance*. (Code of Practice 3:60, p. 56.) The LEA should seek clear, recorded evidence of the child's academic attainment and ask, for example, whether . . . expectations of the child . . . supported . . . by appropriately administered standardised tests of *cognitive ability* or oral comprehension are significantly above . . . the results of appropriately administered standardised reading, spelling or mathematics tests. (Code of Practice 3:61, p. 57.) Where the balance of evidence . . . suggests that the child's learning difficulties . . . are significant and/or complex, have not responded to relevant and purposeful measures . . . and may call for special educational provision which cannot reasonably be provided within the *resources* normally available to mainstream schools in the area, the LEA should consider very carefully the case for a statutory assessment of the child's special educational needs. (Code of Practice 3:63, p. 58.)

The statement of special educational needs: the main ground on which an LEA may decide that they must make a statement is when the LEA conclude that all the special educational provision necessary to meet the child's needs *cannot reasonably be provided within the resources* normally available to mainstream schools in the area. (Code of Practice 4:2, p. 79.) If, as the result of a statutory assessment, the LEA conclude that, for example, the child requires . . . *regular direct teaching* by a specialist teacher . . . the LEA may conclude that the school could not reasonably be expected to make such provision *within its own resources* . . . (Code of Practice 4:11, p. 81.)

Statutory special needs assessment: planning provision

The psychological assessment has emerged as the most authoritative single contribution to the form that special education arrangements should take in any individual case. All parties to disputes are aware that the psychological advice is sensitive and take special pains to determine the views, independent or otherwise, of its providers.

Impressive though this is, it should not obscure the fact that psychological expertise, especially in matters of measurement, has no discernible impact at present on public policy. Decisions in individual cases are very largely influenced by well-argued psychological views, such that the policy framework is pulled altogether out of shape, especially as the number of such cases grows. But the opinions of the one group that appears to understand what is going on in special needs provision is neither heeded nor sought.

Consider, for instance, a variation of the well-known experiment, the Turing test, applied to the question of whether someone has a reading problem or not. A person with a reading age of 7 years is hidden behind a screen. What must be known in order to determine whether this individual has a reading problem? Is it necessary to know his or her name? No. His or her sex? No. The first question is likely to be his or her age. If the child is 6, there is by common consent no problem, but a superior ability. Before considering such niceties as whether the person, reading in English, happens to be Chinese, important questions occur. If the person is 8, is there a problem? Not necessarily. This child might be over- or underachieving, or achieving appropriately. Why? Because expectations are set in relation to a person's *age*, first, and *ability*, second. Other considerations flock in their wake, but these two are the first pieces of information essential to an evaluation of a possible learning difficulty.

Though local education authorities are in general responsible for the education of about 6 077 500 pupils in England and Wales, and the special education of about 212 700 of them, they studiously ignore the second consideration, that of ability. This is a specimen of an egalitarian and comprehensive approach that has virtually no support outside the world of education, and probably only minority support within it. An absolute or level criterion is applied to *all* children who may be candidates for special assessment and provision. A principal educational psychologist was recently quoted in interview as follows:

> In the case of his own [Colwill's] authority, Cornwall, for example, psychologists will expect an 11-year-old to have a reading age of seven-and-a-half or lower before they conduct an assessment for dyslexia. (Pyke, 1994, p. 5, quoting Steve Colwill, president of the Association of Educational Psychologists)

One authority which is said to spend £2 million annually fighting tribunal appeals[6] has published its criteria for formal assessment for dyslexia 'in co-operation with other south of England authorities' in a booklet from which Table 12.1 is adapted.

Table 12:1: 'Reading age' criteria for statutory assessment at seven age-levels, together with the percentile value this represents if the test given is BAS Word Reading. *Source:* Buckinghamshire LEA: *Code of Practice*, March 1996

Child's age	Reading age: Years	Months	BAS Percentile
7–8	5	8	3
8–9	5	11	2
9–10	6	2	2
10–11	6	5	2
11–12	6	11	2
12–13	7	4	2
13–14	7	6	2

Clearly there is a pressing need to have *some* publicly stated policy principles in this area, as with admissions criteria for different schools, in the interest of fairness to candidates competing for opportunities, and of the responsible management of scarce resources. Nevertheless this particular approach is fraught with misunderstanding of the measurement issues involved, not to mention the question of what problem, if any, the child behind the screen may have.

To begin with, every lay person is puzzled by what appears to be a paradox: in order to receive an assessment, the outcome of the assessment must be known in advance! To be sure, children who eventually obtain special services through a statement of special needs must first have received a statutory 'stage four' assessment under section 167 of the 1993 Act. Yet to prejudge the outcome, to reduce the process to going through the legal motions, is to empty it to an extent Parliament did not intend.

Second, dyslexia (at least) is not a matter of reading only. Indeed it will have become clear from data presented in previous chapters that in many circumstances a literacy-learning difficulty remains most acute in spelling, number and writing problems. Most children who have reading problems are not dyslexic and progress with conventional remedial teaching. A reading-centred approach to dyslexia today seems somewhat antiquated.

Third, to announce any policy in terms of age equivalent scores is to sacrifice serious administrative credibility. We have seen in Chapter 6 that the problems with this unit of measurement are intractable; only a loose impression of the data is conveyed. Notwithstanding that age-equivalent scores are common currency among lay persons, responsible management of educational destinies for those lay persons' children requires valid and reliable measurement.

Further on reliability, Table 12.1 shows that reading age-equivalent cut-off scores for initiating formal assessment are based, actually, on standard scores of –2.0 standard deviations, or standard scores of 70. Such scores meet the objection in the previous paragraph, as they are an optimum form of measurement. Nevertheless each standard score of 70 represents a *true* score, within a range delineated by the reliability of the test used, 95% of the time. Any single measure, for instance a reading test result, is valid only within a margin of error derived from empirically established reliabilities, test–retest or coefficient alpha. Table 12.2 shows that the percentage of children thus described may be expected to range from 1% to nearly 5%, depending on the reliability of the test used at the age concerned. These values are produced using the reliable technology of the BAS Word Reading test (long form A); most 'reading age tests' are far less reliable and agree with each other only to a disappointing extent. The solution to this problem – to combine scores for reading, spelling and number into *composites* with higher reliability – also overcomes the objection (above) to a reading-only measure.

Table 12.2: Confidence limits for standard reading scores (Mean 100, SD 15) obtained using the British Ability Scales Word Reading Test A.

Child's age	Standard Scores			
	Confidence limit		Percentages below each value	
	From	To		
7–8	69	74	1.94	4.15
8–9	72	75	3.10	4.78
9–10	65	72	0.98	3.10
10–11	65	72	0.98	3.10
11–12	69	72	1.94	3.10
12–13	65	72	0.98	3.10
13–14	65	69	0.98	1.94

Most unsatisfactory of all, the published policy ignores considerations of general intellectual ability, the problem of the child behind the screen. This is to ignore basic scientific methodology, because the unknown reading problem may be regarded as a *dependent variable* and the strongest known predictors[7] of reading achievement are, as discussed, age and general ability. The practitioner is at liberty to take plentiful *other* considerations into account as well. One would be unwise indeed to generalise about the many personal circumstances that contribute to administrative decision making but psychometric criteria are the common ones, those with the best claim to impartial objectivity, in so far as any measures of human performance may be said to be objective. Tests of cognitive ability have already been discussed rather fully (Chapter 3). Their main utility, perhaps, is in special education in just such situations as this. Moreover:

. . . such tests tap the most important, general way in which people differ psychologically . . . [I]n normal circumstances the reliability of Binet and Wechsler IQs is still around .93: such reliability is far higher than is found for any other important individual, non-biographical measurement across the entire range of twentieth-century psychology and indeed social science. (Brand, 1996, pp. 1–2, 33)

Even if one does not accept the full methodology argued for in this book, a low given level of reading must be accepted as simply more rare at higher levels of ability, as Table 12.3 shows.

Table 12.3: Expected frequencies of reading standard scores of 70 at different IQ levels (100 is average ability, 85 below average, 115 above average)

	IQ 85	IQ 100	IQ 115
Reading standard score	70	70	70
Expected frequency (%)	4.00	0.62	0.07

Thus among children of below-average ability, the incidence of such reading levels is more common – at or beyond the upper levels described by the margins of error in Table 12.2. With children of above-average ability such a level of reading would be expected only in about one child in 1400. This is nearly 60 times as rare. Phenomena with such differing incidence rates should be treated with at least agnostic respect as proceeding possibly from different causes.

A suggested psychometric methodology for decision making in cases of dyslexia

Given that psychological advice at present largely determines both the view of the problem of dyslexia (identification) and the educational planning for it (provision), it is incumbent upon psychologists to propose a basis for public policy that is both rational and equitable. This may be done using psychometric criteria, the ones that are already public, objective (within known limits), valid and reliable, and sensitive, comparing the individual with all others of his or her own age.

There is a minor literature on the disappointments inherent in screening programmes (e.g. Potton, 1983); and some points have already been touched upon in Chapter 10. However, it is not necessary to embark on a costly mass screening programme whose results fall far short of perfection. The best referral procedure – nomination – is free and works at least as well as a screening checklist (Potton, op. cit., p. 48). In the event of a desire to institute group screening tests at 7 (the strategic age for dyslexia identification), group tests of spelling and non-verbal ability ought to produce a manageable minority of children among whom will be candidates for a fuller dyslexia assessment. The results for Standard Assessment Tasks[8] are available for most children and though such testing has unknown psychometric properties, the raw score (out of 30 or so) on the spelling test ought to be useful. In addition, differences as large as a whole level between achievement in literacy and in speaking and listening ought to identify the least subtle cases.

Once selected for a fuller assessment, psychometric methodology provides a full, fair, impartial and efficient methodology which takes account of the most important variable in dyslexia, that of *severity*. There are, as described, two principal criteria for dyslexia:

- an unexpected underachievement in one or more basic skill area (reading, spelling, number);
- positive evidence of inefficiency in the management of information, for instance in short-term memory.

To accommodate the enormous individual variation in strengths and weaknesses at all ages, a comprehensive approach needs to be taken. Also, use of combined or composite scores provides higher reliability and tighter confidence limits.

The following proposed methodology turns on a three-way separation of co-normed ability, achievement and diagnostic measures, such as is possible using DAS and BAS-2, and WISC-III Index scores.[9]

(1) At least six core or ability tests should be given; at least four diagnostic tests; and at least three achievement tests – i.e. reading, spelling and number. (All such tests have been discussed fully in this book, each category with its own chapter.)

(2) All results should be reported in a common metric, perhaps standard scores with a mean of 100 and a standard deviation of 15.

(3) The developmental distance between *average* scores on both groups of abstract thinking and low-level information management skills should be expressed in SD units.

(4) The *average* distance between observed scores on all three achievement measures and scores expected on the basis of GCA or full scale IQ using regression should be expressed in SD units.

(5) These two scores should be averaged as follows: the academic underachievement measure should be multiplied by two, added to the diagnostic measure, and the sum divided by three. This gives a positive weighting to the academic underachievement.

(6) The result, a Dyslexia Index, may be evaluated for severity as follows:
(a) less than 0.0 SD: no dyslexia signs;

(b) 0.0–0.4: few dyslexia signs;
(c) 0.5–0.9: mild dyslexia;
(d) 1.00–1.4: moderate dyslexia;
(e) 1.5–1.9: severe dyslexia;
(f) above 2.0: very severe dyslexia.

This methodology incorporates all the major considerations we have been looking at: reliability and stability of composites; discrepancy based on regression rather than simple difference; inclusiveness of varieties of learning difficulty in different domains and in different aspects of information management; and agnosticism with respect to whether dyslexia ultimately comes to be viewed as categorical or dimensional.

It may help to provide a worked example of a girl with a 'moderate' degree of dyslexia. HL was aged 15 at the time of her assessment. On the Differential Ability Scales (with two WISC-III supplementary diagnostic tests), she obtained scores as follows (all are given in common standard score units – mean 100, SD 15):

Word Definitions	127	Recall of Digits	90	Reading	101
Similarities	145	Objects 1 mm	79	Spelling	88
Matrices	100	Objects Del	88	Number	91
Seq and Quant Reas	97	Speed of Inf Proc	76		
Recall of Designs	103	Coding (WISC-3)	85		
Pattern Construction	111	Digit Span (WISC-3)	81		

The means, again in standard score units, are:

Ability scores ($\times 6$)	114
Diagnostic scores ($\times 6$)	83
Attainment scores ($\times 3$)	93

HL's GCA or IQ of 118 predicts scores as follows:

	Expected	Observed	Difference	Frequency
Reading	110	101	9	23% (NS)
Spelling	110	88	22	5%
Number	111	91	20	5%

With the weighting ($\times 2$) applied to the difference between the observed (O) and expected (E) attainment scores, the arithmetic is as follows:

Difference	Standard units	With weighting	In SD units
Abil–Diag	31	31	
O–E	17	34	
Mean (of 3)		21.7	1.44

Overall, then, using the Dyslexia Index as a means of evaluating anomalous performance on diagnostic tests, together with underachievement on *all* attainment tests of basic skills, HL may be described as showing a *moderate* degree of dyslexia because she has a final index score in SD units of 1.44.[10]

In the data set whose major properties were discussed in Chapter 8, further analysis reveals the following incidences of individuals from this clinical sample in the six proposed class intervals, ranging from non-dyslexic through to very severely dyslexic:

Table 12.4: Numbers of individuals in the Dyslexia Institute data set with varying degrees of dyslexia described using the proposed Dyslexia Index.

Dyslexia Index frequencies Class interval	*n*	%
<0.0	45	11.7
0.0–0.4	88	22.8
0.5–0.9	121	31.3
1.0–1.4	73	18.9
1.5–1.9	43	11.1
>2.0	16	4.1
Totals	386	100

These frequencies, it will be noted, are not unlike those obtained using one or other method (but not both) in Chapter 8. However, it seems fairest to include all the known factors relevant to a dyslexia diagnosis, though weighting those that most concern people, the manifest failure to achieve in basic skills at expected levels.

Such calculations, committed to spreadsheet, are a bagatelle to the psychologist preparing advice on the basis of his or her analysis of the individual's skills and abilities. They can be repeated for large numbers of individuals with accuracy, fairness and consistency, avoiding border effects contingent upon unreliable single measures.

Finally, the practising psychologist is entitled to ask what the actual frequencies might be in the normal population, rather than a biased clinical sample, of individuals with a given Dyslexia Index. Indeed local education authorities, mindful of the limited specialist teaching resources available, might wish to draw up criteria on the basis of observed index levels in the population of school-aged children. Timely help with this concern is afforded with the 1995–96 standardisation of the new edition of the British Ability Scales (BAS-2), for which fresh data of exactly the kind described are available. It is unlikely that the NFER statisticians, unless asked, will think to provide what is effectively a quantitative apparatus for special needs policy making but they would no doubt respond positively to any request to do so.

Policies on provision for pupils with identified special needs

Local education authorities in Britain have spent a long time resisting the recognition of and provision for dyslexia. Given that dyslexia is in all probability the largest single category of learning difficulty, they have had a pressing financial motive for doing so. Increasingly, though, this stance has become untenable and only a minority of authorities still hope that dyslexia will go away. If some such methodology as the above is accepted as a *fair* determination of dyslexia in any individual case, there remains the dilemma of funding.

Roughly £1.00 in £12.00 in the local authority's budget is spent at present on special education (Turner, 1991b). Even enthusiasts for such education can hardly wish the proportion higher. If more money is clawed away from the provision for normal children in mainstream classes, there is the risk that more 'special needs' will be *created*. For the most part, the bulk of these large sums is spent on fully maintained day special schools, a direct labour sector of education in which little in the way of competitive pressure has ever been experienced. To close, or even to rationalise, these special schools is regarded by most elected councillors as political *hara-kiri*.

At present the *statementing* process[11] is the main arena for struggle between authorities reluctant to provide the quite inexpensive education dyslexics for the most part require. Furthermore, suspicions are widespread that resources tend to go to those who exert the most pressure. What is lacking is an explicit policy for resourcing levels of special needs of all kinds in the mainstream school short of the formal statement. The explicit methodology for evaluating intensity of dyslexic need, outlined above, is of course a prerequisite for such a policy.

What might such an explicit policy look like? In the 1980s the education board for Edmonton, Canada, trialled and continuously modified just such a system of explicit levels of funding and found that a policy involving 11 levels worked well. Adapted for Britain and reduced to nine levels, with figures only roughly accurate for capitation funding for infant, junior and secondary *non-special* pupils, we arrive at the descriptions of support with associated costs given in Table 12.5.

This gives only approximately costings, all of which can be finessed appropriately. Moreover, because such figures vary from place to place and over time, it may be more important to work with *weightings* as the constant factors. Column 4 in Table 12.5 represents the weighting applied for each level of special service to the capitation for the junior pupil.

To summarise: dyslexic, along with other, pupils can have their teaching needs met, for the most part, within their ordinary schools, although not in the classroom. Withdrawal for specialist tuition is an irreducible

Table 12.5: Explicit levels of resourcing of pupils with and without special educational needs in mainstream schools

Level	Service provided	Annual cost	Weighting
Level 1	Pupils in mainstream infant or nursery classes	£1250.00	0.88
Level 2	Pupils in mainstream junior classes	£1400.00	0.99
Level 3	Pupils in mainstream secondary classes	£1600.00	1.13
Level 4	Pupils in any school who have English as an additional language	£1750.00	1.24
Level 5	Pupils with learning difficulties who need additional small group tuition	£1900.00	1.34
Level 6	Pupils who need 2–4 hours per week of specialist tuition	£2000.00	1.41
Level 7	Pupils who need 3–5 hours per week of specialist tuition	£2400.00	1.69
Level 8	Pupils attending within-school specialist unit provision part-time	£3000.00	2.12
Level 9	Pupils with severe physically handicapping conditions who require extensive personal assistance for the majority of the school day	£6000.00	4.24

Source: after Edmonton Education Department paper, Alberta, Canada, 1987.

element within the necessary ensemble of measures. Dyslexic children can be identified, following screening or nomination, by means of a full psychometric assessment using publicly verifiable methods fair to all. A number of levels of severity – the feature critical for planning – can be identified. A nine-level categorisation in terms of resource intensity is described, with dyslexic pupils located mostly at levels 5 to 8, and, within these, at levels 6 and 7.[12] If statutory assessment and statementing were reserved for levels 8 and above, then the fiction of assessment (for which eligibility is determined by assessment) could be avoided, with its costly, contentious and bureaucratic negotiations. Appeals could be accommodated by a flexible review system, with recourse to statutory procedures as a last resort. In the main, parents would respond favourably to evidence that their children's dyslexic needs were being satisfactorily provided for. The explicit and objective basis for identification and resourcing would provide the best defence in the face of criticism and special pleading alike: full accountability.

Special examination arrangements

There remains a final popular use to which the psychological assessment of dyslexia may be put. The allowance of special arrangements in examinations requires no statutory assessment or statement of special educational need, but instead provision of a recent psychological assessment of the candidate. For many years the examination boards have accepted that pupils with disabilities need accommodating in timed, written, public examinations, if they are to compete fairly and give a reliable account of their knowledge, skills and understanding. Dyslexic individuals now form the largest single group benefiting from this dispensation.

In their definitive document, which currently governs practice in this area, the GCSE Secretaries state the general principles involved:

Special arrangements are intended:

(a)   to enable the candidate to demonstrate his or her level of attainment;

(b)   to ensure that the special arrangement does not give the candidate an unfair advantage over the other candidates in the same examination;

(c)   to avoid misleading the user of the certificate about the candidate's attainment in the subject concerned. (GCSE Secretaries, 1993)

As in other areas of educational administration, the discovery process involved would benefit from a standard methodology and accepted criteria. There is a suspicion that the arrangement has led to some questionable cases, disproportionately concerning pupils in the private sector whose 'dyslexia' becomes apparent for the first time at exam season, aged 16 or even 18. Each case deserves consideration on its merits, and the professional opinions of psychologists, open to regulation and complaint through chartering,[13] can be trusted in most cases.[14] But the imputation that families are *buying advantage* for their children is a slur that those working professionally with dyslexia are anxious to neutralise. Unseen, equally, are those candidates whose serious and undoubted disadvantage goes unrecognised because they persist in viewing their own dyslexia as an *excuse*.

A consultative committee including psychologists has for some time advised the examination boards well. In 1994 an explicit policy statement referred for the first time to a discrepancy between 'reading and reasoning'. It proposed for psychologists, who had hitherto advanced a variety of reporting formats varying from the sketchy to the detailed, a common form requiring evidence – names and dates of tests given with results – to substantiate the claim for special treatment. This progress has been generally welcomed, but there are still almost annual developments in practice by examination boards and, whatever is claimed to the contrary (Hedderly, 1996, p. 38), requests for special arrangements are mostly dealt with at a clerical level at which understanding of the assessment arguments is often lacking. For instance board officials telephone schools[15] to request 'reading ages' after receiving reports which include standard scores, even though:

It is also recommended that psychologists use tests appropriate for older pupils and use standard scores rather than relatively meaningless reading ages (Hedderly, op. cit., p. 38)

Further, there is no unanimity among psychology professionals as to what is an appropriate methodology. Writing speed, for example, is 'a measure of motivation' (Hedderly, op. cit., p. 41), whilst for other authors in the same journal issue, it is 'a particular motor co-ordination task' (Sawyer, Gray and Champness, 1996, p. 20). The latter authors argue that:

> special arrangements which aid the candidate in what the examinations are assessing [information retention and language processing] are not permitted on the grounds of giving unfair advantage.

They thus conclude that:

> a 20 minute free writing measure is inappropriate. (Sawyer et al., 1996, p. 20)

Others strive, on the contrary, for measures that, in representing candidates' performance in conditions as like those of examinations as possible, seem to offer ecological validity.

Profiles of actual dyslexic candidates for special arrangements

Disagreement is inevitable even in a debate noted for the quality of its constructive and ingeniously practical contributions.[16] It may be helpful, therefore, to seek to carry matters forward by looking at group profiles on tests of the kind discussed in this book of actual GCSE candidates applying for extra time in exams.

The data shown in Figure 12.1 are rescaled to the group mean, and therefore represent only relative levels of, for instance, intelligence. A short form of the Differential Ability Scales was used. Clearly one implication of these data is that reading is not the area to highlight. All these students (one was rejected as a suitable candidate for special arrangements) have overcome earlier reading difficulties and now manifest problems neither with word recognition nor comprehension. High spatial ability is, as so often, a feature strikingly in contrast with the problem areas in dyslexia. However, spelling and Digit Symbol, the Coding analogue on the WAIS-R with fewer verbalisable elements, clearly identify a continuing problem with aspects of *writing*.

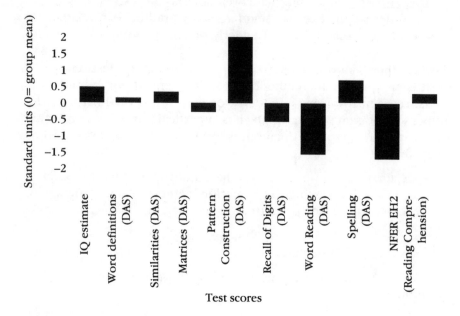

Figure 12.1: Aggregated psychometric results on a selection of tests given to 12 students at a sixth-form college for whom special arrangements in exams were sought.

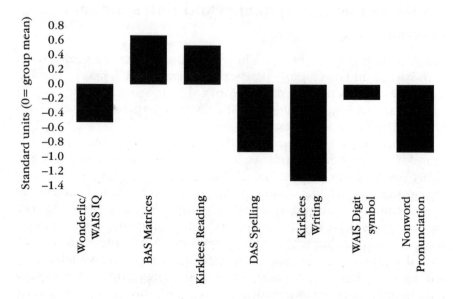

Figure 12.2: Mean test scores for a group 13 boys aged 15–18, candidates for special examination arrangements, March 1996.

The data shown in Figure 12.2 are *not* rescaled to their group mean and so represent this second group of 13 secondary age pupils, all boys, in terms of population standards. The Wonderlic test (Wonderlic and Howland, 1937–95) is a 12-minute multiple-choice test of basic attainments in vocabulary, verbal and numerical reasoning. Though highly *g*-loaded and correlated with WAIS-R (whose IQ equivalents are used here), this is clearly a test of *crystallised* or culture-specific ability with a premium on fast, efficient processing of information. These 13 boys, most with long dyslexic histories, are clearly at a disadvantage on such a measure. On the other hand the BAS Matrices Test E of non-verbal reasoning allows them better to express their abilities. Reading is, again, not a significant problem on the Kirklees test of sentence completion; nor, this time, is the WAIS Digit Symbol but measures of *writing* once more obviously touch the area of difficulty: DAS Spelling and speed of writing in words per minute (Kirklees Incomplete Sentences) are now the focus of the problem. Finally, my own experimental Written Test of Non-word Pronunciation captures continuing difficulties with phonological processing.

Where *disabling* levels of literacy difficulty coexist with measurable competence in one or more GCSE subjects, a tariff of compensatory measures, from questions read and spellings given to full reading of questions and transcription of answers by an amanuensis, is accepted practice, rarely questioned. It is not these candidates who are controversial. Rather, it is the milder and more marginal dyslexic individuals, many of whom are able to read quite well, whose application for special arrangements is of concern. The data reported above show, I hope, that their difficulties reside mainly in aspects of the *writing* process. Where there is a well-established history of assessment and specialist teaching, together with current data showing a persistence of such difficulties, their needs should meet with informed acceptance. It is likely that they can be accommodated with the provision of extra time alone.

We may now return to the argument of Sawyer (Sawyer and Potter, 1994; Sawyer et al., 1996) that language processing partakes of *that which is to be assessed* in, for instance, the GCSE examination. As we have seen at intervals throughout this book, the particular skills which dyslexic people lack are those of information management, in particular those of written communication. Written language skills are particularly associated with *cognitive* operations of immediate verbal memory and speed of processing. These cognitive processes are thought to subserve efficient management of information, for instance in written form, as reading and writing subserve learning more generally, and reading and writing in examinations subserve the demonstration of the level of a candidate's attainment. This looks very much like a hierarchy of *carrier skills* in which lower communication functions serve higher academic ones, just as speech conveys a message. However, management of this medium, speech, or, in the case of GCSE examinations, the English language, is of interest in its own right. Mastery of the resources of English, from fastidious spelling to Shakespearean eloquence, is an objective of great worth and such skills enhance communication ability across the curriculum.

This double view – of English language skills as both an aim of study and the vehicle of written communication – has already been taken by the examination boards. Word-processing and spell-checking are *not* allowed in English language exams because these aid abilities that are being assessed. Where mastery of English is incidental, then a tariff of compensatory arrangements, roughly commensurate with *severity* of disability, is permitted.

The data presented above show, I think, that lower level or mechanical aspects of writing are those for which special arrangements are principally sought: spelling and productivity. Spelling should not, perhaps, be set aside in exams of English language, for the internal structure of words is intimately associated with vocabulary, grammatical structure and punctuation.[17] These are rightly said to be integral aspects of English language competence and any advantage conferred in them would be unfair. Productivity is remarkably independent of *quality* of content being expressed in writing and stems not only from motivation and motor co-ordination, as mentioned above, but habit, attitude and cognitive control in multitasking situations. Because there is usually a trade-off between speed and accuracy, greater productivity is often achieved at the cost of illegibility, confusion and language poverty. This being so, examiners' attention should be drawn to the quality, rather than quantity, of dyslexic candidates' writing. Productivity should be supported across all subjects, and spelling in all subjects but English language.

Epilogue: beyond assessment

This completes the purpose of this book. With the special consideration to be given to dyslexic candidates in examinations, we are brought to the limit of what current assessment practices can demonstrate with reasonable objectivity, so that regardless of their beliefs and idiosyncrasies, psychologists may ' . . . try to avoid talking at cross purposes'.[18]

The culture of the word is in decline. The *Book of Common Prayer*, the 'English liturgy',[19] with the Archbishopric of Canterbury one of only two vehicles for unity in the Anglican communion,[20] is no longer to be heard in parish churches, where its lofty imprecations have been replaced by the English of the infant school assembly set, on guitars, to melodies borrowed from Capital Radio. The progressive restriction in the vocabulary in use with schoolchildren, patiently revealed by Jeanne Chall's quantitative methods in the 1960s (Chall, 1967), has continued. A recent analysis by an examination board of the mean length of sentence achieved in English examinations by 16-year-olds across a 14-year interval proved impossible, using computer methods, because less able children in 1994–95 did not demarcate their sentences with capital letters and full-stops. However, an analysis of the mean length of words used showed clear erosion in the employment of more elaborate vocabulary (see Figure 12.3).

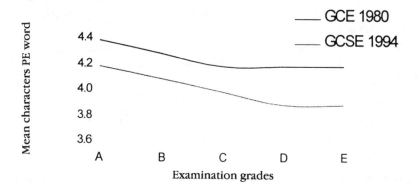

Length of words used in English exams: 1980 GCE and 1994 GCSE

Figure 12.3: Mean length of words used in English examination scripts across a 14-year interval. *Source:* After Massey and Elliott (1996).

What this might mean in the life of a family, where change is not always slow and imperceptible, is demonstrated in the following account by a journalist mother of her 13-year-old son:

> Reading is a torture for him and for anyone around him. He sighs; he shifts and slouches. He turns his baseball hat backwards, then sideways, then backwards again. Then he takes the hat off and smoothes his hair. That means having to get up to check the hair in the mirror, which means going into the kitchen to find an apple, which means going outside and staring vacantly down into the pond . . . Over the years we have battled to make him read and failed . . . If taken to the library, he will leave empty-handed ('there's nothing I want'). When he goes to bed he goes to sleep ('too tired to read') . . . Yet this is a bright child who is neither ill-educated nor emotionally malnourished. It's simply that, born into the electronic age, he prefers to get his information from computer, his stories from movies and his entertainment from CDs . . . Should I worry that he can't keep his nose in a book for more than five minutes on end? No. Good luck to him. His life might well be the richer because of it. (Wilce, 1996, p. 80)

Vivid though this description is, it demonstrates a failure not of parenting but of reflection. To examine why the culture of the book is misunderstood as a technology, and its importance diminished as 'information . . . stories . . . [and] entertainment', would, this close to the end of our journey, be an unwarrantable digression. Suffice it to say that reading is not one easy option among others for consumer gratification, but the necessarily patient and difficult progress of *thought* itself. Indeed, from what glimpses may be had of an increasingly technological future, it is clear that education, at least, will consist in a lot less talking, and vastly more reading and writing, than in the past.[21] The anti-intellectual and anti-aesthetic traditions in English Protestantism will have had, since the Reformation, a lot to answer for.[22]

Notice, however, that though the reluctant teenager with untouched *Julius Caesar* homework is described, also, as follows, no reference is made to the possibility of dyslexia.

> . . . energetic, restless and allergy-prone . . . [who] came to read-ing slowly, struggling with difficulties like sorting a *b* from a *d* . . . [a] hopeless spelle . . . [who] can't read very fast 'and that's annoying'

There is a gradual shading from the anti-lexic culture which increasingly prevails and the clinical symptomatology of dyslexia in families not very different from the one described. Moreover, many problem areas in dyslexia remain out of reach. It is often said that dyslexic individuals are disorganised, lack all sense of time, have 'comprehension' problems because they have to read questions seven times (Bradley, 1993) or 'often look for straightforward . . . interpretations of words' (Hedderly, 1996, p. 40) when metaphoric or ironic meanings are intended. More than one researcher in higher education reports compensated dyslexic students performing diligently in departmental assessments, with extra time allowed and scripts delivered in impeccable cursive hand, but with content somehow like that of individuals writing English as a foreign language.[23] Whilst there is no reason to doubt, and every reason to believe, such anecdotal descriptions from those who live or work closely with dyslexic people, there is as yet no manageable definition of what any of them means, let alone agreement on how to obtain data on them for assessment purposes.

Many developments in assessment technique seem entirely feasible and experimental efforts must be encouraged. Understanding of other, more fugitive aspects of dyslexia must remain for a distant future, when with Jacques Prévert the dyslexic individual will at last be able to say:

> And the classroom walls crumble softly away
> The windows become sand again
> the ink water again

the desks trees again
the chalk cliffs again
the pen-shaft a bird again.[24]

Notes

1 Educational psychologists easily remember formal procedures of many vintages. To take just the forms for the psychological contribution to statutory assessment of learning difficulties, there have been: HP, SE, FA, SEN, Appendix C and Appendix F.

2 As there used to be in the realm of corrective detention of juveniles, who would be assigned to work groups in community homes with education (CHEs) on the basis of their WISC subtest scores.

3 Only recently has the dyslexic seriously been put forward as the *model* for all readers.

4 See Appendix 2, and further references there, for Direct Instruction programmes, for instance.

5 A compilation of research that evaluates teaching is presented in Appendix 4. This list, necessarily partial, may lead the interested reader in fruitful directions.

6 According to the senior official responsible in the Department for Education and Employment as at December 1995.

7 These may also be thought of as *controls* on the phenomenon, literacy skill, in which we are interested.

8 National Curriculum assessment at Key Stage 1.

9 Further refinement in terms of numbers of statistically discrepant single scales of all three types could not be equally accommodated by all major psychometric instruments.

10 That she is towards the upper end of this class, and verges on the 'severe', merely illustrates the limitations of applying words – classificatory epithets – to continuous functions. Indeed the same calculation done using the 'simple difference' method boosts her into the next higher category.

11 The production of statements of special educational need under the terms of the 1993 Education Act.

12 A comparable system of level of special needs activity and support is given in Hinnigan and Forrest (1996). Although even notional cost levels are not included, this system of six levels, four to five being statutory, operates successfully in Northamptonshire LEA.

13 It is open to all psychologists in Britain to become members of the British Psychological Society, the appropriate learned body, and to seek chartered status. This implies a common standard of qualification and post-qualification practice under supervision and entails adherence to a Code of Conduct. Complaints against chartered psychologists are investigated and there is a tariff of penalties if upheld. Though this is at present a voluntary arrangement, parliamentary authority is being sought for statutory registration, which would restrict use of the designation *psychologist* to those recognised by the Society and registered as chartered.

14 The proposal that dyslexia assessment for examination purposes be opened up to the wider professional group of teachers would, at a stroke, introduce massive inflation of numbers through abandonment of any rigorous common standard of methodology.

15 All such requests must for convenience be processed through the schools or examination centres.

16 Sawyer et al., for instance, report that 41 Year 10 pupils asked to write rapidly 0 +
    0 + (etc.) managed a mean of 96.44 (SD 18.12) in one minute. Their mixed
    Dorset comprehensive school, with 60% of pupils achieving 5 or more GCSEs at
    grades A to C in 1995, is representative of, or somewhat above, the national
    average.
17 A product-moment correlation of 0.561 was found for 91 students, resitting GCSE
    English, between Schonell spelling and other aspects of their English papers,
    independently second-marked: punctuation, grammar, vocabulary. I am
    indebted to Jennifer Chew and her sixth-form college students for this analysis.
18 Popper (1945), Chapter 23, reprinted in Popper (1983), p. 372. A fall-back
    position is afforded by Ludwig Wittgenstein: 'Don't *for heaven's sake*, be afraid of
    talking nonsense! But you must pay attention to your nonsense' (Wittgenstein,
    1994, p. 301).
19 Quiller-Couch (1925), pp. 59–64.
20 Most Reverend Ralph Stanley Dean, Archbishop of Cariboo and Metropolitan of
    the Anglican Province of British Columbia: 'Anglican Communion'.
    Encyclopaedia Britannica, 15th edn (1974).
21 See, for example, Hutchison (1996).
22 'The Reformation . . . I do not mean the inferior piece given under that name, by
    Henry the Eighth and a second rate company, in this island, but the real
    Reformation . . . ' Matthew Arnold, in Pagan and Religious Medieval Sentiment, a
    lecture delivered in Oxford on 5 March 1864; excerpted in Allott, M (ed.) (1978)
    Matthew Arnold: Selected Poems and Prose. London: Everyman's Library (J.M.
    Dent), p. 185.
23 Prof. S Gathercole, personal communication.
24 *Paroles*, 1949.

Appendix 1: KEY TO ABBREVIATIONS FOR TESTS USED

A. ADULTS

Wechsler Adult Intelligence Scale – Revised (WAIS-R)

VIQ	Verbal IQ
PIQ	Performance IQ
FIQ	Full Scale IQ
Inf	Information
DSp	Digit Span
Voc	Vocabulary
Ari	Arithmetic
Com	Comprehension
Sim	Similarities
PCo	Picture Completion
PAr	Picture Arrangement
BDe	Block Design
OAs	Object Assembly
DSy	Digit Symbol

WAIS-R further factorial groupings

VCo	Verbal Comprehension (Kaufman)
POr	Perceptual Organisation (Kaufman)
FDi	Freedom from Distractibility (Kaufman)
VCon	Verbal Conceptualisation (Bannatyne)
SAb	Spatial ability (Bannatyne)
Seq	Sequential ability (Bannatyne)
AKn	Acquired Knowledge (Bannatyne)
FIn	Fluid Intelligence (Horn)
CIn	Crystallised Intelligence (Horn)
Ret	Retention (Horn)

Jastak Cluster Analysis

Lex	Lexigraphics
Lin	Linguistics
Sem	Semantic
Rea	Reality
Mot	Motivation
Psm	Psychomotor
Ela	Elation
Dep	Depression
Jud	Judgement
Rea	Reasoning

Attainment tests

Ari	Arithmetic (WRAT-3)
Spe	Spelling (WRAT-3) or Spelling (WORD)
Rea	Reading (WRAT-3)
WId	Word Identification (WRMT-R)
WAt	Word Attack (non-word reading) (WJ-R, WRMT-R)
PCom	Passage Comprehension (WRMT-R)
WEx	Written Expression (WIAT)
BRe	Basic Reading (WORD)

B. CHILDREN

Differential Ability Scales

GCA	General Conceptual Ability (IQ)	All ages
VC	Verbal Ability Cluster	All ages
NC	Non-verbal Ability Cluster	Below 6 years only
NRC	Non-verbal Reasoning Ability Cluster	Ages 6–17:11 only
SC	Spatial Ability Cluster	Ages 6–17:11 only
VCo	Verbal Comprehension	Below 6 years only
NVo	Naming Vocabulary	Below 6 years only
PSi	Picture Similarities	Below 6 years only
Cop	Copying	Below 6 years only
ENC	Early Number Concepts	Below 6 years only
WDe	Word Definitions	Ages 6–17:11 only
Sim	Similarities	Ages 6–17:11 only

Mat	Matrices	Ages 6–17:11 only
SQR	Sequential and Quantitative Reasoning	Ages 6–17:11 only
RDe	Recall of Designs	Ages 6–17:11 only
PCo	Pattern Construction (Block Design)	All ages
MLF	Matching Letter-like Forms	Below 6 years only
RDi	Recall of Digits	All ages
ROI	Recall of Objects – Immediate	All ages
ROD	Recall of Objects – Delayed	All ages
SIP	Speed of Information Processing	Ages 6–17:11 only
RPi	Recognition of Pictures	Below 6 years only
BNS	Basic Number Skills	Ages 6–17:11 only
Spe	Spelling	Ages 6–17:11 only
WRe	Word Reading	Ages 5–17:11 only

Other diagnostic testing

| NWR | Non-word Repetition (CNRep) | Ages 4–10 only |
| SBl | Sound Blending (WJ-R) | All ages |

Other attainment testing

OMN+	One Minute Number (addition)	Ages 6–11 only
OMN–	One Minute Number (subtraction)	Ages 6–11 only
WId	Word Identification (WRMT-R)	All ages
WAt	Word Attack (non-word reading) (WJ-R, WRMT-R)	All ages
PCom	Passage Comprehension (WRMT-R)	all ages
WEx	Written Expression (WIAT)	All ages
BRe	Basic Reading (WORD)	Ages 6–16:11
Spe	Spelling (WORD)	Ages 6–16:11
RCo	Reading Comprehension (WORD)	Ages 6–16:11
CCT	MacMillan 9–14 Group Reading: Context Comprehension Test	Ages 8–15 only
SCT	MacMillan 9–14 Group Reading: Sentence Completion Test	Ages 8–15 only
EH1	NFER sentence completion test	Ages 11–16:11 only
EH2	NFER passage reading comprehension	Ages 11–16:11 only
Spa	SPAR Reading Test (sentence completion)	Ages 6–13 only
KIRK	Kirklees Reading Assessmet Schedule (KRAS); formerly Vernon-Warden Reading Test	Ages 9–adult

Wechsler Intelligence Scale for Children – 3rd Edition with UK norms (WISC-IIIUK)

PCo	Picture Completion	Ages 6–16:11	PO
Inf	Information	Ages 6–16:11	VC
Cod	Coding A	Ages 6–7 only	PS
Cod	Coding B	Ages 8–16:11 only	PS
Sim	Similarities	Ages 6–16:11	VC
PAr	Picture Arrangement	Ages 6–16:11	PO
Ari	Arithmetic	Ages 6–16:11	FD
BDe	Block Design	Ages 6–16:11	PO
Voc	Vocabulary	Ages 6–16:11	VC
OAs	Object Assembly	Ages 6–16:11	PO
Com	Comprehension	Ages 6–16:11	VC
SSe	Symbol Search A	Ages 6–7 only	PS
SSe	Symbol Search B	Ages 8–16:11 only	PS
DSp	Digit Span	Ages 6–16:11	FD
Maz	Mazes	Ages 6–7 only	
Maz	Mazes	Ages 8–16:11 only	

Index Scores

VC	Verbal Comprehension (language ability, including production)
PO	Perceptual Organisation (visuo-spatial ability)
FD	Freedom from Distractibility (learning difficulty, mental control)
PS	Processing Speed (speed of information processing)

Appendix 2: A select bibliography of literature on direct instruction

Becker W (1977) Teaching reading and language to the disadvantaged – what we have learned from field research. Harvard Educational Review 47(4): 518–543.

Becker W Engelmann S (1977) The Oregon Direct Instruction Model. Eugene OR: University of Oregon Follow Through Project.

Becker WC Gersten R (1982) A follow-up of Follow Through: the later effects of the Direct Instruction model on children in fifth and sixth grades. American Educational Research Journal 19(1): 75–92.

Bereiter C Kurland M (1981–82) A constructive look at Follow Through results. Interchange 12(1): 1–22.

Branwhite AB (1983) Boosting reading skills by direct instruction. British Journal of Educational Psychology 53: 291–298.

Carnine D, Silbert J, Kameenui EJ (1990) Direct Reading Instruction. 2nd edn. Toronto, Ontario: Merrill.

Dixon R, Engelmann S (1979) Corrective Spelling Through Morphographs. Chicago: Science Research Associates.

Engelmann S (1990) How sensible is your reading program? A closer look at learner verification. Journal for Supervision and Curriculum Improvement 4(1): 16–22.

Engelmann S, Carnine D (1982) Theory Of Instruction: Principles and Applications. New York: Irvington.

Engelmann S, Carnine L, Johnson G (1988) Corrective Reading Programs. Chicago: Science Research Associates.

Engelmann S, Haddox P, Bruner E (1983) Teach Your Child To Read In 100 Easy Lessons. London: Simon and Schuster.

Gregory RP, Hackney C, Gregory NM (1982) Corrective Reading programme: an evaluation. British Journal of Educational Psychology 52: 33–50.

Lewis A (1982) An experimental evaluation of a Direct Instruction programme (Corrective Reading) with remedial readers in a comprehensive school. Educational Psychology 2(2): 121–135.

Meyer LA (1984) Long-term academic effects of the Direct Instruction Project Follow Through. Elementary School Journal 84(4): 380–394.

Moore J (1986) Direct Instruction: a model of instructional design. Educational Psychology 6(3): 201–229.

Somerville DE, Leach DJ (1988) Direct or indirect instruction? An evaluation of three types of intervention programme for assisting students with specific reading difficulties. Educational Research 30(1): 46–53.

Stebbins LB, St Pierre RG, Proper EG, Anderson RB, Cerva TR (1977) Education As Experimentation: A Planned Variation Model. Vol. 4. Cambridge MA.

Appendix 3: Table of normal distribution values

Centile	T score	Z score	WISC scaled score	Standard score	Regressed standard score	1/x or one individual in:	% falling at or below this level
1	27	−2.33	3	65	<50	2330	0.043
2	29	−2.05	4	69	56	596	0.168
3	31	−1.88		72	61	215	0.466
4	32	−1.75		74	64	123	0.820
5	33	−1.65	5	75	66	85	1.19
6	34	−1.56		77	67	72	1.39
7	35	−1.48		78	69	52	1.94
8	36	−1.41		79	71	38	2.7
9	37	−1.34	6	80	73	28	3.6
10	37	−1.28		81	73	28	3.6
11	38	−1.23		82	75	21	5.0
12	38	−1.18		82	75	21	5.0
13	39	−1.13		83	77	16	6.0
14	39	−1.08		84	77	16	6.0
15	40	−1.04		84	79	12	8.0
16	40	−0.99	7	85	79	12	8.0
17	40	−0.95		86	79	12	8.0
18	41	−0.92		86	81	10	10.0
19	41	−0.88		87	81	10	10.0
20	42	−0.84		87	83	8	13.0
21	42	−0.81		88	83	8	13.0
22	42	−0.77		88	83	8	13.0
23	43	−0.74		89	85	6	16.0
24	43	−0.71		89	85	6	16.0
25	43	−0.67	8	90	85	6	16.0
26	44	−0.64		90	87	5	19.0
27	44	−0.61		91	87	5	19.0
28	44	−0.58		91	87	5	19.0

Centile	T score	Z score	WISC scaled score	Standard score	Regressed standard score	1/x or one individual in:	% falling at or below this level
29	44	−0.55		92	87	5	19.0
30	45	−0.52		92	89	4	23.0
31	45	−0.50		93	89	4	23.0
32	45	−0.47		93	89	4	23.0
33	46	−0.44		93	92	3	30.0
34	46	−0.41		94	92	3	30.0
35	46	−0.38		94	92	3	30.0
36	46	−0.36	9	95	92	3	30.0
37	47	−0.33		95	94	3	34.0
38	47	−0.31		95	94	3	34.0
39	47	−0.28		96	94	3	34.0
40	47	−0.25		96	94	3	34.0
41	48	−0.23		97	96	3	39.0
42	48	−0.23		97	96	3	39.0
43	48	−0.18		97	96	3	39.0
44	48	−0.15		98	96	3	39.0
45	49	−0.13		98	98	2	45.0
46	49	−0.10		99	98	2	45.0
47	49	−0.00		99	98	2	45.0
48	49	−0.05		99	98	2	45.0
49	50	−0.03		100	100	2	50.0
50	50	0.00	10	100	100	2	50.0
51	50	0.03		100	100	2	50.0
52	51	0.05		101	102	2	52.0
53	51	0.08		101	102	2	53.0
54	51	0.10		102	102	2	55.0
55	51	0.13		102	102	2	55.0
56	52	0.15		102	104	3	61.0
57	52	0.18		103	104	3	61.0
58	52	0.20		103	104	3	61.0
59	52	0.23		103	104	3	61.0
60	53	0.25		104	106	3	66.0
61	53	0.28		104	106	3	66.0
62	53	0.31		105	106	3	66.0
63	53	0.33	11	105	106	3	66.0
64	54	0.36		105	108	3	70.0
65	54	0.38		106	108	3	70.0
66	54	0.41		106	108	3	70.0
67	54	0.44		107	108	3	70.0
68	55	0.47		107	111	4	77.0
69	55	0.50		108	111	4	77.0

Centile	T score	Z score	WISC scaled score	Standard score	Regressed standard score	1/x or one individual in:	% falling at or below this level
70	55	0.52		108	111	4	77.0
71	56	0.55		108	113	5	81.0
72	56	0.58		109	113	5	81.0
73	56	0.61		109	113	5	81.0
74	56	0.64	12	110	113	5	81.0
75	57	0.67		110	115	6	81.0
76	57	0.71		111	115	6	84.0
77	57	0.74		111	115	6	84.0
78	58	0.77		112	117	8	87.0
79	58	0.81		112	117	8	87.0
80	58	0.84		113	117	8	87.0
81	59	0.88		113	119	10	90.0
82	59	0.92		114	119	10	90.0
83	60	0.95		114	121	12	92.0
84	60	0.99	13	115	121	12	92.0
85	60	1.04		116	121	12	92.0
86	61	1.08		116	123	16	94.0
87	61	1.13		117	123	16	94.0
88	62	1.18		118	126	24	96.0
89	62	1.23		118	126	24	96.0
90	63	1.28		119	128	32	96.9
91	63	1.34	14	120	128	32	96.9
92	64	1.41		121	130	44	97.7
93	65	1.48		122	132	61	98.36
94	66	1.56		123	134	85	98.83
95	67	1.65	15	125	136	122	99.18
96	68	1.75		126	138	177	99.435
97	69	1.88		128	140	261	99.617
98	71	2.05	16	131	145	741	99.865
99	73	2.33	17	135	>150	2330	99.957

Some of the Rare Literature that Objectively Evaluates the Effectiveness of Teaching, Specialist or Otherwise

Arter J, Jenkins JR (1979) Differential Diagnosis – Prescriptive Teaching: a critical appraisal. Review of Educational Research 49(4): 517–55.

Becker WC, Gersten R (1982) A follow-up of Follow Through: the later effects of the Direct Instruction model on children in fifth and sixth grades. American Educational Research Journal 19(1): 75–92.

Biggs JB, Collis KF (1990) Evaluating The Quality Of Learning: The SOLO Taxonomy (Structure of the Observed Learning Outcomes). New York: Academic Press.

Clay MM (1990) The Reading Recovery programme 1984–88: coverage outcomes and Education Board district figures. New Zealand Journal of Educational Studies 25(1): 61–70.

Engelmann S, Carnine D (1982) Theory Of Instruction: Principles and Applications. New York: Irvington.

Gregory RP, Hackney C, Gregory NM (1982) Corrective Reading programme: an evaluation. British Journal of Educational Psychology 52: 33–50.

Hornsby B, Miles TR (1980) The effects of a dyslexia-centred teaching programme. British Journal of Educationa Psychology 50: 236–42.

Hulme C, Monk A, Ives S (1987) Some experimental studies of multisensory teaching: the effects of manual tracing on children's paired associate learning. British Journal of Developmental Psychology 5: 299–307.

Lewis A (1982) An experimental evaluation of a Direct Instruction programme (Corrective Reading) with remedial readers in a comprehensive school. Educational Psychology 2(2): 121–35.

Mason M, Mason B, Quayle T (1992) Illuminating English: how explicit language teaching improved public examination results in a comprehensive school. Educational Studies 18(3): 341–53.

Meyer LA (1984) Long-term academic effects of the Direct Instruction Project Follow Through. The Elementary School Journal 84(4): 380–94.

Moore J (1986) Direct Instruction: a model of instructional design. Educational Psychology 6(3): 201–229.

Rack J, Walker J (1994) Does Dyslexia Institute teaching work? Dyslexia Review 6(2): 12–17.

Rack J, Rooms M (1995) Hackney morning. Special Children (88): 8–13.

Symons S, Woloshyn V, Pressley M. (Eds) (1994) The scientific evaluation of the Whole Language approach to literacy development. Educational Psychologist (special issue) 29(4); and (1995) Hove, East Sussex: Lawrence Erlbaum.

Thomson ME (1988) Preliminary findings concerning the effects of specialized teaching on dyslexic children. Applied Cognitive Psychology 2: 19–31.

Thomson ME (1990) Evaluating teaching programmes for children with specific learning difficulties. In Pumfrey PD, Elliott CD (Eds) Children's Difficulties in Reading Spelling and Writing. Basingstoke Hants: Falmer Press.

Thomson ME (1994) How children with dyslexia respond to specialized teaching: some practical an theoretical issues. In Hales G (Ed.) Dyslexia Matters. London: Whurr.

References

Aaron PG (1994) Differential diagnosis of reading disabilities. In Hales G (Ed) Dyslexia Matters. London: Whurr.

Aaron PG, Joshi RM (1992) Reading Problems: Consultation and Remediation. New York: Guilford Press.

Adams, MJ (1990) Beginning to Read: Thinking and Learning about Print. Boston: MIT Press.

Adams MJ (1994) Learning to read: modelling the reader versus modelling the learner. In Hulme C, Snowling M (Eds) Reading Development and Dyslexia. London: Whurr.

Advisory Centre for Education (ACE) (1994) Special Education Handbook 6th edition. London: ACE Publications.

Alston J (1994) Written output and writing speeds. Dyslexia Review 6(2): 6–12.

Ames T (1980) Diagnostic reading checklists (Stages 1–4). Basingstoke Hants: Macmillan Education.

Annett M (1985) Left Right Hand and Brain: The Right Shift Theory. Hove, East Sussex: Lawrence Erlbaum Associates.

Ansara A, Geschwind N, Galaburda A, Albert M, Gartrell N (Eds) (1981) Sex Differences In Dyslexia. Towson, MD: The Orton Dyslexia Society.

Baddeley AD (1986) Working Memory. London: Oxford University Press.

Baddeley AD, Hitch GJ (1974) Working memory. In Bower G (Ed) The Psychology Of Learning and Motivation 8: 47–90. New York: Academic Press.

Bannatyne A (1971) Language Reading and Learning Disabilities. Springfield Illinois: Charles Thomas.

Bannatyne A (1974) Diagnosis: a note on recategorization of the WISC scaled scores. Journal of Learning Disabilities 7: 272–4.

Barnard PJ (1995) Specifying the 'central executive'. Proceedings of the British Psychological Society 3(2): 90.

Barrett P, Eysenck HJ, and Lucking S (1986) Reaction time and intelligence: a replicated study. Intelligence 10: 9–40.

Bedford-Feuell C, Geiger S, Moyse S, Turner M.(1995) Use of listening comprehension in the identification and assessment of specific learning difficulties. Educational Psychology in Practice 10(4): 207–4.

Bishop DVM (1982) Test For The Reception Of Grammar. Cambridge: MRC Applied Psychology Unit.

Boder E, Jarrico S (1982) The Boder Test Of Reading–Spelling Patterns: A Diagnostic Screening Test For Subtypes Of Reading Disability. New York: Harcourt Brace Jovanovitch/Psychological Corporation.

Bodien P (1996) Scrambled Reading: a case history. Dyslexia Review (in press).

Bookbinder GE (1976) Salford Sentence Reading Test. Sevenoaks Kent: Hodder and Stoughton .

Born M P, Lynn R (1994) Sex differences on the Dutch WISC-R: a comparison with the USA and Scotland. Educational Psychology 14(2): 249–54.

Bouchard TJ, Lykken DT, McGue M, Segal NL, Tellegen A (1990) Sources of human psychological differences: the Minnesota study of twins reared apart. Science 250 (12 October).

Boulton-Lewis GM (1993) Young children's representations and strategies for sub-traction. British Journal of Educational Psychology 63: 441–56.

Bradley L (1980) Assessing Reading Difficulties. Windsor Berkshire: NFER-Nelson.

Bradley L (1993) Paper presented to a meeting on Speed of Processing at the Royal Society, October.

Brand C (1996) The G Factor. Chichester, West Sussex: Wiley.

Brereton A, Cann P (Eds) (1993) Opening The Door: Guidance On Recognizing and Helping The Dyslexic Child. Reading Berkshire: British Dyslexia Association.

British Dyslexia Association (1995) Dyslexia Early Help Better Future. A video about the early recognition of dyslexia. Reading Berkshire: British Dyslexia Association.

Brook P, Dalton D (1995) The spoonerism test. In Phonological Assessment Battery [PhAB]. London: University College.

Brooks G, Gorman T, Kendall L. (1993) The Spelling Abilities Of 11- and 15-Year Olds. Slough Berkshire: National Foundation for Educational Research.

Brown EN (1990) Children with spelling and writing difficulties: an alternative approach. In Pumfrey PD, Elliott CD (Eds) Children's Difficulties in Reading Spelling and Writing. Basingstoke, Hants: Falmer Press.

Buckhalt JA, Jensen AR (1989) The British Ability Scales speed of information process-ing subtest: what does it measure? British Journal of Educational Psychology 59: 100–7.

Burt CL (1921) Mental and Scholastic Tests. London: King and Son.

Cardon LR, Smith SD, Fulker DW, Kimberling WJ, Pennington.F, DeFries JC (1994) Quantitative trait locus for reading disability on chromosome 6. Science 266: 276–9.

Carnine DW (1976) Similar sound separation and cumulative introduction in learn-ing letter–sound correspondence. Journal of Educational Research 69: 368–72.

Carnine DW (1977) Phonics versus look–say: transfer to new words. Reading Teacher 30: 636–40

Carnine DW, Kameenui EJ (1978) Cited but not referenced in Carnine et al. (1990), p. 26.

Carnine DW, Kameenui EJ, Woolfson N (1982) Training of textual dimensions related to text-based inferences. Journal of Reading Behaviour 14: 182–7.

Carnine DW, Silbert J, Kameenui EJ (1990) Direct Reading Instruction. 2nd edn. Toronto Ontario: Merrill.

Carpenter PA, Just MA, Shell P (1990) What one intelligence test measures: a theoretical account of the processing in the Raven Progressive Matrices Test. Psychological Review 97: 404–31.

Carroll JB (1993) Human Cognitive Abilities. Cambridge: Cambridge University Press.

Chall JS (1967) Learning to Read: the Great Debate. New York: McGraw-Hill.

Chall J (1983) Stages of Reading Development. New York: McGraw Hill.

Chall J, Curtis ME (1990) Diagnostic achievement testing in reading. In Reynolds CR, Kamphaus RW (Eds) Handbook of Psychological and Educational Assessment Of Children: Intelligence and Achievement. New York: Guildford Press.

Chew J (1994) Professional Expertise and Parental Experience In The Teaching Of Reading (Or Mother Often Knows Best). York: Campaign for Real Education September.

Chubb JE, Moe TM (1990) Politics Markets and America's Schools. Washington DC: Brookings Institution.

Clampit MK, Adair J, Strenio J (1983) Frequency of discrepancies between deviation quotients on the WISC-R: a table for clinicians. Journal of Consulting and Clinical Psychology 51: 795–6.

Cleary TA, Humphreys LG, Kendrick SA, Wesman AG (1975) Educational uses of tests with disadvantaged students. American Psychologist 30: 15–41.

Cline T (1983) Educational assessment of bilingual pupils: getting the context right. In Elliott J, Figg J (Eds) Assessment Issues. Educational and Child Psychology 10(4): 59–68. Leicester: British Psychological Society (DECP).

Cole KN, Dale PS, Mills PE (1990) Defining language delay in young children by cognitive referencing: are we saying more than we know? Applied Psycholinguistics 11: 291–302.

Cox CB (1991) Cox On Cox: An English Curriculum For The 1990s. London: Hodder and Stoughton.

Critchley M (1970) The Dyslexic Child. Springfield, IL: Thomas.

Daly M, Wilson M (1983) Sex Evolution and Behavior. 2nd edn. Boston: Willard Grant Press.

Daniels JC, Diack H (1958) The Standard Reading Tests. London: Chatto and Windus.

Darch C, Carnine .W, Gersten R (1984) Explicit instruction in mathematics problem-solving. Journal of Educational Research 77: 350–9.

Das JP, Naglieri JA (in press) Das-Naglieri Cognitive Assessment System. Chicago: Riverside.

Dearing R (1993a) The National Curriculum and Its Assessment: An Interim Report. York: National Curriculum Council; and London: School Examinations and Assessment Council.

Dearing R (1993b) The National Curriculum and Its Assessment: Final Report. London: School Curriculum and Assessment Authority.

Delis DC, Kramer JH, Kaplan E, Ober BA (1994) California Test of Verbal Learning (Children's Version) (CVLT-C). San Antonio Texas: Harcourt Brace Jovanovitch/Psychological Corporation.

Denckla M, Rudel R (1976) Rapid automatized naming: dyslexia differentiated from other learning disabilities. Neuropsychologia 14: 471–9.

Department for Education (1994) Code Of Practice On The Identification and Assessment Of Special Educational Needs. London: Central Office of Information.

Department of Education and Science Assessment of Performance Unit (1988) Language Performance in Schools: Review of APU Language Monitoring 1979–1983. London: HMSO.

Dixon R, Engelmann S (1979) Corrective Spelling Through Morphographs. Chicago: Science Research Associates.

Dockrell J, McShane J (1993) Children's Learning Difficulties: A Cognitive Approach. Oxford: Blackwell.

Doctor L, Stuart M (1995) Prospectus for the Birkbeck Literacy Assessment Centre. London: University of London Birkbeck College.

Dodds J (1994) Spelling skills and causal attributions in children. Educational Psychology in Practice 102: 111–19.

Dodds J (1995) Self-esteem and motivation in the dyslexic child and adult. Dyslexia Review 6(3): 7–9.

Draycott SG, Kline P (1994) Speed and ability: a research note. Personality and Individual Differences 17(6): 763–8 December.

Dunn LlM, Dunn LM, Whetton C, Pintillie D (1982) British Picture Vocabulary Scale (BPVS). Windsor Berks: NFER-Nelson 1982.

Dutton KP (1991) Writing under examination conditions: establishing a baseline. In: SED/Regional Psychological Services: Professional Development Initiatives 1989–90. Edinburgh: Scottish Education Department.

Edwards J (1994) The Scars Of Dyslexia. London: Cassell.

Elbro C (1989) Morphological awareness in dyslexia. In Von Euler C, Lundberg I, Lennerstrand G (Eds) The Brain and Reading. London: Macmillan.

Elliott CD (1983) British Ability Scales Manual 2: Technical Handbook. Windsor Berks: NFER-Nelson.

Elliott CD (1990) Differential Ability Scales: Introductory and Technical Handbook. New York: Harcourt Brace Jovanovitch/Psychological Corporation.

Elliott CD (1982) British Ability Scales Spelling Scale. Windsor Berks: NFER-Nelson.

Elliott CD (1995) British Ability Scales: a g-enhanced Short Form IQ. Windsor Berks: NFER-Nelson.

Elliott CD (1996) Loadings for first two WISC-R factors. Personal communication, January.

Elliott CD, Murray DJ, Pearson LS (1979, 1983) The British Ability Scales. Windsor Berks: NFER-Nelson.

Ellis AW (1995) Cognitive neuropsychology and rehabilitation. The Psychologist 8(7): 303–4.

Ellis AW, Young A (1988) Human Cognitive Neuropsychology. Hove East Sussex: Lawrence Erlbaum.

Ellis N (1981) Visual and name coding in dyslexic children. Psychological Research 43: 201–18.

Engelmann S, Carnine D (1982) Theory Of Instruction: Principles and Applications. New York: Irvington.

Engelmann S, Carnine L, Johnson G (1988) Corrective Reading Programs. Chicago: Science Research Associates.

Ericsson KA, Oliver WL (1989) A methodology for assessing the detailed structure of memory skills. In Colley AM, Beech JR (Eds) Acquisition and Performance Of Cognitive Skills. Chichester Sussex: Wiley, pp. 193–215.

Eysenck HJ, Eysenck SBG (1975) Eysenck Personality Questionnaire (Junior and Adult). London: Hodder and Stoughton.

Fawcett A, Nicolson R (Eds) (1994) Dyslexia In Children: Multidisciplinary Perspectives. Hemel Hempstead Herts: Harvester Wheatsheaf (Simon and Schuster International).

Fawcett AJ, Pickering S, Nicolson RI (1992) Development of the DEST test for the early screening of dyslexia. In Groner R, Kaufmann-Hayoz R, Wright SF (Eds) Reading and Reading Disorders: International Perspectives. North Holland: Elsevier.

Fennell EB (1994) Issues in child neuropsychological assessment. In Vanderploeg RD (Ed) Clinician's Guide To Neuropsychological Assessment. Hove Sussex: Lawrence Erlbaum.

Fielding GD, Kameenui EJ, Gersten R (1983) A comparison of an enquiry and a direct instruction approach to teaching legal concepts and applications to secondary school students. Journal of Educational Research 76(5): 387–93.

Fletcher JM (1985) External validation of learning disability typologies. In Rourke BP (Ed) Neuropsychology Of Learning Disabilities. New York: Guilford Press.

Fletcher JM, Shaywitz SE, Shankweiler D, Katz L, Liberman IY, Stuebling KK, Francis JM, Fouler AE, Shaywitz BA (1994) Cognitive profiles of reading disability: comparison of discrepancy and low achievement definitions. Journal of Educational Psychology 86: 6–24.

Flew AGN (1994) Shephard's Warning: Setting Schools Back On Course. London: Adam Smith Institute.

Flynn JR (1984) The mean IQ of Americans: massive gains 1932–1978. Psychological Bulletin 95: 29–51.

Flynn JR (1987a) Massive IQ gains in 14 nations: what IQ tests really measure. Psychological Bulletin 101(2): 171–91.

Flynn JR (1987b)The ontology of intelligence. In Forge J (Ed) Measurement Realism and Objectivity. New York: Reidel.

Frank G (1983) The Wechsler Enterprise: An Assessment Of The Development Structure and Use Of The Wechsler Tests Of Intelligence. New York: Pergamon.

Frederickson N, Reason R (1995) Discrepancy definitions of specific learning difficulties. Educational Psychology in Practice 10(4): 195–205.

Friedenberg L (1995) Psychological Testing: Design Analysis and Use. Boston: Allyn and Bacon.

Friel J (1995) Children With Special Needs: Assessment Law and Practice – Caught In The Acts. 3rd edn. London: Jessica Kingsley.

Frith U (1985) Beneath the surface of developmental dyslexia. In Patterson KE, Marshall JC, Coltheart M (Eds) Surface Dyslexia: Neuropsychological and Cognitive Studies Of Phonological Reading. Hove East Sussex: Lawrence Erlbaum.

Frith U (1992) Cognitive development and cognitive deficit. The Psychologist: Bulletin of the British Psychological Society 5(1): 13–19.

Frith U (1995) Dyslexia: can we have a shared theoretical framework? In Frederickson N, Reason R (Eds) Phonological Assessment Of Specific Learning Difficulties. Educational and Child Psychology 12(1): 6–17. Leicester: British Psychological Society (DECP).

Frith U, Landerl K, Frith C (1995) Dyslexia and verbal fluency: more evidence for a phonological deficit. Dyslexia 1(1): 2–11.

Garnham A, Oakhill JV (1994) Thinking and Reasoning. Oxford: Blackwell.

Gathercole SE (1995a) Is nonword repetition a test of phonological memory or lexical knowledge? It all depends on the nonwords. Memory and Cognition 23: 83–94.

Gathercole SE (1995b) The assessment of phonological memory skills in preschool children. British Journal of Educational Psychology 65 Part 2: 155–64.

Gathercole SE, Baddeley AD (1993) Working Memory and Language. Hove East Sussex: Lawrence Erlbaum.

Gathercole SE, Willis CS, Baddeley AD, Emslie H (1994) The children's test of nonword repetition: a test of phonological working memory. Memory 2: 103–28.

GCSE Secretaries (1993) Standing Agreement No. 4. GCSE Examinations: Special Arrangements and Special Considerations. Bristol: Joint Council for the GCSE, 24 September.

Gillham WEC, Hesse KA (1973) The Nottingham Number Test. Sevenoaks, Kent: Hodder and Stoughton.

Gillham WEC, Hesse KA (1976) Basic Number Screening Test. Sevenoaks, Kent: Hodder and Stoughton.

Godfrey Thomson Unit University of Edinburgh (1972–77). Edinburgh Reading Tests (Stages 1–4). Sevenoaks, Kent: Hodder and Stoughton.

Godfrey Thomson Unit University of Edinburgh (1986) Word Search. Sevenoaks, Kent: Hodder and Stoughton.

Gorman T (1989) What Teachers in Training Read about Reading. Occasional paper 4. Windsor, Berks: National Foundation for Educational Research.

Goswami U (1992) Paper presented to the British Psychological Society London Conference, City University, December.

Gould SJ (1981) The Mismeasure of Man. Harmondsworth, Middlesex: Penguin.

Grant ECG, Howard JM, Chasty H, Hornsby B, Galbraith S (1988) Zinc deficiency in children with dyslexia: concentrations of zinc and other minerals in sweat and hair. British Medical Journal 269: 607–9.

Gregory HM, Gregory AH (1994) A comparison of the Neale and the BAS reading tests. Educational Psychology in Practice 10(1): 15–18.

Gudjonnson GH (1995a) The Standard Progressive Matrices: methodological problems associated with the administration of the 1992 adult standardization sample. Personality and Individual Differences 183: 441–2.

Gudjonnson GH (1995b) Raven's norms on the SPM revisited: a reply to Raven. Personality and Individual Differences 183: 447.

Hagley F (1987) Suffolk Reading Scale. Windsor, Berks: NFER-Nelson.

Hagues N, Courtenay D (1993) Verbal Reasoning 8–9, 10–11, 12–13. Windsor, Berks: NFER-Nelson.

Hales G (1994) The human aspects of dyslexia. In Hales G (Ed) Dyslexia Matters. London: Whurr.

Halliwell M, Feltham R (1995). Comparing the Neale and BAS reading tests: a reply to Gregory and Gregory. Educational Psychology in Practice 10(4): 228–30.

Halpern DF (1992) Sex Differences In Cognitive Abilities. 2nd edn. Hove East Sussex: Lawrence Erlbaum.

Hammill DD (1990) On learning disabilities: an emerging consensus. Journal of Learning Disabilities 23(2): 74–84.

Hammill DD (1991) Detroit Tests of Learning Aptitude – Third Edition (Detroit-3). Austin, TX: Pro-Ed.

Hatcher PJ (1994) Test Of Phonological Awareness. In Sound Linkage: An Integrated Programme For Overcoming Reading Difficulties. London: Whurr.

Hatcher PJ (1996) A field study of the Sound Linkage Test of Phonological Awareness. Dyslexia (in press).

Hatcher P, Hulme C, Ellis A (1994) Ameliorating early reading failure by integrating the teaching of reading and phonological skills: the phonological linkage hypothesis. Child Development 65: 41–57.

Hedderly RG (1992) Psychologists' assessments of specific learning difficulties (dyslexia) and examinations boards: policies and practices. Educational Psychology in Practice 81(April).

Hedderly RG (1992) Suggested procedure for the assessment of pupils requiring special arrangements in public examinations because of specific learning difficulties. Oldgate House, 2 Oldgate, Huddersfield HD1 6QW: Kirklees Education Authoity.

Hedderly RG (1995) The assessment of SpLD pupils for examination arrangements. Dyslexia Review 7(2): 12–16; 19–21.

Hedderly RG (1996) Assessing pupils with Specific Learning Difficulties for examination special arrangements at GCSE 'A' Level and degree level. Educational Psychology in Practice 12(1): 36–44.

Henchman J, Hendry E (1963) English Progress Test F2. Windsor, Berkshire: NFER-Nelson.

Henderson SE, Sugden DA (1992) Movement Assessment Battery For Children. New York: Harcourt Brace Jovanovitch/Psychological Corporation.

Herrnstein RJ, Murray C (1994) The Bell Curve: Intelligence and Class Structure In American Life. New York: Free Press (Macmillan).

Hieronymus AN, Lindquist EF, France N (1988) Richmond Tests of Basic Skills (RTBS). 2nd edn. Windsor, Berks: NFER-Nelson.

Hinnigan L, Forrest J (1996) An integrated LEA framework for resourcing special educational arrangements to meet individual needs. Educational Psychology in Practice 12(1): 50–1.

Hitch GJ (1990) Developmental fractionation of working memory. In Vallar G, Shallice T (Eds) Neuropsychological Impairments of Short-term Memory. Cambridge: Cambridge University Press.

Horn JL (1989) Cognitive diversity: a framework of learning. In Ackerman PL, Sternberg RJ, Glaser R (Eds) Learning and Individual Differences. New York: Freeman.

Horn JL (1991) Measurement of intellectual capabilities: a review of theory. In McGrew KS, Werder JK, Woodcock RW (Eds) Woodcock–Johnson Technical Manual: A Reference On Theory and Current Research. Allen, TX: DLM Teaching Resources.

Horn JL (1985) Remodeling old models of intelligence. In Wolman BB (Ed) Handbook Of Intelligence: Theories Measurements and Applications. New York: Wiley.

Horn JL, Cattell RB (1966) Refinement and test of the theory of fluid and crystallized intelligence. Journal of Educational Psychology 57: 253–70.

Hornsby B (1989) Before Alpha. London: Souvenir Press.

Hornsby B (1995) Overcoming Dyslexia: A Straightforward Guide For Parents and Teachers. 3rd edn. London: Optima.

Hulme C, Maughan S, Brown GDA (1991) Memory for familiar and unfamiliar words: evidence for a long-term contribution to short-term memory span. Journal of Memory and Language 30: 685–701.

Hunter-Grundin E, Grundin U (1980) Hunter-Grundin Literacy Profiles. High Wycombe, Bucks: The Test Agency.

Hutchison C (1996) Snares in the charmed circle. Times Higher Education Supplement, 12 April.

Jansons KM (1988) A personal view of dyslexia and of thought without language. In Weiskrantz L (Ed) Thought Without Language. Oxford: Clarendon Press.

Jastak F, Jastak S (1979) Meanings and Measures Of Mental Tests (Manual: Jastak Cluster Analysis). Wilmington, DE: Jastak Associates.

Jastak S, Wilkinson GS (1984) The Wide Range Achievement Test – Revised (WRAT-R). Wilmington, DE: Wide Range.

Jensen AR (1968) Patterns of mental ability and socioeconomic status. Proceedings of the National Academy of Sciences 60: 1330–7.

Jensen AR (1970) Hierarchical theories of mental ability. In Dockrell WB (Ed) On Intelligence: The Toronto Symposium On Intelligence 1969. London: Methuen.

Jensen AR (1981) Straight Talk About Mental Tests. London: Methuen.

Jensen AR (1984) The black–white difference on the K-ABC: implications for future tests. Journal of Special Education 18: 377–408.

Johnston RS, Thompson GB (1989) Is dependence on phonological information in children's reading a product of instructional approach? Journal of Experimental Child Psychology 48: 131–45.

Johnston R, Connelly V, Watson J (1995) Some effects of phonics teaching on early reading development. In Owen P, Pumfrey P (Eds) Children Learning To Read: International Concerns. 1: Emergent and Developing Reading: Messages For Teachers. Basingstoke, Hants: Falmer Press.

Kaufman AS (1975) Factor analysis of the WISC-R at eleven age-levels between 612 and 1612 years. Journal of Consulting and Clinical Psychology 43: 138–40.

Kaufman AS (1976a) Do normal children have 'flat' ability profiles? Psychology in the Schools 13: 284–5.

Kaufman AS (1976b) Verbal-Performance IQ discrepancies on the WISC-R. Journal of Consulting and Clinical Psychology 44: 739–44.

Kaufman AS (1979) Intelligent Testing With The WISC-R. New York: Wiley.

Kaufman AS (1990) Assessing Adolescent and Adult Intelligence. Boston: Allyn and Bacon.

Kaufman AS (1994) Intelligent Testing With The WISC-III. New York: Wiley.

Kaufman AS, Kaufman NL (1983) Kaufman Assessment Battery For Children (K-ABC). Circle Pines, MN: American Guidance Service.

Kaufman AS, Kaufman NL (1985) Kaufman Test of Educational Achievement (K-TEA). Circle Pines, MN: American Guidance Service.

Kaufman AS, Kaufman NL (1990) Kaufman Brief Intelligence Test (K-BIT). Circle Pines MN: American Guidance Service.

Kaufman AS, Kaufman NL (1993) Kaufman Adolescent and Adult Intelligence Test (KAIT). Circle Pines, MN: American Guidance Service.

Kaufman AS, Kaufman NL (1994) Kaufman Functional Academic Skills Test (K-FAST). Circle Pines, MN: American Guidance Service.

Kavale KA, Forness SR (1984) A meta-analysis of the validity of Wechsler scale profiles and recategorizations: patterns or parodies? Learning Disabilities Quarterly 7: 136–56.

Kay SR (1989) Cognitive diagnostic assessment. In Wetzler S, Katz MM (Eds) Contemporary Approaches To Psychological Assessment. New York: Brunner Mazel.

Kay J, Lesser R, Coltheart M (1992) PALPA: Psycholinguistic Assessments of Language Processing In Aphasia. Hove, Sussex: Lawrence Erlbaum.

Keith TZ (1985) Questioning the K-ABC: what does it measure? School Psychology Review 14: 9–20.

Keith TZ (1990) Confirmatory and hierarchical confirmatory analysis of the Differential Ability Scales. Journal of Psychoeducational Assessment 8: 391–405.

Kispal A, Tate A, Gorman T, Whetton C (1989a) Test Of Initial Literacy (TOIL). Windsor Berks: NFER-Nelson.

Kispal A, Gorman T, Whetton C (1989b) Reading Ability Series. Windsor Berks: NFER-Nelson.

Klasen E (1972) The Syndrome Of Specific Dyslexia. Baltimore, MD: University Park Press.

Klein C (1993) Diagnosing Dyslexia: A Guide To The Assessment Of Adults With Specific Learning Difficulties. London: Adult Literacy and Basic Skills Unit.

Kline P (1991) Intelligence: The Psychometric View. London: Routledge.

Kline P (1993) The Handbook of Psychological Testing. London: Routledge.

LaBerge D, Samuels SJ (1974) Toward a theory of automatic information processing in reading. Cognitive Psychology 6: 293–323.

Lea M (1986) A British Supplement To The Manual Of The Wechsler Adult Intelligence Scale – Revised. Sidcup. Kent: Harcourt Brace Jovanovitch/ Psychological Corporation.

Lewis CS (1960) Studies In Words. Cambridge University Press.

London Borough of Havering Education Psychology Service (1995) Dyslexia: An EPS View. Romford Essex: London Borough of Havering Education and Community Services.

Lossky V (1957) The Mystical Theology Of The Eastern Church. London: James Clarke.

Lovett MW (1986) Sentential structure and the perceptual spans of two samples of disabled readers. Journal of Psycholinguistic Research 15(2): 153–75.

Lucas A, Morley R, Cole TJ, Lister G, Leeson-Payne C (1992) Breast milk and subsequent intelligence quotient in children born preterm. Lancet 339(8788): 261–4.

Lynn R (1994) Sex differences in intelligence and brain size: a paradox resolved. Personality and Individual Differences 17: 257–71.

Lynn R (1996) Racial and ethnic differences in intelligence in the United States on the Differential Ability Scale. Personality and Individual Differences 20(2): 271–3.

Lynn R, Hampson SL (1986) Further evidence for secular increases in intelligence in Britain Japan and the United States. Behavioural and Brain Sciences 9: 203–4.

Lynn R, Hampson SL (1989) Secular increases in reasoning and mathematical abilities in Britain 1972–84. School Psychology International 10: 301–4.

Lynn R, Hampson SL, Mullineux JC (1987) A long-term increase in the fluid intelligence of English children. Nature 328: 797.

Maccoby EE, Jacklin CN (1974) The Psychology Of Sex Differences. Stanford, CA: Stanford University Press.

MacIntyre A (1981) After Virtue: A Study In Moral Theory. London: Duckworth.

Macmillan Test Unit (1985a) Macmillan Graded Word Reading Test. Basingstoke, Hants: Macmillan Education. Now distributed by: Windsor, Berks: NFER-Nelson.

Macmillan Test Unit (1985b) Macmillan Group Reading Test. Basingstoke, Hants: Macmillan Education. Now distributed by: Windsor, Berks: NFER-Nelson.

Macmillan Test Unit (1990) Macmillan Group Reading Test 9–14. Basingstoke, Hants: Macmillan Education. Now distributed by: Windsor Berks: NFER-Nelson.

Manrique AMB, Signorini A (1994) Phonological awareness spelling and reading abilities in Spanish-speaking children. British Journal of Educational Psychology 64: 429–39.

Marshall JC (1987) The cultural and biological context of written languages: their acquisition deployment and breakdown. In Beech JR, Colley AM (Eds) Cognitive Approaches To Reading. Chichester, Sussex: Wiley.

Massey J, Elliott GL (1996) Aspects of Writing in 16+ English Examinations between 1980 and 1994. Occasional Research Paper 1. Cambridge: University of Cambridge Local Examinations Syndicate.

Matarazzo JD (1985) Review of Wechsler Adult Intelligence Scale – Revised. In Mitchell JV (Ed) The Ninth Mental Measurements Yearbook. Lincoln, NE: University of Nebraska Buros Institute of Mental Measurements, pp. 1703–5.

Maughan B, Yule W (1994) Reading and other learning disabilities. In Rutter M, Taylor E, Hersov L (Eds) Child and Adolescent Psychiatry: Modern Approaches. 3rd edn. Oxford: Blackwell Scientific.

McCarthy D (1972) McCarthy Scales Of Children's Abilities. San Antonio, TX: Psychological Corporation.

McCrum R, Cran W, MacNeil R (1992) The Story Of English. 2nd edition. London: Faber and Faber.

McDougall S, Hulme C (1994) Short-term memory speech rate and phonological awareness as predictors of learning to read. In Hulme C, Snowling M (Eds) Reading Development and Dyslexia. London: Whurr.

McGhee R (1993) Fluid and crystallized intelligence: confirmatory factor analysis of the Differential Ability Scales Detroit Tests of Learning Aptitude-3 and Woodcock–Johnson Psycho-Educational Battery – Revised. In Bracken BA, McCallum RS (Eds) Journal of Psychoeducational Assessment Monograph Series: Advances in Psycho-educational Assessment. Germantown, TN: Psychoeducational Corporation.

McGrew KS (1986) Clinical Interpretation Of The Woodcock-Johnson Tests Of Cognitive Ability. Orlando, FL: Grune and Stratton.

McLeod J, Anderson J (1973) GAPADOL Reading Comprehension. Oxford: Heinemann Educational.

McLeod J, Unwin D (1973) GAP Reading Comprehension Test. Oxford: Heinemann Educational.

Mehler J (1994) Address to 'The Acquisition of Language and its Dissolution': a discussion meeting at the Royal Society, London, 23–24 March.

Mehler J, Dupoux E (1994) What Infants Know. Trans. Southgate P. Oxford: Blackwell 1994.

Miles TR (1982) The Bangor Dyslexia Test. Wisbech, Cambridgeshire: Learning Development Aids.

Miles TR (1993) Dyslexia: The Pattern Of Difficulties. 2nd edn. London: Whurr.

Miles TR (1994) Paper presented to the Third Internation Conference of the British Dyslexia Association. Manchester, April.

Moerk EL (1992) A First Language: Taught and Learned. Baltimore, MD: Paul H Brookes.

Moir A, Jessel D (1989) Brainsex. London: Mandarin/Octopus.

Morgan WP (1896) A case of congenital word-blindness. British Medical Journal 11: 378.

Muter V, Snowling MJ, Taylor S (1994) Orthographic analogies and phonological awareness: their role and significance in early reading development. Journal of Child Psychology and Psychiatry 35(2): 293–310.

Naglieri JA (1985) Matrix Analogies Test (MAT) (Short Form). Columbus, OH: Charles Merrill.

National Foundation for Educational Research (NFER) (1959) English Progress Test B2. Windsor, Berkshire: NFER-Nelson.

National Foundation for Educational Research (NFER) (1961) English Progress Test C2. Windsor, Berkshire: NFER-Nelson.

National Foundation for Educational Research (NFER) (1963) English Progress Test E2. Windsor, Berkshire: NFER-Nelson.

National Foundation for Educational Research (NFER) (1966) English Progress Test A2. Windsor, Berkshire: NFER-Nelson.

National Foundation for Educational Research (NFER) (1970a) English Progress Test C3. Windsor, Berkshire: NFER-Nelson.

National Foundation for Educational Research (NFER) (1970b) English Progress Test D3. Windsor, Berkshire: NFER-Nelson.

National Foundation for Educational Research (NFER) (1971) English Progress Test D2. Windsor, Berkshire: NFER-Nelson.

National Foundation for Educational Research (NFER) (1970) Reading Test A. Windsor, Berkshire: NFER-Nelson.

National Foundation for Educational Research (NFER) (1971) Reading Test BD. Windsor, Berkshire: NFER-Nelson.

National Foundation For Educational Research (NFER) (1975) Reading Tests EH1 and EH2. Windsor, Berks: NFER-Nelson.

National Foundation for Educational Research (NFER) (1976) Reading Comprehension Test DE. Windsor, Berkshire: NFER-Nelson.

National Foundation for Educational Research (NFER) (1978) Reading Test AD. Windsor, Berkshire: NFER-Nelson.

Neale MD (1989) Neale Analysis Of Reading Ability – Revised (NARA-R) (British Edition revised by Christophers U, Whetton C). Windsor, Berks: NFER-Nelson.

Nelson HE (1982) National Adult Reading Test (NART). Windsor, Berks: NFER-Nelson.

Nichols EG, Inglis J, Lawson JS, MacKay I (1988) A cross-validation study of patterns of cognitive ability in children with learning difficulties as described by factorially defined WISC-R Verbal and Performance IQs. Journal of Learning Disabilities 21: 504–8.

Nicolson RI, Fawcett AJ (1990) Automaticity: a new framework for dyslexia research? Cognition 35: 159–82.

Nicolson RI, Fawcett AJ (1995) Balance phonological skill and dyslexia: towards the Dyslexia Early Screening Test. Dyslexia Review 7(1): 8–11.

Nicolson RI, Fawcett AJ, Baddeley AD (1992) Working memory and dyslexia. Sheffield: University of Sheffield Department of Psychology.

Oakhill J, Yuill N (1991) The remediation of reading comprehension difficulties. In Snowling MJ, Thomson ME (Eds) Dyslexia: Integrating Theory and Practice. London: Whurr.

Olson RK, Wise BW, Conners F, Rack JP, Fulker D (1989) Specific deficits in component reading and language skills: genetic and environmental influences. Journal of Hearing Disabilities 22: 339–40.

Olson RK, Wise BW, Conners F, Rack JP, (1990) Organisation, heritability and remediation of component word recognition and language skills in disabled readers. In Carr TH and Levy BA (Eds) Reading and its Development Component Skills Approaches. New York: Academic press, pp. 261–2.

O'Neill GP (1988) Teaching effectiveness: a review of the research. Canadian Journal of Education 13(1): 162–85.

Orton Dyslexia Society (1994) A new definition of dyslexia. Bulletin of the Orton Dyslexia Society (Fall).

Osman BB (1982) No One To Play With: The Social Side of Learning Disabilities. Novato, CA: Academic Therapy Publications.

Pennington BF (1991) Diagnosing Learning Disorders: A Neuropsychological Framework. Hove, East Sussex: Lawrence Erlbaum (Guilford Press).

Perfetti C (1985) Reading Ability. New York: Oxford University Press.

Perin D (1983) Phonemic segmentation and spelling. British Journal of Psychology 74: 129–44.

Peters ML (1985) Spelling: Caught Or Taught? A New Look. London: Routledge and Kegan Paul.

Pyke N (1994) Councils tighten up on special needs costs. Times Educational Supplement, 5 August.

Pinker S (1995) The Language Instinct. Harmondsworth, Middlesex: Penguin.

Plomin R, Rende R (1991) Human behavioural genetics. Annual Review of Psychology 42: 161–90.

Polanyi M (1958) Personal Knowledge. London: Routledge and Kegan Paul.

Popper KR (1945) The Open Society and Its Enemies. London: Routledge and Kegan Paul.

Popper KR (1953/1963/1979) The problem of induction. From 'Philosophy of Science: A Personal Report' a lecture given at PeterhouseCambridge in 1953, later

Chapter 1 in Conjectures and Refutations (1963); and sections 13 and 14 of 'Replies to My Critics' in The Philosophy of Karl Popper in The Library of Living Philosophers, Ed. P.A. Schilpp, Vol. 2. La Salle, IL: Open Court; reprinted as section 7 in Popper (1979).

Popper KR (1979) Objective Knowledge: An Evolutionary Approach. Rev. edn. Oxford: Clarendon Press.

Popper KR (1983) A Pocket Popper, Ed David Miller. Glasgow: Collins (Fontana).

Potton A (1983) Screening. Guides to Assessment in Education series. Basingstoke, Hants: Macmillan Education.

Pritchard B (1971) Reading Test SR-A and SR-B. Windsor, Berkshire: NFER-Nelson.

Pumfrey P (1985) Reading Tests and Assessment Techniques. 2nd edn. London: Hodder and Stoughton.

Pumfrey PD, Reason R (1991) Specific Learning Difficulties (Dyslexia): Challenges and Responses. Windsor, Berks: NFER-Nelson.

Quiller-Couch A (Ed) (1925)The Oxford Book Of English Prose. Oxford: Clarendon Press.

Rack JP (1995) Paper given to a symposium on specific learning difficulties at the London Conference of the British Psychological Society Institute of Education, 20 December.

Rack JP, Hulme C, Snowling MJ (1993) Learning to read: a theoretical synthesis. In Rees H (Ed) Advances in Child Development and Behavior (Academic Press) 24: 99–132.

Rack JP, Snowling MJ, Olson RK (1992) The nonword reading deficit in developmental dyslexia: a review. Reading Research Quarterly 27(1): 29–53.

Ramsden M (1993) Rescuing Spelling. Crediton, Devon: Southgate.

Raven JC (1947) Advanced Progressive Matrices (APM). London: HK Lewis.

Raven JC (1956, 1962) Coloured Progressive Matrices (CPM). London: HK Lewis.

Raven JC (1958) Standard Progressive Matrices (SPM). London: HK Lewis.

Raven J (1995) Methodological problems with the 1992 standardization of the SPM: a response. Personality and Individual Differences 18(3): 443–5.

Raven JC, Court JH (1989) Manual For Raven's Progressive Matrices and Vocabulary Scales. Research Supplement No. 4. London: HK Lewis.

Raven JC, Court JH, Raven J (1978) Manual For Raven's Progressive Matrices and Vocabulary Scales. London: HK Lewis.

Reynolds CR (1990) Conceptual and technical problems in learning disability diagnosis. In Reynolds CR, Kamphaus RW (Eds) Handbook Of Psychological and Educational Assessment Of Children: Intelligence and Achievement. New York: Guilford Press.

Reynolds CR, Bigler ED (1994) Test Of Memory and Learning (TOMAL). Chicago: Riverside.

Reynolds WM (1987) Auditory Discrimination Test. 2nd edn. Los Angeles, CA: Western Psychological Services.

Richardson SO (1992) Historical perspectives on dyslexia. Journal of Learning Disabilities 25(1): 40–7 January.

Richardson E, DiBenedetto B (19185) Decoding Skills Test. Parkton, MD: York Press.

Riddoch MJ, Humphreys GW (Eds) (1994) Cognitive Neuropsychology and Cognitive Rehabilitation. Hove, East Sussex: Lawrence Erlbaum.

Rosenshine B, Stevens R (19184) Classroom instruction in reading. In Pearson D (Ed) Handbook Of Research On Reading. New York: Longman.

Rosner J (1993) Helping Children Overcome Learning Difficulties. 3rd edn. New York: Walker.

Rourke BP (1989) Nonverbal Learning Disabilities: The Syndrome and The Model. Hove, East Sussex: Lawrence Erlbaum (Guilford Press).

Rourke BP, Fuerst DE (1991) Learning Disabilities and Psychosocial Functioning: A Neuropsychological Perspective. Hove, East Sussex: Lawrence Erlbaum (Guilford Press).

Rust J (1996) Manual. Wechsler Objective Language Dimensions; and Manual. Wechsler Objective Numerical Dimensions. London: Psychological Corporation (Harcourt Brace).

Rust J, Golombok S, Trickey G (1993) WORD: Wechsler Objective Reading Dimension. Sidcup, Kent: Harcourt Brace Jovanovitch/Psychological Corporation.

Sattler JM (1988) Assessment of Children. 3rd edn. San Diego, CA: Jerome M. Sattler.

Sawyer C, Potter V (1994) Estimating standardised scores for MIRA. Educational Psychology in Practice 10(1): 46–7.

Sawyer C, Gray F, Champness M (1996) Measuring speed of handwriting for the GCSE candidates. Educational Psychology in Practice 12(1): 19–23.

Schonell FJ (1932) Essentials In Teaching and Testing Spelling. London: Macmillan.

Schonell FJ, Schonell FE (1950) Diagnostic and Attainment Testing. Edinburgh: Oliver and Boyd.

Scottish Council for Research in Education (1976) Manual For the Burt Reading Tests (1974 Revision). London: Hodder and Stoughton.

Scottish Council for Research in Education (1987) Wechsler Intelligence Scale for Children – Revised: Scottish Standardization. Sidcup, Kent: Harcourt Brace Jovanovitch/Psychological Corporation.

Shallice T (1988) From Neuropsychology To Mental Structure. Cambridge University Press.

Shaywitz SE, Escobar MD, Shaywitz BA, Fletcher JM, Makuch R (1992) Evidence that dyslexia may represent the lower tail of a normal distribution of reading ability. New England Journal of Medicine 326(3) (16 January).

Shaywitz SE, Fletcher JM, Shaywitz BA (in press) A conceptual model and definition of dyslexia: findings emerging from the Connecticut longitudinal study. In Beitchman JH, Cohen N, Konstantarias MM, Tannock R (Eds) Language Learning and Behaviour Disorders. New York: Cambridge University Press.

Shearer E, Apps A (1975) A restandardization of the Burt-Vernon and Schonell Graded Word Reading Tests. Educational Research 181: 67–73.

thSheslow D, Adams W (1990) Wide Range Assessment Of Memory and Learning (WRAML). Wilmington, DE: Jastak Associates.

Silver LB (1984) The Misunderstood Child: A Guide For Parents of Learning Disabled Children. New York: McGraw Hill.

Silverman I, Eals M (1992) Sex differences in spatial abilities: evolutionary theory and data. In Barkow JH, Cosmides L, Tooby J (Eds) The Adapted Mind: Evolutionary Psychology and The Generation Of Culture. New York: Oxford University Press.

Singleton C (1995) Paper given to a symposium on specific learning difficulties at the London Conference of the British Psychological Society, Institute of Education, 20 December.

Singleton C, Thomas K, Leedale R (1995) Humberside Early Screening Research Project: Final Report. Hull: Dyslexia Computer Resource Centre Department of Psychology University of Hull.

Slingerland B (1974). Screening Tests For Identifying Children With Specific Language Disability. Cambridge, MA: Educators Publishing Service.

Slingerland B (1977) Pre-Reading Screening Procedures. Cambridge, MA: Educators Publishing Service.

Smith P, Hagues N (1993) Non-Verbal Reasoning 8–9 10–11 12–13. Windsor, Berks: NFER-Nelson.

Smith P, Whetton C (1988) Basic Skills Tests. Windsor Berks: NFER-Nelson.

Snow RE, Yalow E (1982) Education and intelligence. In Sternberg R (Ed) Handbook Of Human Intelligence. Cambridge: Cambridge University Press: 493–585.

Snowling MJ (1987) Dyslexia: A Cognitive Developmental Perspective. Oxford: Blackwell.

Snowling MJ (1994) Paper presented to 'The Acquisition of Language and its Dissolution': a discussion meeting at the Royal Society, London, 23–24 March.

Snowling MJ (in press) Nonword Reading Test. Thames Valley Test Publishing.

Snyderman M, Rothman S (1988) The IQ Controversy The Media and Public Policy. New Brunswick, NJ: Transaction Books.

Somerville DE, Leach DJ (1988) Direct or indirect instruction? An evaluation of three types of intervention programme for assisting students with specific reading difficulties. Educational Research 30(1): 46–53.

Spruill J (1984) Wechsler Adult Intelligence Scale – Revised. In Keyser DJ, Sweetland RC (Eds) Test Critiques. Kansas City, MO: Test Corporation of America.

Stanovich KE (1988) Explaining the difference between dyslexic and garden-variety poor readers: the phonological-core variable-difference model. Journal of Learning Disabilities 21: 590–604.

Stanovich KE (1991a) Discrepancy definitions of reading disability: has intelligence led us astray? Reading Research Quarterly 26(1): 7–29.

Stanovich KE (1991b) The theoretical and practical consequences of discrepancy definitions of dyslexia. In Snowling MJ, Thomson ME (Eds) Dyslexia: Integrating Theory and Practice. London: Whurr.

Stanovich KE, Cunningham AE, Cramer BB (1984) Assessing phonological awareness in kindergarten children: issues of task comparability. Journal of Experimental Child Psychology 38: 175–90.

Stanovich KE, Siegel LS (1994) Phenotypic performance profile of children with reading disabilities: a regression-based test of the phonological-core–variable-difference model. Journal of Educational Psychology 86: 24–53.

Steinberg DD, Steinberg MT (1975) Reading before speaking. Visible Language 9: 197–224.

Sternberg RJ, Detterman DK (Eds) What Is Intelligence? Norwood, NJ: Ablex.

Sternberg RJ, Conway BE, Ketron JL, Bernstein M (1981) People's conceptions of intelligence. Journal of Personality and Social Psychology 41: 37–55.

Stone BJ (1992) Joint confirmatory factor analyses of the DAS and WISC-R. Journal of School Psychology 30: 185–95.

Stothard S (1994) The nature and treatment of reading comprehension difficulties in children. In Hulme C, Snowling M (Eds) Reading Development and Dyslexia. London: Whurr.

Stothard S, Hulme C (1991) A note of caution concerning the Neale Analysis of Reading Ability (Revised). British Journal of Educational Psychology 61: 226–9.

Sylva K, Hurry J (1995) Early Intervention in Children with Reading Difficulties: an Evaluation of Reading Recovery and a Phonological Training (short report). London: Thomas Coram Research Unit.

Tallal P (1994) Integrative studies of temporal integration. Paper presented to the 23rd International Rodin Remediation Academy Conference, Malta, September.

Taylor I, Taylor MM (1983) The Psychology Of Reading. London: Academic Press.

Tellegen A, Briggs PF (19167) Old wine in new skins: grouping Wechsler subtests into new scales. Journal of Consulting Psychology 31: 499–506.

Thomson ME (1982) The assessment of children with specific reading difficulties (dyslexia) using the British Ability Scales. British Journal of Psychology 73: 461–78.

Thomson ME (1990) Developmental Dyslexia. 3rd edn. London: Whurr.

Thomson ME, Newton M (1982) Aston Index (Revised). Cambridge: Learning Development Aids.

Thorndike RL, Hagen E, France N (1986) Cognitive Abilities Test (CAT). 2nd edn. Windsor, Berks: NFER-Nelson.

Thorndike RL, Hagen EP, Sattler JM (1986) Stanford-Binet Intelligence Scale: Fourth Edition (Binet-4 or SB:FE). Chicago: Riverside.

Thorstad G (1991) The effect of orthography on the acquisition of literacy skills. British Journal of Psychology 82: 527–37.

Todman J (1993) Vitamins and IQ. The Psychologist 68: 357–9.

Townend J (1994) Syllable Perception Task – experimental version. Staines, Middlesex: Dyslexia Institute (unpubilshed).

Transvaal Education Department (1987) One Minute Reading Test. Pretoria: Transvaal Education Department.

Trevarthen C, Murray L, Hubley P (1981) Psychology of infants. In Davies JD, Dobbing J (Eds) Scientific Foundations Of Paediatrics. 2nd edn. London: Heinemann.

Trickey G (Ed) (1983) Barking Reading Project Assessment and Remediation Manuals. Rev. edn. Barking East London: Schools Psychological Service.

Turner M (1991a) Spelling Project. Staines, Middlesex: Dyslexia Institute.

Turner M (991b) Just another education industry. Independent, 26 September.

Turner M (1993) Testing times (two-part review of tests of literacy). Part 1, Special Children 65: 12–16 April; Part 2, Special Children 66: 12–14 May.

Turner M (1994a) Quantifying exceptionality: issues in the psychological assessment of dyslexia. In Hales G (Ed) Dyslexia Matters. London: Whurr.

Turner M (1994b) South Africans spell it out: old ways are best. Sunday Times, 27 November.

Turner M (1994c) Streamlining Raven. Dyslexia Review 6(1): 20–2.

Turner M (1994d) The Nonword Decoding Test. Dyslexia Review 6(2): 23–4.

Turner M (1995a) Children learn to read by being taught. In Owen P, Pumfrey P (Eds) Children Learning To Read: International Concerns. 1: Emergent and Developing Reading: Messages For Teachers. Basingstoke, Hants: Falmer Press.

Turner M (1995b) Assessing reading: layers and levels. Dyslexia Review 7(1): 15–19.

Turner M (1995c) Rhyming and non-rhyming sentences: an assessment resource for teachers. Dyslexia Review 6(3): 13–16.

Turner M (1996) Assessment by educational psychologists. In Beech J, Singleton C (Eds) Psychological Assessment of Reading. London: Routledge (in press).

Valdes G, Figueroa R (1994) Bilingualism and Testing: A Special Case of Bias. Hove, East Sussex: Lawrence Erlbaum.

Valdois S, Gerard C, Vanault P, Dugas M (1995) Peripheral developmental dyslexia: a visual attentional account? Cognitive Neuropsychology 12(1): 31–67.

Venezky RL (1993) History of interest in the visual component of reading. In Willows D, Kruk R, Corcos E (Eds) Visual Processes In Reading and Reading Disabilities. Hove, East Sussex: Lawrence Erlbaum.

Vernon PE (1969) The Standardization Of A Graded Word Reading Test. London: University of London Press (now Hodder and Stoughton).

Vernon PE (1977) Graded Word Spelling Test. Sevenoaks, Kent: Hodder and Stoughton.

Vincent D, Claydon J (1982) Diagnostic Spelling Test. Windsor, Berks: NFER-Nelson.

Vincent D, de la Mare M (1985) New Macmillan Reading Analysis (NMRA). Basingstoke, Hants: Macmillan Education. Now distributed as the New Reading Analysis (NRA) by: Windsor, Berks: NFER-Nelson.

Vincent D, de la Mare M (1990) Macmillan Individual Reading Analysis (MIRA). Basingstoke, Hants: Macmillan Education. Now distributed as the Individual Reading Analysis (IRA) by: Windsor, Berks: NFER-Nelson.

Vincent D, Green L, Francis J, Powney J (1983) A Review of Reading Tests. Windsor, Berks: NFER-Nelson.

Vinegrad M (1994) A revised adult dyslexia checklist. Educare (48): 21–23 March.

Vogler GP, De Frées JC, Decker SN (1985) Family history as an indicator of risk for reading disability. Journal of Learning Disabilities 18: 419–21.

Walker J, Brooks L and others (1993) Dyslexia Institute Literacy Programme. London: James and James.

Watts AF (1948) The Holborn Reading Scale. London: Harrap.

Wechsler Individual Achievement Test (WIAT) (1992) San Antonio, Tx: Psychological Corporation.

Wechsler D (1939) The Measurement Of Adult Intelligence. Baltimore, MD: Williams and Wilkins.

Wechsler D (1974) The Wechsler Intelligence Scale For Children – Revised (WISC-R). San Antonio, TX: Psychological Corporation.

Wechsler D (1981) Wechsler Adult Intelligence Scale – Revised (WAIS-R). New York: Harcourt Brace Jovanovitch/Psychological Corporation.

Wechsler D (1987) The Wechsler Memory Scale – Revised (WMS-R). San Antonio, TX: Psychological Corporation.

Wechsler D (1992) Wechsler Intelligence Scale For Children – Third Edition (WISC-III). New York: Harcourt Brace Jovanovitch/Psychological Corporation.

Wechsler D, Golombok S, Rust J, Trickey G (1992) Manual For The Wechsler Intelligence Scale For Children – Third Edition UK (WISC-IIIUK). Sidcup, Kent: Harcourt Brace Jovanovitch/Psychological Corporation.

Wepman JM (1973) Auditory Discrimination Test. Los Angeles, CA: Western Psychological Services. Rev. edn.

Westwood P, Harris-Hughes M, Lucas G, Nolan J, Scrymgeour K (1974) One minute addition test – one minute subtraction test. Remedial Education 9(2): 71–2.

Whyte J (1994) Attentional processes and dyslexia. Cognitive Neuropsychology 11(2): 99–116.

Wilce H (1996) So what's so great about reading? Times Educational Supplement, 26 April.

Wiliam D (1992) Special needs and the distribution of attainment in the National Curriculum. British Journal of Educational Psychology 62: 397–403.

Wilkins A (1992) Presentation to the Dyslexia Institute conference, Leeds, October.

Wilkinson GS (1993) The Wide Range Achievement Test–3rd Edition (WRAT-3). Wilmington, DE: Wide Range.

Wittgenstein L (1994) The Wittgenstein Reader, Ed Anthony Kenny. Oxford: Blackwell.

Wonderlic EF, Hovland CI (1937–95) Wonderlic Personnel Test and Scholastic Level Exam. Libertyville, IL: Wonderlic Personnel Test Inc.

Woodcock RW (1985) Oral Language and Broad Reasoning clusters for the Woodcock-Johnson Psycho-Educational Battery. Assessment Service Bulletin (2). Allen, TX: DLM.

Woodcock RW (1987) Woodcock Reading Mastery Tests – Revised Edition (WRMT-R). Circle Pines, MN: American Guidance Service.

Woodcock RW, Johnson MB (1977) Woodcock–Johnson Psycho-Educational Battery. Allen, TXs: DLM.

Woodcock RW, Johnson MB (1989, 1990) Woodcock–Johnson Psycho-Educational Battery – Revised. Allen, TX: DLM.

Woodcock RW, Mather N (1989a, 1990a) WJ-R Tests Of Cognitive Ability – Standard and Supplemental Batteries: Examiner's Manual. In Woodcock RW, Johnson MB, Woodcock-Johnson Psycho-Educational Battery – Revised. Allen, TX: DLM.

Woodcock RW, Mather N (1989b, 1990b) WJ-R Tests Of Achievement: Examiner's Manual. In Woodcock RW, Johnson MB,. Woodcock-Johnson Psycho-Educational Battery – Revised. Allen, TX: DLM.

Wooldridge A (1994) Measuring The Mind: Education and Psychology In England c. 1860 – c. 1990. Cambridge: Cambridge University Press.

Wynn K (1992) Addition and subtraction in human infants. Nature 358: 749–50.

Young D (1969) Group Reading Test. London: University of London Press (subsequently Hodder and Stoughton).

Young D (1976) SPAR: Spelling and Reading Tests. Sevenoaks, Kent: Hodder and Stoughton.

Young D (1983) Parallel Spelling Tests. Sevenoaks, Kent: Hodder & Stoughton.

Yule W, Rutter M (1976) Epidemiology and social implications of specific reading retardation. In Knights RM, Bakker DJ (Eds) The Neuropsychology Of Learning Disorders. Baltimore, MD: University Park Press.

Zindi F (1994) Differences In Psychometric Performance. The Psychologist 7(12): 549–52.

Index